W9-BSF-097

Mastering Photoshop 5 for the Web

Mastering™ Photoshop® 5 for the Web

Matt Straznitskas

SYBEX®

San Francisco • Paris • Düsseldorf • Soest

Associate Publisher: Amy Romanoff
Contracts and Licensing Manager: Kristine Plachy
Acquisitions & Developmental Editors: Richard Mills,
    Suzanne Rotondo
Editors: Anamary Ehlen, Kim Crowder, Alison Moncrieff
Project Editor: Dann McDorman
Technical Editor: Ben K. DeLong
Book Designers: Patrick Dintino, Catalin Dulfu
Desktop Publisher: Franz Baumhackl
Production Coordinators: Grey Magauran, Blythe Woolston
Indexer: Matthew Spence
Companion CD: Molly Sharp, Ginger Warner
Cover Designer: Design Site
Cover Illustrator/Photographer: Design Site

Screen reproductions produced with Collage Complete.

Collage Complete is a trademark of Inner Media Inc.

SYBEX is a registered trademark of SYBEX Inc.

Mastering is a trademark of SYBEX Inc.

TRADEMARKS: SYBEX has attempted throughout this book to
distinguish proprietary trademarks from descriptive terms by
following the capitalization style used by the manufacturer.

Netscape Communications, the Netscape Communications
logo, Netscape, and Netscape Navigator are trademarks of
Netscape Communications Corporation.

Netscape Communications Corporation has not authorized,
sponsored, endorsed, or approved this publication and is not
responsible for its content. Netscape and the Netscape Communications Corporate Logos are trademarks and trade names
of Netscape Communications Corporation. All other product
names and/or logos are trademarks of their respective owners.

The CD Interface music is from GIRA Sound AURIA Music
Library © GIRA Sound 1996.

The author and publisher have made their best efforts to prepare
this book, and the content is based upon final release software
whenever possible. Portions of the manuscript may be based upon
pre-release versions supplied by software manufacturer(s). The
author and the publisher make no representation or warranties of
any kind with regard to the completeness or accuracy of the contents herein and accept no liability of any kind including but not
limited to performance, merchantability, fitness for any particular
purpose, or any losses or damages of any kind caused or alleged to
be caused directly or indirectly from this book.

Photographs and illustrations used in this book have been
downloaded from publicly accessible file archives and are used
in this book for news reportage purposes only to demonstrate
the variety of graphics resources available via electronic access.
Text and images available over the Internet may be subject to
copyright and other rights owned by third parties. Online avail-
ability of text and images does not imply that they may be
reused without the permission of rights holders, although the
Copyright Act does permit certain unauthorized reuse as fair use
under 17 U.S.C. Section 107.

Copyright ©1998 SYBEX Inc., 1151 Marina Village Parkway,
Alameda, CA 94501. World rights reserved. No part of this publication may be stored in a retrieval system, transmitted, or
reproduced in any way, including but not limited to photocopy, photograph, magnetic or other record, without the prior
agreement and written permission of the publisher.

Library of Congress Card Number: 98-85475
ISBN: 0-7821-2230-2

Manufactured in the United States of America

10 9 8 7 6 5 4 3 2 1

To Sharon, for insisting
that a computer might be a
good way to pass the time

Acknowledgments

This book would have never happened had my great friend and fellow author Molly Holzschlag not (1) convinced me that I could write a book, (2) lobbied Sybex to give me a tryout, and (3) made significant contributions to the manuscript. Molly's fingerprints are all over Chapters 14, 15, 16, and 17 and the gorgeous Web palette that sits in the color section of this book. In addition, Appendix G is adapted from her book *Web by Design*. Thanks for everything, Mol.

B.K. DeLong, Stephen Romaniello, and Gail Wolff also made valuable additions to the manuscript, and Photoshop Master Amy Burnham designed the Web palette. Thank you all.

Lots of fine folks at Sybex made this tome possible, including Suzanne Rotondo, Richard Mills, Heather O'Connor, Amy Romanoff, Alison Moncrieff, Kim Crowder, Dann McDorman, Anamary Ehlen, Kristine Plachy, Grey Magauran, Blythe Woolston, and Franz Baumhackl. You are wonderful people to work with.

I am very appreciative to Adobe for providing me with the Photoshop 5 beta. Computing would be a better place if companies released software as solid as Adobe's betas.

I'm grateful to the 14 Photoshop Masters—Amy, Craig, Heather, Eric, Anna, Sabine, Elisabeth, Irene, Joe, Auriea, Alisha, Claudio, Vivian, and Peter—for taking time out of their very busy lives to talk about how they do what they do so well. It's been a pleasure to get to know each of you better.

All of the people at my company, BrainBug, deserve kudos. Your enthusiasm, creativity, and humor kept me going. Special thanks go to Andy Weatherwax—the deity of DHTML—for his great work in Chapter 18.

I'd like to thank my family, who remained incredibly supportive through the development of this book and during a far more difficult time a few years ago. I love you.

Finally, I'd like to express my gratitude to the following people who have helped me professionally. Whether it was a chance to design your Web site, enduring friendship, marketing smarts, or your business acumen, your support has been invaluable: Susan Brereton, Eve Broderick, Michelle Carrier, Carla Carpenter, Chip Caton, Bill Cronin, Mark Del Vecchio, Bill Derrig, Ken Dixon, Mary Ann Dostler, Jeanine Graf, Bill Hathaway, Ed Isenberg, Dave Johndrow, Ken Johndrow, Don Josephson, Rachel Medbury, Linda O'Connell, Denis O'Shea, Steve Pelletier, Stephanie Riefe, Amy Robinson, Mike Salius, Larry Schwartz, Maria Scotti, Bill Seymour, Ian Warhaftig, Julie Winkelman, Ira Yellen, Eric Zachs, and Henry Zachs.

About the Author

Matt Straznitskas is founder and President of BrainBug, a pioneering Web development agency headquartered in Hartford, Connecticut. A veteran developer of interactive Internet applications, Matt has been described as "...unquestionably one of the finest graphic designers around... his ideas will undoubtedly become foundations of future media" (Molly Holzschlag, *Professional Web Design*).

A born entrepreneur, Matt founded BrainBug in 1994 with the goal of providing the highest quality design and marketing for the emerging medium known as the World Wide Web. Recently, Matt was named one of Connecticut's top business people under the age of 40.

With a passion to share his experience, Matt writes regularly about the Web and emerging technologies for a number of business publications. *Mastering Photoshop 5 for the Web* is his first book.

About This Book

This book is the key to unlocking the power of the latest and greatest version of the best Web graphics tool on the market. It's the street-smart guide to Photoshop's key Web design tools, including hot new features like editable text, multiple levels of Undo, and killer new Layer Effects. This book also provides everything you'll need to know to create great Web sites. You'll get complete lessons on how to make Web pages with cutting-edge technologies like HTML, Cascading Style Sheets, and Dynamic HTML—plus an understanding of what the Web is and how it works.

Mastering Photoshop 5 for the Web is the result of developing thousands of Web graphics for hundreds of sites since 1994. Whether it was a mammoth site for a corporate giant or an award-winning animation for an independent publisher, I've taken all of the hard-won info I've gained and packed it into these pages. I've also included lots of samples of my Photoshop work—everything from cut paper and linocut-type illustrations to realistic 3D graphics.

Here's a more detailed look at this unique book.

Part I: Photoshop 5 Fundamentals

Part I provides a thorough lesson in all of Photoshop's major graphic creation tools. Chapters include getting to know the Photoshop workspace, creating images with the selection tools, breaking graphics down into layers, and using the program's powerful filters for stunning visual effects.

NOTE Notes, Tips, and Warnings are woven throughout this book to provide critical information about the topic at hand.

Part II: Photoshop and the Web

Once you know how to create graphics, the next step is to process those images into the correct Web formats. In Part II, I cover the pros and cons of the GIF, JPEG, PNG, and FPX file formats, plus show you everything you need to know about Web color, type, and graphics. There's even a whole chapter on what the Web is, how it works, and where it is headed.

N O T E   Every chapter in this book is wrapped up with an insightful section called "Conclusion." Just these 18 pieces alone provide a wealth of information about Photoshop and how to design for the Web.

Part III: Web Page Design

The final step is to take all of those images you created and processed with Photoshop and build some stunning Web sites. Part III provides exercises in all the latest Web page technologies, including HTML, CSS, and DHTML. You'll also find an invaluable section on organizing and managing your Web files.

N O T E   This book covers both the Macintosh and Windows (PC) version of Photoshop 5. Most of the screen shots shown here are from the PC, despite the fact that most Web designers still work on the Mac. I thought it would be useful for Mac users to see the PC interface and how similar it is to the Mac.

Photoshop Masters

From New York to Seattle, this book profiles 14 people from across the country who are doing great Web design with Photoshop. The profiles conclude each of the first 10 chapters and provide real world examples of where the Web design profession can take you.

Mastering the Medium

Included in this book is career advice that I've gleaned firsthand from my years of working as a Web designer. These Mastering the Medium segments conclude the final eight chapters of the book and will provide you with new insight into the issues facing every Web designer working today.

Appendices

The appendices at the end of this book are so rich with original information that they are more like bonus chapters than standard backmatter. Don't miss Appendix A—all about Adobe's new ImageReady program—and Appendix F, which details everything you can find on the companion Web site to *Mastering Photoshop 5 for the Web*.

CD-ROM

This book ships with a CD-ROM that is chock full of great Web design and production programs, including GIF Movie Gear, GIFbuilder, WS_FTP, and Microsoft Internet Explorer 4.0—the browser you'll need to view the DHTML effects covered in Chapter 18. Armed with a copy of Photoshop and this book, you'll have all the software you'll need for a long time to come.

Color Insert

This special color section is a reference to Photoshop's key color tools, features, and the 216-color palette for the Web. There's also a look at the portfolios of some of the best Photoshop Web designers working today, and even a peek at the special companion Web site to this book.

More Than Just Another Application Book

Ultimately, this book will do more for you than simply teach you another application. I've brought together a wide range of information—some of it well beyond the scope of Photoshop—because it is my sincere hope that *Mastering Photoshop 5 for the Web* will lead you to a successful, lucrative, and personally satisfying career in Web design.

Contents at a Glance

Table of Contents

Foreword

Eight years ago I became extremely ill, and the sickness persisted for a very long time. During this period, computers were my lifeline to the rest of the world—a way to communicate with others when I was too sick to leave my bed.

Computers were also the way that I planned an escape from my days of boredom and meager disability benefits. By learning to use programs like Adobe Photoshop and code pages for the World Wide Web, I could imagine a future when I would be paid to design from my home. And when my freelance design career began to become a reality, I saw computers as a way of building a much larger business, one that would employ lots of creative people like myself.

When my health returned, everything that I had conceived of happened. I now run a respected interactive agency, conduct frequent seminars about Web marketing and technology, and even get asked to write books like this one. A decade that began with staggering disability and despair has ended in unimaginable good fortune and opportunity.

This book is my way of contributing to a profession and community that has given me so much. I hope you will find as I have that learning can make life better.

PART I

PHOTOSHOP 5 FUNDAMENTALS

BASIC PAINTING

Featuring

CHAPTER 1

BASIC PAINTING

When you're learning how to use Photoshop, or any program for that matter, it is common to alternate between perusing the program's documentation and diving into the application with reckless abandon. While it's easier to learn from a book or manual if you have some specific questions in mind, fooling around with Photoshop and hitting brick walls is a good way to come up with the questions that need answers.

If you've worked in traditional photography and layout, then the way Photoshop's tools work may be familiar to you. Photoshop often uses traditional techniques as metaphors to describe its tools and functions. For instance, the Dodge and Burn tools are similar in nature to age-old darkroom techniques of the same names, and Layers work a lot like the acetate overlays that designers used to create color layouts before computers came along.

This chapter introduces you to the program's workspace and the Paintbrush tool. I highly recommend getting familiar with the Paintbrush because all of Photoshop's painting and drawing tools work in a similar way. Once you learn how to use the Paintbrush, all the other tools will be a snap!

Photoshop's Workspace

Every design program has its own personality and workspace. Some programs are developed on a limited budget and have clunky interfaces. Other programs are budget behemoths with ornate controls. Adobe Photoshop avoids these scenarios with a well-organized, understated workspace.

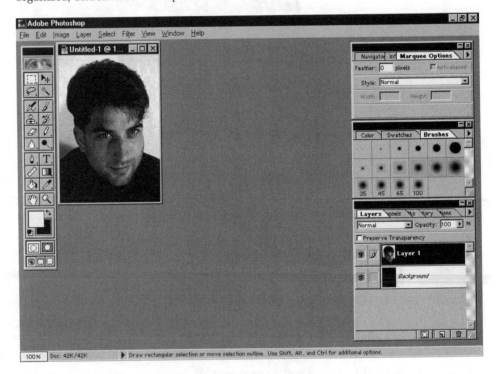

Photoshop was created with the designer in mind. Once the program is launched, your artwork is presented as the main focus. The program offers menus, palettes, a Toolbar, and a Status Bar—all of which the designer uses to customize the workspace and create graphics.

The Menu Bar

Running along the top of the Photoshop interface, the Menu Bar provides nine main options.

As with any program with menus, each one contains a host of additional options that will either open a submenu, launch a dialog, or carry out a command.

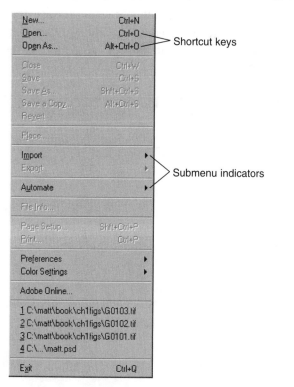

A small triangle to the right of a menu option indicates the presence of a submenu. If applicable, a shortcut key will also be displayed; this will show you a keyboard equivalent to access the command. For instance, the keyboard command for Save is Ctrl+S. If you want to save a file, you can simply hold down the Command/Ctrl key and press the letter "S" rather than take the time to navigate through the menu.

Three small dots next to a menu item indicate a dialog will be launched if this command is chosen. Sometimes commands off the Menu Bar will appear dimmed. This means that they are disabled and not available based on the capacities of the file that is currently open.

N O T E   For information about all of the individual Menu Bar options, see Appendix B.

PART

Photoshop
Fundamentals

Preferences

Photoshop's most underused menu item has to be Preferences. This feature provides dozens of ways to customize the operation of the program and save time. You can determine not only how images are displayed, saved, and measured, but also what resources the program uses on the host computer. You can get to Preferences from the Menu Bar by selecting File ➤ Preferences.

 N O T E   See Appendix E for details on Photoshop's Preferences settings.

The Toolbar

Photoshop's Toolbar is divided up into seven distinct groups of tools and controls.

The first four groups are dedicated to individual tools. A small triangle to the right of a Toolbar icon indicates a submenu. As you can see, there are lots of tools to choose from. But don't worry—it won't take long for you to get familiar with them.

 N O T E   For information about each tool, see Appendix C.

Palettes

Palettes sit on top of your workspace, providing quick access to commands and features. Organized into palette groups, palettes can be re-organized according to your preferences.

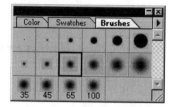

One of the nice features about palettes is that you can display only the ones that you use most often. For example, many Web designers keep the Layers and Swatches palettes open because they use them so much during the design process. Other palettes can be hidden until you need them.

Unless you have a large monitor, keeping all of the palettes open can take up a lot of screen real estate and can interfere with the design process. As a general rule, just keep the palettes that you use the most open—it will make your life a lot easier.

 N O T E   For a detailed list of all of Photoshop's palettes, see Appendix D.

The Status Bar

When you're working on an image in Photoshop, you might not notice some special features along the bottom of the workspace. These inconspicuous items are located in the Status Bar and provide key information about the file you are working on and information about your computer as it relates to Photoshop.

| 100% | Doc: 126K/126K | ▶ Draw rectangular selection or move selection outline. Use Shift, Alt, and Ctrl for additional options. |

 N O T E   On the Macintosh, the Status Bar is embedded into the bottom of the image window.

Here's a more detailed look at each Status Bar item.

Zoom

The bottom-left corner of the Status Bar displays the current zoom percentage. The default zoom is 100%—a 1:1 ratio of the size of the image's pixels to the size of your monitor's pixels.

N O T E   The term "pixel" is shorthand for picture element. It is the primary unit of measurement for all Web graphics.

Indicator Area

To the right of the zoom field is an area for displaying information about the graphic you're working on or information about your computer as it relates to Photoshop.

Indicator Menu

To the right of the indicator area is a triangle you can click to access the indicator menu. The menu offers five options:

Document Sizes   If you're dealing with a layered document and you select this option, two values will display. The first value is the file size of the image as a flattened file, and the second is the size of the file as a layered image.

N O T E   For more about the Layers feature, see Chapter 7.

Scratch Sizes   This option displays two values. The number on the left indicates the amount of RAM currently being used; the number on the right represents the total amount of RAM available. When the amount of RAM being used exceeds the amount available, you'll notice a decrease in system performance, because Photoshop will be using space on your hard drive to make up the difference.

Efficiency   Here's an alternate way to check system performance. When this value reads 100%, Photoshop has enough RAM to process the image you're working on. When lower values are displayed, you will be using space on your hard drive and may be compromising performance.

Timing   This option displays how much time it took for Photoshop to process the last command.

Current Tool   This option displays a simple notation of the tool you're currently working with.

Status Bar Message

This area will display information about the current image, as well as other information, such as the meaning of a command. Think of it as a simple online help system.

T I P   The Status Bar can be hidden by selecting Window ➤ Hide Status Bar from the Menu Bar.

Painting a Seascape

For the remainder of this chapter, you'll get to know the Paintbrush tool by creating the seascape shown in Figure 1.1. You'll start with the creation of a new file, thoroughly explore the Photoshop Paintbrush tool, and end with saving the file to disk.

FIGURE 1.1

A seascape painted in
Photoshop

You may ask yourself why we're painting a seascape when this sort of painting has little to do with creating Web graphics like menu buttons and animations. The truth is that Photoshop is just as valuable for sketching ideas as it is for designing individual Web graphics. Many Web designers play around in Photoshop until they develop an idea that can be used for the Web. So look at this exercise as a way to loosen up and think visually with the aid of a computer.

Creating a New File

To begin painting the seascape, launch the Photoshop application and follow these steps to create a new file:

1. Select File ➤ New from the Menu Bar.

TIP   If you've been working on another image and you want to use the same settings for the new image, hold down Alt (Windows) or Option (Macintosh) as you select File ➤ New.

2. The New dialog will appear. In the Name field, the default title of "Untitled" will appear. You can optionally enter your own title. It's a good idea to name it something you'll remember, otherwise you'll waste a lot of time opening files named `cool.psd` and `kitty.psd` trying to find the one you need. For our purposes, name the file `seascape.psd` (`.psd` is the file extension used in Windows to identify a file as a Photoshop document).

TIP   Select File ➤ Preferences ➤ Saving Files to set the Append File Extension option.

3. Select pixels as the unit of measure from the Height and Width drop-down menus. The pixel is the standard unit of measure for all Web graphics; it's the only one you'll need to use.

4. Enter the desired on-screen dimensions in the Height and Width text boxes. Play it safe and stick with a graphic size that is no more than 600 pixels wide and 300 pixels tall. Anything larger will result in a Web graphic that is too big to be viewed in its entirety on smaller monitors.

TIP   Photoshop defaults to a resolution of 72 pixels per inch (PPI) because most monitors display roughly 72 pixels for every inch of screen area.

5. Select RGB (Red/Green/Blue) color from the Mode drop-down menu. This is the standard color model used by video monitors to display color and should be used for all Web graphics. The RGB color model also works well for editing images on-screen because it provides access to the entire range of 24-bit screen colors.

6. Consider the appropriate Contents option for your image. This is the color that will appear on your canvas. The New dialog offers three Contents options:

White   Fills the background color with white. (This is the default background color.)

Background Color   Fills the image with the current (or last used) background color. As Figure 1.2 demonstrates, having black set as the background color will result in a new file with a black background.

Transparent   Creates an image containing no color value, indicated by a gray and white checkerboard (see Figure 1.3). A transparent background might be chosen when creating an image that will later overlay another image.

7. Because we want to start with a traditional canvas for our painting, select White from Contents option.

8. Click OK.

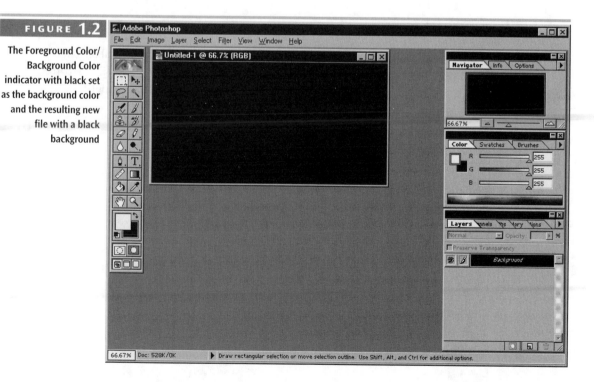

FIGURE 1.2

The Foreground Color/ Background Color indicator with black set as the background color and the resulting new file with a black background

FIGURE **1.3**

A new file with
the Contents set to
Transparent

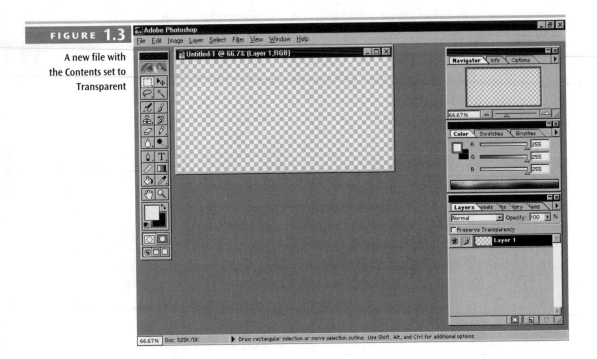

The Photoshop Paintbrush

To begin painting the seascape, you'll need to select a tool from the Toolbar. The
Photoshop Paintbrush is a versatile tool with an infinite number of possible settings.
From the Toolbar, click on the Paintbrush—the third tool down on the right.

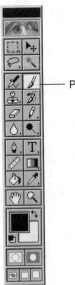

Paintbrush tool

The Paintbrush Pointer

The Photoshop Paintbrush tool includes three possible pointers: Standard, Precise, and Brush Size. The Standard pointer takes the form of a paintbrush and stays the same size regardless of the size of the brush tip. The Precise pointer is a crosshair symbol that is useful for painting very precise shapes. The Brush Size pointer takes the shape of an outlined circle that reflects the size of the current brush tip. Figure 1.4 shows the three possible pointers in action.

FIGURE 1.4

The three Paintbrush
pointers in action

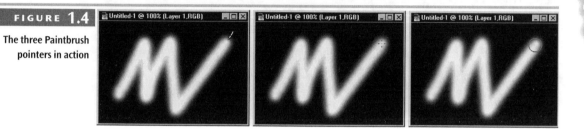

Selecting a particular pointer may seem trivial, but it can make using the Paintbrush a much better experience. Think about the type of painting you'll be doing and what kind of control you require.

To set the Paintbrush tool pointer to reflect your brush size, follow these steps:

1. Select File ➤ Preferences ➤ General from the Menu Bar. The Preferences dialog appears.

2. Select the Display & Cursors option from the drop-down menu.

3. Select the appropriate cursor from the Painting Cursors area in the lower-left corner.

4. Click OK.

While you are working, you can also change the appearance of the tool pointers from one option to another by pressing Caps Lock. The following list outlines the Caps Lock pointer changes:

- Standard changes to Precise.
- Precise changes to Brush Size.
- Brush Size changes to Precise.

To return to the original setting, turn Caps Lock off.

Sketching the Seascape

With a new file created, the Paintbrush tool selected, and a Paintbrush pointer specified, we will begin applying our first brushstrokes to the canvas. The initial strokes will define ocean and coastline (see Figure 1.5).

FIGURE 1.5

The initial brush-strokes define the ocean and coastline.

Before applying the first strokes, we need to load the brush with the appropriate colors:

1. Select the Paintbrush tool from the Toolbar.

2. Select Window ➤ Show Color from the Menu Bar. This will make the Color palette visible.

3. Move your cursor over the rainbow-colored swatch at the bottom of the Color palette. You will notice that the cursor becomes an eyedropper.

4. Click on the color that you would like to paint with.

5. Apply brushstrokes to the canvas by clicking and dragging the mouse over the graphic.

You may notice that the mouse can be a difficult tool to use for applying fluid brushstrokes—like painting with a bar of soap! Using the mouse to apply brushstrokes will become easier with time and practice. For now, apply brushstrokes like the ones you see in Figure 1.5.

TIP   You can constrain your brushstrokes by pressing the Shift key while you click and drag the mouse. Don't release the Shift key until you've reached the end of your stroke or you want to change direction.

Adjusting Brushstrokes

As you paint the seascape, the stroke the Paintbrush tool applies will need to be adjusted depending on the effect you are attempting to achieve. The Paintbrush Options palette provides all of the options for controlling the properties of a brushstroke as it is being applied. The main areas of the palette include Painting Mode (a drop-down menu), Opacity, Fade, Stylus Pressure, and Wet Edges.

Painting Mode

Photoshop provides so many different painting modes that even some experts have never used all of them. The modes are used to change colors and create special effects when painting, or to blend previously colored areas. Each mode defines how the color of a brushstroke combines with the colors in the existing image. The effect of each of these options varies depending on whether you are working on a white, black, translucent, or colored image or background.

In order to describe the differences between the modes, we'll talk about three values:

Base Color   The value of a pixel before you apply a brushstroke. This could be from a background color or other image.

Blend Color   The value you wish to apply. It can be a single value, such as applying the foreground color, or a series of colors.

Result Color   The value ultimately determined by a brush mode, or the color that results from combining the blend color and the base color.

Below is a very brief overview of each mode. The best way to find out what they really do is to try a few of them out for yourself.

Normal   The base color of every underlying pixel will be changed to the blend color. The normal painting mode is used unless you are trying to create a special effect.

Dissolve   This mode scatters the applied color randomly across the targeted pixels. It produces the most pronounced effects when used with large, soft brushes.

Behind   This mode produces the effect of painting behind an image. It is useful when you want to apply a shadow to an image, without eliminating the color of shaded areas in the layers underneath.

Multiply   Many people liken this mode to drawing with felt tip pens. When used with a shade of gray, it's a good shadowing tool.

T I P   Multiply will have no effect when the Wet Edges option is selected because this option already multiplies.

Screen   This mode is the opposite of Multiply. It is used to lighten an area by reducing the brightness values of the underlying pixels.

Overlay   This mode produces either a Multiply or Screen effect, depending on the color value of the base color. As with the Multiply and Screen modes, repeated applications over the same area will increase the effect.

Soft Light   This mode produces effects similar to Overlay, with less intensity. As the name indicates, it's like shining a soft or diffused light on an image.

Hard Light   This mode applies color to the underlying pixels, resulting in higher levels of color saturation. Both Soft Light and Hard Light are valuable tools for adding highlights and shadows to an image.

Color Dodge   This mode is used to produce an overall lightening effect. As you make a brushstroke, any underlying pixels that are darker than the blend color selected will be lightened.

Color Burn   This mode is the opposite of the Color Dodge mode. It is used to produce an overall darkening effect.

Darken   As you pass your brush over an image using this mode, only targeted pixels with colors lighter than the color you are applying will be affected.

Lighten   The opposite of the Darken mode. Under your brushstroke, only pixels darker than the color you are applying are changed.

Difference   This mode will split the difference between the base color and the blend color, producing dramatic effects. Repeated strokes over the same area will continue to change the effect.

Exclusion   This mode works in a similar way to the Difference mode, but the resulting color is softer than that achieved when using Difference.

Hue   A good mode for shifting color without changing brightness or value.

Saturation   This mode intensifies colors.

Color   This mode is often used to convert a black and white image to a color image as it preserves the gray levels in the image while color is applied. It can also be used to tint a color image.

Luminosity This mode is the opposite of the Color mode. The tone or lightness and darkness values of the base color will change, while the color value will not.

To set the painting mode, follow these steps:

1. Double-click on the Paintbrush icon in the Toolbar. This will launch the Paintbrush Options palette.

2. Select the painting mode of choice from the drop-down menu in the upper-left corner of the Paintbrush Options palette.

Opacity

This control is used by Web designers to create graphics with beveled edges. The opacity slider gives you the ability to control the opacity of the brushstroke. A brushstroke with 0% opacity is completely transparent or clear, while a brushstroke with 100% opacity is completely opaque or solid. Figure 1.6 shows brushstrokes using the same tip at different opacity levels.

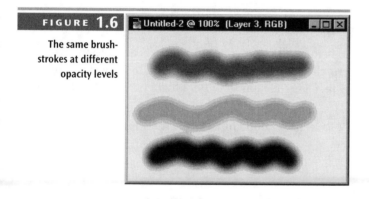

FIGURE 1.6

The same brush-strokes at different opacity levels

To adjust the opacity of a brushstroke, simply double-click on the Paintbrush icon in the Toolbar. This will launch the Paintbrush Options palette. Adjust the triangle under the Opacity option as necessary.

TIP You can also select a specific opacity by typing in the desired percentage on the keyboard while the painting tool is selected.

Fade

The Fade option lets you specify whether a brushstroke should gradually disappear (Fade: transparent) or gradually turn into the background color (Fade: background). The Fade option is useful in emulating real brushstrokes, but less so if you are attempting to paint an area with consistent color. Figure 1.7 demonstrates strokes with and without the Fade option applied.

FIGURE 1.7

Fade- and non–Fade-enabled brushstrokes

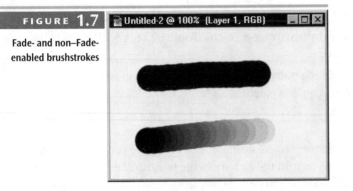

Here's how to use the Fade option:

1. Double-click on the Paintbrush icon in the Toolbar. This will launch the Paintbrush Options palette.

2. Select Fade in the Paintbrush Options palette.

3. Enter the number of steps before the fade-out begins. A step is equal to the size of the brush tip. By entering the number of steps, you are also indicating the length of the brushstroke. Increase the number of steps to increase the length of the stroke.

4. Select Fade: transparent or Fade: background by selecting the appropriate option from the drop-down menu.

Stylus Pressure

If you find using a mouse an annoying way to paint and draw, you're not alone. Many of the top digital illustrators—people like comic book artists and professional illustrators—use pressure-sensitive drawing tablets as a more natural way to input brushstrokes. Photoshop supports pressure-sensitive digitizing tablets, and the Stylus Pressure options in the Paintbrush Options palette offer control over the size, color, and opacity of your brushstrokes.

N O T E   The Stylus Pressure options can only be used if you have a stylus and graphics tablet connected to your computer.

To use Photoshop's Stylus Pressure options, do the following:

1. Double-click on the Paintbrush icon in the Toolbar to launch the Paintbrush Options palette.

2. Select options to get the stroke you're after. The following options are available for the Paintbrush:

   Size   Select this option to control the size of your brushstrokes by applying different pressure with the stylus. Light pressure will create a smaller brushstroke, and heavier pressure will result in a bigger brushstroke.

   Color   Select this option to control the color of the stroke. Light pressure on a stroke will reflect the background color, while heavy pressure will reflect the foreground color. The pressure range, between light and heavy, will reflect an intermediate color or a blend of the foreground and background colors.

   Opacity   Select this option to control how opaque or transparent your brushstrokes will be. Heavy pressure will produce a more opaque or intense effect. Lighter pressure will produce a more translucent color.

T I P   The Stylus Pressure options apply not only to the Paintbrush tool, but also to the Pencil, Airbrush, Eraser, Rubber Stamp, Smudge, Blur, Sharpen, Dodge, Burn and Sponge tools.

Wet Edges

Wet Edges produces a brushstroke with a slightly darker edge and a washed out center, similar to a watercolor effect.

To use the Wet Edges effect, do the following:

1. Double-click on the Paintbrush icon in the Toolbar to launch the Paintbrush Options palette.

2. Select Wet Edges from the lower-left corner of the Paintbrush Options palette and apply a brushstroke.

Building Up the Seascape

As you begin to flesh out the seascape, adjust brushstrokes depending on the effect you're after. As shown in Figure 1.8, we'll highlight the ocean to give the impression of reflected sunlight, and we'll add subtle shading to the coastline to give the landscape some form.

FIGURE **1.8**

Brushstrokes applied
to the seascape give the
impression of water
and land.

Bring out ocean highlights with a stroke set to Color Dodge in the Color Mode portion of the Paintbrush Options palette. Use the Fade option to create strokes that fade out in the direction in which they were applied. Give the coastline form by applying subtle dark strokes with the Opacity set to 50% in the Paintbrush Options palette.

Changing Brushes

As you create the image, you'll need to use different brushes to paint strokes of various width and quality. Photoshop's Brushes palette gives all of the options for controlling the properties of a brush tip that is used with the Paintbrush tool. From this palette, you can select another Photoshop brush, create a new brush, and define a brush.

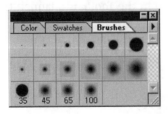

Photoshop Brushes

Round brush shapes are available in several sizes, and you can use them to apply a brushstroke with uniform width. When a brush size is too large to fit in a square on the palette, it will appear in a reduced size with a number indicating the brush diameter in pixels.

To select a Photoshop brush, follow these steps:

1. Select Window ➤ Show Brushes from the Menu Bar.

2. Click on a new brush type from the palette.

TIP   When Brush Size is selected, only the parts of the brush with opacity of 50% are indicated in the Paintbrush pointer. The pointers for very soft brushes will appear smaller than the area they affect.

New Brush

In addition to the default brushes in Photoshop, you can also create new brushes. If you plan to do a lot of painting, consider building a library of your own.

To create a new brush, follow these steps:

1. Select the Paintbrush from the Toolbar.

2. Select Window ➤ Show Brushes from the Menu Bar.

3. Select and click once on a brush that you want to use as a model.

4. Hold down the mouse button on the triangle in the upper-right corner of the palette tabs. Select New Brush to display the New Brush dialog.

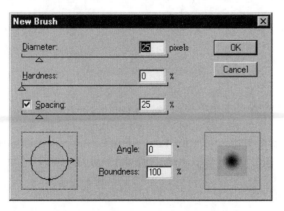

5. In the New Brush dialog, enter the diameter of the new brush or adjust the slider to increase or decrease the size of the brush.

6. While all brush shapes have soft edges, you can further increase the softness of an edge by decreasing the hardness. Adjust the slider to the left to decrease hardness and increase the transparency of the stroke towards the edge of the brush, or enter the percentage desired.

7. Select a spacing option. Spacing controls the distance the brush will paint as you make a stroke. You can think of this as the length of a brushstroke before you need to re-dip into the paint. A spacing of 1 percent provides continuous coverage. However, this option is labor intensive for Photoshop because of the number of times it has to create a brushstroke, which could definitely slow you down. For most brushes, a spacing of 25 percent will produce a brushstroke that appears solid. As you increase the spacing past 30 percent, ridges will begin to appear on the outside of the stroke. If you increase spacing past 100 percent, evenly spaced gaps will begin to appear.

8. To paint strokes without a spacing option, deselect the option. When spacing is deselected, the speed of your stroke will define the spacing. A fast drag will appear broken, a slow drag will appear solid.

9. Select the angle of your brush. On a round brush, changing the angle will not produce any change in the stroke. If you plan to change the roundness to a more elliptical shape, however, you can apply an angle to the brush to alter the brushstroke. The effect will be much like painting with a flat-edged paintbrush. You can enter a numeric angle, or click and drag within the circle in the left preview box to define a new angle.

10. Select the roundness to define the shape of your brush. A roundness value of 100 percent is a circle. A roundness value of 0 percent is a line. To modify the shape of the brush to achieve a more elliptical shape, enter a percentage between 0 and 100. You can enter a numeric percentage, or click and drag on one of the dots on the vertical axis in the preview window to change.

11. Click OK.

Custom Brush

Custom brushes are one of those Photoshop features that are so cool that the fact that they have little practical application is irrelevant. You create custom brushes from any active selection and then apply them with the Paintbrush. The effect is similar to using a rubber stamp. See Figure 1.9 for an example of a brush tip that was saved in the shape of a star.

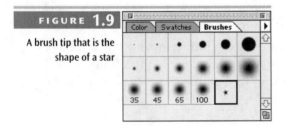

FIGURE 1.9

A brush tip that is the shape of a star

TIP   When using a pressure-sensitive tablet, only standard brushes vary in size depending on the pressure you apply. The size of custom brushes remains constant, regardless of the pressure applied.

To create a custom brush, follow these steps:

1. Select part of an image that you want to use as a custom brush. You can use any of the selection tools available. These tools will be discussed in detail in Chapter 4.

2. Select Window ➤ Show Brushes from the Menu Bar.

3. Choose Define Brush from the drop-down menu on the Brushes palette. A new brush will be added to the Brushes palette.

4. Double-click on the new brush to open the Brush Options dialog.

Brush Options	☒
Diameter: `17` pixels	OK
Hardness: `0` %	Cancel
☑ Spacing: `25` %	
Angle: `0` °	
Roundness: `100` %	

5. Specify a Spacing percentage.

6. Click OK.

You can now use your custom brush just like you would use any other.

Adding Details to the Seascape

With the ocean and coastline defined, it's time to finish the painting by adding some detail. You are going to add houses and other structures to the coastline, and add stars to the sky (see Figure 1.10).

FIGURE **1.10**

Details added to the
seascape with specific
brushes

To paint the houses, choose a new, smaller brush from Photoshop's Brushes palette. Apply the stars to the image by creating a custom brush in the shape of a star. Do this by drawing a star, then selecting it and using it as a custom brush tip. Choose a bright yellow color for the stars and apply the brush randomly over the sky with quick clicks of the mouse.

File Saves

As you know, computer technology can be imperfect. For obvious reasons, it is important to *constantly* save the files that you are working on. Any work that wasn't saved before an unexpected computer shutdown will be lost permanently. Photoshop has three main options for saving files: Save, Save As, and Save a Copy.

Save

The Save command saves files in their current format. For example, if you have opened a JPEG file and use the Save command, the file will remain as a JPEG and incorporate any changes that you have made to the file. Because of this, you will want to use the Save command often to retain the changes that you are making and avoid any data loss due to an unexpected shutdown.

The first time you attempt to save an image, the Save As dialog appears, asking how you want to save the image. Options include where on your computer the file will be saved, the name of the file, and file type.

If the file has not yet been saved, follow these steps:

1. Select File ➤ Save from the Menu Bar.

2. Select a directory to save the file to by navigating through your drive via the large main window and Save In drop-down menu.

3. Make up a filename and enter it into the File Name entry field.

4. Select Photoshop as the file type in the Save As drop-down menu.

5. Click on Save Thumbnail if you would like to have the file's icon be a small graphic that looks like the completed image.

6. Click on Save.

If the file has been saved and you would like to do an incremental save:

1. Select File ➤ Save from the Menu Bar.

2. Alternatively, you can hold down Ctrl+S (Windows) or Command+S (Macintosh).

Save As

The Save As command is useful when you want to create a new document that includes all of your most recent unsaved changes. The original file that you were working on is left intact, with no unsaved changes applied to it. This can be very helpful when you're not sure if the most recent edits should be applied to an original file.

To use the Save As command, do this:

1. Select File ➤ Save As from the Menu Bar.

2. Select a directory to save the file to by navigating through your drive via the large main window and Save In drop-down menu.

3. Make up a filename and enter it into the File Name entry field.

4. Select the file type you would like to save to in the Save As drop-down menu.

5. Click on Save Thumbnail if you would like to have the file's icon be a small graphic that looks like the completed image.

6. Click on Save.

TIP   Note that the file that you will now be working on is the Save As version, not the previously saved file.

Save a Copy

The Save a Copy command is most useful when you're processing Web graphics and saving them as either GIFs or JPEGs. Typically, your original Web graphics will be in the form of layered RGB files. It is very important that these files not be permanently flattened or converted to Indexed Color mode. In most cases you will take your RGB file, convert it to Indexed Color mode (which will flatten the file), and then save a copy as a GIF. Immediately after, use Photoshop's File ➤ Revert command to insure that your RGB file keeps its layers and color intact.

Save a Copy			? ☒
Save in: 🗀 graphics ▾			
File name:	seascape copy.psd		Save
Save As	Photoshop (*.PSD;*.PDD) ▾		Cancel
☐ Flatten Image	☐ Exclude Alpha Channels		
☑ Save Thumbnail	☐ Exclude Non-Image Data		
☑ Use Lower Case Extension			

NOTE   For more information about saving Web graphics, see Chapter 12.

To use the Save a Copy command, follow these steps:

1. Select File ➤ Save a Copy from the Menu Bar. Alternatively, you can use the keyboard shortcut: Shft+Ctrl+S.

2. Select a directory to save the file to by navigating through your drive via the large main window and Save In drop-down menu.

3. Conceive of a filename and enter it into the File Name entry field.

4. Select the file type you would like to save to in the Save As drop-down menu.

5. Select Flatten Image to merge all of the visible layers. For more information about flattening a file, see Chapter 7.

6. Select Don't Include Alpha Channels if you would like the alpha channels removed. For more information about alpha channels, see Chapter 6.

7. Click Save Thumbnail if you would like to have the file's icon be a small graphic that looks like the completed image.

8. Click Save.

WARNING   Saving a thumbnail when creating a Web graphic like a JPEG or GIF can increase file size, sometimes dramatically. (See Chapter 12 for more about these formats.)

Conclusion

Are you starting to get the hang of Photoshop yet? If you've used other graphics applications—even simple paint programs—the techniques mentioned in this chapter should be easy to learn. If they're too easy for you, don't worry; things are going to get hairier in the chapters to come.

If this is your first graphics program, make sure you are comfortable with the principles of creating new files, working with the Paintbrush, and saving files before moving on to other chapters. These features are the foundation for working in Photoshop.

Regardless of your skill level, Photoshop provides an interface that is clear, capable, and consistent. This is important as you begin to create increasingly more complicated graphics.

Up Next

Now that you've gotten your feet wet in Photoshop by creating and saving files and using the Paintbrush, I'll unveil some more exotic tools for image editing. Plus, I'll show you how to move around your image and undo any mistakes you might make.

Photoshop Master: Amy Burnham

Tucked away in Tucson, Arizona, Amy Burnham is one of the hottest Web designers in the desert southwest. Amy is the Art Director for DesertNet, the Web publishing company that focuses on alternative press. DesertNet's Weekly Wire online publication (see Figure 1.11) is designed by Amy and features content from papers like the Boston Phoenix, the Austin Chronicle, and the Chicago NewCityNet.

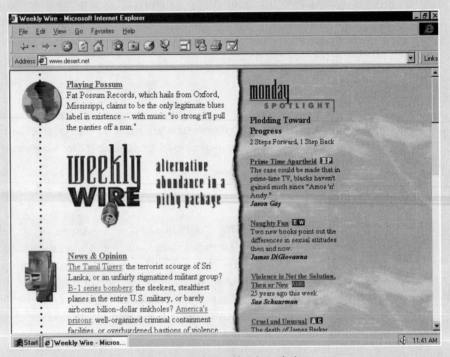

Figure 1.11 The Weekly Wire Web site

Weekly Wire also includes special content areas like the 1950s-inspired Film Vault (Figure 1.12) and the Arizona-Sonora Desert Museum Web Site (Figure 1.13). The Museum is a world famous zoo, museum, and garden located in Tucson, and its online presence continues to expand under Amy's artistic direction.

Before arriving at DesertNet, the 29-year-old designer earned her degree in Graphic Design from Drexel University in Philadelphia, PA. After an informative tenure at a print shop, Amy became an Art Director for a Tucson advertising agency. While at the agency, she became fluent in all types of print, direct mail, and outdoor and broadcast media.

In 1996, Amy began attending various Internet conferences, and her interest in the Web medium grew. Soon after, she took the leap into Web media and accepted a position at DesertNet.

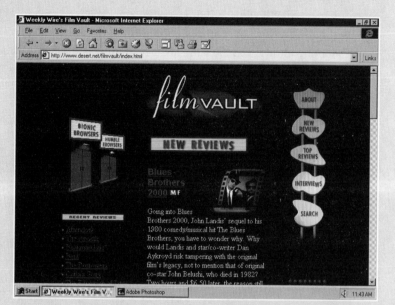

Figure 1.12 The Film Vault Web site

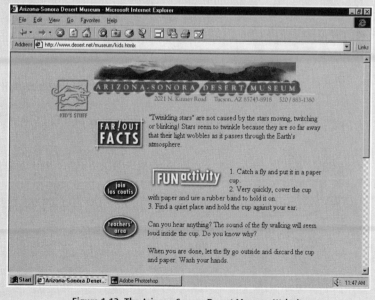

Figure 1.13 The Arizona-Sonora Desert Museum Web site

Unlike other Web designers, Amy prefers to leave the HTML layout and coding issues to DesertNet's team of programmers. Instead, she concentrates on the purely creative and conceptual end of Web design. While concessions sometimes need to be made due to bandwidth and other technical issues, Amy manages to get most of her Web designs produced intact.

Starting with version 2.0, Amy first began using Photoshop over seven years ago. Her frequently used features include Layers, Lighting Effects, and Sharpening. Layers are a particular favorite because of the interesting visual effects that can be achieved by combining commands such as overlay, soft light, and color.

Amy believes strongly that the computer shouldn't drive the initial stages of the design process. Good design starts by carefully thinking about a problem—far away from any production tools. In this respect, Amy's approach to Web design isn't any different from her previous work in print and broadcast media.

Portfolio:

- www.weeklywire.com
- www.weeklywire.com/filmvault/
- www.weeklywire.com/museum

IMAGE EDITING

Featuring

IMAGE EDITING

t's rare that you will render an image perfectly on the first try. No matter how carefully you apply a tool, the results will probably need to be tweaked or cleaned up. Photoshop provides lots of tools for editing images. In fact, Photoshop was originally intended as a tool for modifying photo-based images. So it is well-suited for things like erasing, sharpening, and smudging.

In this chapter, I'll discuss a variety of Photoshop tools for editing and enhancing an image. Later, I'll cover the various ways to completely reverse an edit. First, though, I'll show you how to navigate through an image to get to the part you want to fix.

Getting Around an Image

As you painted the seascape in the previous chapter, you may have been frustrated because you couldn't increase the magnification on different parts of your image, especially when painting in details. Fortunately, Photoshop provides a number of ways to navigate an image.

The primary scrolling and zooming tools are the Hand tool, Zoom tool, and Navigator palette. The Hand tool is used for scrolling, the Zoom tool is for magnifying, and the Navigator is used for both.

The Hand Tool

You use the Hand tool to move around inside an image. Of course, the scroll bars let you scroll through an image vertically or horizontally, but often the Hand tool is more useful because it can move an image both vertically and horizontally at the same time (see Figure 2.1). For artists, it's simply a more natural experience—like moving a piece of paper across a desk.

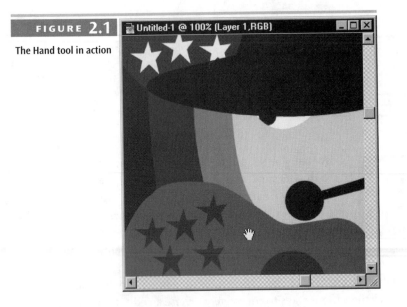

FIGURE 2.1

The Hand tool in action

Using the Hand Tool

To use the Hand tool, follow these steps:

1. Select the Hand tool from the Toolbar.

2. Click and drag over the image to view the area you want to work on.

At any point while you are editing an image, you can double-click the Hand icon in the Toolbar to return to a full screen view.

 TIP   You can also access the Hand tool temporarily by holding down the spacebar while another tool is active.

Zoom

If you're part of Generation X, you may remember a TV show called Zoom—a 1970s PBS program with lots of kids wearing ugly striped shirts. Unfortunately, Photoshop's Zoom isn't nearly as exciting—all it does is provide a way to increase or decrease the magnification of the image you're working on (see Figure 2.2).

FIGURE 2.2

The simple yet useful
Zoom tool

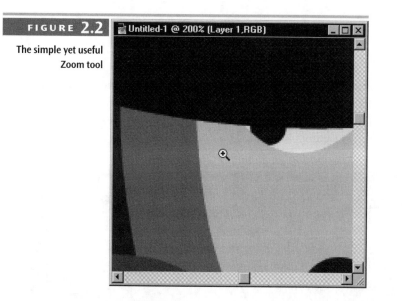

At a 1:1 zoom ratio (the default setting), an image is displayed at a ratio of one screen pixel per each image pixel, or 100 percent view size. You can access the Zoom tool using the Toolbar icon, the keyboard command, or the Zoom In/Zoom Out options on the View menu.

Photoshop provides a maximum zoom of 1600 percent. At any point in the editing process, you can double-click the Zoom tool icon to return to 100 percent view size.

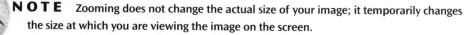

N O T E   Zooming does not change the actual size of your image; it temporarily changes the size at which you are viewing the image on the screen.

Using the Zoom Tool

1. Select the Zoom tool in the Toolbar.

2. Click on the image to zoom in at increments of 100 percent.

3. Press and hold down the Alt (Windows) or Option (Macintosh) key and click while the Zoom tool is active to reverse direction and zoom out.

To zoom in while another tool is active, press and hold the Ctrl key and spacebar (Windows) or the Command key and spacebar (Macintosh). To zoom out, press and hold the Alt key and spacebar (Windows) or the Option key and spacebar (Macintosh).

 T I P   You can also enter an exact Zoom percentage in the lower-left corner of the Photoshop interface.

The Navigator

The idea behind the Navigator is that you often need to reposition an image on your screen as you magnify it. The Navigator window offers a proportionally accurate thumbnail view of the full image and a red outline that represents the boundaries of the current viewing area (see Figure 2.3).

FIGURE 2.3

The Navigator palette with an image loaded

Using the Navigator, you can move the viewing area around the image. You can also enter an exact Zoom percentage in the text entry field at the bottom of the Navigator, or you can use the slider.

Using the Navigator Palette

To change the viewing area of the image using the Navigator, follow these steps:

1. Select Window ➤ Show Navigator from the Menu Bar. The Navigator palette appears.

2. Place the pointer over the viewing area within the thumbnail. The cursor will change to the Hand tool. You will then be able to scroll the viewing area over any area of the image, while you see the result on your screen.

3. Alternatively, you can point and click to any area of the image outside the viewing area to jump to that view. Outside of the viewing area, the pointer will appear as a pointing finger.

To change the magnification of the view using the Navigator, you can do any of the following:

- Click the Zoom In or Zoom Out button. These buttons are located on either side of the Zoom slider on the bottom of the Navigator palette.

- Drag the Zoom slider to the right to zoom in, to the left to zoom out.

- Enter a new Zoom percentage in the lower-left corner of the palette. If you wish to enter a series of percentages until you get the desired magnification, hold down Shift, and the field will remain highlighted after you press Enter (Windows) or Return (Macintosh).

- Hold down Ctrl (Windows) or Command (Macintosh) while your pointer is over the thumbnail view. This is an all-in-one reposition and zoom option. The pointer will change to a magnifying glass. Click and drag the glass over the area you would like to magnify to define a rectangle. The selected image will automatically scale to fit the active window.

Some Other Tools

In addition to the Paintbrush tool, Photoshop offers a number of other useful drawing and painting tools, including Pencil, Line, Airbrush, Paint Bucket, Rubber Stamp, and Smudge.

The Pencil

The Pencil is a simple tool that is ideal for drawing freehand or straight lines or for editing an image on a pixel-by-pixel basis. The Pencil tool can also be used as an eraser.

Using the Pencil

To use the Pencil as a drawing tool, follow these steps:

1. Double-click the Pencil icon in the Toolbar. This launches the Pencil Options palette.

2. If desired, specify the number of steps before the fade-out begins in the Fade text box. The option will make a pencil mark gradually get lighter as it is applied.

3. If you set a Fade value, select Fade to Transparent or Fade to Background from the drop-down menu.

4. If you are using a stylus, choose a Stylus Pressure to attain your desired stroke. The following options are available for the Pencil:

   Size   Select this option to control the size of your pencil marks by applying different pressure with the stylus. Light pressure will create a thinner mark, and heavy pressure will result in a thicker mark.

   Color   Select this option to control the color of the mark. Light pressure on a mark will reflect the background color, while heavy pressure will reflect the foreground color. The pressure range between light and heavy will reflect an intermediate color, a blend of the foreground and background colors.

   Opacity   Select this option to control how opaque or transparent your pencil marks will be. Heavy pressure will produce a more opaque or intense effect; light pressure will produce a more translucent effect.

5. Select Window ➤ Show Brushes and select a brush size.

6. Click and drag the Pencil tool over the image to apply a mark.

Using the Pencil as an Eraser

The Pencil also allows you to do simple erasing:

1. Double-click the Pencil icon in the Toolbar to launch the Pencil Options palette.

2. From the Pencil Options palette, select Auto Erase from the bottom-left corner.

3. Click and drag the Pencil over an image. If the mark begins on a foreground color, it will be replaced with the background color.

The Line Tool

In Photoshop 5, the Line tool is under the Pencil tool in the Toolbar.

Like the Pencil tool, the Line tool is simple, and I use it constantly when creating Web graphics. Use the Line tool to create straight, solid lines using the foreground color. When you combine it with other drawing tools, you can create almost any geometric shape you want. As demonstrated in Figure 2.4, the Line tool is great for creating thin horizontal or vertical rule graphics for a Web page.

FIGURE 2.4

Use the Line tool to create some simple rules.

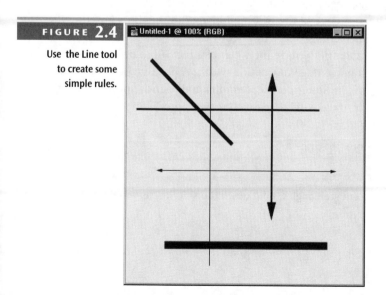

Using the Line Tool

To use the Line tool, follow these steps:

1. Select the Line tool from under the Pencil tool and double-click its icon. This will launch the Line Options palette.

2. Select the appropriate Mode name and Opacity value.

3. Select the line width by entering the desired thickness in pixels in the Weight text box.

4. Select Anti-aliased if you want the line edges to appear smooth.

T I P   You don't need to apply Anti-aliased to lines drawn on horizontal or vertical axes.

5. If you would like the line to have one or two arrowheads, select Start to add an arrowhead to the beginning of the line and/or End to add an arrowhead to the end of the line.

6. If you elected to add arrowheads, click Shape to define the shape of the arrowhead. Enter a percentage between 10 and 5000 to define the width and length of the arrowhead as a percentage of the width and length of the line. Entering the width and shape as a percentage keeps the arrowhead proportional to the size of the line. Enter a concavity percentage [between –50 and 50] to define the shape of the arrowhead as a percentage of the line width. A positive percentage will increase the concavity, producing a more traditional, slender pointed arrowhead. A negative percentage will decrease concavity, producing a diamond or spear-shaped arrowhead.

7. Click and drag the mouse to draw a line.

T I P   To confine lines to 45-degree angles, hold down the Shift key as you draw them.

The Airbrush

The Photoshop Airbrush and Paintbrush are basically the same tool with only one major difference. While the Paintbrush stops applying paint when you stop dragging, the Airbrush continues to apply paint as long as you are pressing the mouse button or stylus. Figure 2.5 shows the dark glob of paint that results if you hold the mouse in place at the end of a stroke.

FIGURE 2.5

The Airbrush continues to apply paint at the end of a stroke until the mouse is released.

Using the Airbrush

To use the Airbrush, follow these steps:

1. Double-click the Airbrush icon in the Toolbar to launch the Airbrush Options palette.

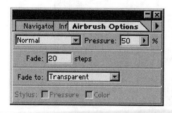

2. Select the appropriate Mode name and Pressure value.

TIP If you're using a stylus rather than a mouse, the Pressure option allows you to control the responsiveness of the tool.

3. Select Fade in the Airbrush Options palette if you would like to make the stroke gradually fade out.

4. Enter the number of steps before the fade-out begins.

5. Select Fade to Transparent or Fade to Background from the drop-down menu.

6. If you are using a stylus, select from the various Stylus Pressures to attain your desired stroke. The following options are available for the Airbrush:

   Color   Select this option to control the color of the stroke. Light pressure on a stroke will reflect the background color, while heavy pressure will reflect the foreground color. A pressure range between light and heavy will reflect an intermediate color, a blend of the foreground and background colors.

   Opacity   Select this option to control how opaque or transparent your brush strokes will be. Heavy pressure will produce a more opaque or intense effect; light pressure will produce a more translucent effect.

7. Select Window ➤ Show Brushes and select a brush size.

8. Click and drag the Airbrush tool over the image to apply a stroke.

The Paint Bucket

The Paint Bucket tool is unlike any of the tools discussed so far. You use it to quickly fill large areas with a single replacement color (see Figure 2.6).

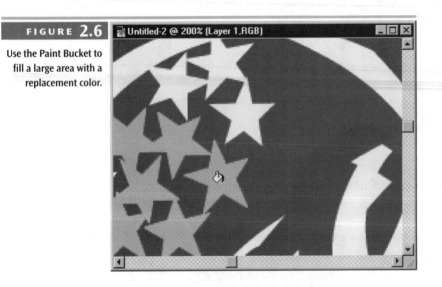

FIGURE 2.6

Use the Paint Bucket to fill a large area with a replacement color.

Untitled-2 @ 200% (Layer 1,RGB)

Using the Paint Bucket

To use the Paint Bucket, follow these steps:

1. Activate the Paint Bucket tool by double-clicking its icon in the Toolbar. This launches the Paint Bucket Options palette.

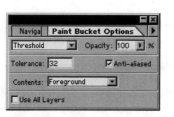

2. In the Paint Bucket Options palette, select the appropriate Mode name and Opacity value.

3. Set the Tolerance level for the fill. Tolerance settings range from 0 to 255. Using these settings, you can affect the range of the pixels that will be changed when you paint. Contiguous pixels are selected by Photoshop by calculating each color's brightness and adding and subtracting the Tolerance setting to create a range of target pixels. A low Tolerance setting will only affect pixels that are close in color to the target pixel. A high Tolerance setting will affect a wide range of color values that may vary greatly from the target pixel.

4. Select Anti-aliased if you want the edges of the area you fill to appear smooth.

5. Select the contents for the fill from the Contents drop-down menu. The two options are Foreground and Pattern. Unless you have defined a pattern using Edit ➤ Define Pattern, Foreground will be the only available option and will use the upper color in the Foreground Color/Background Color indicator.

N O T E   See Chapter 3 for more information about the Foreground Color/Background Color indicator.

6. Select Use All Layers if you are working on a multilayered image and wish to sample colors from all layers, not just the active layer. (See Chapter 7 for more information on the Layers feature.)

7. Click to apply the Paint Bucket to an area.

The Eraser Tool

As depicted in Figure 2.7, the Eraser tool erases part or all of an existing image. It is also an additive tool, offering many of the same options as the Paintbrush.

In fact, the best way to think of the Eraser is like a Paintbrush, Airbrush, or Pencil with transparency capabilities. As the Eraser passes over a graphic, it is in fact painting the image with the background color, a transparent background, or the last saved version of the image. So while it appears to erase the foreground color, it is actually painting over it.

FIGURE 2.7

Using the Eraser on an image

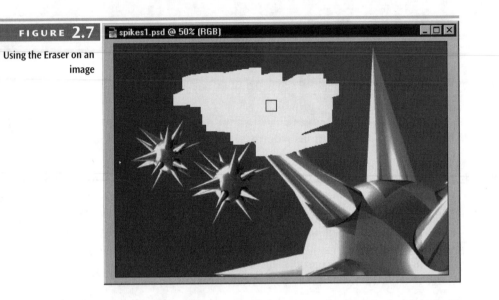

spikes1.psd @ 50% (RGB)

TIP   I use the Eraser when creating soft, realistic images such as beveled buttons. Otherwise, if I'm creating hard-edged graphics, I remove portions of an image with the Rectangular Marquee tool, which I'll cover in Chapter 4.

Using the Eraser Tool

To erase a portion of an image, follow these steps:

1. Double-click the Eraser tool in the Toolbar to launch the Eraser Options palette.

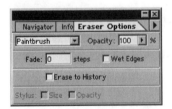

2. In the Eraser Options palette, select Block from the Mode drop-down menu on the upper-left.

3. Click and drag the tool around the image. The Eraser will paint the background color over the underlying pixels.

Erasing with the Paintbrush, Airbrush, or Pencil

You can also erase using other tools' characteristics:

1. Double-click the Eraser tool in the Toolbar to launch the Eraser Options palette.

2. Select Paintbrush, Airbrush, or Pencil from the Mode drop-down menu.

PART

Photoshop
Fundamentals

3. Select the desired Opacity, Fade, Stylus Pressure (if installed), Wet Edges (Paintbrush only), and Brush Size (from the Brushes palette).

4. When you pass your pointer over the image, it appears as an eraser.

Erasing to History

As detailed later in this chapter, Photoshop now includes a feature called History, which allows you to restore previous edits or changes to an image. The Eraser provides a link to the History feature with the Erase to History option, found in the middle of the Eraser Options palette. Figure 2.8 shows the Erase to History option in use.

FIGURE 2.8

The Eraser was used to expose a previous state of an image (the Then type).

The Rubber Stamp Tool

As shown in Figure 2.9, the Rubber Stamp tool is used to sample one area of an image and duplicate it in another location. It's one of my favorite tools. You might use it to remove a crack on a vase or conceal a facial blemish. I've also used it quite often to expand the size of a stock photo in a particular dimension.

FIGURE 2.9

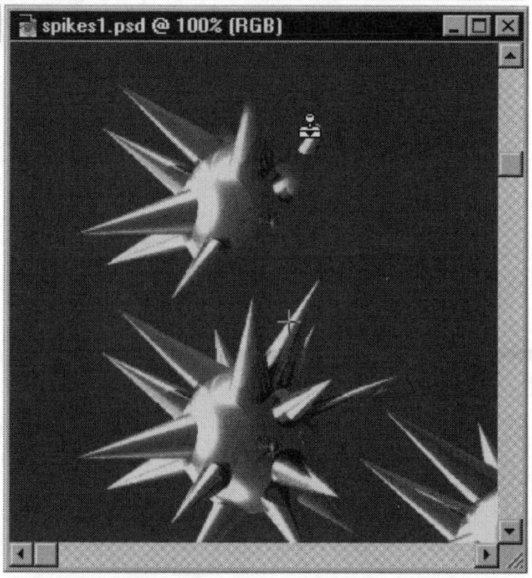

Use the Rubber Stamp tool to duplicate areas of an image in another location.

Using the Rubber Stamp

To use the Rubber Stamp, follow these steps:

1. Click the Rubber Stamp icon on the Toolbar.

2. Select Window ➤ Show Brushes to display the Brushes palette.

3. Select the brush size with which you would like to stamp.

4. Move the pointer over the image area you wish to duplicate. The pointer will look like a rubber stamp.

5. Press Alt+click (Windows) or Option+click (Macintosh) to define the point in the image you will be cloning.

6. Move the cursor to the location where you would like to stamp the cloned pixels.

7. Hold down the mouse button and move the mouse around. A crosshair will appear on the spot where you are cloning pixels.

The Smudge Tool

In Photoshop 5, Adobe has moved the Smudge tool under the Blur tool in the Toolbar.

The Smudge tool simulates the act of intentionally dragging a finger through charcoal or partially dry paint (see Figure 2.10). The tool samples the color on which you begin the brushstroke and pushes it in the direction you drag it. Smudging is often used to imply motion or to extend a shadow. I often use it to smooth out rounded or beveled edges.

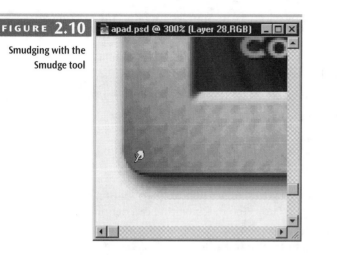

FIGURE 2.10

Smudging with the
Smudge tool

Using the Smudge Tool

To use the Smudge tool, follow these steps:

1. Select the Smudge tool from under the Blur tool and double-click its icon to launch the Smudge Options palette.

2. Select Window ➤ Show Brushes from the Menu Bar to display the Brushes palette.

3. Select the brush size with which you would like to smudge.

4. On the Smudge Options palette, select the appropriate Mode name and (if a stylus is installed) Stylus Pressure.

5. Select the Pressure value. Pressure controls the length and intensity of the stroke, similar to the pressure of your finger as you rub it across wet paint. The lower the pressure, the shorter the smear. The higher the pressure, the longer and more visible the smear. At 100 percent pressure, the Smudge tool copies the portion of the image you initially clicked on and repeats it along the full length of the stroke.

6. Select the Finger Painting option if you would like the Smudge tool to use the foreground color at the beginning of every stroke, adding color to the image area. When this option is not selected, the Smudge tool uses the existing image color (not the foreground color) under your pointer.

7. Select Use All Layers if you are working on a multilayered image and wish to sample colors from all layers, not just from the active layer.

8. Place the pointer over an image.

9. Click and drag to smudge the image.

Turning Back the Clock

One of the problems with Photoshop is that it provides so many editing options and effects that it's hard to know when to stop. Too much editing can definitely be a bad thing. But rather than curse the fact that you didn't stop futzing around with an image sooner, now you can go back and restore an image to its previous state—even if you've just saved it.

The Undo Command

The Undo command is the simplest way to restore a graphic to its previous state. Unfortunately, Photoshop can only remember the very last thing you did to the image, so if you applied a brush stroke and then the Rubber Stamp, you can only get rid of the Rubber Stamp, not the brush stroke, with the Undo command.

To use the Undo command, simply select Edit ➤ Undo from the Menu Bar. Alternatively, you can select Ctrl+Z (Windows) or Apple+Z (Macintosh).

 WARNING   If the last thing you did was save an image, you can't use Undo until you've performed another edit.

Revert to Last Saved

As the name implies, Revert to Last Saved restores your file to the state it was in the last time you saved it. To invoke this command, select File ➤ Revert from the Menu Bar.

 WARNING   You can't undo Revert to Last Saved.

The History Feature

For many years, Photoshop users have been requesting a more capable feature to restore an image to its previous state. There are far too many times when one level of Undo simply doesn't cut it but when Revert to Last Saved is too drastic. Photoshop 5's new History feature contains vastly enhanced Undo capabilities. The History palette is shown below.

The other important component of History is the History Brush. Located directly under the Paintbrush in the Toolbar, this tool allows you to paint back previous changes into an image.

One reason the History feature was only recently added to the application is because it makes significant hardware demands. Rather than putting all the edits in memory and forcing people to buy additional RAM, Adobe opted to record each edit on a "scratch disk." If you want to use the History feature, you may need more hard disk capacity. Adobe allows you to specify up to four scratch disks, and these hard drives can be internal or external.

 TIP   Scratch disks are specified in Preferences. From the Menu Bar, select File ➤ Preferences ➤ Plug Ins & Scratch Disks.

Using History...As Easy as 1, 2, 3

Actually, the History feature takes some getting used to. Think of it as an automated version of Layers (see Chapter 7). Layers is a Photoshop feature that allows you to separate out different parts of an image. The History feature records everything that you do to an image as a specific "instance." At any time, you can click one of these instances and the image will revert to its condition at that time.

To use History, follow these steps:

1. Create a new image to work on.

2. Select Window ➤ Show History to display the History palette.

3. Select the Paintbrush tool.

4. Use three brush strokes to paint the numbers 1, 2, 3 onto the image (see Figure 2.11).

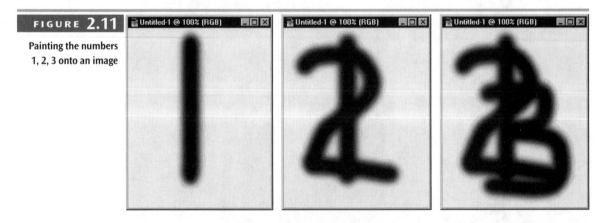

FIGURE 2.11

Painting the numbers 1, 2, 3 onto an image

5. In the History palette, click the uppermost instance of the Paintbrush. As shown in Figure 2.12, the numbers 2 and 3 have disappeared and their instances in the History palette have been dimmed.

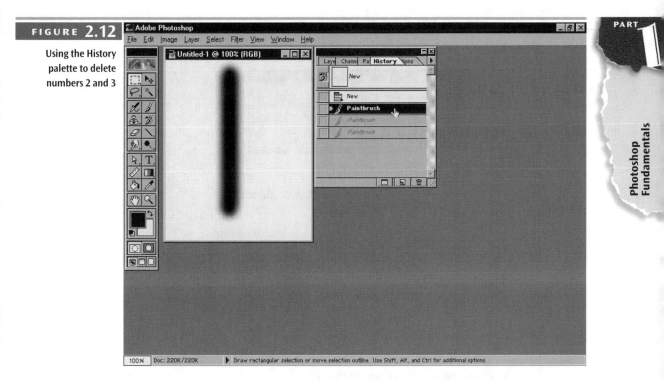

FIGURE 2.12

Using the History
palette to delete
numbers 2 and 3

If at this point you edit the image, the numbers 2 and 3 will be permanently removed
from the image. However, you can adjust the History Options to change this.

Adjusting the History Options

To adjust the History Options, follow these steps:

1. Click the arrow in the upper-right corner of the History palette to access the
   History drop-down menu. Select History Options to open the History Options
   dialog.

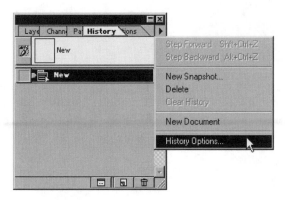

2. In the Maximum History States text box, enter the number of edits you want History to remember.

History Options

Maximum History States: **20**   OK

☑ Automatically Create First Snapshot   Cancel

☐ Allow Non-Linear History

3. Select Automatically Create First Snapshot if you want to see a thumbnail of the original image before any editing occurred.

4. Select Allow Non-Linear History if you would like History to retain previous edits even after you've applied the History brush.

5. Select OK.

WARNING   While the Allow Non-Linear History option is powerful, it can make unraveling the history of edits more complex.

Using the History Brush

As you've seen, you can use the History palette to restore an image to a previous state; however, the History palette alone cannot restore *portions* of an edit. That's where the History Brush comes in. Use the History Brush to paint back part of an image's previous state.

Double-clicking the History Brush launches the History Brush Options palette.

Navig| **History Brush Options** ▶

Threshold ▼ Opacity: 100 ▶ %

☐ Impressionist

Stylus: ☐ Size ☐ Opacity

This palette provides many of the same options as the Paintbrush Options palette, including painting modes and Opacity. Unique to the History Brush Options palette is the Impressionist option. As you might imagine, painting edits back with this brush results in a soft, blurry effect (see Figure 2.13).

FIGURE 2.13

Use the History Brush's
Impressionist option to
paint back an edit with
a soft, blurry effect.

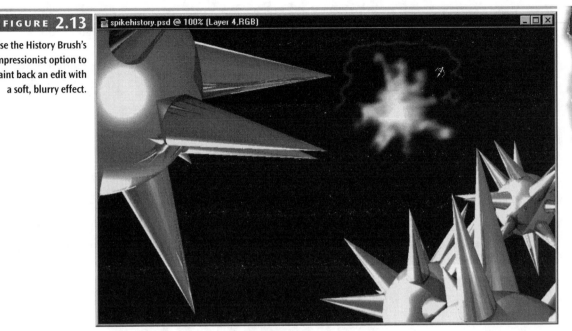

To use the History Brush, follow these steps:

1. In the History palette, click a previous state.

2. Click in the box next to the edit you would like to paint back. The History Brush icon will appear in the box (Figure 2.14).

FIGURE 2.14

The History palette
with a previous state
activated and the
source for the History
Brush set

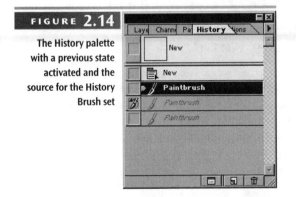

3. Select the History Brush.

4. Paint back the edit.

If this all seems a little confusing, don't worry. When the Layers feature was added to Photoshop, it took months for people to get used to it. Now Web designers can't live without it.

Continue to practice with History and the History Brush using the previous examples. Once you get comfortable performing these simple exercises, practice using History for more complex imagery.

Conclusion

Photoshop is extremely flexible and, as you're probably starting to see, provides multiple ways to accomplish just about everything. In fact, one of the biggest issues for new Photoshop users is figuring out which tool is the best and most comfortable to use.

Photoshop not only gives you multiple ways to navigate and edit an image, but also multiple ways to restore previous changes. With the advent of History, users now have the all-powerful Undo feature that they have been looking for. The only issue may be finding the time to get truly comfortable with it.

Up Next

This book is mostly in black and white, but Photoshop users like to work in color. In the next chapter, I'll discuss how to add some hues to your images.

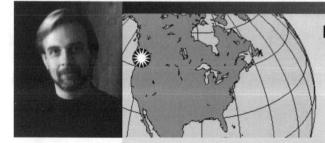

Photoshop Master: Craig Kosak

With a background in corporate print design, Craig Kosak entered the field of professional Web design three years ago with Microsoft. Today, this 40-year-old art director provides design and direction for some of Microsoft's most popular Web sites. His Web work includes Microsoft's Internet Start page, the Microsoft Internet Explorer download site, the Microsoft Channel Guide, the Microsoft Intranet site, and Microsoft SiteBuilder—one of the premiere online resources for Web designers.

Creating and maintaining all of these Microsoft sites takes far more resources than one person can provide. Craig leads a Seattle-based team that includes Kristin Easterbrook, Wendy Tapper, Sharman Armstrong, and Hannah Adams—highly talented Microsoft designers who work together to create well-designed information-based Web sites. Let's take a look at how Craig and his team created some of these sites.

In developing the Internet Start page, Craig created an initial concept with Photoshop (see Figure 2.15). Microsoft sites need to work on even the smallest monitors, so Craig typically produces sketches in Photoshop that are 621 pixels wide.

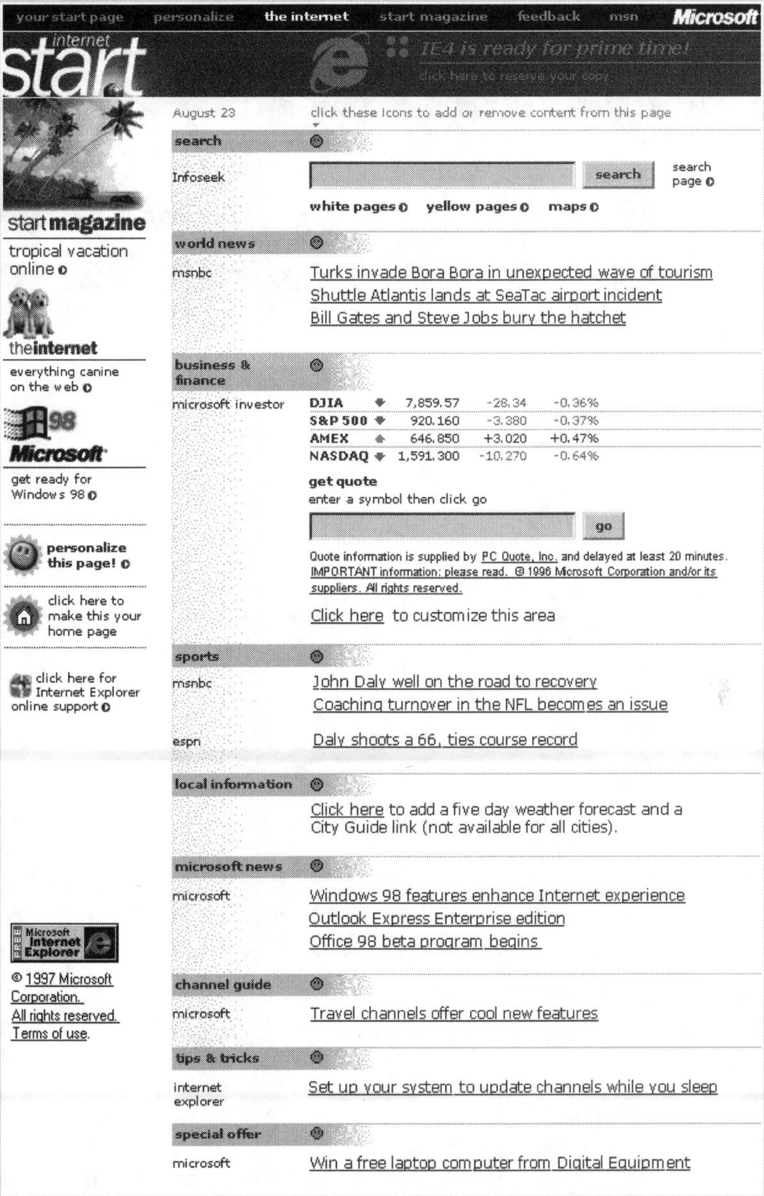

Figure 2.15 Craig's initial concept for the Microsoft Start page

As the Internet Start site began to take shape, Craig consulted with Hannah Adams to refine the site's look. Because the site serves as the default home page for people who use the IE Web browser, the design needed to be particularly sensitive to users with low bandwidth connections. Craig and Hannah worked on a layout and set of graphics that emphasized content over flash. Ultimately, a final design emerged and the graphics were arranged into a completed Web page layout (see Figure 2.16).

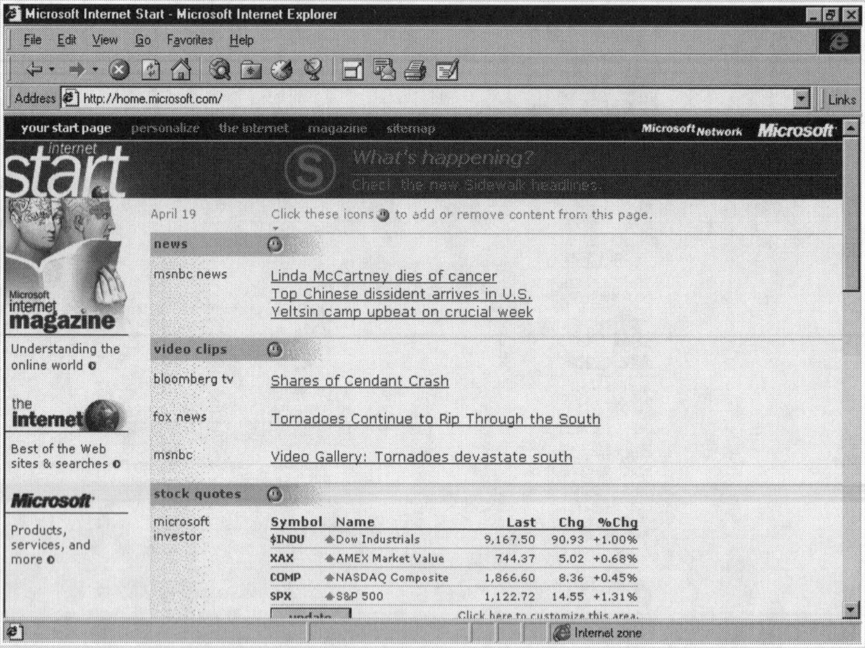

Figure 2.16 The completed Microsoft Start page

For the Microsoft SiteBuilder project, Craig created textured navigation globes to give the pages additional interest (see Figure 2.17). First, he developed unique textures using Photoshop's filters and effects. Craig then took the textures and applied them to spheres that he had designed in Caligari Truespace—a 3D-modeling program. The resulting graphics provided color and dimension to the cleanly designed SiteBuilder site (see Figure 2.18).

Figure 2.17 A navigation globe designed for the SiteBuilder Web site

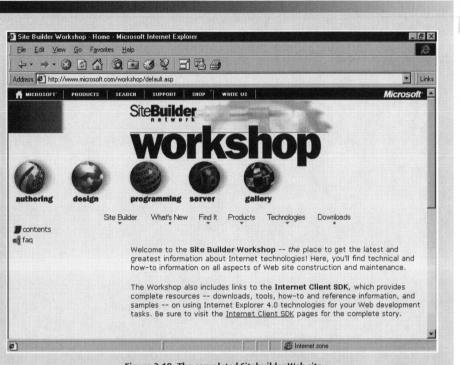

Figure 2.18 The completed Sitebuilder Web site

Craig began designing with Photoshop three years ago using version 3. Some of his favorite features include Filters, especially the Lighting effects and Blurs. Craig also finds the Layers feature to be a great time-saver if a graphic needs to be updated.

Craig's Web design philosophy is that content drives design. He feels that people use the Web to get information, and design should enhance that process, not impede it. Craig and his staff have clearly embraced this philosophy and have created some of the most informative, user-friendly sites on the Web.

Portfolio:

- home.microsoft.com
- www.microsoft.com/ie
- www.microsoft.com/sitebuilder
- www.iechannelguide.com/guide/en/en_us.asp

chapter 3

COLOR

Featuring

CHAPTER 3

COLOR

Back before the Web was invented, people used Photoshop to manipulate color images that were going to be printed in ink on a printing press. As any print designer can tell you, getting an image's color to print accurately is a major problem. Thus, Photoshop was developed with many tools to help with the color matching process—everything from CMYK and Lab modes to special Pantone swatches.

Fortunately, *Web* designers don't have these problems, nor do they need to use the tools. There are only a couple of color modes and a handful of tools that you absolutely must know how to use to design for the Web. In this chapter, I'll discuss the primary color display modes that Web designers use. I'll also cover how color is indicated and adjusted. Finally, I'll show you a tool that can apply a rainbow of colors to your images.

NOTE   Many of the figures and graphics in this chapter can be seen in full color in the color insert.

Color Modes

Photoshop provides many different color modes—ways of describing color—but few of them apply to Web design. Unless you plan on printing an image, don't bother with any of them except RGB and Indexed Color.

RGB Color Mode

RGB mode is based on the RGB color model that relies on mixing different values of red, green, and blue to create most of the colors in the spectrum. RGB mode is intended for use with images that are displayed on a computer. In RGB mode, every picture element (pixel) in an image is assigned a value of 0 to 255 for red, green, and blue. For example, in Figure 3.1, Photoshop's Color palette indicates that the currently selected color has a red value of 100, a green value of 255, and a blue value of 0. This results in a very bright green color because the green value is at its maximum and the red and blue values are quite low.

FIGURE **3.1**

The Color palette indicating a bright green color

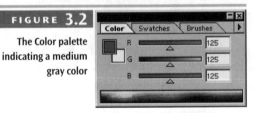

In the RGB mode, the three levels can be adjusted to represent almost any color, including black, white, and various shades of gray. For pure black, the three RGB values are set to 0. For white, all three values are set to 255—the maximum number. Grays are created by setting each of the three values to the same number. For example, a medium gray color would be created by setting the RGB values to 125 (see Figure 3.2).

FIGURE **3.2**

The Color palette indicating a medium gray color

All Web images are originally developed in RGB mode because the format was intended for computer-based graphics. As you'll learn in Chapter 13, computers render color on monitors by combining red, green, and blue light. Also, RGB files can be saved with their layers intact.

N O T E   As detailed in Chapter 7, Photoshop provides a Layers feature that allows different parts of an image to be conveniently arranged for later editing.

Once an RGB image is complete, a copy of the image is processed for the Web and either (1) flattened and saved as a JPEG or (2) converted to Indexed Color mode so it can be saved as a GIF.

NOTE   See Chapter 12 for detailed information about the JPEG and GIF Web file formats.

Indexed Color Mode

Indexed Color mode was specifically developed for images that appear on Web pages and other computer-based multimedia. The mode limits images to no more than 256 colors, primarily to insure that files will be small in size.

When an image is converted to Indexed Color mode, Photoshop creates a color lookup table (CLUT) that contains the 256 (or fewer) colors that make up the image. Because the image is forced into this palette, many of Photoshop's effects and filters cannot be applied while in this mode.

WARNING   Switching to Indexed Color mode "flattens" the file, destroying the document's Layer information.

The Foreground Color/Background Color Indicator

The Foreground Color/Background Color indicator is Photoshop's way of noting current color selections.

Located at the bottom of the Toolbar, the indicator notes two colors. The first color is uppermost and is the foreground color. This color is the one that is applied by the various painting and drawing tools. For example, when you use the Paintbrush tool, the current foreground color is applied to the image (see Figure 3.3).

The Foreground Color/Background Color indicator provides the option for switching the two colors by clicking on the double-headed arrow in the upper-right corner. If at any time you would like to switch back to the default colors, simply click on the Default Colors icon in the lower-left corner.

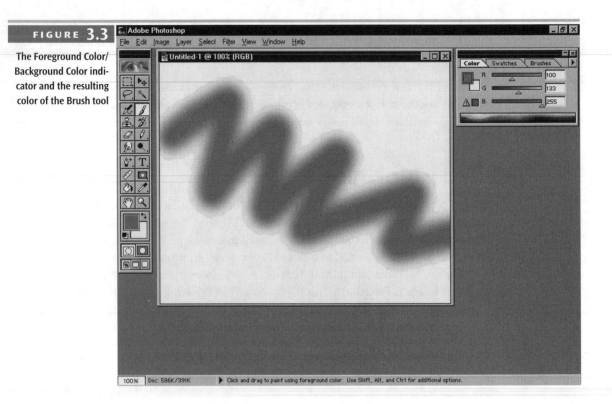

FIGURE 3.3

The Foreground Color/
Background Color indi-
cator and the resulting
color of the Brush tool

Specifying Color

Unless you plan on only painting black and white images with Photoshop, you'll
need to specify colors to work with. The Color Picker, Color palette, and Swatches
palette can all be used to change the current foreground and background colors.

The Color Picker

Photoshop's Color Picker is a powerful tool that allows you to choose from over 16
million colors. As is typical with Photoshop, the program offers a number of options
to select a new color. There are color spectrums, systems, and numeric entry fields
from which to specify colors.

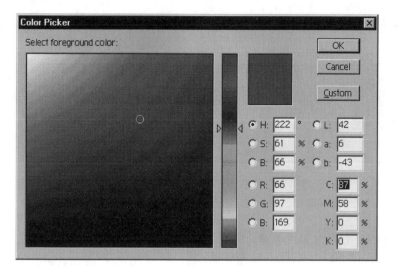

First, you should familiarize yourself with the color indicator window. This window is located in the upper-right side of the Color Picker dialog. When you select a new color, it is displayed in the top part of the window and the current foreground color moves to the lower part of the window (see Figure 3.4).

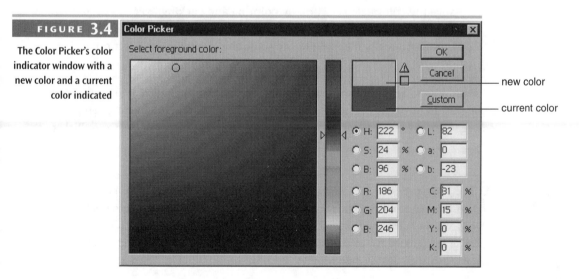

FIGURE 3.4

The Color Picker's color indicator window with a new color and a current color indicated

new color

current color

The Color Picker also contains a large color field that dominates the left side of the dialog. This swatch is used to manually pick a desired color. The color that is displayed in the swatch is controlled by the slider in the middle of the dialog.

When selecting colors from the color field, it is possible that a color will be picked that is not printable on a printing press. Such colors will be noted with an Alert warning above the small color swatch indicator.

TIP   Since you are creating images for the Web, you do not need to heed the Alert warning.

Using the Color Picker

To use the large color indicator window in the Color Picker to change the foreground color, follow these steps:

1. Click on the top swatch in the Foreground Color/Background Color indicator in the Toolbar. The Color Picker dialog will appear.

2. Move your pointer over the color field—it will appear as a circular marker.

3. Change the color field selection by pointing and clicking over the swatch. This will replace the color in the upper swatch indicator (above the HSB settings). The lower swatch will remain to show you the original color selection.

4. Click OK.

You can also select a color by using any of four color models: HSB (Hue, Saturation, and Brightness), RGB (Red, Green, Blue), Lab, and CMYK (Cyan, Magenta, Yellow, and Black). Each of these models is available at the lower-right corner of the Color Picker dialog.

NOTE   The Lab color model is based on a color model developed in 1931 and refined in 1976 as a way to create colors that are not specific to a particular type of computer. Lab stands for Luminance and two color elements: the "a" component, which ranges from green to red, and the "b" component, which ranges from blue to yellow. Today, Lab mode is not widely used by Web designers.

The HSB radio buttons allow you to isolate one of the color property values at a time. The selected color property will be reflected in the upper color swatch in the middle of the dialog and can be adjusted using the slider. The remaining two properties can be adjusted based on the currently selected color. If saturation is selected, you can adjust it simply by moving the slider bar, or entering a numeric value. No changes will be made to hue or brightness as a result. Alternatively, to adjust the hue and/or brightness of a color, you can make changes using the color selection marker in the color field. No changes will be made to saturation.

The RGB numeric radio buttons work the same way as the HSB radio buttons—you can isolate each one of the color values at a time. For example, if you select the color red you can increase or decrease the red value using the slider bar or by entering in a numeric value for red. Any changes to green or blue values would be made in relation to the currently selected value for red.

Lab and CMYK color models are also available, as are a plethora of other color libraries (accessible from the Custom button in the Color Picker dialog). However, these models and libraries are used in print design and are not of significance to Web designers.

The Color Palette

Photoshop's Color palette lets you define colors in three ways: with RGB sliders, numerically, and with an eyedropper. You will notice that the colors in the Foreground Color/ Background Color icon that appears on the bottom of the Toolbar are duplicated on a similar icon in the Color palette. Changes made in one of these indicators are automatically reflected on the other.

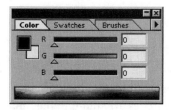

Using the Color Palette

To pick a color using the Color palette, do the following:

1. Select Window ➤ Show Color from the Menu Bar.

2. Adjust the color sliders by doing any of the following:

- Click and drag over the small triangle under each color bar.

- Enter numeric values for each color in each of the three input boxes to the right of the color bars. The allowable range for each box is 0 to 255, with 0 being darkest and 255 being lightest.

- Move the pointer over the colored band on the bottom of the palette and click on the desired color. The pointer will become an eyedropper when it is over the band.

In the Color palette, you will notice that a black border surrounds the top color in the Foreground Color/Background Color indicator. This will reflect your current color selection.

TIP   The Color palette's numeric fields are a good way to quickly select specific colors.

The Swatches Palette

Because of the nature of color on the Web, most designers use the Swatches palette to specify color. As the name indicates, the Swatches window displays blocks of pre-defined colors. They can be used to change the foreground or background color very quickly and conveniently. While you cannot create new colors from the Swatches window, you can add existing swatches to the palette. Photoshop provides a default swatch from which to work.

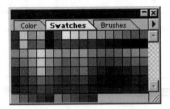

NOTE   On the PC, swatch files are appended with .aco and located in the Extras ➤ Color Palettes directory. On the Mac, swatches are found in the Goodies ➤ Color Palettes directory.

Using the Swatches Palette

To choose a color using the Swatches palette, follow these steps:

1. Select Window ➤ Show Swatches from the Menu Bar.
2. Move your pointer over the Swatches palette. The pointer will convert to an eyedropper.
3. Click on any swatch color to make it the active color.

NOTE   Web graphics are designed from a palette of 216 specific colors. These colors are loaded into the Swatches palette before work begins on a Web graphic. Further information about loading and working with these colors is provided in Chapter 13.

The Eyedropper Tool

The Eyedropper tool is useful for selecting a color directly from an existing image. The tool needs as little as a single pixel from which to select a color. The Eyedropper Options palette (accessed by double-clicking on the Eyedropper tool) provides the following selection possibilities.

| Navigat | **Eyedropper Options** | ▶ |
| Sample Size: | Point Sample | ▼ |

Point Sample   The Eyedropper copies a color from a single pixel.

3 by 3 Average   The Eyedropper averages the colors in a nine-pixel square around the targeted pixel.

5 by 5 Average   The Eyedropper averages the colors in a 25-pixel square around the targeted pixel.

Using the Eyedropper Tool

To use the Eyedropper tool, follow these steps:

1. Double-click on the Eyedropper tool in the Toolbar. This will launch the Eyedropper Options palette.

2. From the Eyedropper Options palette, select an option from the Sample Size drop-down menu.

3. Move your pointer over the image you intend to select a color from. The pointer will transform into an eyedropper while it is over the image.

4. Click when you have found the color you would like to use. This color will now be the foreground color in the Foreground Color/Background Color indicator.

Adjusting Color

While tools like the Color Picker and Eyedropper allow you to specify new colors to work with, it is often helpful to adjust the color in a whole image or layer. Typical color adjustment scenarios in the development of Web graphics include:

- Changing an image from full color to monochromatic in order to achieve a unique style

- Altering the brightness of an image to increase the legibility of overlaid text
- Inverting an image's color to create a special effect
- Fixing the color value of a scanned image

NOTE   For more information about color-correcting scanned images, see Chapter 6.

This section will detail Brightness/Contrast, Hue/Saturation, Desaturate, Invert, Threshold, and Posterize. Examples of these color tools in action can be found in the color insert in this book.

Brightness/Contrast

As the name indicates, the Brightness/Contrast tool allows you to alter the brightness and contrast in an image and can be found off the Image ➤ Adjust menu option. The Brightness/Contrast dialog provides two sliders that can be adjusted by hand or numerically with the keypad.

Using the Brightness/Contrast Tool

To adjust an image's brightness and contrast, follow these steps:

1. Select Image ➤ Adjust ➤ Brightness/Contrast. The Brightness/Contrast dialog appears.
2. Adjust the Brightness and Contrast sliders.
3. Select the Preview box to view the results of your adjustments.
4. Click OK.

Hue/Saturation

Of all the color adjustment tools, this is the one I have found to be the most valuable in developing Web graphics. Unlike print, where special effects like duotones need to be painstakingly created, the Hue/Saturation tool can be used to quickly experiment with different colorizations. One of my favorite techniques is to use the tool's Colorize command to convert a full-color image to a single hue. The Hue/Saturation dialog is shown below.

Using the Hue/Saturation Tool

To change an image's hue and saturation levels, do the following:

1. Select Image ➤ Adjust ➤ Hue/Saturation. The Hue/Saturation dialog appears.

2. From the Edit drop-down menu, select Reds, Yellows, Greens, Cyans, Blues, or Magentas to target specific colors to be adjusted, or leave the target set to Master to edit all colors.

3. Adjust the Hue, Saturation, and Lightness sliders manually or with the keypad.

4. Select the Colorize box if you would prefer to strip out the image's color information and apply a single hue to the image.

5. Select the Preview box to view the results of your adjustments.

6. Click OK.

Desaturate

Desaturate is a very simple tool that removes all the color from an image. The effect is the same as converting the image to grayscale without having to actually change color modes. The command is so simple, in fact, that there is no dialog. Simply select Image ➤ Adjust ➤ Desaturate, and all indication of hue will be drained from the image.

Invert

Just as it sounds, the Invert tool inverts the color in an image. Every color is replaced by its compliment, sitting directly across from it on the color wheel—orange becomes blue, red becomes green, and so on.

Like Desaturate, Invert is also a simple command that requires no dialog. To invoke the effect, select Image ➤ Adjust ➤ Invert.

Threshold

This tool forces every color in a graphic to be either white or black. Threshold is most useful in print work when you can only use one color, but it does have certain Web applications—when you need to create graphics with very small file sizes, for example. The Threshold dialog allows you to determine the point at which the image's color will become white or black.

Using the Threshold Tool

To apply the Threshold tool to an image, do the following:

1. Select Image ➤ Adjust ➤ Threshold. The Threshold dialog appears.

2. Enter a number into the Threshold Level field (between 1 and 255) or adjust the level manually via the slider. Note that the lines in the window represent the major areas of color in the image.

3. Select the Preview box to view the results of your adjustments.

4. Click OK.

Posterize

The is one of the few Photoshop tools whose name doesn't provide a very good indication of what it actually does. Posterize allows you to reduce the number of brightness levels in an image, thus creating an image that has larger areas of flat color. In Web graphics, it is mainly used as a special effect. The Posterize dialog is shown below.

Using the Posterize Tool

To apply the Posterize tool to an image, do the following:

1. Select Image ➤ Adjust ➤ Posterize. The Posterize dialog appears.

2. Set the number of levels (between 2 and 255). Fewer levels will result in fewer colors in the image.

3. Select the Preview box to view the results of your adjustments.

4. Click OK.

The Gradient Tools

Because of their intrinsic relationship to color, one set of tools that I haven't discussed thus far in this book are the gradient tools. These tools are used to create a gradual transition between two or more colors. You can create blends with the foreground and background color, as well as from a transparent background to the foreground color and vice versa.

The gradient tools can be used to fill a selection or an entire layer. They are often used to produce a backdrop for an image or to create subtle shading. The toolset originally included just the Linear and Radial Gradient tools, but with the release of Photoshop 5, the Angle, Reflected, and Diamond tools are also available.

Linear Gradient Tool

The Linear Gradient tool produces transitions of color along a straight path (see Figure 3.5). This is the most widely used type of gradient and is most commonly seen as backdrops in presentations.

FIGURE 3.5

The Linear Gradient
tool applied to an image

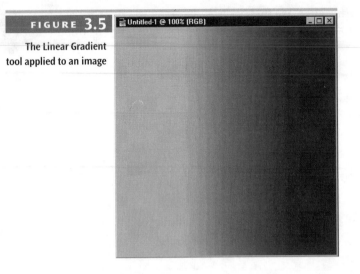

Radial Gradient Tool

The Radial Gradient tool creates spherical transitions between two or more colors, which you can see in Figure 3.6. The effect is often used to give circular objects some dimension and interest.

FIGURE 3.6

The Radial Gradient
tool applied to an image

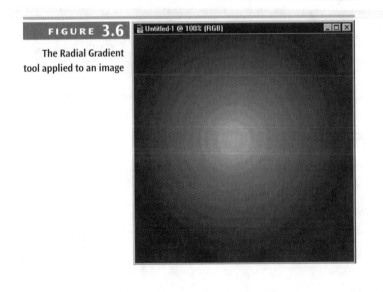

Angle Gradient Tool

The Angle Gradient tool creates a spectrum of color from dark to light set in a specified angle. In Figure 3.7 you can see this tool being used at a 360-degree angle.

FIGURE 3.7	
The Angle Gradient tool applied to an image	

Reflected Gradient Tool

The Reflected Gradient tool creates an effect similar to what happens when light strikes a reflective object like a mirror or chrome bumper. You can see this effect in Figure 3.8. The tool applies the foreground or first color as a shaft of light in the center of the image and the other color(s) occupy the remainder of the graphic.

FIGURE 3.8	
The Reflected Gradient tool applied to an image	

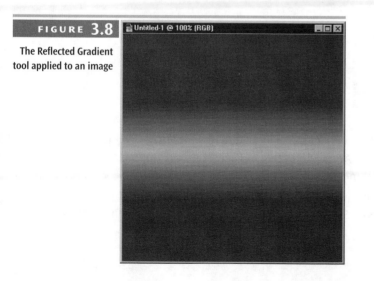

Diamond Gradient Tool

Similar in nature to the Radial tool, the Diamond Gradient tool applies a four-sided, diamond-shaped gradation to an image (see Figure 3.9). It is mainly used for creating graphical patterns or highlights.

FIGURE **3.9**

The Diamond Gradient tool applied to an image

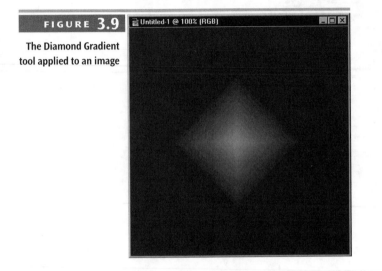

Gradient Options

Like most of the tools in the Photoshop Toolbar, the gradient tools have special options that are available for each type of tool. The Linear Gradient Options palette is shown here.

Despite the fact that the Gradient Options palette renames itself depending on the tool selected (Linear, Radial, Angle, Reflected, or Diamond), the options for each tool are exactly the same. They include:

Painting Mode   This is the same set of modes provided to all of the other painting and drawing tools. See Chapter 1 for an explanation of each Painting mode.

Opacity   This controls the overall level of opacity of the colors you are applying with the tool.

Gradient   While the default colors to be applied with the gradient tools are pulled from the Foreground Color/Background Color indicator, the Options palette provides a host of other preset color options. See the color insert in the book for some examples.

Transparency   This option maintains the transparent values of a gradient.

Dither   This option smoothes out gradations, making them more natural in appearance.

Reverse   This option simply reverses the colors in the gradient, so rather than going from orange to blue, the gradient would go from blue to orange.

Edit   This button launches the Gradient Editor dialog, which will be covered in more detail later in this chapter.

Using the Gradient Tools

Here's how to use the gradient tools:

1. If necessary, choose the appropriate foreground or background color using any of the color specification techniques mentioned earlier in this chapter.

2. Select the appropriate gradient tool from the Toolbar (Linear, Radial, Angle, Reflected, or Diamond) and double-click.

3. In the Gradient Tool Options palette, select the appropriate Mode name and Opacity value (as described earlier in this chapter).

4. Select a gradient from the Gradient drop-down menu. The list contains more than a dozen predefined gradients, or you can use the foreground and background colors you selected in step 1.

5. Behind every gradient is a transparent mask that controls the opacity of the fill along the gradient. Select Transparency to maintain the transparent values of a gradient. If you work with a transparent gradient without selecting Transparency, the gradient will appear as a solid fill.

N O T E   For more information about masks, see Chapter 6.

6. Select Dither to create a smoother blend of colors and reduce the chance of banding. Banding can occur when you are using a gradient between two distinct colors over a large distance. In such cases, the individual tones become visible, reducing the transitional effect. There are few reasons that you would disable Dither when using a gradient.

7. Back in your image, click the location you would like to begin the gradient and drag to the end location (see Figure 3.10).

FIGURE **3.10**

Using the Linear
Gradient tool on an
image

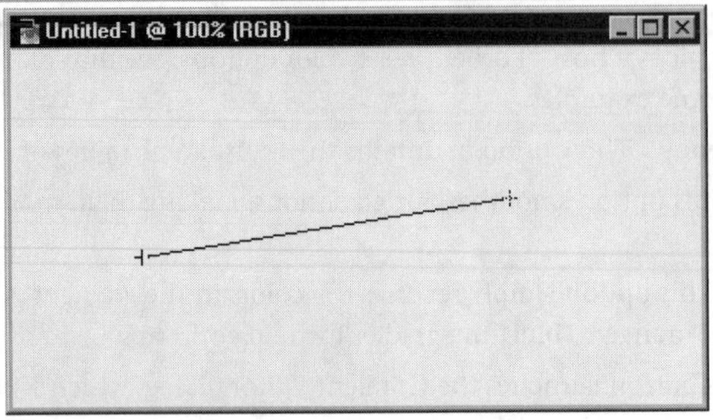

Each of the gradient tools are somewhat unpredictable in their application. Continue to apply the tool to the image until you are happy with the results.

The Gradient Editor

As the name implies, the Gradient Editor dialog provides a way to edit existing gradients that are currently loaded into the program, as well as create new ones.

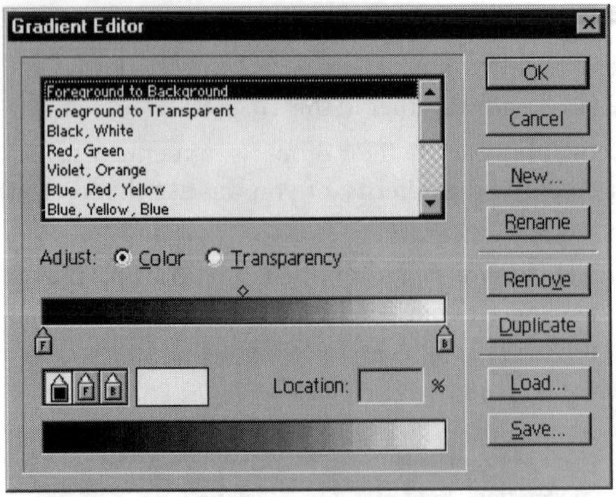

Creating a New Gradient with the Gradient Editor

To create a new gradient that you can save and use again later, do the following:

1. Double-click on a gradient tool in the Toobar. This launches the Gradient Tool Options palette.

2. In the Options palette, select Edit. This launches the Gradient Editor dialog.

3. Click New. This launches the Gradient Name dialog.

4. Input a name for the gradient and click OK.

5. Double-click on the left marker under the upper gradient indicator (see Figure 3.11). This launches the Color Picker dialog.

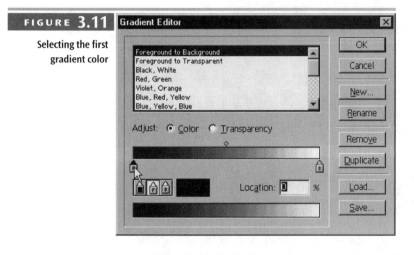

FIGURE **3.11**

Selecting the first gradient color

6. From the Color Picker, select a foreground color for the gradient.

7. Click OK.

8. Double-click on the right marker under the upper gradient indicator (see Figure 3.12). This launches the Color Picker dialog.

FIGURE **3.12**

Selecting the second gradient color

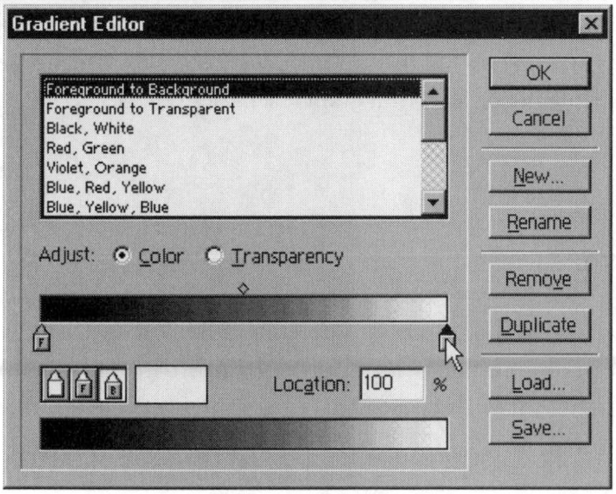

9. From the Color Picker, select a background color for the gradient.

10. Click OK.

11. To adjust the gradient's midpoint, click and drag on the diamond above the gradient indicator (see Figure 3.13).

FIGURE **3.13**

Specifying the
gradient's midpoint

Gradient Editor

Foreground to Background
Foreground to Transparent
Black, White
Red, Green
Violet, Orange
Blue, Red, Yellow
Blue, Yellow, Blue

Adjust: ⦿ Color ○ Transparency

Location: 24 %

OK
Cancel
New...
Rename
Remove
Duplicate
Load...
Save...

12. To save the gradient, click Save. This launches the Save dialog.

13. Name the gradient and append the file with the .grd extension.

At a later date you may want to use the gradient again. If so, simply select Load from the Gradient Editor dialog and load the .grd file into Photoshop. It won't be removed until the Remove command is issued.

N O T E   Gradients can make attractive backgrounds on a Web site, but positioning images like buttons and text on top of such images can be problematic. See Chapter 12 for more about the issues associated with graphical backgrounds.

Conclusion

Now that you know how to specify color, you can apply color with all of the tools that you learned about in Chapters 1 and 2—the Paintbrush, Airbrush, Pencil, and so on. Go back and experiment with these tools in color to get a sense of how color behaves on the computer.

You may notice there are a number of other color tools and dialogs included with Photoshop, and this chapter's coverage of color tools may seem incomplete. If this were a Photoshop book for print, that would indeed be the case. But there is no need to learn much of what Photoshop offers with regard to color because many of its tools are not appropriate to Web work.

However, just because most of Photoshop's color tools aren't necessary in Web work doesn't mean that dealing with color on the Web is a simple issue. As you will learn in Chapter 13, the issues surrounding Web color can sometimes be more troublesome than print.

Up Next

With all of Photoshop's fancy tools, dedicating a whole chapter to the seemingly dry subject of selections might seem like a strange decision. But after completing the next chapter, you may believe as I do that selections are one of Photoshop's most useful tools in the drawing and editing of Web graphics.

Photoshop Master: Heather Champ

Designer, author, speaker, and publisher, Heather Champ epitomizes the special breed of Web designers who have become personalities within the industry. Heather has spoken on a number of panels at technology conferences like Internet World, Web Interactive, and MacWorld and has written design columns for publications such as iWORLD and MIND.

Originally from Canada, Heather began designing for the Web in 1994 after working for five years in graphic design for New York's architecture community. Some of her early Web work included sites for Sony, Chase/Chemical, and the Cool Site of the Day.

Heather also maintains her own award-winning Web site, Jezebel (see Figure 3.14). The site was originally launched in August of 1994 and is currently a mixture of journal entries, holiday greetings, and free Web graphics. Heather views the site as a place to express herself after spending her day designing Web sites for other people. She feels that the site provides a forum for her thoughts and opinions—similar to the exposure one would get in an art gallery.

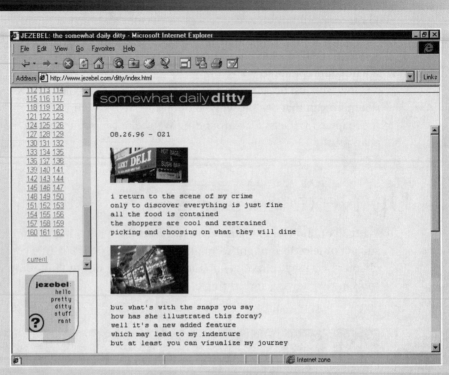

Figure 3.14   The Jezebel Web site

The 34-year-old designer has worked on a number of great projects, including development of the Benetton, Art + Commerce, SPG, Perfumes Isabel, and Sweet'N Low Web sites. Heather is particularly fond of the Benetton site, for which she provided her formidable design and HTML services (see Figure 3.15).

Heather has been using Photoshop for over seven years. She works primarily on the Macintosh platform, and her favorite Photoshop features include filters such as Sharpen that can compensate for low-quality scanned artwork. The designer also finds Pantone's Color Web Plug-in particularly useful in creating graphics that contain browser-safe colors.

The fact that Heather is a recognized personality in the industry is important in changing the notion that good design can be achieved by simply purchasing enough hardware and software. As more personalities emerge, it is more likely that the craft of Web design will be valued by people outside of the industry.

Figure 3.15   The Benetton Web site

Portfolio:

- www.jezebel.com
- www.sweetnlow.com
- www.benetton.com

SELECTIONS

Featuring

CHAPTER 4

SELECTIONS

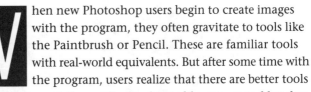

When new Photoshop users begin to create images with the program, they often gravitate to tools like the Paintbrush or Pencil. These are familiar tools with real-world equivalents. But after some time with the program, users realize that there are better tools for drawing most Web graphics, especially rectilinear objects like menus and headers. Selection tools provide the only real way to create crisp, hard-edged graphics.

Selection tools also specify portions of an image for basic editing functions like cutting, copying, and cropping. As you'll learn in Chapter 5, Photoshop's Paths feature is an excellent way to make precise drawings, and you can turn selections into paths.

In this chapter I'll use selections in the creation of Web graphics. I'll also describe all of the selection tools, including Marquee, Lasso, and Magnetic Lasso. Lastly, I'll discuss how selections can be added to, subtracted from, inverted, filled, stroked, pasted into, and transformed.

Let's get started with this very critical chapter.

The Importance of Selections

Without selection tools, creating graphics with Photoshop would be difficult. While the Toolbar contains a vast array of tools, it's hard to imagine how someone could create precise graphics like squares or circles with the Airbrush. You could probably do it pixel by pixel with a tool like the Pencil, but it would take forever.

Figure 4.1 shows a Web page with a left-side menu that allows users to navigate through the site's main levels.

FIGURE **4.1**

A Web page with a
left-column menu

FIGURE **4.1**

A Web page with a
left-column menu

When one of the original menu buttons is displayed in Photoshop as a layered file,
the layers that compose the graphic become visible (see Figure 4.2).

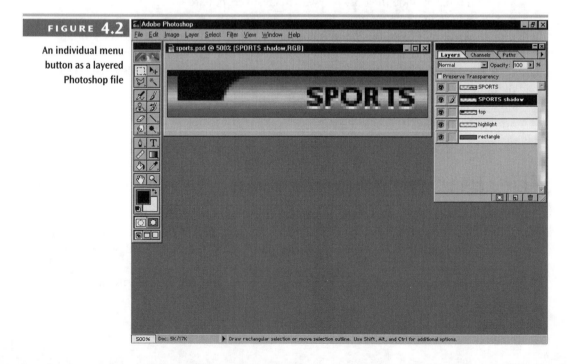

FIGURE **4.2**

An individual menu
button as a layered
Photoshop file

NOTE For more about Layers, see Chapter 7.

In addition to the rectangle, highlight, and text that make up the graphic, a unique shape caps each menu bar item (see Figure 4.3).

FIGURE 4.3	sports.psd @ 500% (Layer 1,RGB)

A shape that caps the
top of each button

This shape was actually drawn in three steps. First, a long rectangle was defined and filled (see Figure 4.4). Next, another rectangle was drawn to form the little tab (see Figure 4.5). Finally, a circular shape was cut out of the tab using an elliptical selection tool (see Figure 4.6).

FIGURE 4.4	sports.psd @ 500% (Layer 2,RGB)

Defining and filling a
long rectangle

FIGURE 4.5	sports.psd @ 500% (Layer 3,RGB)

Defining and filling a
smaller rectangle

FIGURE 4.6	sports.psd @ 500% (top,RGB)

Cutting out an elliptical
shape from the smaller
rectangle

It is important to look at Web graphics and think about how they were actually constructed. Most of the time, they will be comprised of simple geometric shapes put together in unique ways. These kinds of shapes are drawn with selection tools.

N O T E   When a selection is active, only the area inside the selection space will be affected by Photoshop's tools. The area outside the selection space is "masked" from any editing.

The Selection and Move Tools

If you can think of a way to make a selection, Adobe has created it. Whether it's the workhorse Rectangular Marquee or the new and exotic Magnetic Lasso, Photoshop has a selection tool for every job. The selection tools are broken up into three different groups: Marquee, Lasso, and Magic Wand. While not a tool for selecting, the Move tool is vital to adjusting the movements of an object after it is selected.

Marquee Tools

The Marquee tools are so named because they create visible or invisible marquee selection areas (see Figure 4.7).

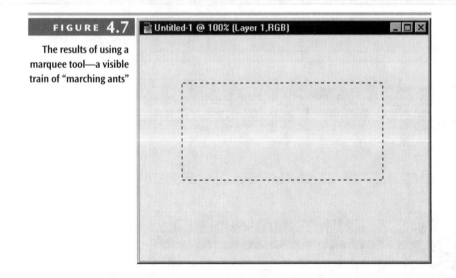

FIGURE 4.7

The results of using a marquee tool—a visible train of "marching ants"

Untitled-1 @ 100% (Layer 1,RGB)

T I P   To turn off the "marching ants" and make the selection outline invisible, select Ctrl+H (Windows) or Command+H (Mac). To make it reappear, use the same command.

The Marquee tools are located in the upper-left corner of the Toolbar and include, from left to right, the Rectangular Marquee, Elliptical Marquee, Single Row Marquee, Single Column Marquee, and Crop tools.

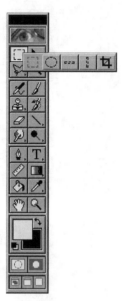

 N O T E   The Crop tool is covered in detail in Chapter 10.

When using the Marquee tools, you'll find the Info palette very helpful.

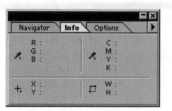

The lower-right corner of the palette displays the selected area's width (W) and height (H). The lower-left corner shows the X and Y coordinates for the current position of the mouse over the image. X refers to the distance from the left margin, and Y refers to the distance from the upper margin.

The other great aid is the context-sensitive tool menu. To access the menu, choose one of the selection tools and either right-click (Windows) or Control+click (Mac) with your mouse on the image. As Figure 4.8 shows, this launches a pop-up menu that provides lots of helpful options—everything from Select All to transformation and layer commands (see Chapter 7 for more about Layers).

FIGURE 4.8

Using the context-
sensitive tool menu

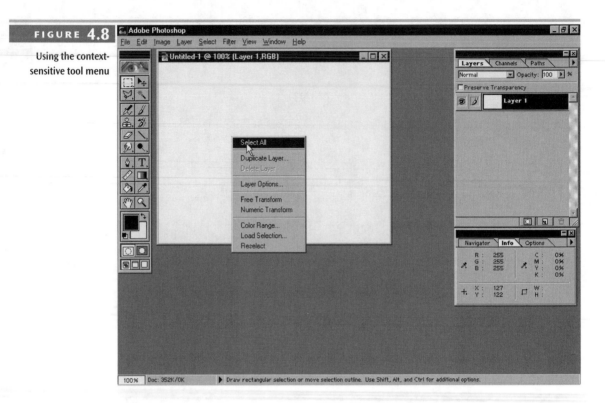

While this feature is available for most of the other Photoshop tools, I use it mainly with the selection tools. Try using these menus with different tools and in different situations. Once you get the hang of it, the way you work in Photoshop will definitely change.

Rectangular Marquee Tool

Use the Recangular Marquee tool to make rectangular and square selections. Select the tool, click, and drag. To make a square, hold down the Shift key while dragging. You'll see that the image has a selection made visible by a series of short, animated line segments, popularly referred to as "marching ants" (see Figure 4.9).

If you already have an active selection in your image, it is important to hold down the Shift key *after* you begin drawing your square. Holding the Shift key down before you start to select will add to any selections you've already got going (see Figure 4.10).

Conversely, holding down the Ctrl (Windows) or Option (Mac) key will *remove* areas from an active selection (see Figure 4.11).

TIP To make an entire selection inactive, press Control+D (Windows) or Command+D (Mac). Alternatively, you can choose Select ➤ Deselect, or right-click (Windows) or Option+click (Mac) on the image with one of the selection tools activated and choose Deselect from the pop-up menu.

FIGURE 4.9

Using the Rectangular
Marquee tool

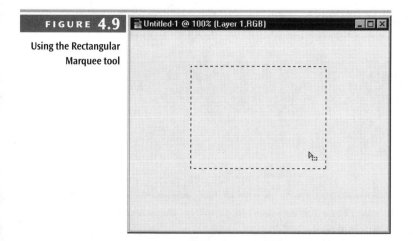

FIGURE 4.10

Adding an area to
the active selection
with the Shift key
and Rectangular
Marquee tool

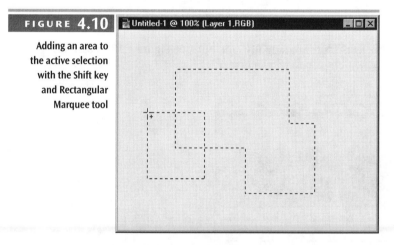

FIGURE 4.11

Removing areas from
the active selection

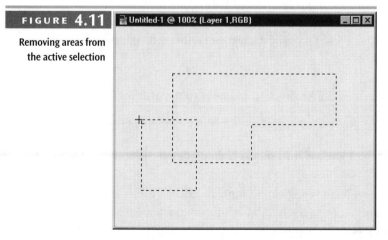

The Rectangular Marquee Options Palette   Like all the selection tools, the Rectangular Marquee tool has a Marquee Options palette. To launch the palette, simply double-click the tool.

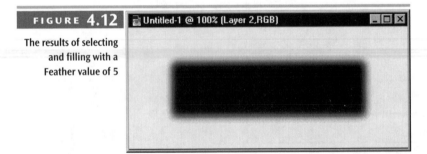

TIP   If you've already got a Photoshop tool selected, simply hit the Return key, and the appropriate Options palette will open.

There are two main features on the palette:

Feather   Makes selections that gradually fade out (see Figure 4.12). Possible pixel values range from 0 (none) to 250 (a lot).

FIGURE 4.12

The results of selecting and filling with a Feather value of 5

WARNING   Making a selection using the highest Feather settings can take a while for Photoshop to process.

Style   Establishes how the Rectangular Marquee tool will draw. Choose from the following options:

- Normal
- Constrain Aspect Ratio is the same as holding down the Shift key to draw a square.
- Fixed Size allows you to enter exact Width and Height dimensions. This little-known feature can be useful in establishing an exact size for a menu button or graphical Web page header.

Elliptical Marquee Tool

The Elliptical Marquee tool selects ovals and circles. Similar to the Rectangular Marquee tool, holding the Shift key forces the selection to be a perfect circle (see Figure 4.13).

FIGURE 4.13	Untitled-1 @ 100% (RGB)

Using the Elliptical Marquee tool to select a perfect circle

TIP   To draw a selection from the center out, rather than from the corner, hold down the Alt (Windows) or Option (Mac) key as you use the selection tool.

If you're having trouble getting the selection exactly where you want it, try holding down the spacebar as you create the outline. This will allow you to position it on the fly!

The Elliptical Marquee Options Palette   The main difference between the Rectangular Marquee Options palette and the Elliptical Marquee Options palette is that the Anti-aliased feature is operable.

Navigator Inf **Marquee Options**
Feather: 0   pixels   ☑ Anti-aliased
Style: Normal
Width: Height:

The Anti-aliased feature is critical for creating Web graphics that have soft, natural edges. Figure 4.14 depicts two circles created with the Elliptical Marquee tool. The one on the left has no anti-aliasing effect applied, while the graphic on the right does. The anti-aliased graphic has a bit more roundness and softness.

FIGURE 4.14

No anti-aliasing (left) vs.
anti-aliasing (right)

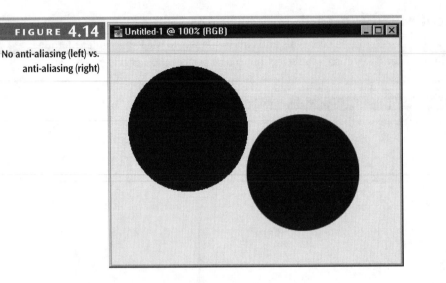

N O T E   All Photoshop images consist of a series of square elements called pixels (picture elements). Because rectangular selections—the kind made by the Rectangular Marquee and Single Row/Column tools—consist of nothing but 90-degree angles (just like the pixels), there is no need for the Anti-aliased feature in such tools.

The term *anti-aliasing* comes from the world of electronics, as is explained by Deke McClelland in his book *Macworld Photoshop Bible*:

> *Where did the term antialias originate? Well, to alias an electronic signal is to dump essential data, thus degrading the quality of a sound or image. Antialiasing boosts the signal and smoothes the rough spots in a way that preserves overall quality.*

N O T E   Information about the drawbacks of anti-aliasing in the creation of transparent Web graphics can be found in Chapter 12.

Single Row/Column Marquee Tools

It's pretty easy to figure out what these two tools do. The Single Row Marquee tool selects every pixel along a one-pixel-high, horizontal area across an image. The Single Column Marquee tool selects every pixel along a one-pixel-wide, vertical area in an image. Use this simple tool for quickly defining thin lines.

Its Options palette provides only one option, Feather. As described earlier in this chapter, feathering creates a softened selection border.

Lasso Tools

While the Marquee tools create geometric selections, the Lasso tools handle more freeform selection tasks. The Lasso selection tools include, from left to right, the Lasso, Polygonal Lasso, and Magnetic Lasso.

Lasso Tool

This quaint tool—dating back to the days of MacPaint, the first Macintosh paint program—makes completely freeform selections. As shown in Figure 4.15, wherever you drag your mouse, the selection path follows. As soon as you stop dragging, the selection is automatically completed.

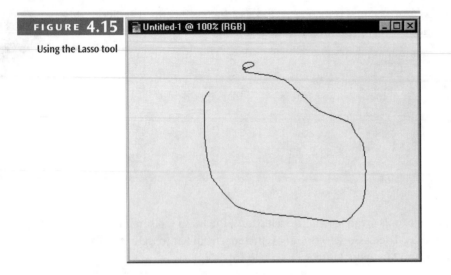

FIGURE **4.15**

Using the Lasso tool

T I P You can nudge an active selection around by using the up, down, right, and left arrows with either the Marquee tools, Lasso tools, or Magic Wand selected. This can be very helpful if your selection is misaligned by just a pixel or two.

The Lasso Options Palette The Lasso Options palette is very straightforward, with only the two familiar options, Feather and Anti-aliased.

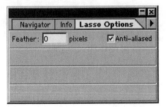

Polygonal Lasso Tool

The Polygonal Lasso tool can only draw straight lines and has the feel of working with a needle and thread. To use the tool, click in different spots on an image, and double-click when you are finished (see Figure 4.16).

N O T E The Polygonal Lasso Options palette is identical to the normal Lasso Options palette.

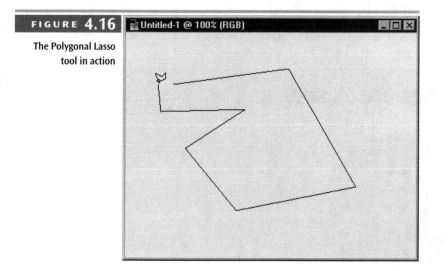

FIGURE 4.16

The Polygonal Lasso tool in action

Magnetic Lasso Tool

For the most part, I've found the Lasso tools to be only somewhat useful. However, with Photoshop 5, Adobe has introduced a new tool called the Magnetic Lasso. This tool does a pretty good job of actually anticipating what you're trying to select. For example, Figure 4.17 shows an image of an eightball. As I drag the Magnetic Lasso tool around the eightball, the selection outline is automatically created.

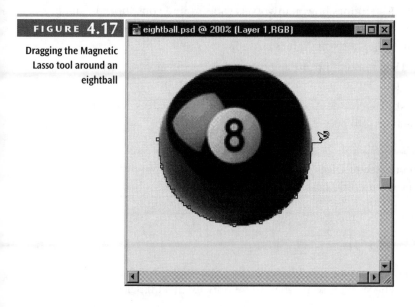

FIGURE 4.17

Dragging the Magnetic Lasso tool around an eightball

The Magnetic Lasso tool is indeed sticky—sometimes it's difficult to make the thing stop drawing selection outlines! The key is to either double-click when you are done selecting or bring the Lasso back to where you started and release (see Figure 4.18).

FIGURE **4.18**

Completing a selection outline with the Magnetic Lasso

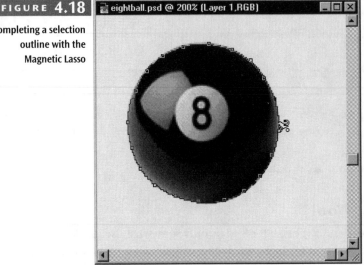

eightball.psd @ 200% (Layer 1,RGB)

The Magnetic Lasso Options Palette   In addition to the Feather and Anti-aliased features, the Magnetic Lasso Options palette has a number of unique controls:

Lasso Width   Determines how many pixels wide around your stroke it should consider prime real estate for finding an edge as you drag the cursor around the object you are trying to select. Values range from 1 to 40.

Frequency   Determines how often points will automatically be inserted into the selection path. Frequency values can be from 0 to 100.

Edge Contrast   Determines the sensitivity of the tool to edges. Edge contrast values can be from 1 to 100.

TIP   Be careful not to set the Edge Contrast too high or too low. A low setting will not be responsive enough, while a very high setting can stick to everything.

Magic Wand Tool

The Magic Wand has a cool name, but it's actually little used when creating hard-edged Web graphics. The Wand is somewhat useful only for making selections in complex, continuous-tone images (scanned photographs and 3D illustrations). To use the Magic Wand in such scenarios, simply select the tool from the Toolbar and click on a portion of the image. As shown in Figure 4.19, some or all of the image is selected.

FIGURE 4.19

Using the Magic Wand to make a selection

The Magic Wand Options Palette   The Magic Wand works by sampling the pixel that you click on and using the Tolerance setting found in the Magic Wand Options palette. The options in this palette are described below.

Tolerance   Determines how many adjacent pixels to include in the selection. The higher the setting, the more pixels will become part of the selection.

Use All Layers   Provides a way for the Magic Wand to base its initial selection value on the average value of all the pixels at a particular set of coordinates in all of the layers of the image. However, the selection that is ultimately made with the Magic Wand can only exist on the currently targeted layer.

Like other selection palettes, the Magic Wand Options palette also provides an Anti-aliased feature that softens the edges of the selection.

NOTE   All of the selection tools and commands can affect only one layer at a time. See Chapter 7 for more information about Layers.

Move Tool

Using the arrow keys with the selection tools I've previously mentioned adjusts the positioning of the "marching ants," but doing the same with the Move tool actually moves the selected image around the canvas. When pixels are moved, one of two things happens: Either the underlying layers of the image are exposed or the raw canvas is made visible. The latter scenario is shown in Figure 4.20.

FIGURE 4.20

The Move tool moves the selection area and the underlying pixels, exposing the canvas below.

eight.tif @ 66.7% (RGB)

Since the Move tool is used a lot with selections, Adobe has made it instantly accessible. Just hold down the Ctrl (Windows) or Command (Mac) key while another tool is in use.

TIP   Hold down the Option key before clicking and dragging with the Move tool to automatically create a duplicate of the selection.

Other Selection Techniques

Beyond the selection tools, you can use a variety of other commands and techniques to make and adjust selection outlines.

The Basics

The Select All command (Select ➤ Select All) provides a simple way to select everything on a layer. The Reselect command (Select ➤ Reselect) reactivates your most recent selection. Finally, the Inverse command (Select ➤ Inverse) is a quick way to select everything that is not selected and deselect everything that *is* selected.

The Nudge Trick

What if you have a layer in an image that has an assortment of graphics—maybe some rectangles, ovals, and circles—and you want to select them all so you can transform or fill them with a single color? The trick is to invoke the Select ➤ Select All command and then use the up and down arrows to nudge everything one pixel up and then one pixel down—right back where everything started. Now you've got ants that are marching only around the objects, not the entire dimensions of the file (see Figure 4.21).

FIGURE 4.21

Selecting all the objects on a layer via the "nudge trick"

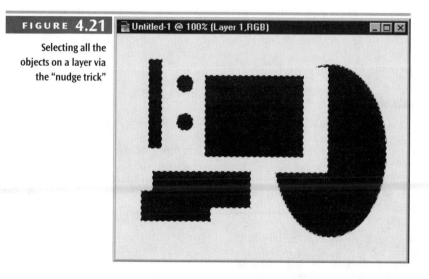

At this point you can fill the entire selection with a color or texture, or warp the whole thing with the transform tools.

N O T E   For more about Layers, see Chapter 7.

Transform Selection

The Transform Selection command in the Select menu modifies a selection outline. In Figure 4.22, a rectangular selection outline has had the Select ➤ Transform Selection command applied and is surrounded by an adjustable frame. When the cursor is outside the frame, it becomes a rotation tool. When the cursor is clicked and dragged on one of the eight handles, the dimensions of the selection outline change. Lastly, when the cursor is double-clicked inside the frame, the changes take effect.

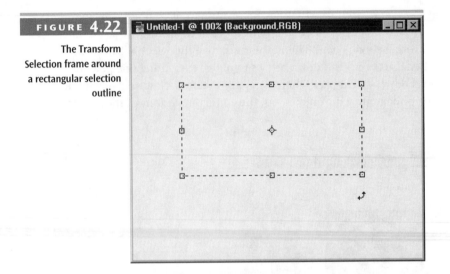

FIGURE 4.22

The Transform Selection frame around a rectangular selection outline

To undo a transformation before it has taken effect, just select another tool from the Toolbar, and Photoshop asks if you want the transformation to take effect.

Coloring Selections

When you're making hard-edged Web graphics, the whole point of using selections is to fill them with color or textures.

The Fill Command

To add color to a selection, select Edit ➤ Fill. The Fill dialog appears.

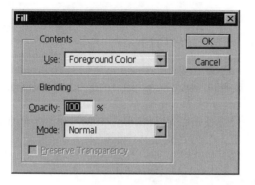

In the Contents area of the dialog, the Use menu offers the following options:

Foreground Color   Fills the selection with the currently selected foreground color.

Background Color   Fills a selection with the currently selected background color.

Pattern   Fills a selection with a graphic pattern when you use the Edit ➤ Define Pattern command.

History   Fills the selection with the currently selected History layer.

N O T E   See Chapter 2 for more information about Photoshop 5's new History feature.

Black   Fills the selection with black.

50% Gray   Fills the selection with an RGB value of 128, 128, 128.

W A R N I N G   50% Gray is not a color setting that can be used reliably in Web graphics. For more on Web color, see Chapter 13.

White   Fills the selection with white.

The Blending portion of the dialog provides the familiar Opacity and Mode settings. The Preserve Transparency command is also available.

N O T E   For more on Photoshop's standard blending options, see Chapter 7.

Nine times out of 10, you'll be filling a selection with the foreground color. In such cases, it's much easier to use the Alt+Backspace (Windows) or Option+Delete (Mac) shortcut. If you want to use the background color, press Ctrl+Backspace (Windows) or Command+Delete (Mac).

The Paste Into Command

If you copy a selection from one part of an image—or a separate image entirely—you can paste that element into another selection by selecting Edit ➤ Paste Into. I pasted the image of Joe Walker (see Figure 4.23), the Photoshop Master profiled in Chapter 6, into a selection of some text created with Photoshop's Type tool (see Figure 4.24). The result is a photo that is clipped in the shape of the text (see Figure 4.25).

FIGURE 4.23

A photo of Joe Walker

joew1.tif @ 66.7% (RGB)

FIGURE 4.24

Some bold type

joe.psd @ 100% (Layer 3,RGB)

FIGURE 4.25

The photo pasted into
the type

In the process, Photoshop created a Layer mask that can be seen in the Layers palette (see Figure 4.26).

FIGURE 4.26

The Layers palette with
the Layer mask

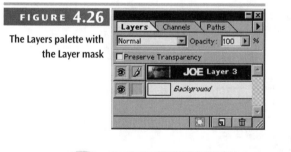

N O T E   Layer masks are covered in Chapter 7.

As you can see in Figure 4.27, by using the Move tool, the precise positioning of the pasted image can be adjusted.

FIGURE 4.27

Positioning the pasted
graphic

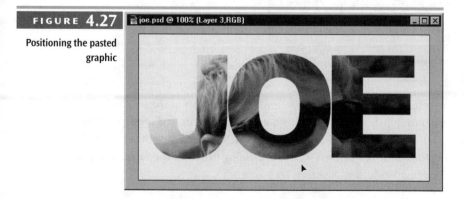

The Stroke Command

The Stroke command applies a line of paint on the selection outline—similar to chalk outlines seen in police work. For example, in Figure 4.28 I have used the Rectangular Marquee tool and applied the Edit ➤ Stroke command, creating a 5-point line around the selection. This is a fantastic way to quickly create geometric outlines—the kind of stuff you see around menu buttons and header graphics.

FIGURE 4.28

Using the Stroke command to create a rectangle with a 5-point line

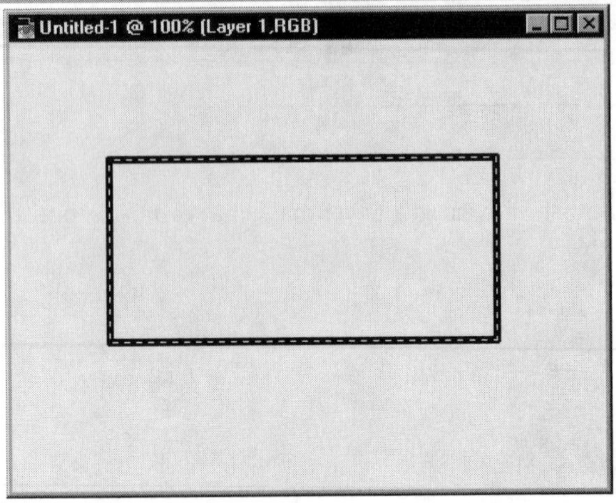

The Stroke command opens the Stroke dialog.

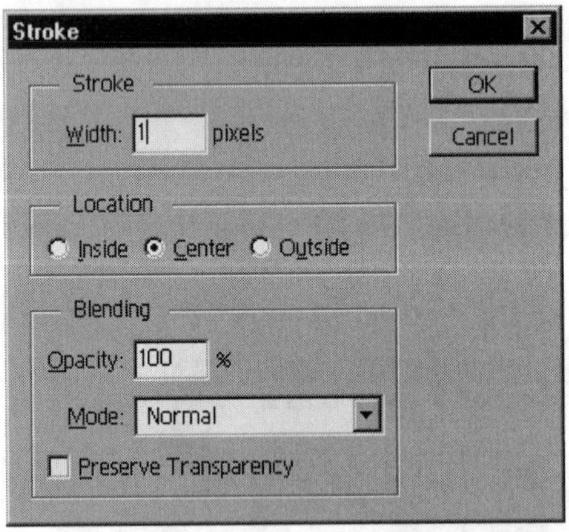

The dialog includes a Stroke area that determines the width of the stroke, in pixels. This feature can be really helpful in creating some thickness around rendered type selections. The Location area specifies where the stroke will be applied—either to the Inside, Center, or Outside of the selection. Finally, the dialog provides the familiar Blending commands (Opacity, Mode, and Preserve Transparency).

WARNING Applying the Stroke command to circular or elliptical selection outlines tends to square off corners. It is often necessary to clean up such areas with the tools mentioned in Chapter 2.

Transforming

As mentioned earlier, it is possible to transform a selection outline. But what about transforming an actual selection—making it bigger, smaller, rotating it, flipping it, or just totally distorting it? Photoshop's Edit menu provides the key to making these kinds of changes.

Scale

To scale a selection, first make a selection and then choose Edit ➤ Transform ➤ Scale. You can scale the selection in any direction and maintain the height/width proportions by holding down the Shift key (see Figure 4.29). Double-click inside the selection area to make the scaling take effect.

FIGURE 4.29
Scaling a selection

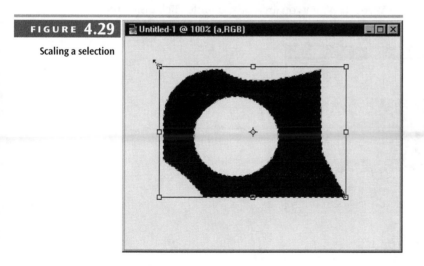

Rotate

Make a selection and then choose Edit ➤ Transform ➤ Rotate to spin the selection around. When you are done, double-click within the selection area to make the rotation take effect. Figure 4.30 demonstrates the rotation technique.

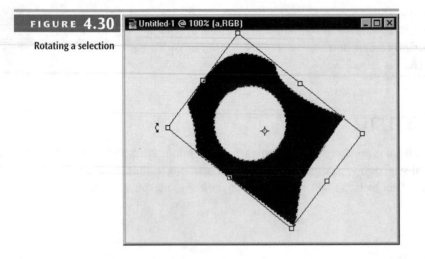

FIGURE **4.30**

Rotating a selection

Flip Horizontal/Vertical

Flipping a selection vertically or horizontally is particularly useful when you want to change the orientation of a photograph (see Figure 4.31). Select Edit ➤ Transform ➤ Flip Horizontal or Flip Vertical. When you are done, double-click inside the selection.

FIGURE **4.31**

Flipping a photograph horizontally (compare with Figure 4.23)

Free Transform

Introduced in Photoshop 4, Free Transform is the all-in-one scale, rotate, skew, distort, and perspective tool. Figure 4.32 demonstrates some of the torture that this tool can inflict on a selection.

Here are a few notes on the Free Transform tool:

- Pressing the Ctrl/Command key creates a perspective effect.
- Clicking and dragging inside the image repositions the entire selection.
- Selecting Edit ➤ Undo reverses the most recent change.

FIGURE **4.32**

The Free Transform
tool in action

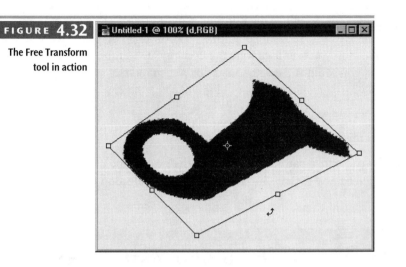
Untitled-1 @ 100% (d,RGB)

TIP   The Flip Horizontal/Flip Vertical commands work while you are using the Free
Transform command.

Duplicating

In addition to the savvy technique of using the Alt (Windows)/Option (Mac) and
Move tool combination to duplicate a selection, you can also use the basic Cut, Copy,
and Paste functions in the Edit menu. As you can probably guess, using the Cut command removes all of the selected area from the image and places it into memory. The
Copy command does the same thing but leaves the image intact. Finally, the Paste
command takes whatever was put into memory and pastes it into the current image.

NOTE   Every time you use the Paste command, Photoshop places the pasted element
on a new layer. For more about Layers, see Chapter 7.

Conclusion

This chapter has introduced you to an array of selection tools, commands, and features. Some you will use often, like the Rectangular Marquee tool and Fill command,
while the Lasso tool will be used only occasionally. The important thing is to learn as
much as possible about Photoshop's selection features because they are so key in the
Web graphics design process.

Casual users may think that tools like the Paintbrush and Airbrush classify Photoshop as an illustration or image editing program, but now you know that Photoshop is also a great design tool. Even if all you ever used were the Rectangular Marquee tool, Fill, and Paste Into commands, you could still create some cool Web graphics.

Up Next

If you like selections, you'll love paths. The subject of the next chapter, the Paths feature provides an advanced way to draw and make very robust selection outlines.

Photoshop Masters: Eric Eaton, Anna McMillan, and Sabine Messner

In a former coffee bean warehouse located at the heart of San Francisco's famed Multimedia Gulch, Eric Eaton, Anna McMillan, and Sabine Messner develop the latest and greatest incarnation of Hotwired. The Hotwired site, part of a family of Web sites that includes Wired News, Hotbot, and Suck, is *the* place for design information, opinions, and culture. Eric (age 28), Anna (24), and Sabine (32), form a close-knit team that is responsible for giving form to one of the most stylish and useful sites on the Web (see Figure 4.33).

In an approach that is best compared to television production, development on the Hotwired site involves multiple disciplines, including designers, writers, marketers, researchers, and producers. When a new portion of the site goes into production, a producer is selected who assembles a development team from the talented Hotwired staff. The producer runs an initial meeting that defines for each team member the goals of the new project.

Once a visual concept has been agreed upon, the designers create individual Web graphics in Photoshop. Having used the program for more than half a decade, Eric, Anna, and Sabine are each expert Photoshop users. Favorite features include Layers and Masks. Besides Photoshop, the Hotwired design team also has other favorites. Anna finds Adobe After Effects to be particularly useful in developing animations. Eric likes Equilibrium Debabelizer for optimizing color palettes and file sizes.

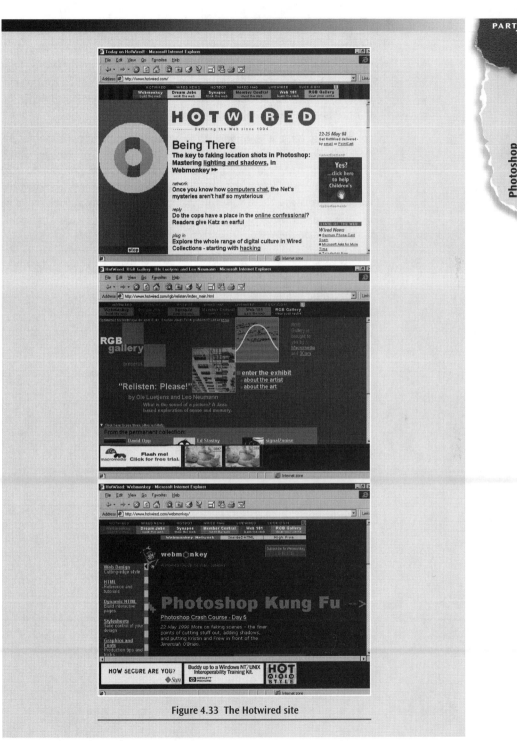

Figure 4.33 The Hotwired site

While the graphics are under development, the designers start to flesh out the layout of the pages with HTML. Eric, Anna, and Sabine do all of their HTML by hand, eschewing WYSIWYG tools like FrontPage that don't provide the level of control the team insists upon. One exception is Dreamweaver, a software tool from Macromedia that has proven to be helpful in the creation of DHTML effects.

For every project, the team adheres to a Web design philosophy that asserts the goals of attaining absolute clarity. The designers use bright colors, rough edges, and bold graphics. They also shy away from anti-aliasing—blending the edges of type and graphics to make them appear more subtle and print-like. As Eric explains, "We see anti-aliasing as a technique that creates unnecessary information. In our designs, a pixel should be either on or off." This rigorous and economical approach to design has resulted in one of the most distinctive sites on the Web.

Portfolio:

- www.hotwired.com
- www.hotwired.com/rgb
- www.hotwired.com/webmonkey

PATHS

Featuring

PATHS

As you saw in Chapter 4, Photoshop has several methods for making selections, including the Marquee, Magic Wand, and Lasso tools. One technique for making selections that I didn't cover in that chapter was Paths.

Paths enhance your selection-making capabilities by using a type of technology seen most often in drawing programs like Adobe Illustrator and Macromedia Freehand. These programs use vector-based objects to define shapes and describe the elements in a drawing.

I begin this chapter by explaining the difference between painting and drawing programs. Next, I'll cover all seven of Photoshop's Paths tools in detail. Last, I'll discuss how you can turn paths into selections (and vice versa) with the Paths palette.

Painting vs. Drawing

One of the reasons paint programs such as Photoshop are so popular is that they're intuitive. The process of painting in Photoshop is similar to working with real paint. You can select different brushes and colors, apply strokes to the canvas, and rework the images with a series of tools and effects.

Drawing programs, on the other hand, are nothing like the real thing. Applications such as Adobe Illustrator and Macromedia Freehand require you to be a geometry major, carefully placing and dragging points along a path to create lines and shapes. Figure 5.1 displays a look at one of these vector-based objects.

FIGURE **5.1**

A typical vector object being created with anchor points, curved line segments, and direction handles

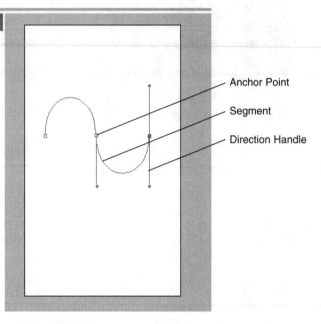

Anchor Point

Segment

Direction Handle

The points and lines that you see are actually just graphic representations of underlying algorithms that tell output devices such as printers how to render the images on paper. This method of storing drawings as algorithms is very powerful because the drawings can scale up or down with absolutely no loss in resolution. In Figure 5.2, the image on the left was created with a paint program while the image on the right was created in a drawing program. Both look pretty good. But when each image is magnified, as in Figure 5.3, the painted image becomes very jagged and rough while the drawn image maintains its clean lines.

FIGURE **5.2**

A painted image (left) and a drawn image (right)

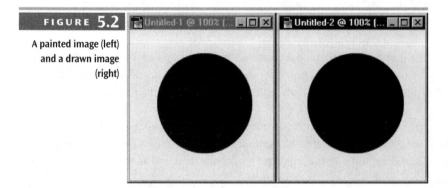

FIGURE 5.3

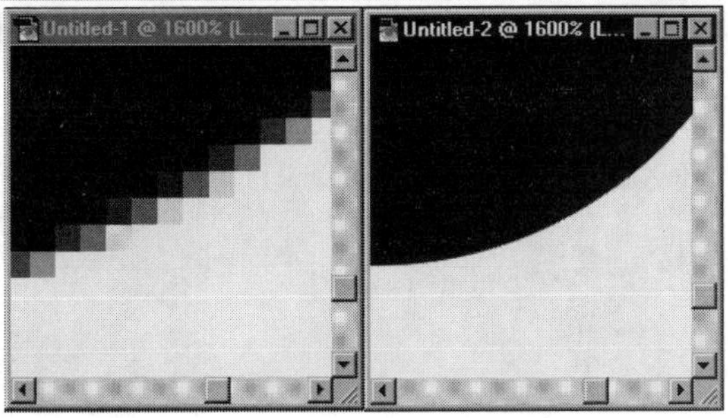

The same images magnified

Even though paint programs are more intuitive, drawing programs clearly have their advantages and are very popular with designers.

N O T E Because drawing programs store files as algorithms, file sizes are far smaller than comparable paint-based images.

Do Web Designers Need to Draw?

The answer is yes. The Web is a pixel-based medium, and Photoshop is a superior tool for pushing these little squares around. But Web designers also need to draw in a vector-based format, especially when they have to create precise selections around irregularly shaped objects. For example, imagine having a photograph of a bunch of people in a crowd. Now imagine having to select only one of those people using Photoshop's standard selection tools. This would be a difficult task.

In fact, digital stock photography providers like Photodisc ship some of their imagery with paths already included, making it very easy to make selections. Figure 5.4 shows a Photodisc image of a piece of bread. By accessing Photoshop's Paths palette, turning the path on, and making it into a selection, you can see how easy it is to isolate the bread.

With the path turned into a selection, I can easily cut and paste this isolated element into another document (see Figure 5.5).

With the Paths feature, you can not only draw outlines around objects to make precise selections, but you can also create vector-based artwork. In fact, Photoshop's biggest secret is that it's a paint program with drawing-application–like features.

FIGURE 5.4

A Photodisc image with a path included in the file

FIGURE 5.5

The object cut and pasted into a new document

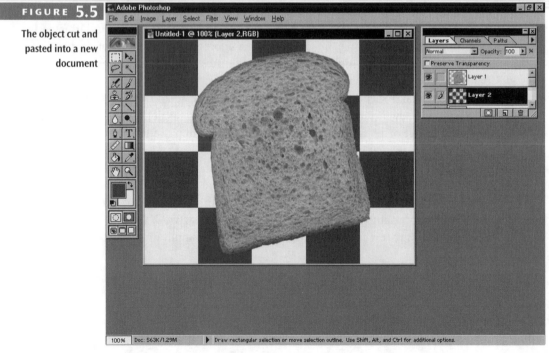

As shown in Figure 5.6, I made a stylized illustration with Photoshop. The illustration is done in a hard-edged, cut paper style, which is perfectly suited to Paths.

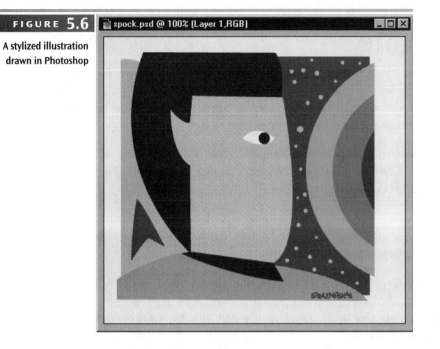

PART

Photoshop Fundamentals

FIGURE 5.6

A stylized illustration drawn in Photoshop

To make the illustration, I created a series of paths that isolated each element in the illustration. Figure 5.7 shows all the paths that went into the drawing.

FIGURE 5.7

All of the paths that make up the illustration

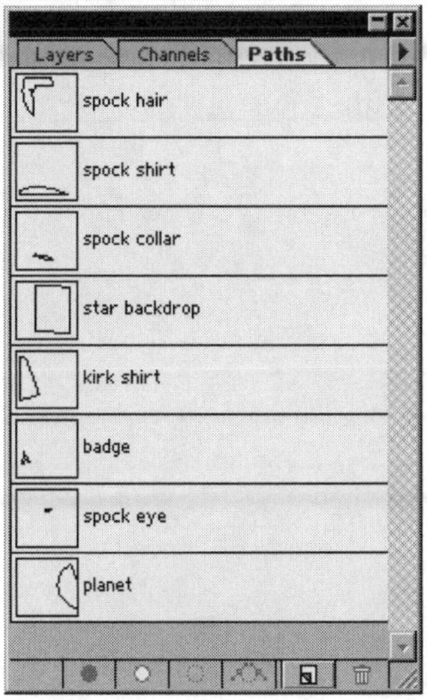

	spock hair
	spock shirt
	spock collar
	star backdrop
	kirk shirt
	badge
	spock eye
	planet

Once the paths were created, I made them each into selections and did a simple color fill. These same techniques can be used to make fun menu buttons, headers, and other graphical elements for Web pages.

Be the Line

Learning to draw with the Paths tools can be a challenge, because creating vector-based art is unlike any form of traditional drawing. With a little practice, however, your speed and skill will increase. As Olav Martin Kvern discusses in his book *Real World Freehand 3*, to understand drawing tools, you must first start thinking like a line:

> *Imagine that, through some mysterious potion or errant cosmic ray, you've been reduced in size so that you're a little smaller than one of the dots in the connect-the-dots puzzle...*
>
> *The only way out is to complete the puzzle. As you walk, a line extends behind you. As you reach each dot in the puzzle, a sign tells you where you are in the puzzle, and how to get to the next dot.*
>
> *Get the idea? The dots in the puzzle are points. The route you walk from one dot to another, as instructed by the signs at each point, is a line segment. Each series of connected dots is a path. As you walk from one dot to another, you're thinking like a line.*

The Paths Tools

In order to make paths, Photoshop provides seven tools, which fall into two general categories: path drawing tools and path editing tools. All of these tools are available via the Toolbar. Figure 5.8 shows the seven Paths tools.

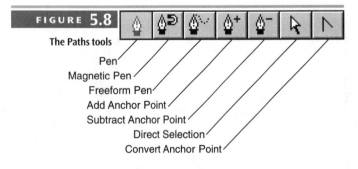

FIGURE 5.8

The Paths tools

Pen
Magnetic Pen
Freeform Pen
Add Anchor Point
Subtract Anchor Point
Direct Selection
Convert Anchor Point

The Path Drawing Tools

With version 5, Adobe has significantly expanded the lineup of path drawing tools, adding both the Magnetic Pen and Freeform Pen tools. Each of the three path drawing tools has a unique method of creating a path outline.

Pen   Draws paths by clicking and dragging.

Magnetic Pen   Attaches itself to real-life objects within the image.

Freeform Pen   Draws a freeform line that converts itself to a path when the mouse is released.

The Pen Tool

If you've ever used Adobe Illustrator's drawing tools, then the Pen tool will be familiar to you. As shown in Figure 5.9, the Pen tool lets you draw straight lines and smooth curves with more control than with the freehand path tools. Then you can edit the path and refine it with a high degree of accuracy. Using the Zoom tool or the Navigator to view the image more closely when editing greatly enhances your ability to draw with precision.

FIGURE 5.9

Straight and
curved paths

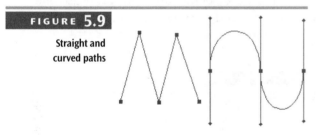

Drawing a Straight Path   A straight path consists of one or more line segments and anchor points. An anchor point is either a smooth point, when the line segments it connects flow together, or a corner point, when the line segments change direction. To create a straight path, do this:

1. Select the Pen tool.
2. Place the cursor on the image where you want the path to begin.
3. Click your mouse. An anchor point appears.
4. Release the mouse button and move the cursor to the next point on the image.
5. Click your mouse. A line segment with another anchor point appears.
6. Continue to click and move your mouse to produce a series of straight segments connected by corner anchor points.

Drawing a Curved Path   A curved path consists of one or more line segments and anchor points from which direction handles are dragged. Direction handles determine the position and length of the line segment. To draw a curved path, follow these steps:

1. Select the Pen tool.

2. Place the cursor on the image where you want the path to begin.

3. Click your mouse and drag. An anchor point with a direction handle appears. Without releasing the mouse button, adjust the direction handle to the direction in which you want the bump of the curve.

4. Release the mouse and move the cursor to the next point on the image.

5. Click your mouse and drag. A curved segment with another anchor point and direction line appears. Drag in the direction of the next curve, or the opposite direction, of the first direction handle.

6. Adjust the direction handle until the line segment is in the desired position and release the mouse button.

Here are some additional tips for drawing curved paths:

- Drag the first point in the direction of the top of the curve and drag the second point in the opposite direction. Dragging the first and second point in the same direction produces an S curve (see Figure 5.10).

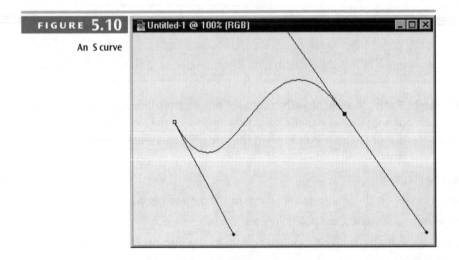

FIGURE **5.10**

An S curve

- Use as few anchor points as possible to assure a smooth path.

- Anchor points should be placed on the valleys of a curve and not on the peaks.

- A path is a continuous series of segments connected by anchor points. You can only add segments to the end points and not to the middle of a segment.

- An anchor point can only connect two segments.
- If you should stop drawing and want to add a new segment to a path, resume drawing by first clicking on one of the end points with the Pen tool.
- If you are drawing an open path and want to begin a second path that is not connected to the first, click the Pen tool before starting the new path.

Changing the Direction of a Curved Path   To change the direction of a curved path, follow these steps:

1. Follow steps 1 through 6 from the preceding section, "Drawing a Curved Path."
2. Place your cursor on the last anchor point and press the Option key while dragging the direction handle in the direction of the next curve.
3. Move your cursor to the next location and click your mouse.
4. Adjust the segment so that the curve is the desired length and position (see Figure 5.11).

FIGURE 5.11

A scalloped path

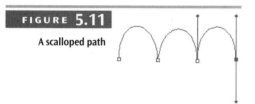

Adding a Curved Path to a Straight Path   To add a curve to a straight path, follow these steps:

1. Follow steps 1 through 5 from the earlier section, "Drawing a Straight Path."
2. Place your cursor on the last anchor point and press the Option key while holding down the mouse button and dragging in the direction of the next curve.
3. Release your mouse button and move your cursor to the next location.
4. Click your mouse and drag in the opposite direction.

Adding a Straight Path to a Curved Path   To add a straight path to a curved one, do this:

1. Follow steps 1 through 4 under the earlier section, "Drawing a Curved Path."
2. Place your cursor on the last anchor point, press the Alt (Windows) or Option (Mac) key, and click your mouse.
3. Move your cursor to the next location and click your mouse to complete the segment (see Figure 5.12).

FIGURE **5.12**

A straight path to
curved path and
vice versa

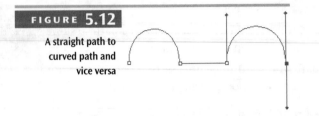

Ending a Path   To end an open path, simply stop drawing. To end with a closed path, place the cursor on the first anchor point. A little circle appears beside the cursor to indicate that the path is ready to be closed (see Figure 5.13). Click your mouse to close the path.

FIGURE **5.13**

Ending a path

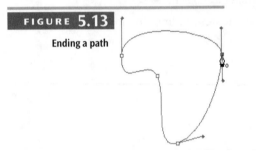

The Magnetic Pen Tool

As mentioned, the Magnetic Pen tool is a new feature to Photoshop 5. It shares the same performance characteristics as the Magnetic Lasso tool (see Chapter 4). It intuitively snaps to defined areas within an image as you drag and converts these areas to paths. You can set the sensitivity and the complexity of the tool's performance with the Magnetic Pen Options palette.

To set options for the Magnetic Pen tool, follow these steps:

1. Double-click on the Magnetic Pen tool to display its palette.

Navigat	**Magnetic Pen Options**	▶
Curve Fit: 2	pixels	
Pen Width: 10	pixels	
Frequency: 20	Edge Contrast: 10 %	
Stylus: ☐ Pressure		

2. Specify the Curve Fit between .5 and 10 to control the sensitivity of the pen to the movement of your mouse. A higher number creates a less complex path with fewer anchor points.

3. Enter a Pen Width value between 1 and 40 to control the width in pixels where the Magnetic Pen will detect a border.

TIP You can increase the detection width in one-pixel increments while drawing by pressing the Open Bracket key ([). You can decrease the width by pressing the Close Bracket key (]).

4. Enter a Frequency value between 1 and 100 to establish the rate at which the Magnetic Pen places anchor points. Higher values place anchor points more rapidly.

5. Enter an Edge Contrast value between 1 and 100% to determine the tool's sensitivity detecting contrasting borders. Higher values detect edges of greater contrast, while lower values increase the tool's sensitivity to low-contrast edges.

TIP If you are working with a stylus tablet, you can set the pressure to correspond with the Pen Width setting. An increase of pressure on the stylus will narrow the pen width.

To draw with the Magnetic Pen tool, do the following:

1. Place your cursor on the image.

2. Click your mouse to set the starting point for the path.

3. Release the mouse button and drag. A path will follow along the most distinct edge within the pen width.

4. Periodically, the Magnetic Pen places anchor points along the specified border while the most recent segment remains active.

5. Click once on the first path's starting point to complete the path.

TIP You can temporarily turn off the Magnetic Pen by holding down Alt (Windows) or Option (Mac) with the mouse button depressed to draw a straight path, or with the mouse button released to draw a freeform path.

End an open Magnetic Pen path by pressing Enter/Return. You can end a closed Magnetic Pen path by double-clicking on the first anchor point.

The Freeform Pen Tool

Another new version 5 feature, the Freeform Pen tool has many of the same characteristics as the Freeform Lasso tool (see Chapter 4). When you place your cursor on the image and click and drag your mouse, the Freeform Pen is followed by a trail that, when the mouse is released, produces a path. The Freeform Pen tool is a fast way to draw a loose, natural curve.

WARNING   You cannot precisely control the number or placement of anchor points with the Freeform Pen tool. Paths created using this tool usually require editing and removing excess anchor points.

To set options for the Freeform Pen tool, follow these steps:

1. Double-click on the Freeform Pen tool to display its palette.

2. Specify the Curve Fit between .5 and 10 to control the sensitivity of the pen to the movement of your mouse. A higher number produces a simpler path with fewer anchor points.

3. Click your mouse on the image and drag. A trail follows the tool as you drag.

4. Release the mouse button, and the trail turns into a path.

NOTE   What's the best way to draw? It's a personal preference. I prefer to draw as few points as possible and then add in curves and other points later. Other people like to draw very freeform and then clean up excess points.

Path Editing Tools

The advantage of paths is that once a path has been drawn, all or part of it can be moved or reshaped. Anchor points can be added or omitted, and corners can be converted into curves or curves into corners.

Photoshop offers four path editing tools:

Add Anchor Point   Adds anchor points to existing paths.

Subtract Anchor Point   Removes anchor points from existing paths.

Direct Selection   Selects anchor points, segments, or direction handles and moves or edits them.

Convert Anchor Point   Changes a corner point to a curve and a curve to a corner point.

Adding and Deleting Anchor Points

After you have drawn a path, you may need to refine it by adding or deleting anchor points. To add an anchor point, select the Add Anchor Point tool and click on the path. A new anchor point will appear. If you want to alter the shape of the line segment, click on the path and drag until the desired shape is achieved.

To omit an anchor point, choose the Delete Anchor Point tool. Click on an anchor point to delete it. The two segments connected by the anchor point join into one. You can reshape a path by clicking on an anchor point and dragging before releasing the mouse button.

The Direct Selection Tool

The Direct Selection tool selects, moves, or modifies a path.

To select paths, do the following:

1. Draw a path with any of the path drawing tools.

2. Choose the Direct Selection tool from the Toolbar.

 T I P You can toggle from any of the Pen tools or path editing tools to the Direct Selection tool by pressing Alt (Win) or Option (Mac).

3. To select an anchor point, click anywhere on the path. The anchor points will appear hollow. Place the cursor on any anchor point or segment and click your mouse. The anchor point will become solid, indicating that it is selected.

4. To select the entire path, place your cursor on the path, hold down the Alt (Win) or Option (Mac) key and click your mouse. You can also draw a marquee around the path with the Direct Selection tool. All the anchor points will appear solid, indicating that the entire path is selected.

5. To deselect the path, click anywhere on the image.

Moving, Copying, and Reshaping Paths

To move or copy a path, follow these steps:

1. To move the entire path, click on the path while holding down the Alt (Win) or Option (Mac) key to select the entire path, then release the key and drag.

2. To copy the path, click on the path and hold down the Alt (Win) or Option (Mac) key while dragging.

3. When the path is in the desired location, click your mouse.

To reshape a path, do this:

1. Place the cursor on an anchor point and click to select it.

2. With the mouse button held down, drag to reposition it.

3. Click on its direction handle and drag to alter the size and position of the segment, or click on any portion of a segment and drag to move, lengthen, or shorten it (see Figure 5.14).

FIGURE 5.14

Moving paths

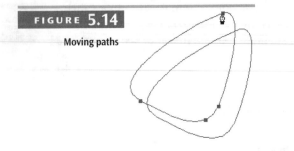

Converting Anchor Points

There are two types of anchor points. *Smooth* points connect curved or straight lines that flow into each other. *Corner* points connect lines that change direction. Anchor points can be converted from corner to smooth or smooth to corner (see Figure 5.15).

FIGURE 5.15

Converting an anchor point

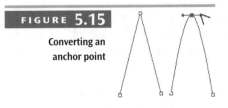

To convert anchor points, choose the Convert Anchor Point tool and do one of the following:

- Click on a smooth point, and it converts to a corner point.
- Click on a corner point and drag the direction handles until the desired shape is achieved, then release the mouse. The corner point changes to a smooth point.

The Paths Palette

The most common use for a path is to convert it to a selection and apply a Photoshop tool. Like layers and channels, paths can be stored to a palette so they can later be loaded. The Paths palette can be accessed by choosing Window ➤ Show Paths from the Menu Bar.

Using the Paths Palette

When you begin drawing a path with the Pen tool, the path appears as a thumbnail in the Paths palette (titled Work Path—the name a path is given until it is saved). As you continue to draw, the thumbnail changes to include new sections of the path. You can increase or decrease the size of the thumbnails or turn them off altogether. Choose Palette Options from the drop-down menu in the upper-right corner of the palette, and click on the radio button next to the desired thumbnail size.

Saving Paths

Once your path has been drawn, you can save it by choosing Save Path from the drop-down menu in the upper-right corner of the palette. A dialog appears so you can name the path. If no name is entered, the path name defaults to Path 1. You can also save a path by dragging the work path to the New Path icon at the bottom of the palette.

The Paths palette lists saved paths from top to bottom in the order in which they were created. The paths can be moved within the list by clicking on the path's name or thumbnail and dragging it to the desired location.

Loading Paths

To load a path, click on the path's name or thumbnail in the Paths palette. Photoshop allows only one path to be loaded at a time. When loaded, it will appear on the image. You can edit or move it, add other paths to it, or delete portions of it. To unload the path, click on the empty portion of the Paths palette.

Deleting Paths

To delete a path, do one of the following:

- Drag a path's thumbnail to the Trash icon at the bottom of the Paths palette. This procedure deletes the path and its thumbnail.

- Click on a path's thumbnail in the Paths palette and press the Delete key. This procedure deletes the path, but does not omit the path's thumbnail from the Paths palette.

- Select an entire path with the Direct Selection tool. (Hold down the Alt (Win) or Option (Mac) key when you click on it). Press the Delete key.

- Select a part of the path with the Direct Selection tool. Press the Delete key once to delete part of the path or twice to delete the entire path.

Using Paths to Apply Color

You can apply color to an area of an image within a closed path or to the edge of a path. To fill a path, do the following:

1. Draw a path or load a path from the Paths palette.

2. Choose a foreground color (see Chapter 3 for more about making color selections).

3. If you are filling a work path, choose Fill Subpath from the Paths palette drop-down menu. If you are filling a saved path, choose Fill Path from the drop-down menu.

4. Select a fill option from the Fill Path dialog.

```
┌──────────────────── Fill Path ────────────────────┐
│                                                    │
│  ┌ Contents ─────────────────┐  ┌──────────┐      │
│  │                           │  │    OK    │      │
│  │  Use: [ Background Color ▲▼]  └──────────┘      │
│  │                           │  ┌──────────┐      │
│  │                           │  │  Cancel  │      │
│  ├ Blending ─────────────────┤  └──────────┘      │
│  │                           │                    │
│  │  Opacity: [100]  %        │                    │
│  │                           │                    │
│  │  Mode: [ Normal      ▲▼]  │                    │
│  │  ☐ Preserve Transparency  │                    │
│  │                           │                    │
│  ├ Rendering ────────────────┤                    │
│  │                           │                    │
│  │  Feather Radius: [0]  pixels                   │
│  │  ☑ Anti-aliased           │                    │
│  └───────────────────────────┘                    │
└────────────────────────────────────────────────────┘
```

5. Click OK.

TIP   You can fill a path with the current Fill Path dialog settings by clicking on the Fill Path icon at the bottom of the Paths palette.

As you saw in Chapter 4, selection outlines can have strokes applied to them, producing an effect similar to the chalk outlines seen in police dramas. Paths can also have strokes applied. To do so follow these steps:

1. Draw a path or load one from the Paths palette.

2. Choose a foreground color.

3. If you are stroking a work path, choose Stroke Subpath from the Paths palette drop-down menu. If you are stroking a saved path, choose Stroke Path from the drop-down menu.

4. A window appears that lets you choose a tool from the submenu. The stroke will paint the characteristics of the chosen tool as defined in the tool's Options palette and the brush from the Brushes palette for the specific tool.

> **Stroke Path**
>
> Tool: ✎ Airbrush ⬍ OK
>
> Cancel

T I P   You can stroke a path with the current tool characteristics set in the Stroke Path window by clicking on the Stroke Path icon at the bottom of the Paths palette.

Turning Paths into Selections

To apply any Photoshop function to an area surrounded by a path other than filling or stroking, you must first convert the path to a selection. Choose Make Selection from the Paths palette drop-down menu. A dialog opens that lets you choose the characteristics of the new selection.

> **Make Selection**
>
> **Rendering**
>
> Feather Radius: 0 pixels   OK
>
> ☑ Anti-aliased   Cancel
>
> **Operation**
>
> ○ New Selection
> ○ Add to Selection
> ● Subtract from Selection
> ○ Intersect with Selection

The Rendering area enables you to feather, or soften, a selection by entering a pixel radius or to anti-alias a selection. If you are converting a path while a selection is active, you can choose an option from the Operation area by clicking on its radio button.

New Selection   Discards the active selection and replaces it with an entirely new selection.

Add to Selection   Has the effect of adding the area defined by the path to the active selection border.

Subtract Selection   Has the effect of omitting the area defined by the path from the active selection border.

Intersect Selection   Makes a selection where the path and the active selection border overlap.

Click OK to convert the path into a selection.

T I P   You can convert a path into a new selection by clicking on the Paths As Selection icon at the bottom of the Paths palette.

Turning Selections into Paths

Active selection borders can be converted to paths. This is a technique sometimes used to modify a typeface in Photoshop. The type is generated with the Type Outline tool and converted to paths. The paths are modified and then reconverted into a selection, and a Photoshop function is applied to the image.

N O T E   For more about type, see Chapter 14.

Drawing a selection border with one of the selection tools and converting it to a path is a way to assure accuracy for the selection when it is reconverted back into a selection. To convert a selection into a path, do the following:

1. Draw a marquee with one of the selection tools.

2. Choose Make Work Path from the Paths palette drop-down menu.

3. Set the tolerance of the path in pixels in the dialog that opens. Tolerances with low values produce more complex paths with greater numbers of anchor points, while tolerances with higher values produce simpler paths.

4. Click OK to convert the selection into a path.

T I P   You can convert a selection into a path by clicking on the Selection As Path icon at the bottom of the Paths palette.

Conclusion

Paths are powerful because once they've been drawn, they remain stored in a Photoshop file until you need them again. Paths can also be scaled without any loss of resolution.

Finally, paths are compact and add very little information to an image, keeping file sizes down.

In many ways, the Paths feature is an application within an application. Paths provide Illustrator-like drawing capabilities without ever having to leave Photoshop. With version 5 of the program, Adobe has beefed up the Paths feature even more. It will be interesting to see how far Adobe will go in blurring the lines between its drawing and painting tools.

Up Next

Don't touch that dial! Channels are a savvy way to adjust color in photographic images and create special effects. It's all coming up in Chapter 6.

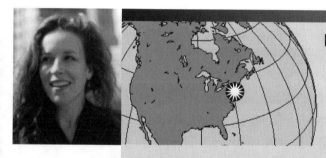

Photoshop Master: Elisabeth Roxby

Elisabeth Roxby lives the life most budding free-lance Web designers dream of. From a New York City loft that serves as both her living quarters and studio, Elisabeth spends her days working on sites that are both challenging and personally rewarding. Her reputation has now grown to the point where she can pick and choose the projects that she wants to work on.

The 30-year-old designer began using Photoshop in 1991 with version 2.0. At that time, she was the Exhibitions Coordinator for Cooper-Hewitt, the Smithsonian Institution's National Design Museum in New York City. Elizabeth's responsibilities included the design of various exhibitions—an experience that she feels prepared her for Web design. "Like a Web site, an exhibit must have very clear navigation systems, because you're never sure how people will move around the space," she explains.

After leaving the museum in 1995, Elisabeth began working with upstart Web firms like Razorfish. While with such agencies, she found that most projects were handled by account executives, leaving little opportunity for designers to have direct contact with clients.

In response to such practices, Elisabeth began freelancing and dealing directly with her own clients. Working on a variety of sites, including MovieLink and Cooper-Hewitt (see Figure 5.16), Elisabeth established herself as one of New York's finest Web designers.

PART 1

Photoshop Fundamentals

Figure 5.16 The MovieLink and Cooper-Hewitt Web sites

The life of a freelancer can be lonesome, but Elisabeth has found ways to break the soli-
tude. She often ventures into the streets below her studio to conduct field research on
new projects. Also, since she works directly with clients, there are plenty of opportunities to work with others and become part of a virtual team. In her spare time, she's part
of a nine-member *a cappella* singing group (see Figure 5.17).

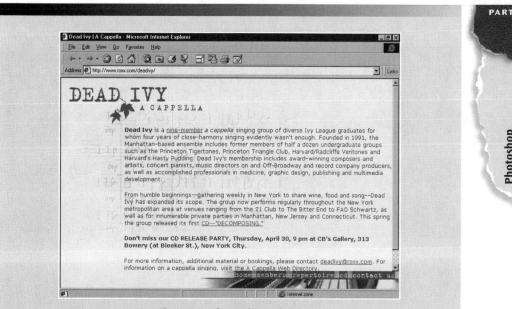

Figure 5.17 The Dead Ivy Web site

Finally, there are her three assistants—two cats and a dog—who keep her company while she works.

Portfolio:

- www.roxx.com
- www.movielink.com
- www.si.edu/ndm
- www.roxx.com/deadivy

chapter 6

CHANNELS

Featuring

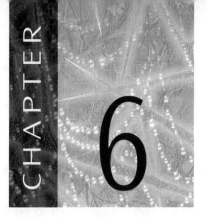

6

CHANNELS

Photoshop's Channels feature is a powerful tool for adjusting color in photographic images and creating the soft, photomontage work that is seen so often on the Web. I must confess that channels were one of the last Photoshop technologies that I learned. As a Web designer, they always seemed too complicated and unnecessary since I wasn't doing print work. However, after watching some print designers in action, it became clear that channels offered advantages over the way I was working.

This chapter is divided into two parts. The first deals with channels and color, particularly as they relate to RGB files. The second part covers alpha channels and their ability to create special effects. First, I'll discuss what channels can actually do for you.

What Are Channels?

Channels do two things: They break down an image's color into distinct, adjustable levels and provide a way to save selections.

In Chapter 3, I discussed a number of ways to adjust an image's color. Channels provide a different way to access and change an image's color information. This is particularly useful when dealing with scanned photographic images that have poor color balance and need to be put on the Web.

Channels also provide a way to save selections into *alpha channels*. As you know from Chapter 4, any time you make a selection, the area outside is masked—you can't paint or draw on it no matter how hard you try. Thus, alpha channels actually serve as masks that you can use to create special effects.

Channels and Color

As you learned in Chapter 3, designers work in RGB mode when creating Web graphics. Figure 6.1 depicts an RGB image and a breakdown of its channels. There are four color channels: red, green, blue, and the RGB channel that is a composite of the three values.

FIGURE 6.1

The three color channels and the composite RGB channel

Because each red, green, and blue channel contains 256 possible shades of each color, an RGB image can display 256^3 or 16,777,216 possible colors. This is what a computer catalog is referring to when it says that a scanner is 24 bit, RGB, and capable of producing millions of colors. It is 24 bit because it can scan three eight-bit color channels, each capable of producing 256 colors.

WARNING   Even though Web graphics are created in RGB mode, you will sometimes need to convert a CMYK image that was used in print. A CMYK image has four channels—cyan, magenta, yellow, and black. These are the ink colors used in the offset printing process to represent full color. Because the CMYK color mode represents the image in four channels instead of three, the image has a larger file size than the same image in RGB mode. When converting files from CMYK to RGB, there is often an unavoidable distortion in the color values, and the channels may need to be adjusted.

The Channels Palette

Channels are accessed via the Channels palette. To open the Channels palette, select Window ➤ View Channels. The contents of each channel will be displayed on-screen when the Eye icon to the left of the channel is visible. When the composite channel's Eye icon is visible, all of the color channels are displayed simultaneously so that the full color image can be seen (see Figure 6.2).

FIGURE 6.2

The Channels palette with the RGB composite channel visible

NOTE When an individual channel is highlighted, it is known as the *target channel*. Photoshop's editing functions will only be applied to the target channel.

Channels Commands

As displayed in Figure 6.3, the Channels palette provides a number of commands via a drop-down menu off the arrow in the upper-right corner of the palette. Commands include duplicating, splitting, and merging channels. Palette options are also provided.

Duplicating Channels   When you duplicate a targeted channel, you get an exact copy of it in the Channels palette. This is helpful if you want to experiment with modifying the channel by painting, applying a filter effect, or using any other editing function without harming the original channel. Also, you will want to duplicate a channel if you need to convert a color channel into a mask.

To use this command, target a channel to be duplicated by clicking on it and select Duplicate Channel from the drop-down menu.

FIGURE 6.3

Accessing the Channels
palette commands

Layers \ **Channels** \ Paths \

New Channel...
Duplicate Channel...
Delete Channel

New Spot Channel...
Merge Spot Channel

Channel Options...

Split Channels
Merge Channels...

Palette Options...

N O T E   The Duplicate Channel option will be dimmed if the RGB composite channel is
targeted, because only one channel can be duplicated at a time.

Splitting Channels   Photoshop can split a document's channels into independent
grayscale images. Each window's title is automatically appended to the channel's color
name as a suffix in the image's title bar at the top of the window. Alpha channels will
appear separately as grayscale images. This option is useful as a first step in redistribut-
ing channels in an image before merging them or for making separate documents of
the channels.

To use this command, simply select Split Channels from the drop-down menu.

Merging Channels   Separate channels can be merged into a single, multi-channel
document. Images to be merged must be single-channel, grayscale images—not RGB.
Images must also be open and the exact same size in height, width, and resolution.
Three open images will produce an RGB, LAB, or a Multi Channel image. Four open
images will produce a CMYK or Multi Channel image.

To use the Merge Channels command, do this:

1. Open three grayscale images that are the exact same size in height, width, and
   resolution.

2. Select Window ➤ View Channels to open the Channels palette, then select
   Merge Channels from the palette's drop-down menu.

3. Since you're a Web designer, assign the RGB color mode to the image in the Merge
   Channels dialog.

4. Click OK.

5. The Merge RGB Channels dialog opens so you can determine the distribution of the color channels. This is helpful if you want to create color distortions by switching color information between channels.

6. Click OK.

Palette Options   Like most Photoshop palettes, the Channels palette provides a Palette Options command. However, the only adjustment you can make is to the size of the thumbnails displayed in the palette. Simply select an appropriate thumbnail size.

N O T E   The Merge Spot Channel feature in the Channels palette is used to create images that are output to film for traditional printing on presses. In other words, it is of no concern to Web designers.

Channels Display Preferences

In RGB mode, individual color channels, by default, are represented on the Channels palette by a red, green, or blue thumbnail icon. When the color channel is viewed on-screen, subtle tonal variations may not necessarily be apparent. It is sometimes desirable to view the color channels in black and white.

To change the channel display, do this:

1. Choose File ➤ Preferences ➤ Display and Cursors. The Display & Cursors Preferences dialog opens.

2. Click on the Color Channels in Color checkbox to turn the option on or off.
3. Click OK.

The Channel Mixer

The Channel Mixer is a brand new addition to Photoshop 5 and enables you to adjust the color information of each channel from one control window. You can establish color values on a specific channel as a mixture of any or all of the color channels' brightness values. The Channel Mixer can be used for a variety of purposes, including the following:

- Creating an optimal grayscale image from an RGB or CMYK file
- Making a high-quality sepia tone from a CMYK or RGB file
- Converting images into alternative color spaces
- Swapping color information from one channel to another
- Making creative color adjustments to images by altering the color information in a specific channel

Tips on Using the Channel Mixer

Photoshop expert Stephen Romaniello, an educator at Pima College in Tucson, Arizona, shares his notes about using the brand new Channel Mixer tool:

- You can adjust color information globally on a particular channel or within a selection marquee so that portions of the image can be quickly altered, corrected, or converted independently while previewing the results.

- When you choose a channel by name from the Output Channel drop-down menu, the value next to the corresponding color slider reads 100% and represents the total amount of that color in the image. The values can be increased to 200% or decreased to –200%.

- The performance of the Color Mixer depends on the color mode of the image. When working in CMYK, increasing the numerical value of the color cyan, for example, by dragging the slider to the right to a maximum of 200%, increases the amount of cyan in the cyan channel. Decreasing the numerical value by dragging the slider to the left to a minimum of –200% omits cyan from the channel.

- Adjusting the color slider of any other color, like magenta for example, while the cyan channel is targeted, changes the amount of the cyan in the cyan channel based on the relationship between the brightness values of magenta and cyan.

- When working in RGB mode, the Channel Mixer performs differently. Increasing the numerical value to a maximum of 200% shifts the color toward the color of that channel, while decreasing the value to a minimum of –200% shifts the color towards its compliment. Therefore, by decreasing the value of red, you can shift the color towards cyan. Decreasing the value of green shifts the color towards magenta, and blue decreases toward yellow.

- The Constant slider is like having an independent black or white channel with an opacity slider added to the targeted color channel to increase or decrease its overall brightness values.

- Converting a color image to grayscale has been a process of trial and error until now. An optimal grayscale image from an RGB or CMYK image can be created by checking the Monochrome box, targeting the black channel, and adjusting the color sliders for each of the colors. With the ability to control brightness and contrast values of each of the color channels while previewing the image, you can create an optimal grayscale image.

Using the Channel Mixer

To use the Channel Mixer, do the following:

1. In the Channels palette, target the RGB composite channel by clicking on it.

2. Choose Image ➤ Adjust ➤ Channel Mixer from the Menu Bar. The Channel Mixer dialog appears.

3. Select the channel to be affected from the Output Channel drop-down menu.

4. Adjust the color sliders to modify the color relationships between channels.

5. Click OK.

Making Color Corrections with Channels

Few people are aware of what constitutes a good, color-balanced image, and even fewer know how to properly correct an image. With the advent of the World Wide Web, many pictures have been published that are in serious need of color correction.

Fortunately, channels let you isolate the red, green, and blue color information and make adjustments to poorly colored images. Images that have an inadequate color range, use color casts, or have poor brightness and contrast can easily be adjusted by targeting a specific color channel and applying one of Photoshop's image adjustment functions.

Let's explore a method of correcting a photograph with a distinct color cast. Typically, a yellow or orange cast on a photograph is the result of taking inside pictures with outdoor film. Correcting this simple mistake requires only a few steps:

1. Inspect the image visually and determine how the color is off balance.

2. Open the Channels palette and highlight the blue channel by clicking on its name. Be sure that the Eye icon is visible next to all of the color channels as shown in Figure 6.4. Even though the blue channel is the only one targeted, you will see the results of your changes on the composite image.

FIGURE **6.4**

The Channels palette with the blue channel targeted

3. Choose Image ➤ Adjust ➤ Levels from the Menu Bar. The Levels window appears, displaying a graph of the color information of the blue channel, called a *histogram*. The histogram notes the relative number of pixels of each of the 256 shades in the image. Each shade is represented by a line. The higher the line on the graph, the more pixels of that shade are present in the image.

4. The blue channel controls the amount of blue or yellow (the opposite of blue in the additive color model) in the image. To reduce the amount of yellow in the image, click on the midtone slider (the gray triangle) and move it towards the right. Be sure to click on the Preview box to observe the results.

5. When you are satisfied with the results, click OK.

Alpha Channels

Beyond the four color channels found in an RGB image, other channels containing selection information can exist. You may recall that when you make a selection using one of Photoshop's selection tools, the area within the marquee is editable. The area outside the marquee is protected or masked. When you store a selection to an alpha channel—also called a mask—it appears in the Channels palette as a grayscale image (see Figure 6.5).

FIGURE 6.5

An alpha channel with a mask indicated

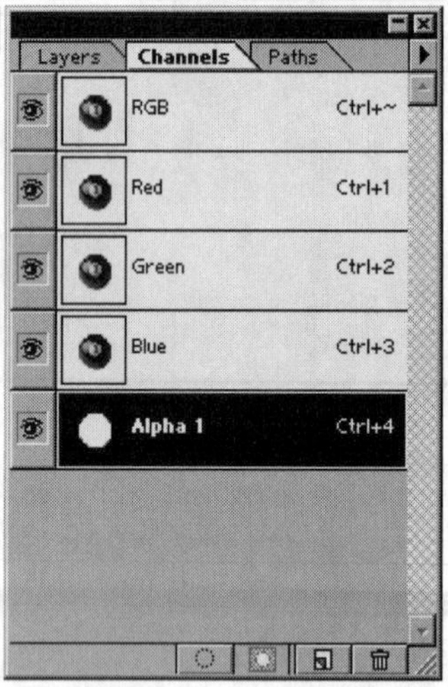

Alpha channels can have up to 256 shades of gray just like any other channel. By default, the white area on the Channel icon represents areas that you selected. The black area indicates areas that are masked. Any intermediate gray values in the channel, like a shadow, can be partially selected.

Using Alpha Channels to Create a Special Effect

Like driving a car with a standard transmission, alpha channels provide a hands-on technique for creating special effects, rather than using Layer Effects or filters.

Figure 6.6 shows two RGB graphics that are exactly the same size (500 pixels wide by 200 pixels tall).

I selected Image ➤ Calculations to launch the Calculations dialog. As you can see in Figure 6.7, I've set Source 1 to be the upper graphic, and source 2 to be the lower, type graphic.

FIGURE 6.6

Two RGB graphics

FIGURE 6.7

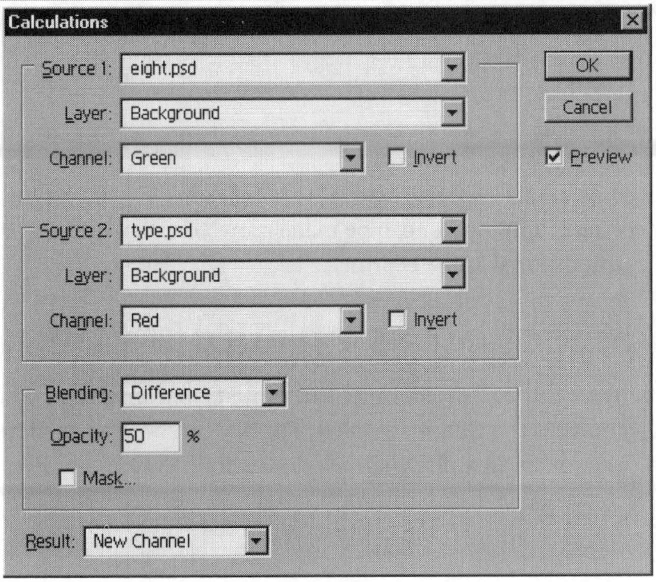

The Calculations dialog

I set Blending to Difference and Opacity to 50%. Finally, I chose New Channel from the Result drop-down list. The final result is that the upper graphic now includes the type, and the background is screened back (see Figure 6.8).

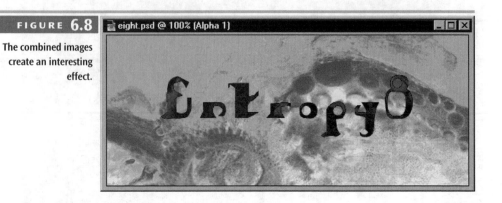

FIGURE 6.8

The combined images create an interesting effect.

All of this information is placed in a new alpha channel (see Figure 6.9).

FIGURE 6.9

The new alpha channel

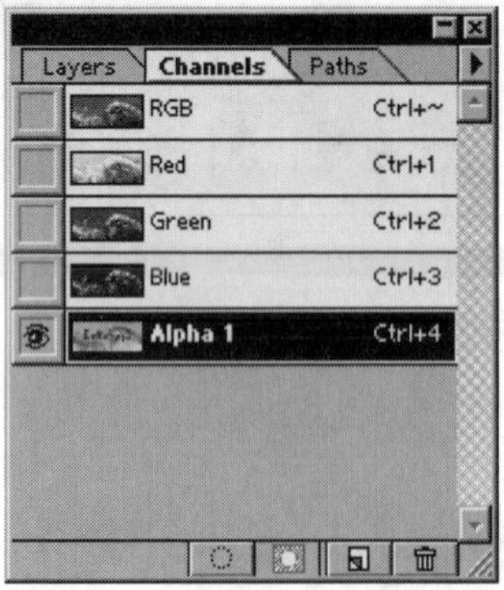

This interesting graphic effect can be made more complex by applying the Calculations feature to additional alpha channels.

Saving a Selection as an Alpha Channel

Because making an intricate selection can be quite time-consuming, Photoshop lets you store selections to the Channels palette so they can be used at a later time.

To save a selection as an alpha channel, do the following:

1. Make a selection.

2. Choose Select ➤ Save Selection from the Menu Bar. The Save Selection dialog appears.

Save Selection

Destination
Document: eightball.psd
Channel: New
Name:

Operation
⦿ New Channel
○ Add to Channel
○ Subtract from Channel
○ Intersect with Channel

OK
Cancel

3. Under Destination, designate the document where the selection will be saved from the Document drop-down menu. You can save a selection as an alpha channel to the document where the selection was made or to any open document that is the exact same size in height, width, and resolution. You can also open it as an independent document by selecting New.

4. Choose the destination channel where the selection will be saved from the Channel drop-down menu. To create a new alpha channel, select New.

5. If you want, type a name for your alpha channel in the Name text box. If you leave the box empty, your saved selection will appear on the Channels palette as Alpha 1, Alpha 2, etc.

6. Click OK.

N O T E   You can quickly save a selection as a new alpha channel by clicking on the New Channel icon (second from left) at the bottom of the Channels palette.

Viewing Alpha Channels

Once a selection has been saved as an alpha channel, it can be viewed independently. If you click on the icon of the channel in the Channels palette, the mask will appear in the main image window (see Figure 6.10). By default, black represents masked areas and white represents selected areas.

FIGURE 6.10

The Channels palette
with the Alpha 1
channel displayed in
main image window

Channel Options

When you double-click on the Mask icon, the Channel Options dialog appears.

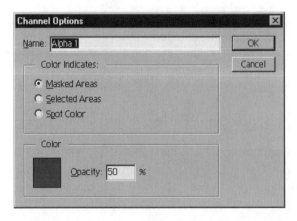

In this dialog, you can choose either Masked Areas or Selected Areas to be displayed as color overlays. By default, these overlays are red and 50% opacity. You can specify an alternate color for the overlay, which is helpful if the image has areas that are the same color as the mask or if you want to color-code your masks. You can also specify the opacity for the mask, which affects the display only and not the masking characteristics. This is necessary if you need to see the image and the mask at the same time.

To change the color and opacity of the overlay, follow these steps:

1. Open the Channel Options dialog.

2. Click on the color swatch in the lower-left corner. The Photoshop Color Picker is displayed.

3. Choose a hue from the hue slider and a saturation and brightness from the color field.

4. Click OK.

5. In the Channel Options dialog, enter a percentage value in the Opacity box.

6. Click OK.

Loading Selections

Once saved, the alpha channel can be loaded to select an area on an image. To load a selection, do this:

1. Choose Select ➤ Load Selection from the Menu Bar. The Load Selection dialog appears.

2. Choose the name of the source document from the Document drop-down menu.

3. Select a channel from the Channel drop-down menu.

4. Select the Invert checkbox to load an inversed selection of the mask.

5. Choose one of the four options from the Operation area:

New Selection   Loads a new selection to the image.

Add to Selection   Adds the loaded selection area to an active selection marquee.

Subtract from Selection   Omits the loaded selection area from an active selection marquee.

Intersect with Selection   Loads the area where the loaded selection and an active selection marquee intersect.

6. Click OK to load the selection.

N O T E   You can quickly load a selection by dragging it to the Load Selection icon at the bottom left of the Channels palette.

Editing Alpha Channels

It is sometimes desirable to adjust the boundaries of a saved mask, and Photoshop gives you the painting tools for such work. For example, if you missed a small part of the selection while using the Lasso tool, you can alter the contents of the mask channel with the Paintbrush to include the areas that were excluded from the original selection.

T I P   Any painting or editing function that can be applied to a grayscale image can be applied to an alpha channel.

To alter the contents of an alpha channel, do this:

1. Target the channel that you want to affect by clicking on its name in the Channels palette.

2. Load the color black into the Foreground Color/Background Color indicator in the Toolbar (see Chapter 3 for more information about specifying color).

3. Choose the Paintbrush, Airbrush, Pencil, or any tool that applies foreground color.

4. Paint directly on the channel.

The resulting painting will, by default, alter the selection to mask the newly painted areas when the selection is loaded.

To produce a more precise selection, you may need to see the image while you are altering the mask channel. You can view the channel as a colored overlay over the image by clicking on the boxes next to the composite channel and the alpha channel in the Channels palette.

NOTE   If you paint with white on an alpha channel, you will erase the masked areas. Painting with a shade of gray will create a partially masked area depending on how light or dark the color is. The darker the shade of gray, the more an area will be masked.

Using Mask Channels in GIFs

As you will learn in Chapter 12, GIF is the most popular graphic format used on the Web. GIF lets you designate certain colors as being transparent. This is often done best with an alpha channel.

To embed a channel in a GIF image, follow these steps:

1. Make a selection in an image.

2. Choose Select ➤ Save Selection and use the Save Selection dialog to save the selection as an alpha channel.

3. Select Image ➤ Mode ➤ Indexed Color from the Menu Bar. The Indexed Color dialog appears.

4. In this dialog, select the Web palette from the Palette drop-down menu.

5. Select File ➤ Export ➤ GIF 89A Export from the Menu Bar. The GIF89a Export Options dialog appears.

6. From the Transparency From drop-down menu, select Alpha 1 or the name of the channel you would like to use as a transparency selection (see Figure 6.11).

FIGURE 6.11

Selecting an alpha channel for transparency

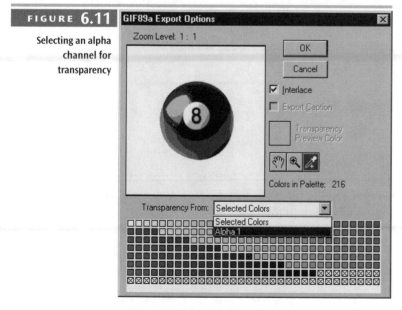

7. Click OK and save the file.

Alpha Channels and File Size

Alpha channels do not affect the way the image appears until they are loaded and an editing function is applied to them. But even if a mask is not visible, it is increasing the overall file size of an image. Images with lots of channels can become quite large and consume lots of disk space and RAM, so be sure to delete them when they no longer serve a purpose.

You can delete a targeted channel by selecting the Delete Channel command off the Channels palette menu.

N O T E   You can only delete alpha channels. The Delete Channel command will be grayed out when the RGB composite channel or any of the individual color channels are selected.

Quick Mask

Quick Masks are an efficient method for making temporary masks using the paint tools and can quickly be converted into selections or be stored as mask channels in the Channels palette for later use. You can toggle directly into the Quick Mask mode on the Toolbar by pressing the letter Q or clicking on the Quick Mask icon (see Figure 6.12).

FIGURE 6.12

The Quick Mask icon activated on the Toolbar

Quick Mask Icon

When you choose Quick Mask mode from the Toolbar, a temporary icon labeled Quick Mask, in italics, appears in the Channels palette (see Figure 6.13). The icon will change appearance as you apply paint to the Quick Mask.

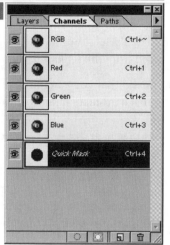

FIGURE 6.13

A Quick Mask noted in
the Channels palette

Quick Mask Options

The Quick Mask Options dialog is essentially identical to the Channel Options dialog described earlier in the chapter and can be accessed by double-clicking on the Quick Mask icon.

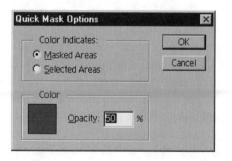

As in the Channel Options dialog, you can choose a specific color for the mask display by clicking on the color swatch and choosing a color from the Color Picker. This is very helpful if areas of the image are predominantly the same color as the mask. The opacity of the mask is determined by the percentage value entered in the Opacity box.

Using Quick Mask

To use the Quick Mask feature, do the following:

1. Select the Quick Mask icon on the Toolbar.

2. Select a tool: The Paintbrush, Airbrush, Pencil, Rubber Stamp, Smudge, Sharpen, Blur, Paint Bucket, Line, and Gradient tools all work in Quick Mask mode.

3. Apply the tool to the image.

4. Select the Normal Mode icon from the Toolbar when you have completed your editing. The painted area will change to a selection marquee. By default, the areas that were painted are now excluded from the selection.

Once you've made a Quick Mask, I recommend that you carefully examine it for missed areas and pinholes. It is quite easy to make mistakes because it can be difficult to see omissions and errors on the image.

The best way to examine the Quick Mask is to view it as a grayscale image. To do this, turn off the Eye icons on all the other channels in the Channels palette except for the one to the left of the Quick Mask. Scrutinize it carefully to assure that the masked areas are solid and opaque. If necessary, apply more paint to deficient areas.

Quick Mask is ideal for cleaning up selections that you have made with one of the selection or marquee tools. Painting a few pixels at a time with a small brush greatly enhances the precision and speed of making selections.

WARNING   If the Opacity slider on the Paintbrush Options palette is set to 50%, it will paint with translucent color. The result will be an area that is only partially masked. To be sure that the area is completely masked, set the Opacity slider to 100%.

Conclusion

Web designers could conceivably get by without ever learning how to use the Channels feature. Indeed, as we'll learn in the next chapter, Photoshop's Layers feature includes a masking feature. But for some types of image creation, channels provide a good way to store selections and compose rich graphics. Masks also provide an excellent way to develop transparency areas for GIF files.

As far as color, channels offer insight into how RGB images are constructed, and many of the photographic images on the Web could benefit from color channel adjustment.

Up Next

Layers are often cited as the most indispensable part of Photoshop. If you've ever tried to create Web graphics with a low-end paint program, you'll know why. Dig into the next chapter to learn how the Layers feature can save you time and increase the quality of every Web graphic you create.

Photoshop Master:
Irene Fazio

What does it take to make corporate America happy? According to Irene Fazio, it takes a Web designer who understands branding and graphic identity. As an art director for my company Brain-Bug, located in Hartford, Connecticut, Irene develops Web communications for some of the area's largest corporations.

In 1992, Irene got her start in design at traditional advertising agencies producing high-end print work. Back then, she worked with Photoshop 2.0—long before convenient features such as Layers were developed. High-resolution photo retouch work provided Irene with invaluable, hands-on training in Photoshop.

In 1996, with successful print work for clients such as Guinness Import Company and AGFA under her belt, Irene took the leap into Web design. One of her first projects was for MedSpan, a fast-growing HMO. Irene combined the company's existing corporate identity and the nuances of the Web to create a site that was integrated into MedSpan's traditional marketing campaign (see Figure 6.14).

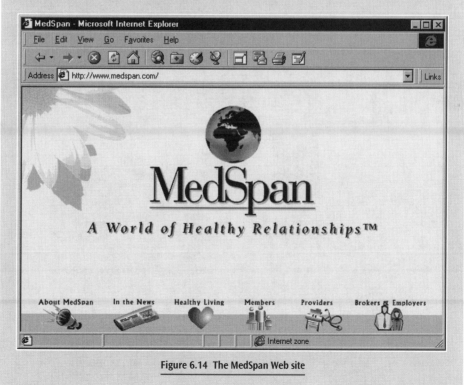

Figure 6.14 The MedSpan Web site

Irene has also developed clean, corporate Web communications for another health care provider, Tufts Health Plan (see Figure 6.15), and Robinson and Cole, a major law firm (see Figure 6.16).

Figure 6.15   Tufts Health Plan Web site

Figure 6.16   Robinson and Cole Web site

The 28-year-old designer got her education at the University of Hartford, where she studied under designer and author Alex White and renowned designer/instructor Jan Kubasiewicz. Irene credits these instructors with providing her with a foundation of strong typography and design, a background that has served her well while venturing into the new medium of the World Wide Web.

Portfolio:

- www.medspan.com
- www.rc.com

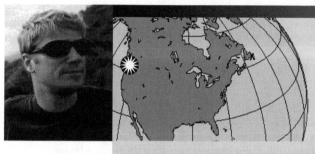

Photoshop Master:
Joe Walker

For me, the best thing about the Web isn't just designing sites, but also getting to know other people who do the same kind of work. A few years ago when the Web was relatively new, I stumbled onto a very unique personal Web site. Its creator was Joe Walker, an artist/designer from Seattle, Washington. In e-mail conversations with Joe, I learned a bit more about how he got started in the medium.

After Joe got his degree from the American Academy of Art in Chicago, he moved to Seattle, Washington, where he did everything from silk screen work and sign painting to CD-ROM development. In 1995, Joe started working on the Web and found a niche for himself, creating some of the best music sites around. His portfolio includes pages for Subpop, the Seattle label that specializes in alternative music (see Figure 6.17).

One of the most challenging things about being a Web designer is keeping up with technology. Joe has developed a strategy of not using any new browser technology until it's been supported by at least two versions of the software. The strategy helps him avoid wasting lots of time testing new technology that often does nothing to enhance a site's overall design. Bells and whistles are fun, but they are not nearly as important as logically organized content and good design.

Joe's platform of choice is the Mac (although he notes that he can function on the PC if need be), and he started using Photoshop in 1994 with version 3 of the program. The 32-year-old designer likes the program because it allows him to explore different looks very quickly. Joe also likes the way the program allows him to optimize images. "I have some really involved processes for crunching things down while still preserving the quality of the graphic—processes that just wouldn't be possible in other image editing programs," he says.

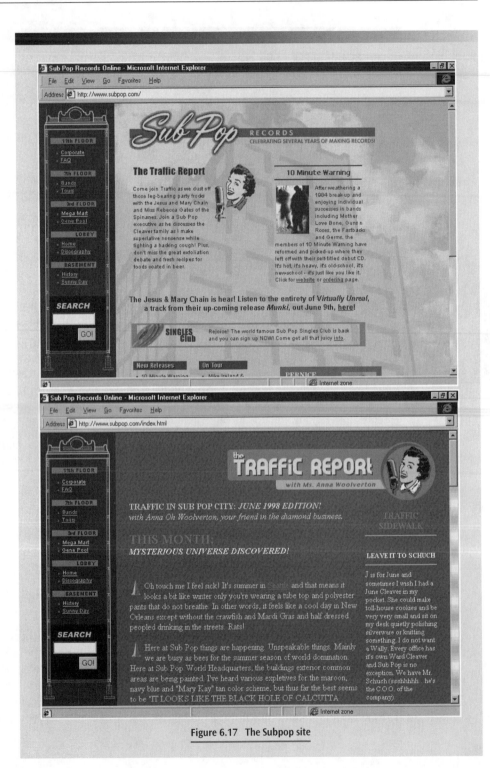

Figure 6.17 The Subpop site

Figure 6.17 (Continued) The Subpop site

Portfolio:

- www.subpop.com
- www.odesigninc.com
- www.cruffphoto.com/cruff

chapter 7

LAYERS

Featuring

LAYERS

And on the seventh day, God created Layers. OK, so maybe that's overly dramatic. Still, for most Web designers, the Layers feature is what makes Photoshop their design tool of choice. More than just a feature, Layers is a unique way of approaching image creation.

In this chapter, I will begin by defining what layers do and how you can create them. Then I'll discuss how you can make different kinds of layers, particularly those that deal with type. The discussion will continue with an exploration of special effects that can be used to create professional Web graphics. I'll conclude with some tips on managing and saving layers.

What Are Layers?

I may think of myself as being young, but I'm old enough to remember a time when graphic design was not done with computers. Back when I started my career, I worked for a theater designing colorful posters for shows like The Preservation Hall Jazz Band, The Cleveland Orchestra, and James Galway. The mechanicals for the posters were actually created on large acetate sheets of plastic, and each sheet represented a different color. So I would paste the text that I wanted to be, say, blue on one sheet, and other text and images on another sheet. If I had a big block of color I wanted printed, I'd use a semi-transparent red plastic called rubylith.

Photoshop's Layers feature is a lot like using those plastic sheets. But instead of using the sheets to indicate color, layers separate elements so they are easier to remove or edit if the need arises. And believe me, when you're creating complex Web graphics for clients who change their mind a lot, the need arises quite often.

The best way to really understand the Layers feature is to fire up Photoshop and inspect a complex layered graphic created with the program. Figure 7.1 shows a 3D-type display device that I created with Photoshop.

FIGURE 7.1

A complex graphic created in Photoshop

By digging through the Layers palette (select Window ➤ Show Layers from the Menu Bar), you can begin to unravel how I created the graphic (see Figure 7.2).

As shown in Figure 7.3, the first thing I did when making the image was create the overall shape of the high-tech device with the Selection and Fill tools. This shape sits on its own separate layer, named Shape.

Above the Shape layer sits the device's surface texture, which was subtly shaded using the Photoshop Lighting Effects filter (see Figure 7.4).

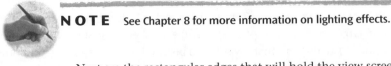

N O T E   See Chapter 8 for more information on lighting effects.

Next are the rectangular edges that will hold the view screen (see Figure 7.5).

FIGURE 7.2

The Layers palette displaying the organization of the image

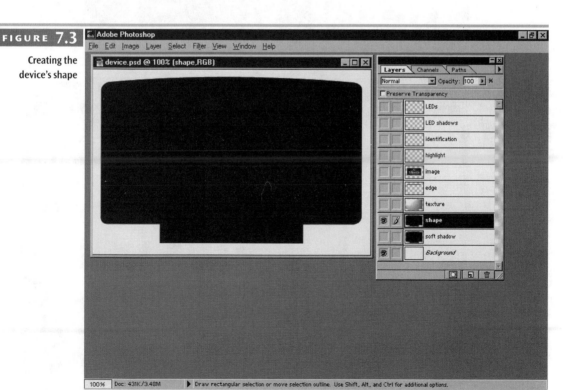

FIGURE 7.3

Creating the device's shape

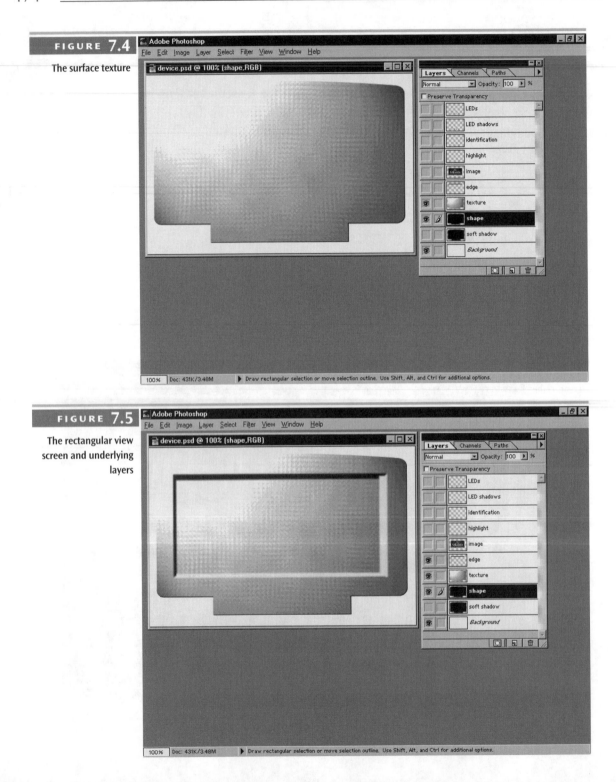

Above the edges is a graphic that provides some text, a logo, and a wavy background. As a special touch, I added some blurred white highlights that give the screen a more rounded feel (see Figure 7.6).

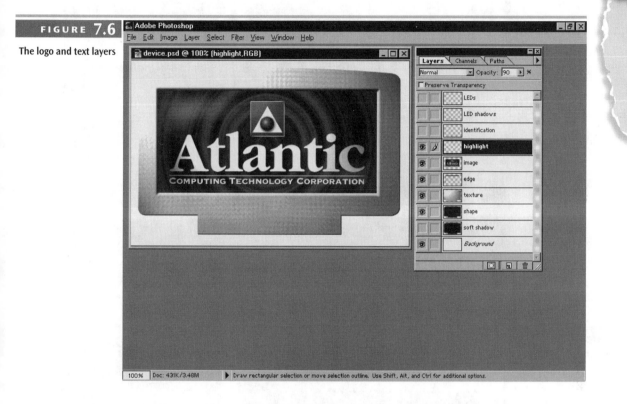

FIGURE 7.6

The logo and text layers

There are also some small LED-type indicators with identifying labels at the bottom of the device (see Figure 7.7).

Finally, a soft drop shadow is put on a layer behind the rest of the image (see Figure 7.8).

As you can see, I broke this image up into a logical series of layers. Layers make it easy to compose such images because each part of the image is insulated from changes made to another part. If I mess up one part of the graphic, I can throw it out and not worry about ruining the rest of the image. And if I ever need to go back and change some text or a button, the Layers feature allows me to alter such information without disturbing the rest of the graphic.

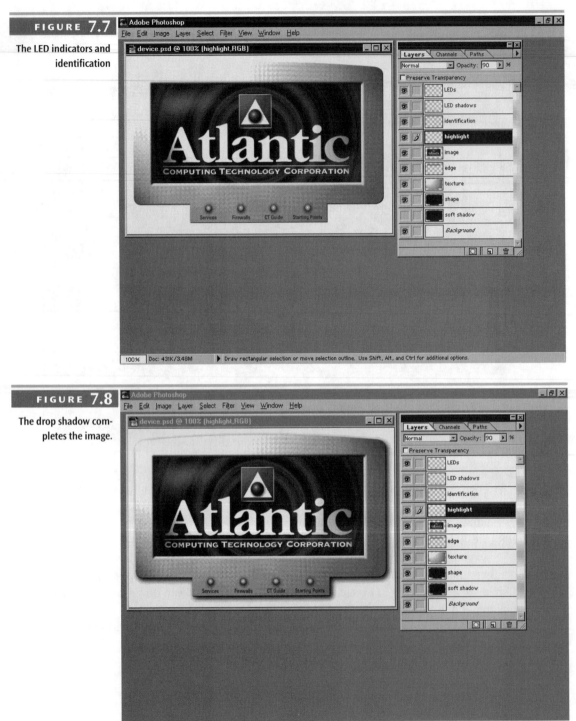

FIGURE 7.7

The LED indicators and
identification

FIGURE 7.8

The drop shadow com-
pletes the image.

The Layers Palette

The Toolbar has no Layers tools, so you use the Layers palette to access most features. Select Window ➤ Show Layers from the Menu Bar to open the Layers palette.

The upper-left corner of the palette provides a drop-down list of different modes. These modes work the same as the Painting modes discussed in Chapter 1. To the right of the drop-down list is the Opacity setting. If you adjust the setting, it will be applied to only the currently selected layer, not the entire document.

In the middle of the palette are the actual layers that comprise the image. Clicking on the Eye icon turns specific layers on and off. Figure 7.9 shows the state change that occurs when the brush stroke layer (Layer 1) is turned off. As you can see, the brush stroke is not visible in the image and the image is blank.

The Paintbrush icon signifies the currently targeted layer, as does the black highlight on the image itself. The small icons at the bottom of the palette allow you to add a layer mask, create a new layer, and delete the current layer.

Using the Layers Palette

The Layers palette is quite powerful and provides ways to do the following:

- Create new layers
- Duplicate layers
- Change the order of layers
- Bind layers together
- Merge different layers into one layer
- Delete layers
- Copy a layer into another document

FIGURE 7.9

A layer can be turned
on or off.

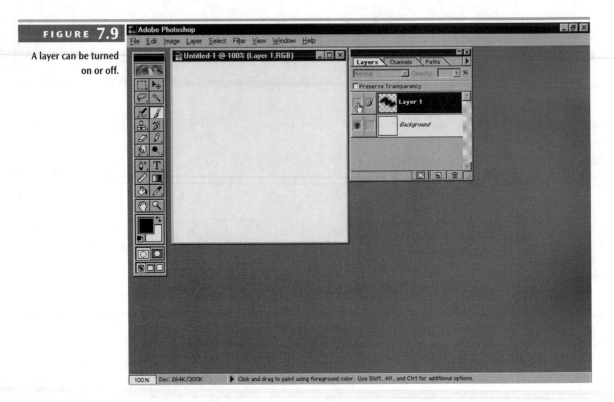

The palette is also a gateway to other special layers-related dialogs and tools, including these:

- Type Options
- Adjustment Layers
- Layer Options
- Palette Options

The rest of this section covers all of these characteristics—and more!

Creating a New Layer

Unless you're using the Paste command or the Type tool, you will need to manually create a new layer before you make each major addition to an image. To create a new layer, do the following:

1. Select Window ➤ Show Layers from the Menu Bar to open the Layers palette.

2. From the Layers palette, click on the Create New Layer icon (see Figure 7.10).

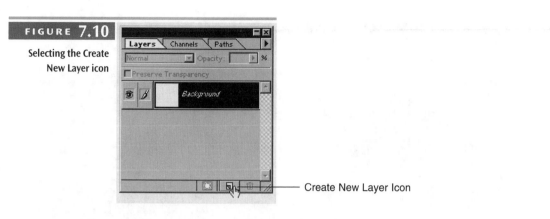

FIGURE 7.10

Selecting the Create
New Layer icon

Create New Layer Icon

N O T E   A new layer is automatically added to the Layers palette each time the Type tool
is used on an image. Only one element of text can be present on a layer.

Duplicating Layers

Sometimes you will want to duplicate a particular layer, especially when you are unsure
about results of a filter or effect. Rather than destroy an original layer, use duplicate layers to experiment and develop variations.

To make a copy of a layer, click and drag the layer to the Create New Layer icon. The
duplicate contains the word *copy* in the layer name (see Figure 7.11).

FIGURE 7.11

A duplicate layer

Linking Layers

When more than one layer is present in a document, it is possible to link different
layers together so that the elements can be moved without disturbing the spatial relationships between them. For example, Figure 7.12 shows two layers that have been
linked together via the Linking icon. If the Move tool is used on one layer, the other
layer will move with it.

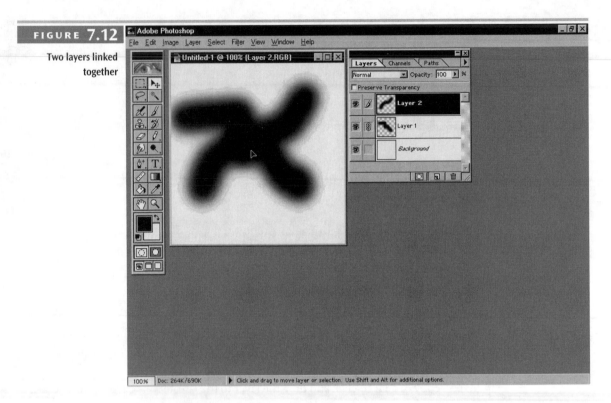

FIGURE 7.12

Two layers linked together

To link a layer to the currently targeted layer, just click in the empty box to the right of the Eye icon. Delinking occurs when the Linking icon is clicked.

Merging Layers

It is possible to merge linked and visible layers into a single layer. This is most often done to optimize file size and better organize an image's layers. To merge linked layers, select Merge Linked from the Layers palette drop-down menu (see Figure 7.13).

It is also possible to merge all of the layers that are visible in a document. Visibility is indicated and turned on or off via the Eye icon to the left of each layer. Like the Merge Linked command, you select Merge Visible from the Layers palette drop-down menu.

NOTE   You can also merge the targeted layer and the layer directly below it by selecting Merge Down from the Layers palette menu.

WARNING   Two or more type layers cannot be merged. However, type layers can be merged with non-type layers, and the text is automatically rendered in the process.

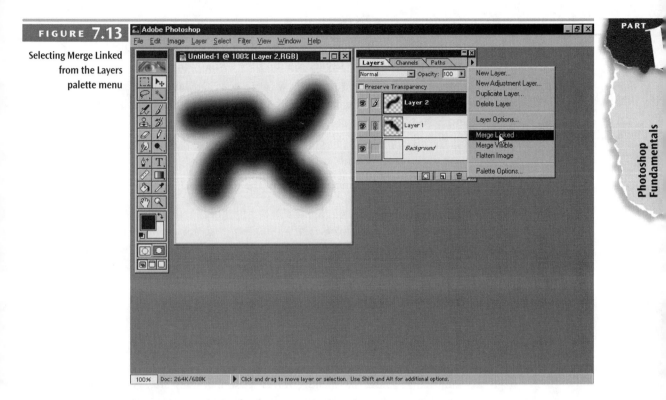

FIGURE 7.13

Selecting Merge Linked
from the Layers
palette menu

Photoshop
Fundamentals

Deleting Layers

To delete a layer, simply click and drag it to the Trash icon in the bottom-right corner
of the Layers palette. As shown in Figure 7.14, the hand icon changes to a clenched
fist when the layer is over the Trash icon and ready to be deleted.

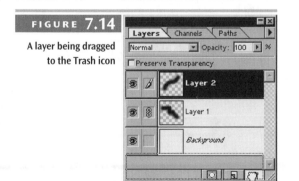

FIGURE 7.14

A layer being dragged
to the Trash icon

Copying Layers to Other Files

Rather than rely on basic Edit tools like Cut, Copy, and Paste, you can quickly copy a layer into another file using the Layers palette. Here's what you do:

1. Open both the document that you want to copy the layer into and the document with the layer to be copied. Make sure at least a portion of the target document is visible.

2. Select the layer you want to copy in the Layers palette and drag it to a visible portion of the target document.

Upon release, the target document jumps to the foreground, and the Layers palette reflects the new addition.

TIP   The layer will be centered on the location where it is released unless the Shift key is pressed while dragging.

Type Layers

As you will learn in Chapter 14, one of the biggest changes to Photoshop is the ability to edit text. Previously, text was rendered as a paint-based element, and it was not possible to go back and change things like spelling, font selection, or point size. With version 5, Photoshop provides text-handling capabilities that are very similar to vector-based drawing programs like Illustrator and Freehand.

NOTE   See Chapter 6 for an explanation of the differences between painting and drawing applications.

Because Photoshop's type capabilities are so different, layers with type on them now have special characteristics, including an icon that allows you to access the Type Tool dialog.

Using Type Layers

To create a type layer, do the following:

1. From the Toolbar, select the Type tool.

2. Click once on your image.

3. Input text into the Type Tool dialog (see Chapter 14 for a description of all of the options).

4. Click OK.

You will notice that a new layer has automatically been added to the Layers palette and that it has a *T* symbol to set it apart from other layers (see Figure 7.15).

FIGURE **7.15**

A type-based layer vs.
regular layers

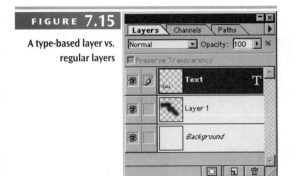

Double-clicking on the symbol will relaunch the Type Tool dialog and allow you to make changes to the text.

N O T E   The Edit ➤ Transform commands can be applied to type layers, and such commands can impact the size of the font. Such changes are reflected in the Type Tool dialog's Size field.

Adjustment Layers

Adjustment layers are one of the features that I never even knew existed until I started working on this book. Perhaps it's because they're buried in the Layers palette menu. After working with them for a while, I could just kick myself—these things make color experimentation and adjustment so incredibly easy!

Adjustment layers don't provide any new color adjustment features, but they do allow you to make temporary (or permanent, if you like what you've done) color tweaks to an entire image. That's the point of this feature: The Adjustment layer impacts every layer beneath it. In contrast, accessing the same features via the Image ➤ Adjust command only affects the particular layer that you're working on.

The other great thing about Adjustment layers is that an infinite number of them can be chained together and applied to an image. You could have one layer that shifts the hues in an image and another one that inverts all of those colors. The possibilities are endless.

Using Adjustment Layers

New Adjustment layers can be created by selecting the New Adjustment Layer option from the Layers palette drop-down menu (see Figure 7.16).

FIGURE 7.16

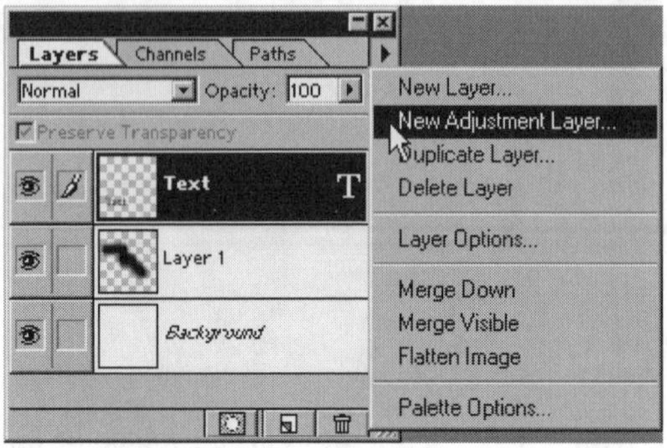

Selecting the New
Adjustment Layer
command

The command launches the appropriately named New Adjustment Layer dialog.

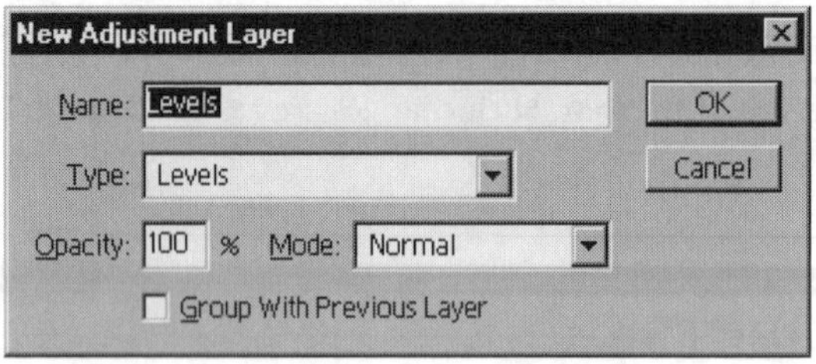

The Type drop-down menu displays the very same color adjustment tool options found in the Image ➤ Adjust menu. The difference is that once the color adjustments are made, the effects become contained in a layer that can be adjusted and deleted, much like any other layer.

NOTE   See Chapter 3 for more information about color adjustment tools like Brightness/Contrast, Hue/Saturation, Invert, Threshold, and Posterize.

Layer Options

The most important thing to know about the Layer Options dialog is that it provides you with a way to change the name of each layer to something more descriptive and identifiable. Other than the Mode and Opacity options, which are more conveniently accessed on the Layers palette, the Layer Options dialog provides tools for adjusting the way a layer can be blended into the rest of the document.

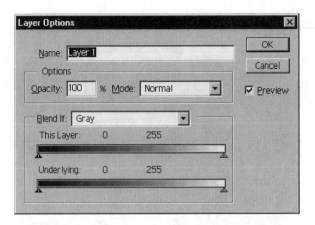

The blend tools consist of a Blend If drop-down menu and two sliders. Early on in my career, before I learned how to use paths and the selection tools, I would often use the blending sliders to drop out the white area surrounding a scanned logo so the logo could be put on another color. Figures 7.17 and 7.18 show this technique in action.

But paths are the more precise way to do this, and I have not found the layer blending options to be tremendously useful in Web work. Most Web graphics tend to be hard-edged and crisp, and the careful blending of layers is rarely used in such images. Still, there may come a time when you will need to quickly remove the light or dark values from an image. If so, the layer blending features are an acceptable, if unsophisticated, way to do this.

FIGURE 7.17

The logo before the white area is dropped

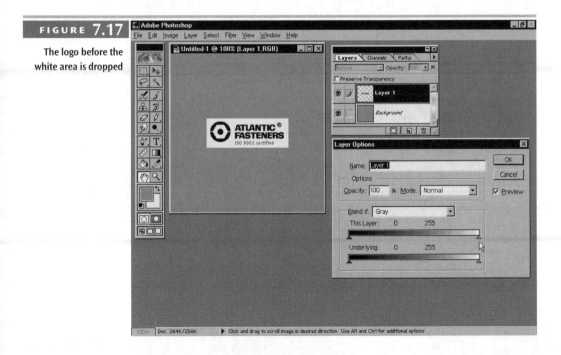

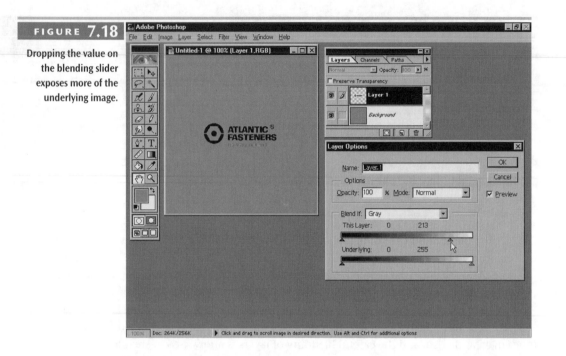

FIGURE **7.18**

Dropping the value on
the blending slider
exposes more of the
underlying image.

Palette Options

Not to be confused with Layer Options, Palette Options are the bottom-most option
available on the Layers palette's drop-down menu. There is only one option available,
and it offers simple radio buttons to adjust the size of the thumbnails displayed in the
palette.

Layers Menu Options

Layers are such an important part of Photoshop that one of the nine options on the Menu Bar is dedicated just to this feature. The Layers menu is shown below.

New ▶
Duplicate Layer...
Delete Layer

Layer Options...
Adjustment Options...

Effects ▶
Type ▶

Add Layer Mask ▶
Enable Layer Mask

Group with Previous   Ctrl+G
Ungroup   Shft+Ctrl+G

Arrange ▶
Align Linked ▶
Distribute Linked ▶

Merge Down   Ctrl+E
Merge Visible   Shft+Ctrl+E
Flatten Image

Matting ▶

The majority of the Layers menu commands are also present in the Layers palette. You'll probably find that the Layers palette is a more natural place from which to create and edit layers. It is critical to be able to see the layers that you are affecting, and only the Layers palette provides this capability. However, in Photoshop 5, three very useful features are found only on the Layers menu: Effects, Type, and Layer Masks.

N O T E In Photoshop 5, Adobe has moved all of the Transform commands to the Edit menu.

Effects

This option provides some excellent highlight and shadowing effects that can be applied to both regular and type layers. But the real secret behind the Effects feature is that *after you've applied an effect to a layer, everything put on the layer thereafter has the effect applied to it.* Not only that, but the settings for the effect can be adjusted at any time, and you can also add or remove other effects. As Figure 7.19 demonstrates, a layer with an effect contains a special *f* symbol. This symbol is actually a functional button that, when clicked, launches the Effects dialog.

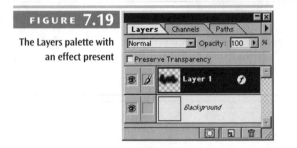

FIGURE 7.19

The Layers palette with an effect present

Photoshop 5 effects include Drop Shadow, Inner Shadow, Outer Glow, Inner Glow, and Bevel & Emboss.

Drop Shadow

As the name indicates, the Drop Shadow effect places a soft, feathered shadow under an element. These sorts of shadows are used most widely behind text. Figure 7.20 provides an example of the effect.

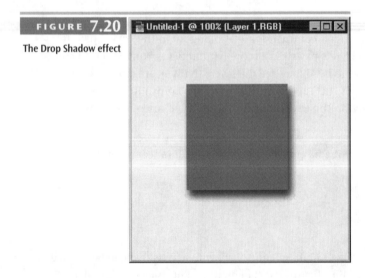

FIGURE 7.20

The Drop Shadow effect

To apply the Drop Shadow effect, select Layer ➤ Effects ➤ Drop Shadow from the Menu Bar. The Effects (Drop Shadow) dialog opens.

Effects

Drop Shadow ▼   ☑ Apply

Mode: Multiply ▼   ■

Opacity: 75 ▸ %

Angle: 120 ▸ ° ☑ Use Global Angle

Distance: 10 ▸ pixels

Blur: 10 ▸ pixels

Intensity: 0 ▸ %

OK
Cancel
Prev
Next
☑ Preview

 (right margin) PART — Photoshop Fundamentals

Options include the following:

Mode   The same set of options you've seen throughout Photoshop, modes allow you to adjust the way the effect is blended into the image.

T I P   All of the various Effects dialogs display a square color swatch from which the effect's hue is drawn. Click on the swatch to launch the Color Picker and select a new color.

Opacity   Just like the other opacity settings, this adjusts the "solidness" of the effect.

Angle   The angle at which the effect is applied, with options from 180 to –180 degrees.

Use Global Angle   Overides the Angle setting and applies the Layer ➤ Effects ➤ Global Angle configurations.

Distance   The distance, in pixels, that the shadow will be offset from the image, with options from 0 to 30,000!

Blur   The overall number of pixels in from the edge of the shadow that will be blurred, with settings from 0 to 50.

Intensity   The relative softness or hardness of the shadow, with settings from 0 to 600.

T I P   The Prev (Previous) and Next buttons in the dialog allow you to cycle through the five effects.

Inner Shadow

The Inner Shadow effect produces the opposite of the Drop Shadow effect, with objects appearing as if they've been carved into the background. Figure 7.21 depicts a simple example of the effect.

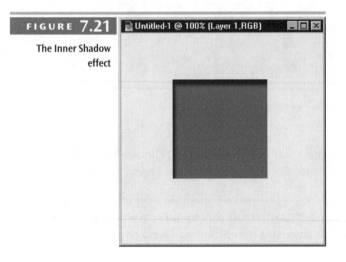

FIGURE 7.21

The Inner Shadow effect

     To apply the Inner Shadow effect, select Layer ➤ Effects ➤ Inner Shadow from the Menu Bar. The Effects (Inner Shadow) dialog opens. This dialog offers the exact same range of options as the Drop Shadow dialog.

Outer Glow

The Outer Glow effect produces a look that is similar to neon, with a soft light emanating from under the object and extending around it (see Figure 7.22).

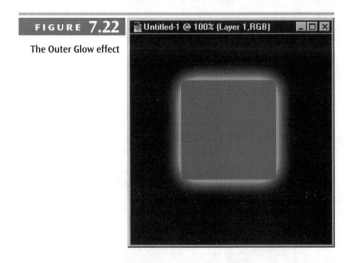

FIGURE 7.22

The Outer Glow effect

To apply the Outer Glow effect, select Layer ➤ Effects ➤ Outer Glow from the Menu Bar. The Effects (Outer Glow) dialog opens.

Options include Mode, Opacity, Blur, and Intensity, and each operates like the options in the Drop Shadow dialog.

Inner Glow

As you might expect, Inner Glow turns the Outer Glow effect inward. As Figure 7.23 demonstrates, the final effect makes an object look semi-transparent and internally lit up.

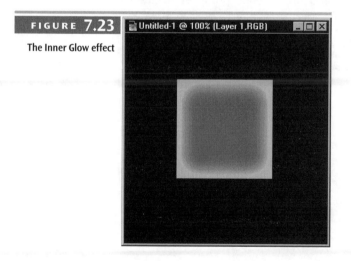

FIGURE 7.23

The Inner Glow effect

PART

Photoshop
Fundamentals

To apply the Inner Glow effect, select Layer ➤ Effects ➤ Inner Glow from the Menu Bar. The Effects (Inner Glow) dialog opens.

The settings for Inner Glow are the same as for Outer Glow, with the exception of the following two options:

Edge   Makes the lighting emanate from the outer edge of the object.

Center   Produces a more focused light source.

Bevel and Emboss

As the name indicates, the Bevel and Emboss effect produces images that have a realistic, 3D feel (see Figure 7.24). The effect is most often used on type and logos.

FIGURE 7.24

The Bevel and Emboss effect

To apply the Bevel and Emboss effect, select Layer ➤ Effects ➤ Bevel and Emboss from the Menu Bar. The Effects (Bevel and Emboss) dialog opens.

Of all the effects, the Bevel and Emboss effect provides the most options. The Highlight and Shadow options both have settings for Mode and Opacity. Other unique features include these:

Style   Provides four options: Outer Bevel, Inner Bevel, Emboss, and Pillow Emboss.

Depth   Provides a way to set the intensity of the 3D effect, with levels from 1 to 20.

Up/Down   Alternates the placement of the effect.

T I P   The five effects in the Effects feature can be chained together in different combinations to provide a single effect. To chain different effects together, just select them from the top drop-down menu in the Effects dialog and click the Apply checkbox.

Other Effects Menu Options

The Effects submenu also provides other options, including these:

Copy Effects   Copies effects from a layer.

Paste Effects   Pastes the copied effect from one layer into another.

Paste Effects to Linked   Pastes copied effects to all of the layers that are linked to the currently targeted layer.

Global Angle   Lets you set an angle for all effects in the file.

Create Layer   Splits off the effect into its own layer.

Hide All Effects   Turns off all of the effects in all layers.

Type

As mentioned earlier in this chapter, layers with type on them behave differently than regular layers. Because type-based layers are composed of vector-based—not paint-based—objects, these layers need to be converted to Paint mode in order to apply Filters—unique Photoshop commands that apply special artistic and image-enhancing effects. Filters are discussed in greater detail in Chapter 8.

 N O T E   A quick way to know if a layer is vector-based is to look at the Menu Bar. If the text layer is selected and the Filter option is grayed out, the layer has not been rendered.

 W A R N I N G   Once a text layer has been rendered, the text is no longer editable.

Rendering Type

To convert an editable text layer to paint status, do the following:

1. Target the text layer in the Layers palette.

2. Select Layer ➤ Type ➤ Render Layer from the Menu Bar.

You will notice that the *T* symbol on the target layer has been removed.

 T I P   The Layers menu also provides a simple way to change the orientation of non-rendered type. Select Layer ➤ Type ➤ Horizontal or Vertical to change the orientation.

Layer Masks

As discussed in Chapter 6, masks let you block out certain areas of an image so you can edit them more precisely. In addition to creating masks in channels, you can also create masks in layers. In fact, creating a mask using the Layers feature is usually more convenient than using other techniques.

As shown in Figure 7.25, the icon to the right in Layer 1 shows that the mask is a grayscale image. White areas represent the "live," nonmasked area, while the black areas are blocked out and masked. Gray areas are portions of the layer that are semi-visible. Notice the small gray Mask icon on the left of the layer, indicating the presence of a layer mask.

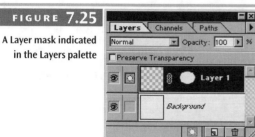

FIGURE 7.25

A Layer mask indicated in the Layers palette

Creating a Layer Mask

To create a layer mask, do this:

1. In the Layers palette, target the layer to which you want to add a mask.

2. Make a selection in the image to define the shape of the mask.

3. Select Layer ➤ Add Layer Mask ➤ Reveal Selection from the Menu Bar.

You now have a layer with a mask. The selected area is "live" and the non-selected area is blocked out. If you paint on the layer, the masked-out area becomes apparent. To view the mask, press Alt+click (Windows) or Option+click (Mac) on the mask thumbnail in the Layers palette.

N O T E   Photoshop lets your create only one mask per layer.

To edit a layer mask, simply click on the layer mask thumbnail in the Layers palette and use any of the painting or selection tools on the image. You can only work in grayscale on the mask.

Saving Layers

When you create a layered document, it is imperative that you save a version of the file in Photoshop format as soon as possible. If you later convert the image to Indexed Color mode for use on the Web, you will see a warning dialog.

If the image is converted to Indexed Color mode and then a save occurs, all of the layer information will be lost (unless you go back and reverse the change using the History palette while the file is still open—see Chapter 2). Clearly, it is very important to save a layered file in Photoshop format before it is converted to Indexed Color mode. Once a graphic is converted to Indexed Color mode, you can use the File ➤ Save a Copy or File ➤ Export ➤ GIF89a Export command to save the file as a GIF.

N O T E   See Chapter 12 for more information about saving graphics to Web file formats.

Keep It Clean

When you're creating graphics with the Layers feature, things can quickly get out of hand. Not only is it easy to lose track of what element is on which layer, but the number of layers in a document can grow to the point where the file is too large to open. Here are a few tips to keep a Layers file tidy:

- When creating a new layer, be sure to name it immediately. It can be difficult to remember where different elements were placed even after only a few minutes of working on a document.
- Name your layers in such a way that they will be easy to identify. For instance, if your file has many types of shadows, name them descriptively—"buttons shadow," "header shadow," and so on.

N O T E   Text layers will automatically be named with the first few words that you type into the Type Tool dialog. If you go back in and edit the text, the name will change on the fly. Fantastic stuff!

- Put discrete elements on different layers so that you can apply the Filters and Effects features to only the parts of the image that require the change.
- Much like writing computer code or HTML, it is important to keep your layer files as lean as possible. Even at the Web resolution of 72 pixels per inch, additional layers can add significantly to the file size of a Photoshop document. When you're sure that you're not going to need it later, throw a layer out.

Conclusion

Photoshop's Layers feature is a huge time saver and a great way to make changes without defacing the other parts of the graphic. Once you get used to isolating image elements and envisioning graphics in terms of layers, you'll never go back to using a simple paint application.

Understanding the concept of layers is important not just for composing images in Photoshop, it's also important when thinking about programming cutting-edge Web pages, as we'll see in Chapter 17. With the advent of Cascading Style Sheets (CSS), Web designers can layer text and graphics much like they would in Photoshop.

Up Next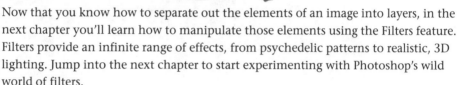

Now that you know how to separate out the elements of an image into layers, in the next chapter you'll learn how to manipulate those elements using the Filters feature. Filters provide an infinite range of effects, from psychedelic patterns to realistic, 3D lighting. Jump into the next chapter to start experimenting with Photoshop's wild world of filters.

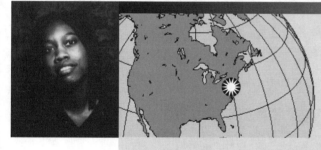

Photoshop Master: Auriea Harvey

If you think you know what a home page is, think again. For the past two years, Auriea Harvey has maintained Entropy8, one of the most beautiful home pages on the Web (see Figure 7.26). A visit to the Entropy8 site will compel even the most talented designer to rethink their Web presence.

Like many Web designers, Auriea came to the medium from fine arts. Although she has a degree from Parsons School of Design, Auriea started out as a sculptor. But while at Parsons, the sculptor was introduced to the Macintosh and the technology changed both her profession and way of working. Some of her first experiments on the Macintosh were with Photoshop, creating illustrations for her drawing classes that challenged most of her professors (see Figure 7.27).

After graduating from Parsons in 1993, Auriea worked as a print designer in the publishing industry. But in 1995, as the Web started to come into its own, she realized that this new medium was better suited to her need for experimentation and self-expression.

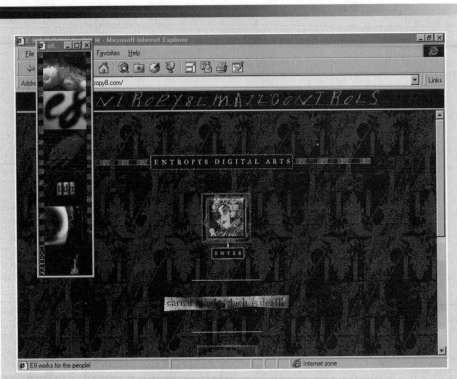

Figure 7.26 The Entropy8 Web site

Figure 7.27 One of Auriea's earliest computer-based works: an illustration for a figure drawing class

Auriea had seen a lot of early Web design, and with Entropy8 she wanted to make a statement. She felt that the Web could be more than just a series of documents—it was a new artistic medium capable of communicating a wide range of messages and emotions. Auriea executed a site that was lush, complex, and like nothing seen before on the Web. The site's notoriety grew quickly and the site won THE WEB Magazine's Webby Award, Arts Category, in both 1997 and 1998.

Today, the 26-year old artist continues to maintain and evolve the site, investing about 10 hours a week to the project. Nothing about the site is planned, and updates occur when the mood strikes her. Auriea's continuing involvement in the project is powered by both her love of the medium and the feedback she receives from the site's admirers.

Entropy8's success has lead to the formation of a business: Entropy8 Digital Arts. Auriea and her partner, Marc Vose, develop Web sites from their New York City office for clients like Virgin Records, Red Hot, and Public Theater (see Figures 7.28 and 7.29).

The success of Entropy8 has vaulted Auriea into the limelight. She's a frequent contributor to design magazines and a speaker at design conferences. No less than David Bowie has cited Auriea's work as among his favorites.

If any of this has you thinking that you should spend more time developing your home page, you're not alone.

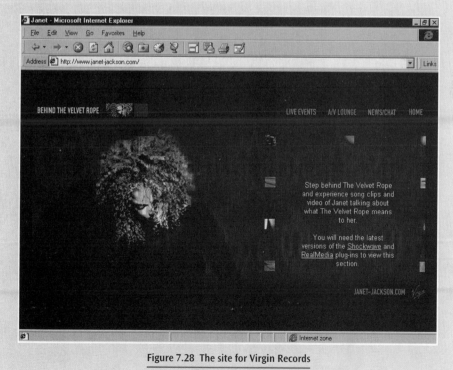

Figure 7.28 The site for Virgin Records

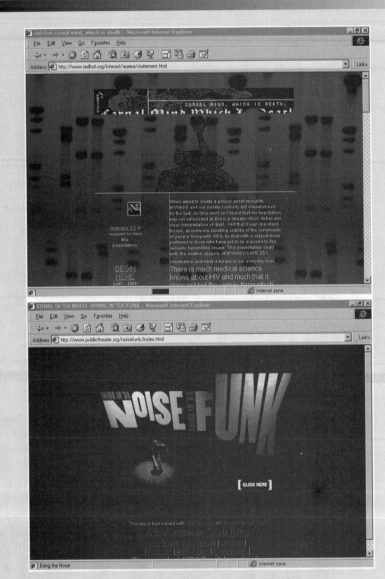

Figure 7.29 Web sites for Red Hot and Public Theater

Portfolio:

- www.entropy8.com
- www.janet-jackson.com
- www.publictheater.org/noisefunk
- www.redhot.org/interact/auriea

FILTERS

Featuring

CHAPTER

8

FILTERS

O f all the Photoshop features, Filters are the easiest to learn and experiment with. Most of the learning is intuitive—moving sliders, adjusting values, and seeing what happens. Photoshop provides dozens of filters, each with sometimes hundreds of different possible settings, so the range of combined effects that can be achieved by applying multiple filters to an image is truly amazing.

The bulk of this chapter is made up of visual examples of what each Photoshop filter can do. Specific filters that I find particularly useful in Web work are covered in more detail. I've also included information about Photoshop's copyright filter, which is particularly relevant when publishing images on the World Wide Web. Finally, information on third-party, plug-in filters is provided.

The Photoshop Filters

Like Layers, the Filters feature is important enough to merit space on the Menu Bar and is located between the Select and View options.

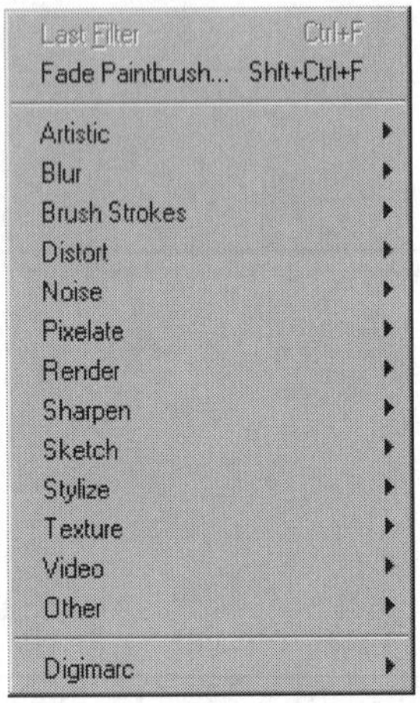

Last Filter	Ctrl+F
Fade Paintbrush...	Shft+Ctrl+F
Artistic	▶
Blur	▶
Brush Strokes	▶
Distort	▶
Noise	▶
Pixelate	▶
Render	▶
Sharpen	▶
Sketch	▶
Stylize	▶
Texture	▶
Video	▶
Other	▶
Digimarc	▶

The menu includes 14 groups of filters plus a Fade command. The most recently used filter is appended to the Fade command (Fade Add Noise, Fade Add Gaussian Blur, and so on). Fade offers a useful control for fading the current version of the image with the filter applied with the original, nonfiltered image (see Figure 8.1).

FIGURE 8.1

The Fade filter dialog

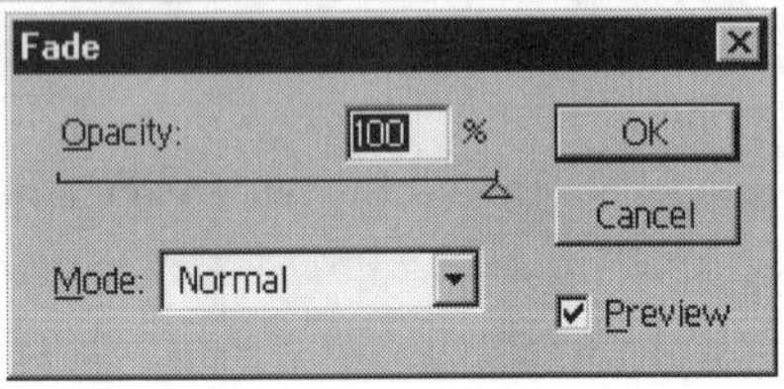

Fade

Opacity: 100 %   OK   Cancel

Mode: Normal   ☑ Preview

The last filter group is Digimarc, which provides a way to embed nearly invisible copyright information in an image. I will cover the Digimarc filter much more thoroughly near the end of this chapter.

TIP   Like most of Photoshop's commands, a filter is applied only to the targeted layer. To affect an entire document, the file must be flattened.

In between Fade and Digimarc are the other 13 filter groups, which range from the highly useful to the truly bizarre. Some of the more artistic filters were acquired by Adobe when it purchased Aldus. These filters, originally known as Gallery Effects, are sprinkled throughout the Filter menu. Perhaps because of this, the Filter menu is poorly organized and unintuitive. Despite working every day in the program for many years, I still can't remember if the Extrude filter is in the Distort or Stylize group.

N O T E   The first computer paint application I used was SuperPaint. Like Gallery Effects, SuperPaint was originally made by a company called Silicon Beach. Silicon Beach was sold to Aldus, which was later bought by Adobe. Got that?

Artistic

The Artistic filters let you experiment with traditional media effects (see Figure 8.2). As you'll see, some of the filters are more natural and realistic than others, but they all apply a painterly effect.

FIGURE 8.2

Artistic: the original and filtered images

The original image

Colored Pencil

Cutout

Dry Brush

Film Grain

Fresco

FIGURE 8.2

(Continued)

Artistic: the original and
filtered images

Neon Glow

Paint Daubs

Palette Knife

Plastic Wrap

Poster Edges

Rough Pastels

Smudge Stick

Sponge

Underpainting

Watercolor

N O T E   Most filters are associated with a dialog that can provide a wide range of adjustments. Filters with a dialog are identified in the Filters menu by an ellipsis (…).

Blur

As the name implies, the Blur filters reduce areas of high contrast and soften the overall appearance of an image (see Figure 8.3). Low settings tend to reduce the graininess of an image, while higher settings produce abstract shapes or exaggerated motion effects. While there are a half dozen blur options, Gaussian is the most useful, providing the greatest amount of control.

FIGURE 8.3

Blur: the original and
filtered images

The original image

Blur

Blur More

Gaussian Blur

Motion Blur

Radial Blur

Smart Blur

Using the Gaussian Blur Filter

The Gaussian Blur filter provides an excellent way to create very soft, diffused shadows. To apply the filter to an image, layer, or selection, select Filter ➤ Blur ➤ Gaussian Blur. The Gaussian Blur dialog appears.

The Gaussian Blur dialog provides a simple numeric/slider control for altering the extent of the effect. See Figure 8.3 for an example of the effect.

 T I P   Soft drop shadows can also be made with the Layer ➤ Effects ➤ Drop Shadow command. See Chapter 7 for more information about layers.

Brush Strokes

The Brush Strokes filters attempt to simulate the hand of an artist, adding color, detail, or texture to an image (see Figure 8.4).

FIGURE 8.4

Brush Strokes: the original and filtered images

The original image   Accented Edges   Angled Strokes

FIGURE 8.4

Brush Strokes: the original and filtered images

Crosshatch

Dark Strokes

Ink Outlines

Spatter

Sprayed Strokes

Sumi-e

NOTE   If there is an active selection in a file, a filter will affect only the selected area, not the entire image or layer.

Distort

The Distort group provides some of the most extreme transformations available (see Figure 8.5). While the Distort filters will change the position of pixels—sometimes radically—they will not change any color values.

FIGURE 8.5

Distort: the original and filtered images

The original image

Diffuse Glow

Displace

FIGURE **8.5**

(Continued)

Distort: the original and
filtered images

Glass

Ocean Ripple

Pinch

Polar Coordinates

Ripple

Shear

Spherize

Twirl

Wave

ZigZag

Using the Glass Filter

I can guarantee that you won't use it often, but the Glass filter provides an excellent way to simulate the effect of looking at an image through various kinds of glass. To apply the filter, select Filter ➤ Distort ➤ Glass. The Glass dialog appears.

Glass	✕
	OK
	Cancel
	+ 100% −

Options
Distortion   5
Smoothness   3

Texture: Frosted ▾
Scaling   100 %
☐ Invert

The Glass dialog offers Distortion and Smoothness controls, plus the choice of four types of glass: Blocks, Canvas, Frosted, and Tiny Lens. You can also load a texture that will influence the glass effect. Scaling provides the final control, letting you change the way light waves are reflected. See Figure 8.5 for an example of the effect.

N O T E   Additional textures can be found in the Photoshop Goodies folder.

Noise

The Noise filters introduce random patterns of pixels into an image, as well as remove such imperfections from graphics like scanned images (see Figure 8.6).

FIGURE 8.6

Noise: the original and
filtered images

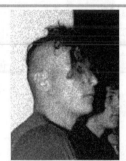

The original image   Add Noise   Despeckle

Dust & Scratches   Median

Using the Add Noise Filter

Most people overlook the simple Add Noise filter, but I use it all the time in the creation of textures that look high-tech. The image shown in Figure 8.7 has a distinct surface treatment. Upon closer inspection, you will see that the texture is the result of using the Add Noise filter (see Figure 8.8).

FIGURE 8.7

This image has a
high-tech look

PART

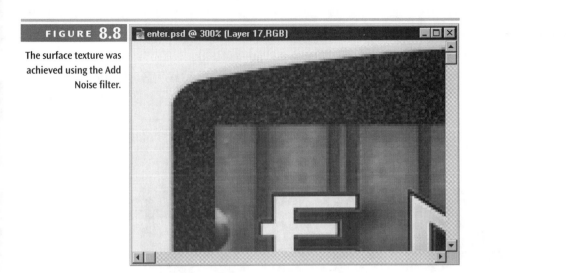

FIGURE 8.8

The surface texture was achieved using the Add Noise filter.

Photoshop
Fundamentals

To create a similar texture, create a new document with a medium gray background. Then select Filter ➤ Noise ➤ Add Noise. The Add Noise dialog appears.

The Add Noise dialog provides Amount, Distribution, and Monochromatic options. I tend to use the Uniform Distribution and Monochromatic options to maintain the most basic possible texture.

Used in combination with the Brightness/Contrast command, the Add Noise filter can create some effective surfaces.

T I P   The Last Filter command, the first item on the Filter menu, lets you quickly reapply the most recently used filter effect.

Pixelate

The Pixelate filters merge small groups of similarly colored pixels into solid areas of color. The effects range from traditional printing methods to stylized painting strokes (see Figure 8.9).

FIGURE 8.9

Pixelate: the original and filtered images

The original image

Color Halftone

Crystallize

Facet

Fragment

Mezzotint

Mosaic

Pointillize

Using the Mosaic Filter

Sometimes it's useful to simulate the effect of Web graphics, especially their coarse, pixelated tones. The Mosaic filter dialog (select Filter ➤ Pixelate ➤ Mosaic) provides a simple option for controlling the coarseness and size of the pixels.

See Figure 8.9 for an example of the effect.

Render

The Render filters add new patterns to an image by either overlaying new detail on an image or altering the existing image. A wide range of natural-looking effects—everything from clouds to lighting effects to 3D rendering—can be achieved (see Figure 8.10).

FIGURE 8.10

Render: the original and filtered images

  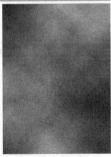

The original image   3D Transform   Clouds

FIGURE 8.10

(Continued)

Render: the original and
filtered images

Difference Clouds

Lens Flare

Lighting Effects

Texture Fill

Using the Lighting Effects Filter

Lighting Effects is a very powerful filter that creates natural tonal changes. As shown in Figure 8.11, I used the filter to make the type and buttons look more realistic.

FIGURE 8.11

The Lighting Effects
filter in action on text
and buttons

To launch the Lighting Effects dialog, select Filter ➤ Render ➤ Lighting Effects from the Menu Bar.

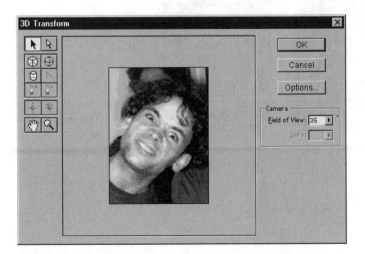

The dialog is packed with features and could easily be an application in its own right. I tend to use the Spotlight most often because it offers a very natural effect, but Directional and Omni are also useful. The Style option comes set to Default, but you can choose from 16 other preprogrammed lighting possibilities. See Figure 8.10 for another example of the Lighting Effects filter.

Using the 3D Transform Filter

New to Photoshop 5 is 3D Transform, a filter that provides effects similar to—though far less capable—3D modeling and rendering capabilities. The 3D Transform dialog is accessed by selecting Filter ➤ Render ➤ 3D Transform.

Like Lighting Effects, 3D Transform is like an application in itself. Cubes, spheres, and cylinders are drawn directly on the dialog's working area and are rotated and moved with specialized tools.

While the ability to do "light" 3D modeling in Photoshop is interesting, 3D Transform is still nowhere near as powerful as industry standard 3D programs like Ray Dream and Strata Studio. Still, with the addition of Lighting Effects in version 4 and 3D Transform in version 5, Photoshop is definitely making a commitment to more dimensional image effects.

Sharpen

The Sharpen filters add focus and detail to an image by increasing the color difference in adjacent pixels (see Figure 8.12). These filters are very effective at sharpening out-of-focus scanned photos, and the king of the Sharpen filters is the oddly named Unsharp Mask.

FIGURE 8.12

Sharpen: the original and filtered images

The original image

Sharpen

Sharpen Edges

Sharpen More

Unsharp Mask

Using the Unsharp Mask Filter

Unsharp Mask is probably Photoshop's most widely used filter, primarily because it sharpens scanned images that are usually blurred and out of focus. To use the filter, select Filter ➤ Sharpen ➤ Unsharp Mask. The Unsharp Mask dialog appears.

The dialog offers Amount, Radius, and Threshold commands to change the degree of sharpening. I tend to Unsharp Mask scanned images destined for the Web with settings of Amount 20%, Radius 1.0, and Threshold zero. See Figure 8.12 for an example of the effect.

Sketch

Like the Artistic and Brush Strokes filters, Sketch emulates traditional media effects (see Figure 8.13). However, all of the Sketch filters replace existing colors with whatever hues are indicated in the Foreground Color/Background Color indicator.

FIGURE 8.13

Sketch: the original and
filtered images

The original image   Bas Relief   Chalk & Charcoal

FIGURE **8.13**

(Continued)

Sketch: the original and filtered images

Charcoal

Chrome

Conte Crayon

Graphic Pencil

Halftone Pattern

Note Paper

Photocopy

Plaster

Reticulation

Stamp

Torn Edges

Water Paper

Using the Plaster Filter

Here's a filter that you may never have any practical use for, but it creates such cool effects that I couldn't resist discussing it. The Plaster filter works best on flattened images with lots of contrast—try black text on a white background. Then launch the Plaster dialog by selecting Filter ➤ Sketch ➤ Plaster.

The dialog provides an Image Balance option, which controls how far above the surface dark objects will sit, and a Smoothness option, which controls how much the image will decompose and slip back into the plaster. Finally, there are eight controls for directing light. See Figure 8.13 for an example of the effect.

Stylize

The Stylize filters provide everything from natural effects like Wind to more mechanical processes like Emboss and Extrude (see Figure 8.14).

FIGURE 8.14

Stylize: the original and
filtered images

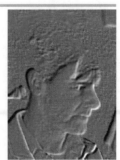

The original image   Diffuse   Emboss

FIGURE 8.14

(Continued)

Stylize: the original and
filtered images

Extrude

Find Edges

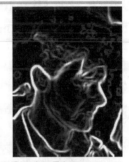

Glowing Edges

Solarize

Tiles

Trace Contour

Wind

Using the Wind Filter

The Wind filter provides some pretty simple yet useful simulations of wind and its effect on objects and people (see Figure 8.14). To use the filter, select Filter ➤ Stylize ➤ Wind. The Wind dialog appears.

The Wind dialog provides increasing amounts of the effect, including Wind, Blast, and Stagger. Wind can also come from the left or the right.

TIP   Most filter dialogs provide a small preview window to show how the image will look after the filter is applied. You can zoom in and out of the swatch, as well as navigate by simply clicking and dragging on the image.

Texture

As the name indicates, the Texture filters add texture to an image (see Figure 8.15). Texture filters can work well in combination with the Artistic filters.

FIGURE 8.15

Texture: the original and filtered images

The original image

Craquelure

Grain

Mosaic Tiles

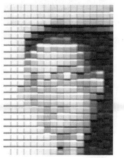

Patchwork

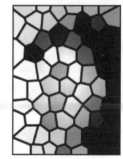

Stained Glass

Texturizer

Using the Texturizer Filter

The Texturizer filter allows you to pick from Brick, Burlap, Canvas, and Sandstone—or you can load another texture of your choice. Select Filter ➤ Texture ➤ Texturizer to open the Texturizer dialog.

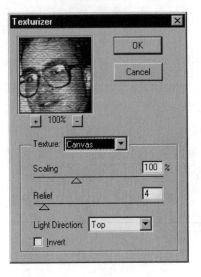

The Scaling and Relief sliders alter the intensity of the effect. Similar to the Plaster filter, the Light Direction command, with eight options, impacts the direction of shadows cast by the effect. See Figure 8.15 for an example of the Texturizer in action.

N O T E   The Texturizer filter can be useful in creating textured backgrounds for use on Web pages. For more information about creating backgrounds, see Chapter 15.

Video

Video filters are used for editing images captured from video or processing images destined for video or television. As such, they are rarely used in the creation of Web graphics.

Other

The Other filters are specialized effects that do not fit nicely into the previously mentioned filter categories (see Figure 8.16). Most simulate printing press effects. Among the Other filters is a Custom option that allows for the creation of new filters via a numeric interface.

FIGURE 8.16

Other: the original and
filtered images

The original image   Custom   High Pass

Maximum   Minimum   Offset

Digimarc

Since Photoshop 4, Adobe has provided the Digimarc filter as a way to embed invisible copyright and other types of information into a file. Called a *watermark*, this technology is intended to protect images from being used without permission. Because the Web is a global publishing system, graphics created for the medium have become ripe for misuse. Photoshop includes the Digimarc filter for both embedding and reading such information.

How It Works

The filter introduces a seemingly random pattern of noise into an image that is actually coded and decoded by the Digimarc software to communicate copyright information. In Figure 8.17, the graphic to the left has not been processed by the Digimarc filter, while the image on the right has the copyright year 1998 inserted into it. As you can see, using the Digimarc filter can have an impact on image quality.

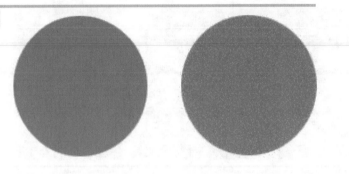

FIGURE 8.17

The same graphic
without (left) and with
(right) the Digimarc
filter applied

It is not possible to directly read copyright information in an Indexed Color image (the type most Web graphics are made of—see Chapter 12 for more info). Such images must be converted to RGB mode. Likewise, it is not possible to insert a watermark into an Indexed Color image. It is also not advisable to insert a watermark into a layered file—the file should be flattened before applying the filter.

WARNING   Converting an RGB image to Indexed Color can degrade the Digimarc copyright information to the point where it cannot be read. Be sure to test the image with the Filter ➤ Digimarc ➤ Read Watermark command before publication on the Web.

Because the Digimarc filter inserts noise and thus makes flat color images larger (in terms of file size), the format is best applied to non-Indexed Color, continuous tone images like photographs. In other words, it's best used in JPEG format imagery that has a critical value to artists, illustrators, and corporations.

WARNING   Very low JPEG quality settings can destroy the Digimarc filter's copyright information.

Using the Digimarc Filter

To see if a file has a Digimarc watermark, open an image and select Filter ➤ Digimarc ➤ Read Watermark. Photoshop also provides an indication, albeit small, of the presence of a watermark. As shown below, Photoshop (Windows) will present a tiny copyright symbol in the lower-left corner of the Status Bar if a Digimarc watermark is present.

© Doc: 118K/118K

To embed a watermark, select Filter ➤ Digimarc ➤ Embed Watermark. This will launch the Embed Watermark dialog.

Unlike Photoshop's other dialogs, this one is more involved than simply clicking buttons and boxes. To make full use of the filter, you will need to pay an annual fee to the Digimarc company. Here's what the service provides:

- A unique Creator ID
- The ability to communicate your copyright, copyright year, and first and last names in images
- Listing in Digimarc's online publication; this includes address, phone number, and links to your e-mail and Web site
- The ability to track your images on the Web with an online, password-protected "spider" that searches the Web for misuse of your images

N O T E   A "lite" version of the Digimarc service is currently available at no cost, but it only provides the first two options.

Once you have a Creator ID, you can make use of the rest of the Embed Watermark dialog. Since the graphics you are creating are for the Web, select Monitor as your Target Output. While a Watermark Durability setting of 1–4 is available, settings 1 and 2 are intended for print use. Web images will need a setting of 3 or 4 to remain legible after image processing.

N O T E   For more information about getting a Creator ID, visit the Digimarc Web site at http://www.digimarc.com.

A Word about Copyright Law on the Web

The following article appeared in the March 11, 1998 issue of the *Hartford Business Journal*.

Attorneys Wear White Hats

By Matt Straznitskas

Everyone knows that the advent of the Web created an incredible opportunity for professionals armed with creative and technological skills. What's gone relatively unnoticed, however, is the Web's propensity to provide opportunities for another group of professionals—intellectual property lawyers.

Each day, an increasing number of words, images, and sounds are published on the Web. With this increase, the potential for disagreement over who owns such information has skyrocketed. In fact, one of the most common questions posed by a good number of my firm's clients is, "How can I protect my Web site's photos, graphics, and copy from online piracy?"

The issue of intellectual property rights is not new. Web publishers from organizations of all kinds have attempted to gain sole "ownership" of their online content. At the same time, groups ranging from popular musicians to the world's largest corporations have been accused of stealing work that was authored by someone else.

The Copyright Act is a federal law that was developed to address the issue of authorship. It protects a wide range of works including pictorial and graphic images, motion pictures and other audiovisual material, sound recordings, and literary works. With this Act in place, a copyright owner can sometimes recover awards up to $100,000 from violators.

Because most people are familiar with the concept of copyrights, it is surprising that both publishers and the judicial system have had trouble interpreting the law. The New York Times recently won a court battle against freelance writers who claimed that they were due royalties for articles republished on the Times' Web site. If the articles were republished in any other medium, it is likely that the judge would have sided with the writers. Clearly, the legal system is struggling with this new medium.

Another looming court battle is one between media companies and the fans who are devoted to the networks' top-flight programs. Producers of the popular TV shows "Star Trek" and "X-Files" demand that creators of "fan club" Web sites comply with copyright law, removing images such as photos of the cast from the Web. Many Web publishers feel that such demands are unreasonable, asserting that their Web sites are intended for personal use with no profit involved. On the other hand, copyright owners—including writers, musicians, and artists—claim that they must maintain control of their work. Without ownership, these professionals feel that they will lose the ability to determine market value.

In anticipation of greater prosecution of copyright offenders, companies such as Digimarc have developed "watermarks" that invisibly stamp digital files—such as graphics

PART

1

Photoshop
Fundamentals

and music—with copyright information. Online publisher Playboy is protecting its assets with Web graphics that include image creation, ownership, and distribution information.

But even with watermark technology, one needs to be mindful that the Web is a global publishing environment. Presently, copyright law is only in effect in the United States. Fortunately, the World Intellectual Property Organization (WIPO) was formed to address the issue of intellectual property on the Web. WIPO has established treaties that provide ownership rights to authors and artists. The treaties are awaiting ratification by at least 30 countries.

If the WIPO treaties are not ratified and amateur publishers are able to freely distribute bootleg copies of everything from music to books, it's possible that artists and legitimate publishers will be stripped of the ability to profit from their work. If the Internet becomes a source for downloading stolen content, no one will buy the actual product. (For example, music fans already have the ability to illegally download entire "albums" for free.) The result could be a deficit of original, artistic output. It's uncommon to root for lawyers, but in this case the intellectual property attorney is wearing the white hat.

Plug-Ins

On your computer inside your Photoshop folder, you will notice a Plug-Ins directory. This is where many of the filters mentioned in this chapter reside. If you remove a filter from the directory, it will no longer be available from the Filters menu when you're in Photoshop. If you know you're never going to use a particular filter, it is a good idea to remove it from the Plug-Ins directory. This reduces the amount of memory necessary to run Photoshop.

Adobe has also made it possible to put other, third-party filters into the Plug-Ins directory. These plug-ins enhance Photoshop with everything from animation tools to the ability to save files as fractals. Development of plug-ins has been wildly successful, and dozens of companies sell such software. Here are a few of the most popular:

Metatools (also known as Kai's Power Tools)	http://www.metatools.com/
Alien Skin Software	http://www.alienskin.com/
Xaos Tools	http://www.xaostools.com/

For a more comprehensive list of plug-in vendors, visit the Adobe site at http://www.adobe.com/prodindex/photoshop/resources.html.

Conclusion

While filters are a lot of fun to experiment with, most Web designers use effects like Charcoal and Fresco rather infrequently. If a client is looking for a traditional media effect, it's far better to hire a professional illustrator than to mechanically process a photograph and imitate a style. Most people can instantly spot a real drawing from a fake.

Filters are effective in optimizing blurry or dirty images. The Unsharp Mask filter is used by thousands of designers every day to improve scanned photos. On the low-resolution environment of the Web, a filter can also be very useful in simulating natural lighting effects and giving graphics some impact.

With every new version of Photoshop, the application evolves. In version 5, the nature of the Filters feature is changing somewhat. As discussed in Chapter 7, Layer Effects has made achieving effects like drop shadows and embossing more convenient than using the traditional Gaussian Blur and Emboss filters.

Up Next

Lights. Cameras. Actions! Photoshop 5 now provides a wide range of functions that can be automated. Read the next chapter to learn how to achieve remarkable productivity gains with the Actions feature.

Photoshop Masters: Alisha and Claudio Vera

Most people would consider running one of Boston's hottest Web agencies a big deal, but for Alisha and Claudio Vera, it's all in a day's work. Over the last few years, this dynamic husband-and-wife team has not only started a profitable design business, but they've also bought a house, started a family, and taught courses in Web design.

Black Bean Studios was founded in April of 1994 and quickly grew to 10 full-time employees. Originally started as a home-based business, Alisha and Claudio moved the company to the third floor of a warehouse on the outskirts of Boston's financial district. The fun, funky work environment contains absolutely no cubicles and is close to historic Boston landmarks like Fanueil Hall and the waterfront.

Alisha, 28, received her design education at both the Massachusetts College of Art and the Rhode Island School of Design (RISD). Claudio, 34, received a BA in Art History at Johns Hopkins and an MBA from Boston University. Despite their divergent educational backgrounds, both Alisha and Claudio serve as Black Bean Creative Directors and share equally in driving the look and feel of the sites they produce.

Alisha and Claudio have adopted a dynamic approach to Web development projects, assembling unique teams of people for every job. The approach clearly works: Black Bean has developed killer sites for Museum of Science (Boston), Digital Equipment Corporation, and Lasertron (see Figure 8.18).

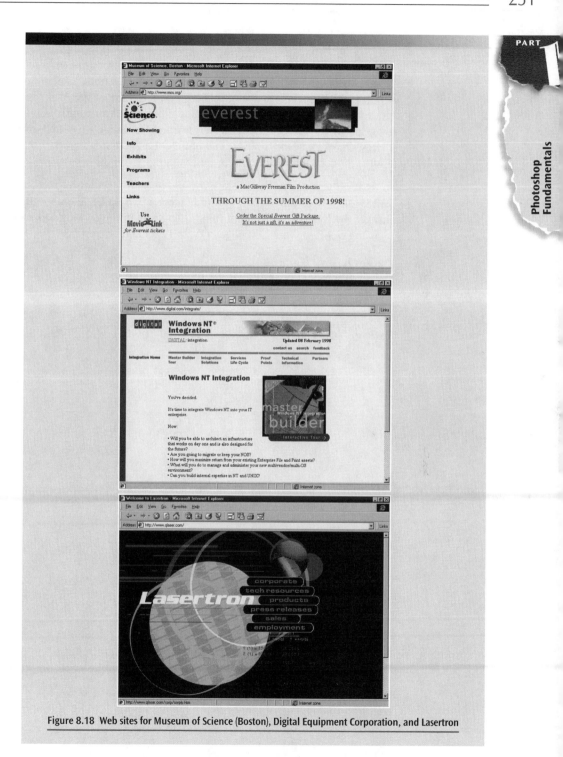

Figure 8.18 Web sites for Museum of Science (Boston), Digital Equipment Corporation, and Lasertron

While Alisha and Claudio are both big fans of Photoshop, they preferred version 3 of the program over version 4, mainly because they had an enormous amount of experience with the old interface. For them, version 4 buried some of the most frequently used functions, particularly indexed colors, color tables, and layer masks. With version 5, the designers are very excited about the new features like editable type and History. Beyond Photoshop, Black Bean also uses state-of-the-art animation programs like Macromedia Flash and Adobe After Effects.

So what do you do for an encore once you've built a successful Web company and started a family? Create work that is truly memorable. As Claudio says, "Having a child changes the way you think about things. Ten years from now, you'd like your child to think the work that you're doing today is still cool and interesting."

Portfolio:

- www.blackbean.com
- www.mos.org
- www.digital.com/integrate
- www.qlaser.com

chapter 9

ACTIONS

Featuring

CHAPTER

9

ACTIONS

Many people go through daily rituals. For example, if you go to an office every morning, you probably turn on the computer, log in to a network, check your e-mail, look at your schedule, and visit one of your favorite Web sites for daily news. What if you could sit in front of your computer, turn it on, and have all those actions done automatically for you? That's the basic idea behind the Actions feature in Photoshop.

This chapter covers everything you'll need to know about actions, including what they are, how they're created, and how to use them as special effects. When you're finished, you'll have a whole new perspective on how actions can be used to make your image processing more efficient and convenient.

The Convenience of Actions

When you create a Web site, you ultimately decide on a single "look and feel." Header graphics will use a certain font with a certain color, and your photographs may have a standard height and width and black or white border. Preparing all of these graphics can get very monotonous.

Actions take some of the drudgery out of creating Web graphics by recording a sequence of commands so that you can repeat them automatically with the click of a single button. The amount of time you can save by creating an action to do the dirty work of processing these images into Web format is amazing! All you have to do is open up your graphic, create a new action, start recording, and do what you'd normally do. Once you're finished with your process, you hit the Stop button and you're ready to use your action.

With Photoshop 5, it is now possible to automate all of the tools in the Toolbar, modify layer modes, and do pretty much everything else in the application. As you'll see, there's almost nothing that can't be included in an action.

Creating an Action

When working with actions, you can either start from scratch or open an existing image and enhance it. The key to creating and maintaining actions is through their palette. Select Window ➤ Show Actions from the Menu Bar to access the Actions palette.

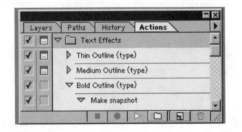

Using the Actions Palette

The Actions palette has several different parts: the list that displays the actions and their parts, the row of option buttons at the bottom, and the palette menu in the upper-right corner of the palette. When working with actions, you will use all three.

T I P   Before creating an action, think it through. It often helps to write down each step before you begin recording. This will prevent you from wasting a lot of time editing your actions after you record them.

Starting a New Action Set

Prior to making your first action, it's a good idea to start your own *action set*. This set is the folder where you store the actions you create. Photoshop comes with its own action set called Default Actions. To create your set, follow these steps:

1. Click on the folder icon at the bottom of the palette. This icon is new to Photoshop 5 and lets you create a new action set. As shown in Figure 9.1, the New Set dialog appears, asking you to name your new set.

2. Enter a name for your action set in the Name text box and click OK. In the example, I've chosen the name My Set.

FIGURE 9.1

The New Set dialog

3. Once your new set appears in the Actions palette list, you should save it. Click on the arrow at the upper-right corner of the palette. A drop-down menu appears.

4. Choose Save Actions from the drop-down menu (see Figure 9.2). A dialog appears, asking you to choose a filename for your set. Type a name and save it.

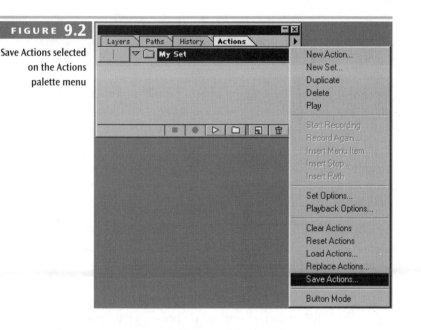

FIGURE 9.2

Save Actions selected on the Actions palette menu

N O T E   Action files are saved in the Goodies ➤ Actions directory.

Making a New Action

Once you've created your own set to store actions in, you're ready to create your first action. Before you start, make sure you are ready to record the action. Once you click the OK button in the New Action dialog, recording begins. Follow these steps:

1. Click on the New Action icon (the paper icon located between the Trash and New Set icons) on the Actions palette. The dialog depicted in Figure 9.3 appears, offering you several options.

FIGURE 9.3

The New Action
dialog

New Action

Name: My First Action   Record

Set: My Set   Cancel

Function Key: F2   ☐ Shift ☐ Control

Color: ☐ Red

2. Type a name for your action in the Name text box. It's a good idea to make it as descriptive as possible. Vague action names often lead to mistakes when choosing an action to use on a particular set of images.

WARNING   Never test an action on original work. Always make a copy of the file you're working on or use something you're not too worried about messing up.

3. Once you've named your action, choose what action set to associate it with. By default, it should say the name entered earlier—My Set, in this example. If you didn't create a new action set, it will default to the Default Actions set.

4. Choose a keyboard shortcut for your action from the Function Key drop-down list. This is a great idea, because you won't have to click on Play every time you want to run your action—you can just use your keyboard shortcut. In the example, I've chosen F2.

NOTE   With version 5, Adobe has tripled the amount of keyboard shortcut options by adding the use of the Ctrl/Command and Shift keys.

5. Choose a color from the Color drop-down list. When the list of actions is in Button mode (shown below), your actions are presented as one-click, color-coded buttons.

Layers	Paths	History	**Actions**	
Large Rectangular Button		Large Square Button		
Large Round Button		Vignette (selection)		
Frame Channel – 50 pixel		Wood Frame – 50 pixel		
Cast Shadow (type)		Clear Emboss (type)		
Custom RGB to Grayscale		Custom CMYK to Graysc...		
Make Clip Path (selection)		Sepia Toning (layer)		

6. Click on the Record button to begin recording your action. When you're finished recording, click on the Stop button (the black square on the Actions palette).

The next section takes you through a recording session exercise.

Recording an Action

This section shows you how to record an action that opens a new file, adds some text, applies a shadow, and rotates and crops the entire image. Prepare to record an action as described in the previous section, click on the Record button, and follow these steps:

1. Choose File ➤ New and make a file that is 400 pixels wide by 100 pixels high, 72 dpi, in RGB color mode, and with a transparent background.

2. Click on OK. You'll notice in the Actions palette that the list item Make appears under the name of your new action (see Figure 9.4).

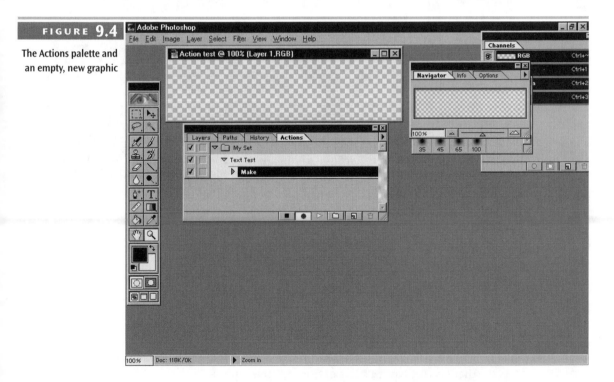

Photoshop Fundamentals

FIGURE **9.4**

The Actions palette and an empty, new graphic

3. Choose the Type tool and click anywhere on your image.

4. Enter all of your desired information including the font, color, and size.

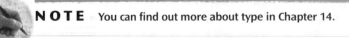

NOTE   You can find out more about type in Chapter 14.

> **5.** Click on OK. Notice that the list item Make Text Layer appears in the Actions palette (see Figure 9.5).

FIGURE **9.5**

The Actions palette and
a graphic with text

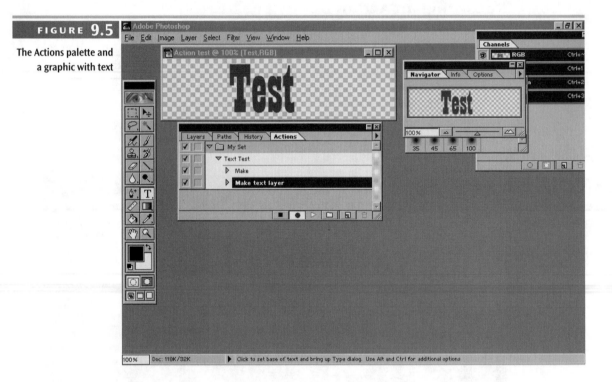

> **6.** Now you're going to add a text effect to your text. Open the Layers palette by selecting Window ➤ Show Layers from the Menu Bar.
>
> **7.** Holding down the Ctrl/Command key, click on your new text layer. Notice that your text is now selected and Set Selection appears in your action.
>
> **8.** Select Layer ➤ Effects from the Menu Bar and choose Drop Shadow.
>
> **9.** Play around with the Drop Shadow options until you're satisfied with how the graphic type looks, then click on OK. As shown in Figure 9.6, a new action item that says Set Layer Effects of Current Layer appears.
>
> **10.** Select Image ➤ Rotate Canvas from the Menu Bar and rotate your canvas to an acceptable point. Click OK. Your current action item says Rotate First Document (see Figure 9.7).

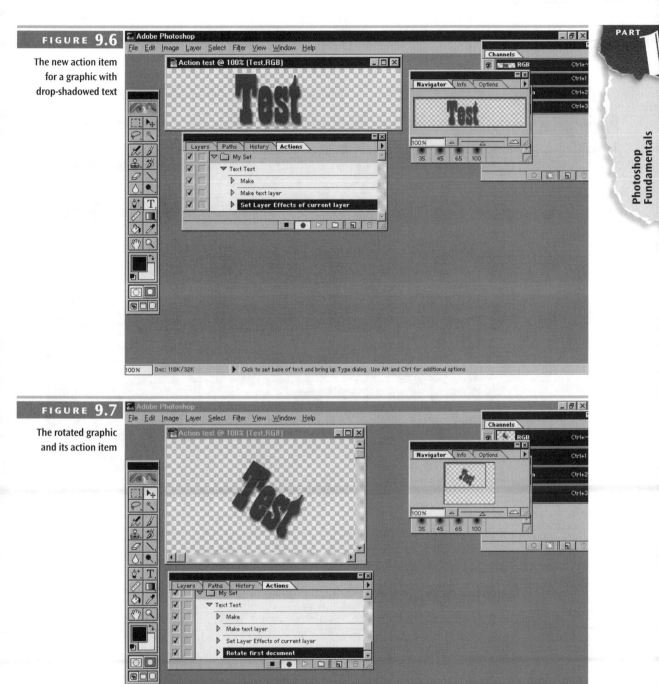

FIGURE 9.6

The new action item for a graphic with drop-shadowed text

FIGURE 9.7

The rotated graphic and its action item

11. Choose the Marquee tool and select your text, eliminating the excess canvas from the selection.

12. Select Image ➤ Crop from the Menu Bar. The finished graphic is shown in Figure 9.8.

FIGURE **9.8**

The finished graphic

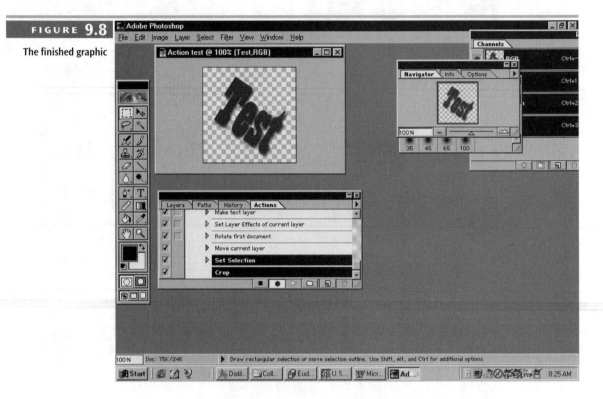

13. Click on the Stop button to end recording.

The above process may seem like a lot of steps, and that's because it is. The point of the exercise is to show you just how many things you can automate using actions. Most of the time, your actions will involve far fewer steps.

Saving Actions

Once your action is complete, it's time to save it. Highlight My Set in the Actions palette and choose Save Actions from the palette's drop-down menu. Notice that Photoshop does not let you save individual actions—it saves them by set.

TIP   As you create more actions, it's a good idea to name your sets by the type of actions that they include. This will make it a lot easier to determine what you're looking for.

Playing Back Actions

When you've finished creating your action, you'll want to view it. Follow these steps:

1. Once you've saved your new action, close the image you used to create your action (you don't need to save it).

2. Select your first action and click on the Play button (the white triangle) on the Actions palette. Notice that it completely re-creates the last graphic you had created, faster than the blink of an eye.

3. Go to the Actions palette menu and choose Playback Options. The Playback Options dialog appears.

4. You have three playback options for your actions:

   Accelerated   This option is the default. This will cruise through your action so you can get on with other things.

   Step by Step   This option slows things down a little.

   Pause For   This lets you choose the number of seconds your action pauses between steps—very useful in seeing just where a potential action snafu may be occurring.

Choose an option and click OK.

Editing Actions

When running the example action, you may notice that you never have the option to change the original text. This action isn't terribly useful if all it does is create a graphic with the exact same text over and over again. It would be best to modify your action so you or someone you're working with can create the same effect using different text. Since you want others to insert their own text, you can have a window appear that allows them to insert unique text. Here's how:

1. In the Actions palette, select the Make Text Layer option within your action and go to the palette menu.

2. Look at the column to the left of the Actions list. You'll see what looks like a depressed button (see Figure 9.9). Click on that space. A small icon has appeared on top of the depression, and other symbols have also been added to the previous parts of the action—it looks like a tiny dialog with three dots in it. This represents modal

control. Modal controls allow you to stop your action and let the user specify options for the text through a dialog.

3. Go back to the name of your action, highlight it, and press the Play button again. When it gets to the Text dialog, it stops, opens up the dialog, and lets you make changes.

4. This time through, change the options. Choose a different font, color, and size and then click OK.

FIGURE 9.9

The Actions palette with modal control selected

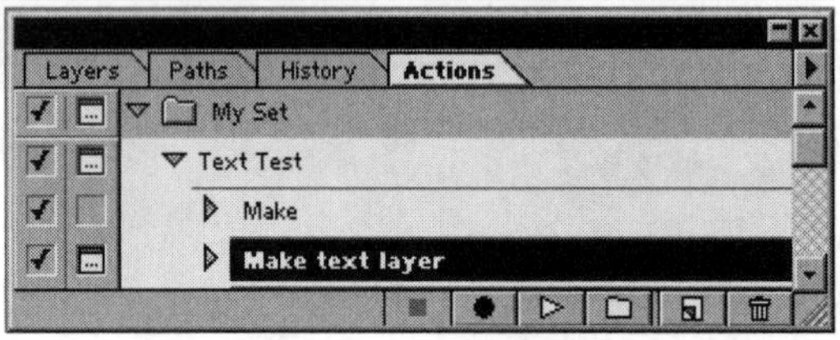

Clicking OK continues the process of the action and although you have different text options, you have a similar effect on the text. You can use modal controls for any option that has a depression next to it.

Excluding Commands

There may be a point when you want to exclude a step or command in a particular action because it's not always appropriate. Deselecting the checkmark in the far-left column of the Actions palette will deactivate the command, and the task will not be performed the next time you run the action. A red checkmark will appear next to actions with excluded commands.

Explaining Steps

Suppose you created a new action for a friend who's not very experienced with Photoshop. You can record a message that will stop the action process and explain the next step to them. Follow these steps:

1. Highlight the appropriate step in the Actions palette (in the example, this would be Make Text Layer) and choose Insert Stop from the palette menu (see Figure 9.10).

2. In the dialog that appears, type in your message (see Figure 9.11).

3. Click the Allow Continue checkbox if you want the action to automatically move on to the next step after the message.

4. Click on OK.

You now have a mini-tutorial that explains how to use this action. This comes in very handy when you're creating complex actions that need explaining. There might also be some instances where you cannot automate a particular procedure. If so, you can explain what the user needs to do.

NOTE   Action messages are effective in letting users know what types of images the action will work on—some might just work on graphics, while others are effective strictly on photographs.

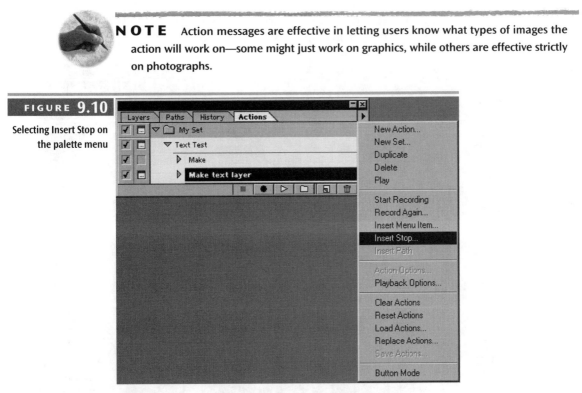

FIGURE 9.10

Selecting Insert Stop on the palette menu

FIGURE 9.11

The Record Stop dialog

Deleting Actions

Sometimes an action won't work properly and will need to be discarded. As an example, close the graphic you have created with your action and run the action again. This time, choose a much larger font size. Notice that by the time the action finishes up, more than half of your image is chopped off (see Figure 9.12). What happened? When I chose the Marquee tool to select the layer and crop it, it was only set to select for the original font size—smaller than the font used the second time around.

How do you remedy the situation? There's not much you can do with modifying the selection process for now. Your best bet is to delete the selection and crop steps of the action. Perhaps you'll stumble across a solution later. Besides, you can always append that new step to your current action. To delete the selection and crop steps, select them with your mouse and drag them to the Trash icon (see Figure 9.13).

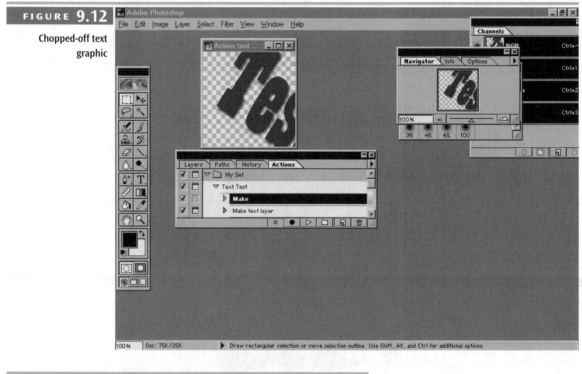

FIGURE 9.12

Chopped-off text graphic

FIGURE 9.13

Dragging action items from the palette into the Trash icon

TIP   To select more than one step at a time, hold down the Ctrl key (PC) or Control key (Mac) as you click on all your desired selections.

Appending Extra Steps to Existing Actions

Even though in the previous example there wasn't a solution to the crop problem, suppose you still want to add more steps to your action. For the sake of example, you decide to give the image a more "plastic" look. Select the action and click Play. This will create an image to use as you add new steps. After it finishes running, click the Record button—the black circle at the bottom of the Actions palette.

To run any filters on the current layer, you have to "render" it. That is, make it so it's no longer specifically a text layer. Select Layers ➤ Type from the Menu Bar and choose Render Layer. Then select Filter ➤ Artistic and choose Plastic Wrap. Play around with the options until you're satisfied, then click OK.

Choose Stop on the Actions palette. Two new options appear in your menu: Render Type Layer and Plastic Wrap. If you want to move these new options anywhere within the action, all you have to do is click and drag. If you try to move the Plastic Wrap option up above Set Layer Effects and run the action from scratch, you'll get an error.

TIP   There are some points during the creation of an action where certain menu items cannot be used. Make sure you test your actions after rearranging options.

Re-recording Actions

Sometimes you don't necessarily want to add a new step to your action, but you want to modify the settings of one of the existing steps. Rather than trashing and re-recording an entire action, you can simply delete just one step, append it, and move it into place.

The Record Again option takes care of this situation quite nicely. Select the action element you wish to re-record and choose Record Again from the Actions palette menu (see Figure 9.14). The dialog for that option opens so you can modify your settings. After you click OK, the recording stops, and your fixed item works.

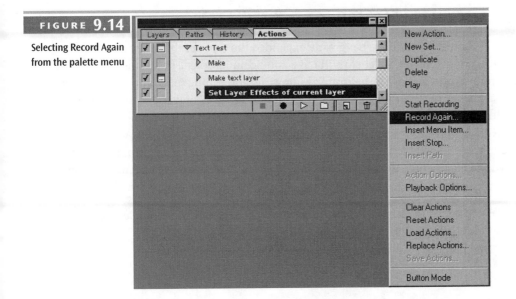

FIGURE 9.14

Selecting Record Again from the palette menu

PART

Photoshop
Fundamentals

There might also be times where you're not so sure about an entire action. You might want to modify several steps, but you're not sure which ones. By selecting the entire action and choosing Record Again from the Actions palette menu, you will be walked step by step through each option until you're finished. You can choose to either modify an option or leave it as is.

When you're re-recording actions, it's a good idea to make a copy of the entire action. To do this, click on an action and select Duplicate from the Actions palette menu. Use the copy to make any changes and, when you're sure it works, delete the original.

Troubleshooting Actions

There are times when an action will go wrong. Maybe it didn't work as you had planned, or you were unsure of the steps involved. That's when troubleshooting kicks in. Also known as "debugging," *troubleshooting* is when you work out the kinks in a program or script; or in this case, an action.

The best way to troubleshoot an action is methodically, step by step. You may notice that each list item within an action has a little triangle pointing to the right. Click on the triangle, and it displays all the specs for that action. If something's wrong with it, you'll probably be able to determine it there.

T I P   Don't forget you can re-record a list item within an action by double-clicking on it or choosing Record Again from the Actions palette menu.

The Limitations of Actions

Unlike Photoshop 4, Adobe has greatly expanded the types of things that can be done in an action. However, version 5 still has a couple limitations. For instance, while you can record the selection of the painting, drawing, and toning tools, you cannot record any actual use of them. Tool options, Photoshop preferences, and any of the View menu options cannot be recorded.

The solution is to insert a menu item into your action. If you go to the Actions palette menu and choose Insert Menu Item, you can then choose something from any drop-down menu. These methods help deal with any limitations that actions might pose.

T I P   The titles of each action list item are the equivalent of what you would type under the Insert Menu dialog for that action.

Importing Existing Actions

Photoshop 5 comes with an amazing amount of prerecorded actions. They are divided into six categories:

Buttons   This set of actions creates some great 3D buttons for use on Web pages.

Commands   This is a set of fairly common menu commands to be inserted in various new actions.

Frames   This is a set of complex actions that create elaborate frames for use with pictures. They can be used for creating unique picture galleries on the Web.

Image Effects   These actions create cool image effects like blizzards, light rain, aged photos, and much more.

Production   These actions are primarily for preparing images for print production. Included is an action for creating a transparent GIF.

Text Effects   These effects can be great for the graphical text used on Web pages.

Texture   This makes some interesting textured swatches that can be applied in the creation of Web backgrounds.

To use these actions, go to the Actions palette menu and choose Load Actions. The Photoshop actions are located in the Goodies ➤ Actions directory.

N O T E   Be sure you read the directions to the actions. Some will have the word "selection" in parentheses. This means part of the graphic you want to modify needs to be selected. Others will specify whether the graphic needs to be grayscale or in color.

Actions as Filters

Avid Photoshop users know that there are dozens of commercial filter products available for sale as Photoshop plug-ins. However, several actions that now come with Photoshop can provide many of the same effects. This section takes an in-depth look at a few.

Buttons

Buttons are popular graphical features on Web sites. Some of the more common types include E-mail, New, and the ever-present Back button. Photoshop has provided a number of new actions for the creation of buttons. Here's how to use one:

1. Open a new document 100×100 pixels, 72 dpi, and transparent.

2. Load the Buttons action set from the Actions directory.

3. Choose a foreground color by clicking on the Foreground Color/Background Color indicator, then select a hue from the Color Picker. This will be the color of your button.

4. In the Actions palette, select the Large Square Button action.

5. Click the Play icon and look at the button that is created. Figure 9.15 shows a sample button.

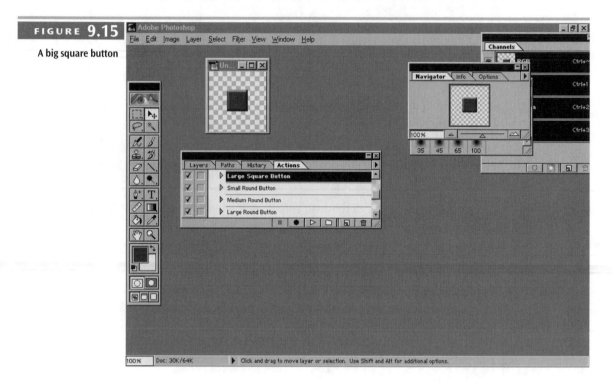

FIGURE 9.15

A big square button

You can also create buttons from photographic elements. Here's how:

1. Open up a photograph in Photoshop.

2. Using the Marquee tool, select the area you want to make into a button (see Figure 9.16).

3. Select the Photo Button action.

4. Click the Play icon and observe the results (see Figure 9.17).

Experiment with certain parts of the image and see what works for you.

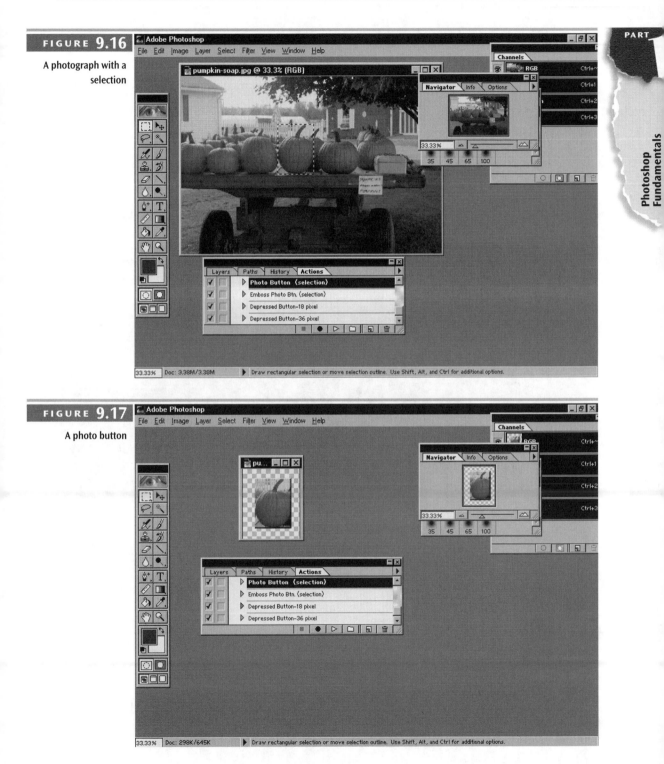

FIGURE 9.16

A photograph with a selection

FIGURE 9.17

A photo button

Photo Effects

Photo galleries are everywhere on the Web, especially on personal home pages. Photoshop's pre-prepared Frames and Image Effects action sets provide some realistic-looking effects for such graphics.

Frames

Here's how to experiment with a few Frame actions provided by Adobe:

1. Replace the current actions with the Frame action set using the Actions palette menu.

2. Open a photograph. Figure 9.18 displays a photo before any effect is applied.

FIGURE 9.18

A photograph before using the Photo Corners action

3. Choose the Photo Corners action.

4. Click the Play icon. Figure 9.19 displays the photo after the effect is applied.

You also have a few choices with selections in photographs:

1. Choose a photograph with a person or animal.

2. Using the Elliptical Marquee tool, select a portion of your photograph. Figure 9.20 displays a photo before any effect is applied.

FIGURE **9.19**

The photograph with
photo corners added

FIGURE **9.20**

A photograph before
using the Vignette
action

3. Select the Vignette action. The higher the feathering amount you select, the better the effect.

4. Click Play. Figure 9.21 displays the results.

FIGURE **9.21**

The photograph after
using Vignette

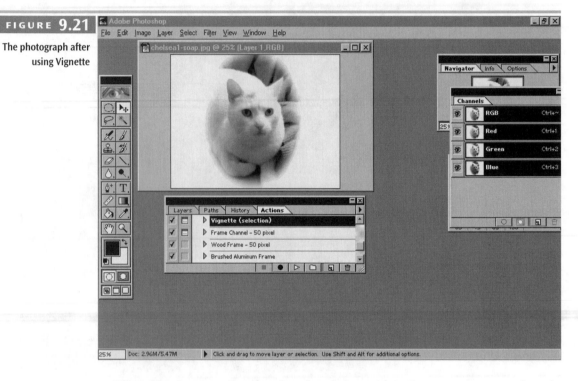

Effects like these usually take a lot of work, but with actions you can create them in just seconds.

Image Effects

The Image Effects action set is a great tool and offers everything from faux weather effects to aged photo effects. Here's how to use it:

1. Replace the current actions with the Image Effects action set by choosing Load Actions from the Actions palette drop-down menu.

2. Open up an outdoor photograph. Figure 9.22 displays a "before" photo.

3. Select the Blizzard action.

4. Click Play. Figure 9.23 displays the "after" version.

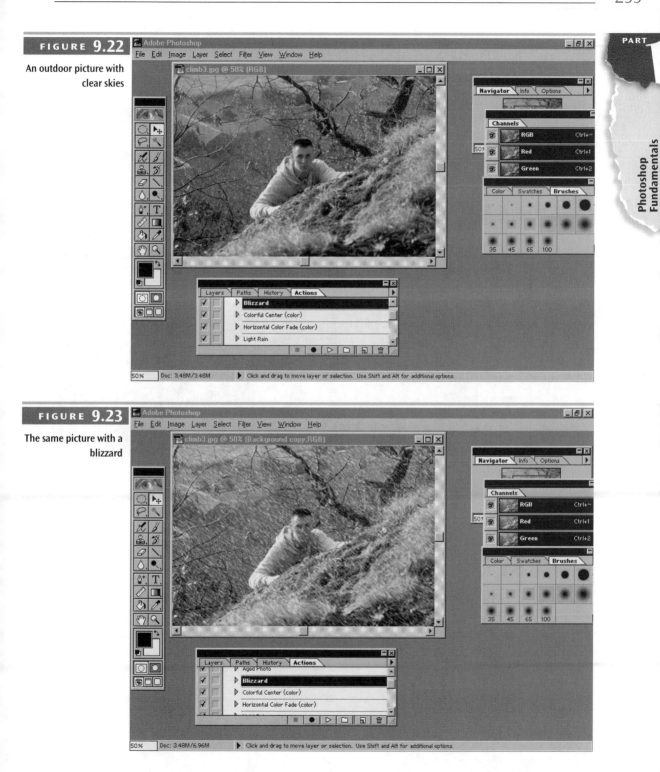

FIGURE 9.22

An outdoor picture with clear skies

FIGURE 9.23

The same picture with a blizzard

OK, so you're probably not going to use this effect all that often. Still, someday you may need to, and it's good to know that it's available. Here's another effect:

1. Open up any photograph (see Figure 9.24).

FIGURE 9.24

A landscape photo before taking action

2. Select the Oil Pastel action.

3. Click Play. See Figure 9.25 for the results.

If all goes well, you've given your photograph a more painterly look.

Text Effects

Photoshop's Text Effects action set gives you ways to create dynamic text graphics. Here's how to implement the Brushed Metal action:

1. Replace current actions with the Text Effects action set using the palette menu.

2. Open a new image.

3. Using the Type tool, create some text in your new image (see Figure 9.26).

4. Select the Brushed Metal action.

5. Click Play and view the results (see Figure 9.27).

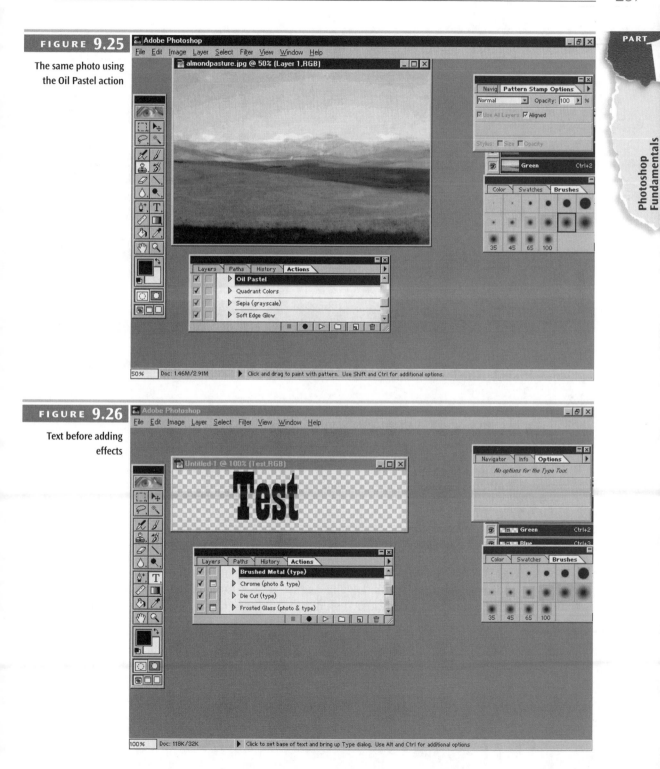

FIGURE 9.25

The same photo using the Oil Pastel action

FIGURE 9.26

Text before adding effects

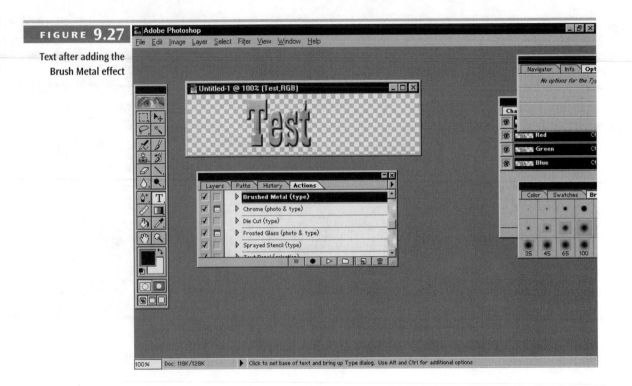

FIGURE 9.27

Text after adding the
Brush Metal effect

Actions on the Web

The Web is an excellent resource for finding Photoshop actions. Web designers across the world share their homemade actions with their peers through several popular Web sites.

Action Xchange   http://www.actionxchange.com/
CoolType.com   http://www.cooltype.com/
Action Addict   http://www.bayweb.com.au/actionaddict/

Many of the actions archived on these Web sites are posted in two ways: an action file and an archived ZIP file. To download either of these formats on the PC, hold down the Shift key and click on the link. Then navigate to your Actions directory and save the file. On the Mac, click on the link and hold down the mouse button until a menu comes up. Choose the Save As option and work your way to your Actions directory.

TIP To "unzip" ZIP files, you will need Winzip for the PC or Unzip for the Mac. Both are available on shareware.com (http://www.shareware.com).

Cleansing the Palette

Once you discover the wonderful world of free, pre-prepared actions, you may get a little overzealous and load several sets into your Actions palette. This can get very messy. The best thing to do is to clear your palette after you're done with each set. If you don't want to choose Clear before you load a new set, choose the Replace Actions option from the Actions palette drop-down menu. This clears the palette, and the new set loads.

TIP You can use the Reset Actions command to restore the default actions settings that shipped with Photoshop.

Conclusion

Actions provide a great way to automate most of the monotonous, repetitive tasks found in Photoshop and Web image creation. As long as you think logically and plan out an action ahead of time, you will be able to develop some very useful shortcuts. In time, you can drastically reduce the amount of time it takes to create a large number of graphics for the Web.

Actions also allow you to apply some cool special effects to text and images. Photoshop ships with lots of these effects, but there is also a growing list of Web sites dedicated to providing homemade actions. And if you're creative enough, you might be one of the people providing such actions to these sites.

Up Next

In the course of the last nine chapters, you've created many graphics. But what about scanning existing photos and artwork and bringing them into Photoshop for editing? What about getting images out of your digital camera and into Photoshop? How about video images? Those questions and more will all be addressed in the next chapter.

Photoshop Master: Vivian Selbo

Some of the most exciting art created in the last few years has been Web-based, and nowhere has Web art been better presented than on the ada'web site. A primary force behind ada'web has been Vivian Selbo, who has served as designer, creative director, and featured artist. Vivian's most notable work for ada'web, Vertical Blanking Interval (see Figure 9.28), represents a new kind of conceptual art. Tom Watson of @NY, a New York City Web developer publication, comments on the piece:

> ...the remote control's wiring has gone awry and the control over what's on the array of video screens is lost. Or is it? With practice and over time, the links and the images make some kind of sense. And as is the case with abstract art, the image in the mind after the experience is as important as the image on the canvas—or in this case, the video screen.

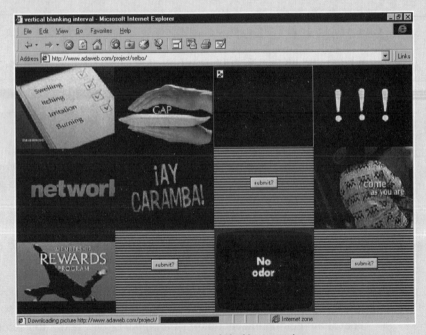

Figure 9.28   Vertical Blanking Interval

The 39-year-old artist began working on the Web in 1995 after a successful career as a print designer. Vivian's first experience with Photoshop was in 1990 with one of the first releases of the program. Today, Vivian combines her thorough knowledge of Photoshop with HTML and scripting technologies to make artwork that is conceptual, challenging, and engaging.

Time moves fast on the Web, and sites don't last forever. After showcasing cutting edge Web artwork for over three years, ada'web ceased commissioning new work in the spring of 1998. But the site, named for Ada Augusta Lovelace—the daughter of Lord Byron and the inventor of the concept of software—will continue to live on. Ada'web has been archived, and thanks to the Walker Art Center of Minneapolis, the site will endure as a snapshot of mid-90s Web art, including groundbreaking work by Jenny Holzer, Darcey Steinke, and Julia Scher (see Figure 9.29).

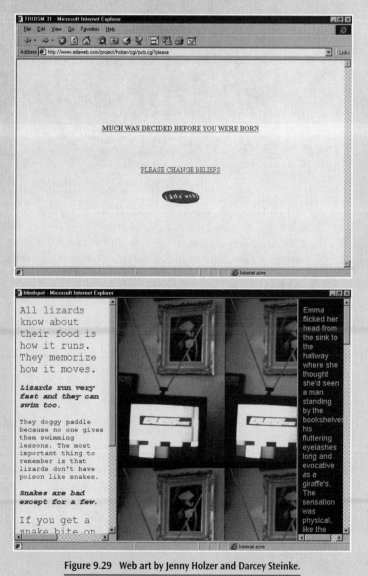

Figure 9.29   Web art by Jenny Holzer and Darcey Steinke.

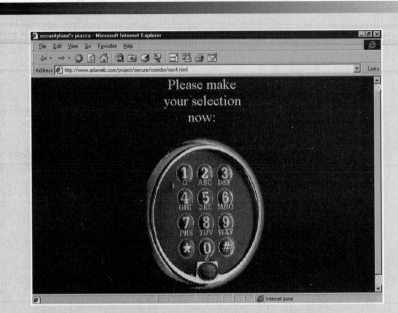

Figure 9.29 (continued)   Web art by Julia Scher

For her part, Vivian remains committed to the Web as a medium for art. It's easy to see why. In many ways, the Web is an ideal artistic medium. It is highly resistant to commercialization, the cost of materials are low, and the whole gallery system is avoided. All that is required is some space on a Web server, talent, and something to say.

Portfolio:

- www.cavil.com
- www.adaweb.com
- www.adaweb.com/project/selbo

DIGITIZING

Featuring

DIGITIZING

I f you want to put photographs and video clips into your designs and onto Web pages, you'll need to get that information into a computer. Today, designers have a whole range of ways to do this—from flatbed scanners to digital cameras and video capture boards. There are even companies that will digitize images for you.

This chapter is dedicated to all of this exciting technology, as well as the more down-to-earth issue of positioning, cropping, and scaling digitized images after they are captured.

What Is Digitizing?

Digitizing is the process of turning real world, analog information into a format that can be used by computers. The converted information is called *digital* because it is made up of strings of ones and zeroes (digits).

Visual information can be digitized in a number of ways. Scanners capture a hard-copy photograph so that it can be edited in Photoshop. Digital cameras skip the scanning process altogether and directly digitize real world objects like people, places, and things. And video capture boards convert analog video media (VCR tapes, Hi8 video, etc.) to a stream of digital frames.

Scanning

When I need to scan an image, I fire up my AGFA Arcus II color scanner and launch Photoshop. The scanner has special scanning software called FotoLook that is accessed via Photoshop's File ➤ Import command. Figure 10.1 presents the FotoLook interface.

FIGURE 10.1

The FotoLook interface

Mode:	Color RGB ▼
Original:	Reflective ▼
Input:	72 ppi ▼
Scale To:	100% ▼
Range:	Automatic ▼
Tone Curve:	Gamma 1.2 ▼
Descreen:	None ▼
Sharpness:	None ▼
ColorLink:	None ▼
Optimize:	Quality ▼
Preferences:	General ▼
Settings:	Current ▼

Rotation   Size: 🔒 5x7" ▼

X: 0; Y: 0; W: 5; H: 7 inch
Image Size: 531.6K; W: 360; H: 504 pixels
Set W/B Rescan

Cancel   ?   Scan   Preview   Zoom   View   Info

While every scanner/software combination is somewhat different, the process of scanning is essentially the same. You put the scanned image on the Web at basically the same size, set Input (also known as Resolution) to 72 ppi (dpi), and Scale to 100%. Rather than do the entire scan first, it's best to test it using the Preview option. Preview does a very quick scan to show you if everything is OK. As you can see in Figure 10.2, I managed to scan in a picture of my truck upside-down.

WARNING   It is important to clean any dust off the scanner's glass surface before scanning. Otherwise, your image will be marred by little white specks.

After a quick manual flip, I preview the image again. This time, I see a lot of space around the image. I use the software's selection tools so that only the photo is scanned (see Figure 10.3).

PART

Photoshop
Fundamentals

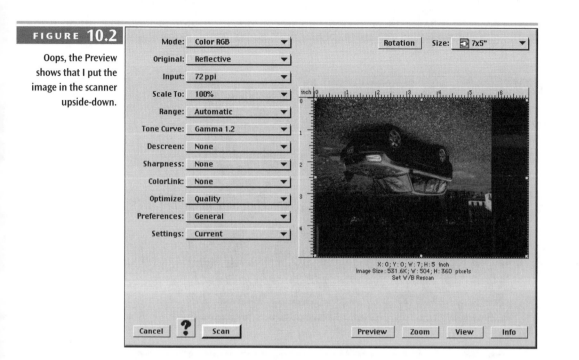

FIGURE 10.2

Oops, the Preview shows that I put the image in the scanner upside-down.

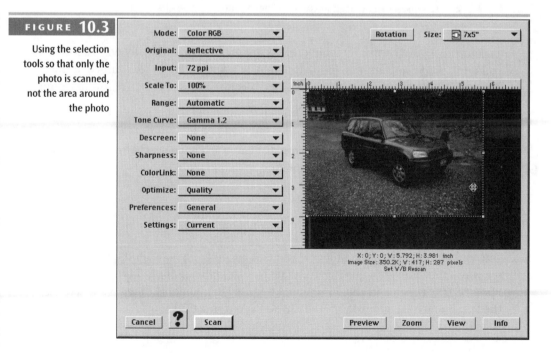

FIGURE 10.3

Using the selection tools so that only the photo is scanned, not the area around the photo

Now I scan in the image for real, and it is automatically dumped into Photoshop as a new file (see Figure 10.4).

FIGURE **10.4**

The software automatically dumps the scan into Photoshop as a new file.

N O T E   Channels can be used to color-correct a bad scan. See Chapter 6.

Sometimes you'll either forget to preview an image or intentionally do so because you think everything is set up properly. Often, the result is an image scanned upside-down or at a 90-degree angle. To reorient the file, just choose Edit ➤ Transform ➤ and whatever rotation command you need.

N O T E   Most scanned images are somewhat blurry and often benefit from having the Unsharp Mask filter applied (see Chapter 8).

Digital Cameras

Due to their popularity, lots of digital cameras are on the market, and it's easy to see why—they provide a quick, immediate way to capture images. I use an Epson PhotoPC 600, which I purchased because I was used to traditional cameras and liked the Epson's familiar zoom, built-in flash, and aperture settings.

Once you take your photos, you need to physically get them into your computer. While some cameras store images on removable floppy disks, the Epson ships with a special software/cable combination to download your pics into either a Mac or Windows computer. Figure 10.5 displays the software interface and a series of photos taken with the camera.

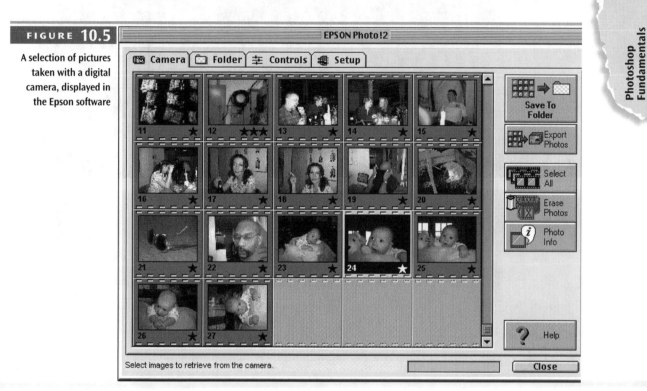

FIGURE 10.5

A selection of pictures taken with a digital camera, displayed in the Epson software

The software provides an Export Photos option that can export the images to a Photoshop-friendly format. I use the PICT format because it retains the maximum amount of image data, unlike the JPEG format that throws out information for the sake of file size. Figure 10.6 shows the result of opening an exported image in Photoshop.

FIGURE **10.6**

An image exported with the Epson software and opened in Photoshop. Photo credit: Michelle Carrier

milo @ 100% (RGB)

100%   Doc: 900K/900K

Video

Outfitted with a special video capture board, computers can capture video and sound from both VCRs and video cameras. As mentioned in Chapter 12, you can now put video on the Web using special plug-ins and Java applications.

Video capture is also very useful for grabbing static images for use on a Web page. Shooting passages of video and then selecting the precise frame is a great way to get the best image possible.

Once you've taken some video that you'd like to digitize, you'll need to launch whatever capture software that you have on hand. Most video boards ship with a capture application. However, I prefer to use Adobe Premiere because it is the industry standard for desktop video.

WARNING   When digitizing, shut down all other programs and get off the network you may be on. Other programs or network activity can interrupt the CPU intensive capture process.

To capture an image from video using Adobe Premiere, follow these steps:

1. Make sure the VCR or video camera is connected to the computer and then launch Premiere.

2. Select File ➤ Capture ➤ Movie Capture. The program will provide a blank Movie Capture window (see Figure 10.7).

FIGURE 10.7

Premiere's Movie
Capture window

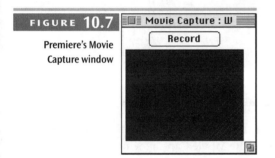

3. Hit the Play button on your VCR or camera to see the video on your screen.

4. Select Movie Capture ➤ Recording Settings. The Recording Settings dialog opens.

5. Set the capture settings. The default capture setting is 160×120 pixels, but if you want to capture a single frame for use on a Web site, 240×180 is probably more useful (see Figure 10.8). Click OK after you've made your settings choice.

FIGURE 10.8

The Recording Settings
dialog with the 240×180
dimensions

Recording Settings

○ Record at current size
● Record at: 240 × 180
   ☒ constrain
☒ Post-Compress Video
☐ Record to RAM
☐ Abort on dropped frames
☐ Report dropped frames
☒ Conform movie to 10.00 fps ▼
☐ Decode burned-in timecode
Audio Block Size: 2 Seconds ▼

[Cancel]   [OK]

6. Select Movie Capture ➤ Video Input. The Video dialog opens (see Figure 10.9).

7. Set Compression and the Compressor to None and set Depth at Thousands of Colors. Click OK.

FIGURE **10.9**

The Video dialog with Compressor set to None and Depth set to Thousands of Colors

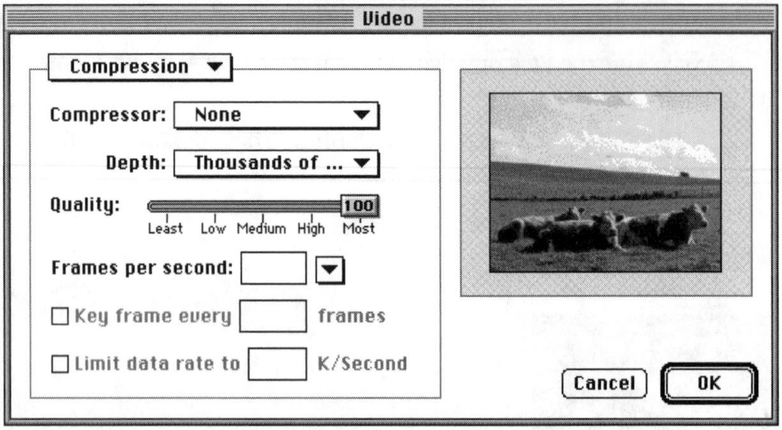

Video

Compression ▼

Compressor: None ▼

Depth: Thousands of ... ▼

Quality: |————————[100]
          Least Low Medium High Most

Frames per second: [   ] [▼]

☐ Key frame every [   ] frames

☐ Limit data rate to [   ] K/Second

[Cancel] [OK]

8. On your VCR or camera, fast-forward or rewind to the portion of the tape you want to capture. Hit the Record button in the Movie Capture window.

9. Click your mouse when you want the capture to end. The Clip window automatically opens (see Figure 10.10).

FIGURE **10.10**

The Clip window

10. Use the Clip window controls to select the frame to output. Then choose File ➤ Export ➤ Save As PICT. Name the image and click OK.

You can now open the image in Photoshop (see Figure 10.11).

PART

1

Photoshop
Fundamentals

FIGURE 10.11

The captured frame in
Photoshop

Predigitized Images

Stock photo houses like Photodisc and Digital Stock provide a vast array of images that can be purchased and delivered to you either online or as a CD-ROM. Also, Kodak's PhotoCD service puts pictures taken with a traditional camera directly on a CD-ROM. There are now Web-based equivalents of this service, providing Internet delivery of your images. All of these services eliminate the need for purchasing a scanner, and they can be a good alternative to purchasing digitizing equipment if you prefer traditional cameras or don't plan on capturing images on a regular basis.

N O T E One of the nice things about some Photodisc images, particularly the object collections, is that they come with paths already created. This makes selecting an object from the background very easy (see Chapter 5).

Positioning

Photoshop provides three ways to help position digitized images and other graphic elements, and they all work together. Rulers provide indicators that sit around the left and top edges of the graphic. Guides are horizontal and vertical rules that you can place around an image area. The Grid feature places a regular structure over an image and makes lining up image elements a snap.

Rulers

To make rulers visible, select View ➤ Show Rulers. As Figure 10.12 shows, rulers are placed along the left and top sides of the image.

FIGURE **10.12**

Rulers visible along the left and top sides of the image

Set the zero point by clicking and dragging from the graphic's upper-left corner. When you release, a new zero point is established. To make the zero point return to its original position, double-click in the square in the upper-left corner.

As detailed in Appendix E, selecting File ➤ Preferences ➤ Units & Rulers provides controls for adjusting this feature's unit of measurement. For Web designers, it's always pixels.

TIP   With version 5, Photoshop now provides the Measure tool to measure non–90-degree angles. To use the tool, simply select it from the Toolbar and click from one point to another. Measurements are reflected in the Info palette.

Guides

Guides are accessed by selecting View ➤ Rulers and then clicking and dragging from the horizontal and vertical ruler area. Figure 10.13 shows four guides dragged onto the image.

To adjust the positioning of a guide, select the Move tool from the Toolbar and place it on the guide you'd like to move. The cursor changes to a different icon, indicating that it's close enough to move the guide (see Figure 10.14).

Guides don't print, but more importantly, they aren't visible when an image is converted to a GIF or JPEG (common Web file formats) and viewed in a Web browser.

FIGURE **10.13**

An image with four guides

FIGURE **10.14**

The Move tool cursor changes to move a guide.

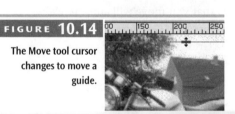

The View menu provides three other guides-related options:

Snap to Guides   Forces any element that you move to automatically snap to a nearby guide.

Lock Guides   Locks all guides into place so you don't mistakenly move them during image editing. Reselect View ➤ Lock Guides to move a guide.

Clear Guides   Allows you to start fresh, which is a convenient housecleaning feature.

T I P   To change the color or style of the guides, select File ➤ Preferences ➤ Guides & Grid.

Grid

The Grid feature is a very helpful option for creating Web layouts with a rigid, modern structure. To activate the Grid feature, select View ➤ Show Grid. A grid of lines is placed over the current image (see Figure 10.15).

FIGURE 10.15

An image with the Grid feature turned on

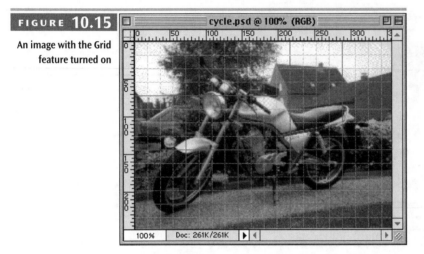

By selecting View ➤ Snap to Grid, any elements that you move will automatically position along the structure. You can adjust the spacing of the Gridlines and Subdivision options by selecting File ➤ Preferences ➤ Guides & Grid.

Cropping

Web designers spend a good deal of their time cropping images so that they (1) precisely mortise together when placed on a Web page, and (2) create the smallest file size possible. Photoshop provides two commands (Canvas Size and Crop) and one tool (Crop) to slice away parts of an image.

The Canvas Size Command

The quickest but least precise way to crop a graphic is with the Edit ➤ Canvas Size command. From the Canvas Size dialog (shown on the facing page), you can adjust the Width and Height values. The Anchor option provides 10 locations from where new canvas space will be added or subtracted.

Canvas Size

Current Size: 344K
Width: 416 pixels
Height: 282 pixels

New Size: 344K
Width: 416 pixels
Height: 282 pixels
Anchor:

OK
Cancel

If you input a Width and/or Height amount that is less than the current value, you will be warned that your image is about to be clipped.

Adobe Photoshop

The new canvas size is smaller than the current canvas size; some clipping will occur.

Proceed   Cancel

Figure 10.16 shows my earlier scan with a new canvas height value of 100 pixels.

FIGURE 10.16

A graphic clipped via the Canvas Size command

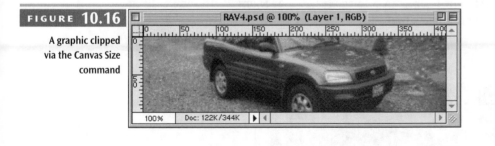

 NOTE   The Canvas Size command is more commonly used to add space around an image.

The Crop Command

The Crop command works in conjunction with the selection tools and is particularly effective when used with the Guides/Snap to Guides feature.

As you may recall, the scan of my truck has a lot of "dead" area. To clip this away, set up four guides around the image and then, with the Snap to Guides feature on, draw a rectangular selection around it (see Figure 10.17).

FIGURE 10.17

The scanned image with guides and an active rectangular selection marquee

To clip the image, select Image ➤ Crop. As Figure 10.18 shows, the graphic is now more appropriately framed.

FIGURE 10.18

The cropped image

T I P The Crop command can only be used when absolutely rectangular selections are active.

The Crop Tool

The main advantage of using the Crop tool is the ability to quickly adjust a selection area and crop an image without using a menu command—it's the "hands on" way to crop.

To use the tool, select it from the Toolbar (the last of the five Marquee tools) and click and drag in an image to define the area to crop. As you can see in Figure 10.19, the result is a selection marquee with handles.

FIGURE 10.19

Using the Crop tool results in a selection with adjustment handles

You can use the Crop tool to adjust the dimensions of the selection area, but the tool's real power is its ability to rotate an area and then crop it with the Image ➤ Crop command. Figure 10.20 shows a rotated selection and the results of using the Crop command.

T I P Double-click on the Crop tool to access the Cropping Tool Options palette and create fixed-size crop selections.

FIGURE 10.20

Rotating a selection area and using the Image ➤ Crop command to crop and reorient the image

Scaling

While Chapter 4 provided exercises in scaling and otherwise transforming selections, adjusting the size of an entire image has yet to be covered—until now. When you adjust the size of an image, all of the action happens in the Image Size dialog.

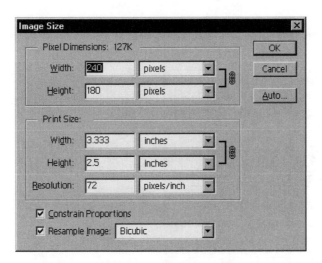

The dialog is broken up into two distinct areas: Pixel Dimensions and Print Size. If you deactivate the Resample Image option, the Pixel Dimensions feature is unavailable. Since the print size of the graphic is irrelevant to Web designers, it is important to keep the Resample Image option activated.

The Resample Image feature is an algorithm that tries to figure out what an image should look like if it is shrunk or enlarged. Because Photoshop images are made up of little colored squares, the program guesses what color the remaining or additional squares should be.

In Figure 10.21, I have taken the captured frame from the cow video and reduced it from 240 pixels wide by 180 pixels high to 100 pixels wide by 75 pixels high. It looks quite good at that size—Photoshop has done an excellent job of figuring out what pixels to remove (compare with Figure 10.11).

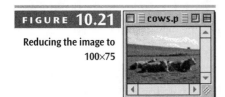

FIGURE 10.21

Reducing the image to 100×75

In Figure 10.22, however, I took the 100×75 image and scaled it up to 300×225. As you can see, the image has lost much of its sharpness. Zooming in on the face of one of the cows shows how much detail has been lost (see Figure 10.23).

FIGURE 10.22

Increasing the size to 300×225

FIGURE 10.23

A close-up of the loss of detail

Clearly, making an image larger is a major no-no in Photoshop. The Scaling feature does a good job figuring out what information to discard, but it can't guess at missing detail. Always scale down, not up. If you need an image to be bigger, scan it at a higher resolution.

T I P Scaling an image down will tend to soften it. Apply the Unsharp Mask filter (select Filter ➤ Sharpen ➤ Unsharp Mask) if it becomes too blurry.

Conclusion

In most cases, Photoshop is of little help when you need to get an image—photographic, video, or otherwise—into a computer. While it allows scanner manufacturers to plug in their capture software, the program itself doesn't digitize anything. Because of this, the exercises shown in the first half of this chapter are only of practical value to people using the same hardware and software. However, the basic principles in scanning, downloading photos from a digital camera, and capturing video are the same no matter what software you're using.

Photoshop does offer great tools for positioning, cropping, scaling, and otherwise cleaning up bad scans or captures. Be sure to refer back to Chapter 6 for information about adjusting the color values in poorly scanned images.

Up Next

Congratulations, you've finished Part One of this book. This book has three parts, so view the completion of Part One as attaining your Bachelors degree. Up next is Part Two, where you'll learn about the Web and how to combine your knowledge of Photoshop with techniques for preparing and processing actual Web graphics.

Photoshop Master: Peter Guagenti

Hard work is essential in becoming a great designer. Usually the hard work comes early on in a career, when inexperience is compensated for with enthusiasm and determination. Peter Guagenti remembers a time when he labored for nearly 60 hours during a three-day span on a Web site for the Super Bowl. "It was difficult work… I hand-coded hundreds of pages of statistics during one of the worst blizzards to ever hit New York City," recalls the designer.

The native New Yorker got his start in his hometown and was one of the pioneers in the city's Web design scene—dubbed "Silicon Alley." After serving for a short time as *People* magazine's Webmaster, Peter joined the interactive agency Avalanche. It was there that the designer became well versed in Photoshop, working on sites for Electra Records, Carnegie Hall, Paper Magazine, and the Super Bowl.

But after successful tenures with local firms Avalanche and Spiral Media, the 22-year-old was burned out and in need of a change. Prior to becoming a Web designer, Peter traveled the country as a photojournalist for action sports like skateboarding (see Figure 10.24). Hoping that a change of location would again do him some good, he began interviewing for various jobs around the country. Ultimately, it was a position with interactive agency Cybersight that made Peter leave New York for Portland, Oregon.

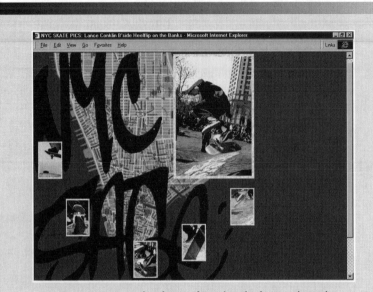

Figure 10.24 Examples of some of Peter's early photography work

Today, Peter is creative director for the fast-growing agency, managing a creative staff of nine people. He has defined his role in the company as a site architect and someone who keeps people on track and provides quality control so that the team can produce great work. The approach certainly seems to be working. In the last year, Cybersight has won awards for its work on projects for Molson, Tektronix, Founders Funds, and Nissan North America (see Figures 10.25 and 10.26).

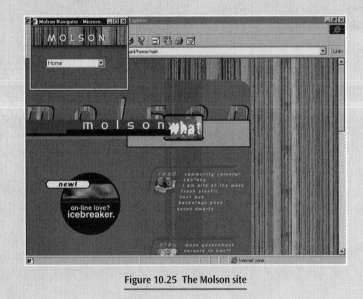

Figure 10.25 The Molson site

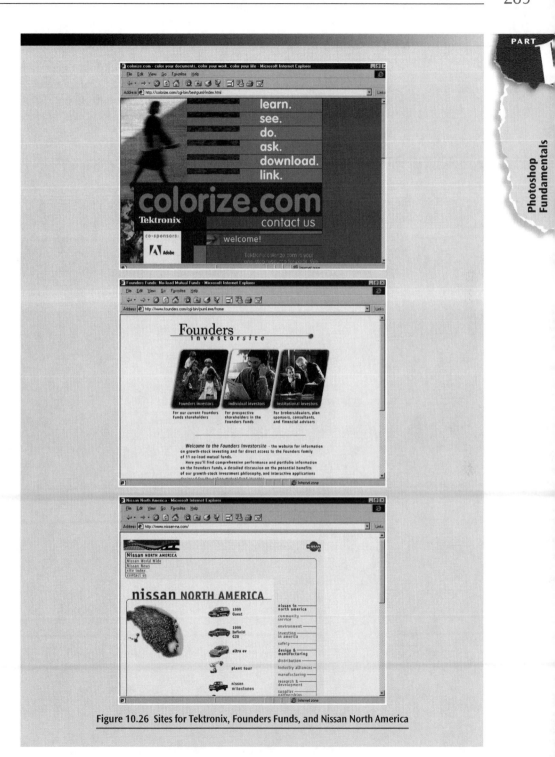

Figure 10.26 Sites for Tektronix, Founders Funds, and Nissan North America

While he misses New York's culture and the peer relationships he formed there, Peter is happy in Portland and relishes the opportunity to help Cybersight grow into an international agency with the highest creative standards. The days (and nights) of slogging through HTML may be over, but Peter's intense work ethic and enthusiasm for the medium endure.

Portfolio:

- www.guagenti.com
- www.molson.com
- www.colorize.com
- www.cybersight.com

PART II

PHOTOSHOP AND THE WEB

THE WORLD WIDE WEB

Featuring

THE WORLD WIDE WEB

Most designers are, by nature, non-technical people. We prefer to concentrate on conceptual and creative development and shy away from things like programming and networking. But the best Web designers understand how the Web works. Like a print designer who knows the printing process, Web designers who understand Web publishing are far more likely to create compelling sites.

While Photoshop is a highly capable tool for creating specific Web graphics, the Web relies on a host of other technologies to design pages and publish sites. These technologies tend to go by acronyms—HTML, HTTP, UNIX, NT, FTP, for example. Some are over a decade old, while others have emerged only in the last couple of years.

This chapter details the technologies that allow Web presentations to be seen by the world. It also provides insight on some of the politics and policies that shape what we can do on the Web. So, put away Photoshop for the time being and take a look at why the Web is like it is.

What Is the Web?

The Web was created in 1989 by Tim Berners-Lee at the CERN Particle Physics Laboratory in Switzerland. Tim's intent was to create a system that could exchange papers and other scientific information between CERN and the Stanford Linear Accelerator Center in California. Because of the cost and slowness of using traditional media, computers networked via the Internet provided the best means of publishing and delivering this information.

The Web was also designed to provide users with a non-linear mode of navigation. Unlike books where the reader is expected to move from page 1 to page 2, on the Web hypertext is used to move from document 1 to document 100. In fact, on the Web the whole notion of numbered documents is irrelevant. The author of a Web document can provide links to any Web document in existence.

Because of its advantages over traditional publishing, the Web has been adopted for a wide range of uses—including some of the more unsavory purposes you've undoubtedly heard about on the evening news. But the real business of the Web *is* business. Companies have become highly reliant on the medium. More than just another marketing tool, the Web provides companies new ways to conduct business. With the Web, businesses can educate the consumer, train staff, sell products, and provide customer support.

The Web's applications for business are so far reaching that it has spawned entirely new business models. Companies have emerged whose only storefront is on the Web. These businesses—Amazon.com and CDNOW, for example—sell items that relate well to the Web's demographic, including books, music, software, and hardware.

Though business has put great demands on the Web, the technology has proven to be up to the task. The Web's client/server architecture provides a mechanism for serving up millions of Web pages each day. The entire system is highly distributed and remarkably efficient.

Clients

Web clients—we usually call them browsers—are the software applications that allow users to visit Web sites. Web clients are so closely associated with the Web that many people mistakenly believe that their browser *is* the Web.

Originally, the Web was just pages and pages of text without any graphics. With the advent of the first graphical Web browser in 1993, the Web really started to take off. Today, Web browsers from Netscape and Microsoft provide even richer user experiences, offering animation, sound, and video.

Until recently, the Navigator browser from Netscape (see Figure 11.1) was by far the most popular browser on the market. But stiff competition from Microsoft's Internet Explorer (IE) browser (see Figure 11.2) has resulted in a user base that is about half of the market.

Netscape Navigator

With the release of Navigator 4.0, Netscape introduced support for Dynamic HTML (DHTML), a new way to provide interactivity on the Web. However, Netscape's implementation of DHTML is different from Microsoft's version.

Netscape Navigator continues to support all standard Web technologies and is available for a wide range of operating systems, including Windows, Macintosh, and UNIX.

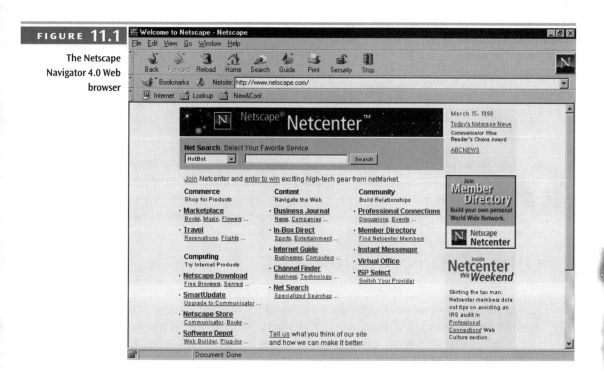

FIGURE 11.1

The Netscape Navigator 4.0 Web browser

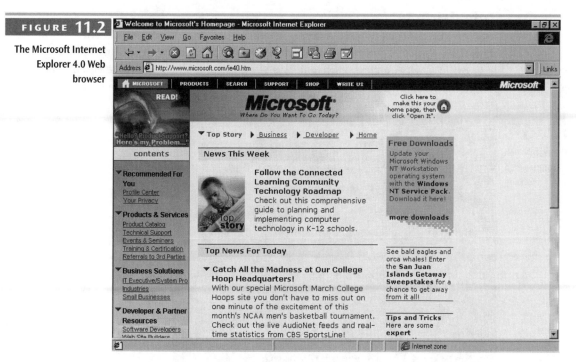

FIGURE 11.2

The Microsoft Internet Explorer 4.0 Web browser

PART

Photoshop and the Web

Microsoft Internet Explorer

First launched in August, 1995, The IE Web browser is now used by about half of the market. Release 4.0 of Explorer has provided support for new technologies such as DHTML, channels, and active desktop components. Like Navigator, the browser also supports all standard Web technologies such as HTML, Java, and plug-ins. Explorer also provides convenience: users of the Windows operating system will find that Explorer is integrated into the overall computing experience.

TIP   Designers should have both Netscape and IE installed on their computers to ensure that the Web sites they create will work on both browsers. It's also a good idea to have different versions of each browser—each one tends to have unique features and bugs.

Other Types of Clients

When a technology like the Web is successful, everyone wants to get in on the action. So companies that make everything from small, handheld computers to televisions are incorporating Web access in their products. For better or for worse, the Web is moving beyond desktop computers, and designers have to consider these devices when they develop a site.

Television

Anyone who has tried to teach a family member with limited technical experience how to use a computer knows that computers can be somewhat difficult to learn. Simple, low-cost TV devices such as Microsoft's WebTV, that use a television as the visual interface to the Web, have emerged on the market to address this problem (see Figure 11.3).

FIGURE 11.3

The WebTV Web browser running on a television

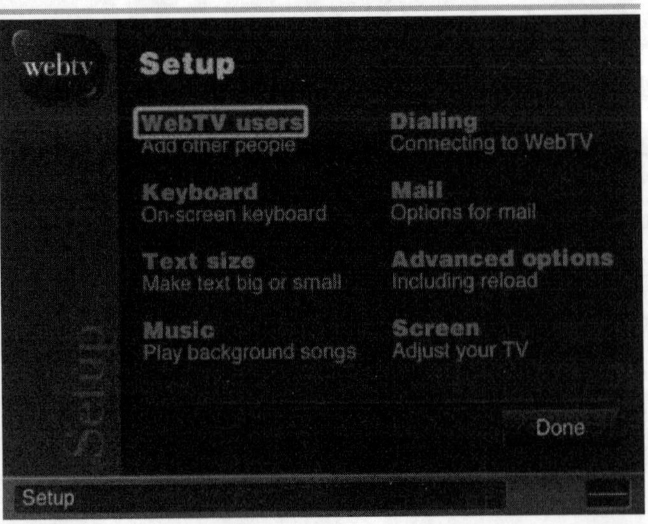

webtv

Setup

WebTV users
Add other people

Dialing
Connecting to WebTV

Keyboard
On-screen keyboard

Mail
Options for mail

Text size
Make text big or small

Advanced options
Including reload

Music
Play background songs

Screen
Adjust your TV

Done

Setup

From a design standpoint, televisions and computers rely on fundamentally different display technologies. Television renders color differently than a computer—some of the colors used on a computer are actually against the law to use on television.

Also, TVs have a different screen scale than computers do. Computers commonly display pages that are over 600 pixels wide, while TVs display pages that are no more than 544 pixels wide. On the other hand, TVs have a vertical display of up to 378 pixels high, while some computers display less than 300. As a result, pages designed for WebTV and other TV-based Web devices need to be narrower and taller in shape, otherwise the TV will force a Web page into the space—without regard to aesthetics.

 NOTE For more information about Web and television-based color, see Chapter 13.

Devices like WebTV are not as technically advanced as computers and usually cannot take full advantage of Web technologies like frames, plug-ins, Java, and Dynamic HTML. Currently, Web multimedia created with programs like Macromedia Director and Flash will not operate on television-based Internet devices.

The number of people using television-based Web interfaces is growing, but it still only represents one-half of a percent of the Web audience. Web professionals need to decide on a case-by-case basis if the potential TV audience is sufficient enough to warrant designing around the limitations of television display.

Handheld PCs

If you've ever wanted to own a Star Trek tricorder, you'll understand why handheld PCs have become so popular. These tiny PCs use either proprietary browsers created by the device manufacturer or a specialized version of the Microsoft Internet Explorer browser developed for the Microsoft Windows CE operating system (see Figure 11.4).

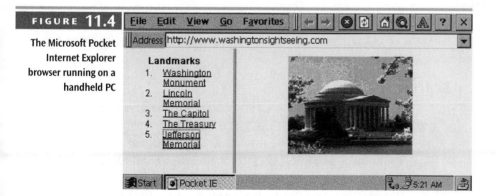

FIGURE 11.4

The Microsoft Pocket Internet Explorer browser running on a handheld PC

PART

Photoshop and the Web

Handheld devices have displays that are half as deep as the smallest computer monitors. Handheld screens typically measure no larger than 640 pixels wide by 240 pixels high. Also, because the devices are often powered by simple, consumer battery technology, most display only in black and white to conserve power. Rather than designing a single Web site that works on both computer and handheld displays, Web designers and handheld PC users are generally better served with the creation of a separate, handheld-specific site that uses simple, black-and-white graphics.

Like the WebTV users, handheld Web browsing users currently account for only a small fraction of the overall Web demographic. However, with an increasing number of small, Web-enabled electronic devices hitting the market, it may make sense to create alternate Web sites for handheld PC users.

Servers

A Web server is a piece of software that is installed on a computer connected to the Internet. Like an obedient dog, servers receive requests from clients (Web browsers), fetch the appropriate files, and bring them to the client.

The HyperText Transfer Protocol (HTTP)

Servers and clients use the HyperText Transfer Protocol (HTTP) as a common language to move Web documents over the Internet. An exchange of bits between the client and server is loosely translated to read something like this:

> Client: "Hi Server. I am looking for the Web page called dogfood.html."
>
> Server: "I got your request. Please wait while I look for it."
>
> Server: "Oh yes, here it is. I'm sending it to you now."

HTTP is called a connectionless protocol because after a client has made a connection to the server and receives the requested Web page, the connection is dropped until the next document request. The connectionless protocol is important because maintaining a constant connection to a server consumes resources and degrades performance. Thus, the connectionless protocol increases the number of people that can be served by a Web server.

Server Software

There are many kinds of computers and operating systems in use today, and most offer excellent Web server software. The most popular operating systems for computers serving Web pages are UNIX and Microsoft Windows NT. UNIX has been in use since the inception of the Web, and the majority of Web servers continue to be of the UNIX variety. Windows NT is a relative newcomer to the business of serving Web pages, but has quickly grown in popularity. From the perspective of the Web designer, the server that is used to deliver a Web site is largely irrelevant, with the following exceptions:

- UNIX is case sensitive and Windows NT is not. Files created for a Web site on a UNIX server must be carefully named—logo.gif would not be the same file as Logo.gif.

- UNIX has been around for a long time and is relatively stable. Windows NT continues to receive major upgrades and can be less stable.

- Many businesses have Microsoft Access databases that they would like to integrate into their Web site. This can only be done in the Windows NT hosting environment.

- Internet service providers (ISPs) tend to charge somewhat less for UNIX-based Web hosting because it is less costly to maintain than Windows NT hosting.

Bandwidth

Web users connect to the Internet at a wide range of speeds. Some use a corporate network that can download Web pages extremely fast because they are connected to a fiber-optic network. Other users, particularly those in residential areas, connect to servers via modems that download pages much slower. Connection speed is commonly referred to as bandwidth and is a major issue in Web design.

When developing a Web site, it is imperative for a designer to understand the site's intended audience. An internal corporate site will most likely have high-bandwidth users and might benefit from advanced graphic treatments and multimedia. However, a Web site intended for the mass consumer market will have an audience that uses low-bandwidth modems, so streamlined designs with low-bandwidth downloads are very important for usability.

 NOTE See Chapter 12 to learn how to create graphics that are optimized for low-bandwidth situations.

Hypertext Markup Language (HTML)

The Web was built upon the idea of hypertext—linking documents together to form complex structures of information. The language that is used to bind these documents together is called the Hypertext Markup Language (HTML). Behind every Web page is HTML, and it can be viewed by selecting the View Source command in a standard Web browser. Figure 11.5 displays a simple Web page and the HTML that makes it happen.

FIGURE 11.5

A Web page and
its HTML

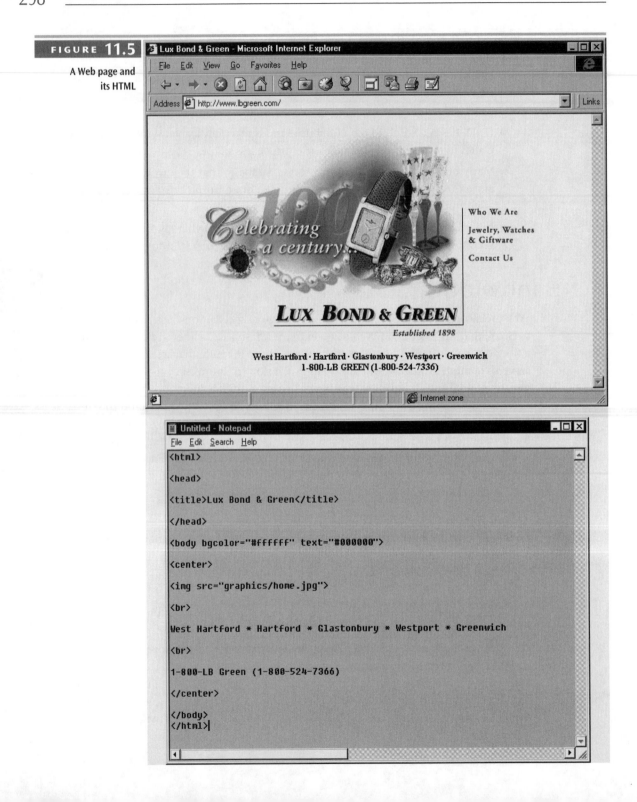

As demonstrated in the previous example, HTML allows you to include text in a document. However, Web designers who want to include images must create them in a separate image-editing program like Photoshop. The graphics are then called out in the HTML and rendered in the browser. For example, in Figure 11.6, you see a logo on a Web page.

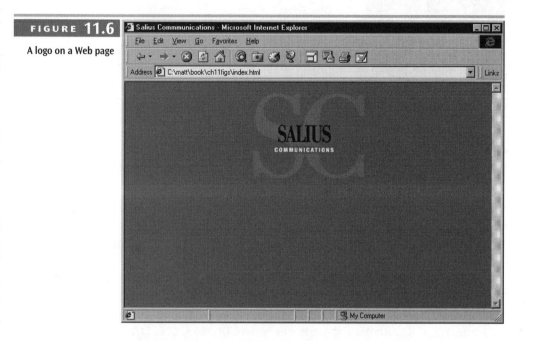

FIGURE **11.6**

A logo on a Web page

In Figure 11.7, the HTML describes a link to a graphic called `logo.gif`. Notice that included in the HTML are tags identifying the height and width of the graphic. This allows the browser to allot the proper space for the graphic on the page.

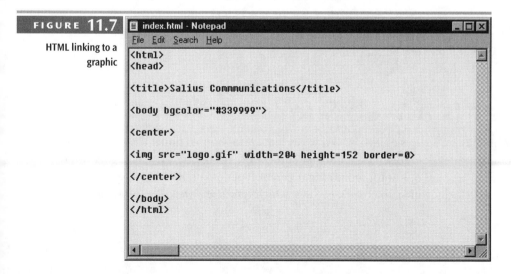

FIGURE **11.7**

HTML linking to a graphic

PART

Photoshop and the Web

Finally, in Figure 11.8 we have the graphic itself that was created in Photoshop and saved in the GIF file format.

FIGURE 11.8

The logo graphic saved as a GIF file

N O T E   See Chapter 12 for more on saving graphics in Web file formats.

The Web was intended to be a cross-platform information publishing system, conforming to every user's hardware. Because fonts, resolution, and monitor size vary from computer to computer, no provisions were made in HTML for standard page layout techniques like drop caps and multiple columns of text.

So when you're thinking about HTML, remember that the language was intended to describe the structure of a document, not the layout of a page itself. If it seems clunky and imprecise, that's because HTML was never intended to be used for design.

Despite HTML's limitations, designers have developed a series of tricks and work-arounds to create more pleasing Web sites. New technologies such as Cascading Style Sheets and downloadable fonts have also emerged, and promise to make the job of designing superior Web pages a more straightforward endeavor.

N O T E   See Chapters 16, 17, and 18 for designing and constructing graphically advanced Web pages.

What Is a Web Site?

Web sites are a series of linked Web pages that are all housed under the same general domain. Sites tend to serve a particular purpose or area of interest—selling hardware, sharing political opinions, promoting different types of entertainment, etc. Web sites can also include links to other Web sites, which results in "webs" of information.

Organization

The first document in a Web site is called the home page. The home page contains links to all of the other primary documents in the presentation. Because the relationships between pages can become complex, Web designers rely on site maps to comprehend all of the possible paths through a presentation. Figure 11.9 demonstrates a schematic for a two-level Web site.

FIGURE **11.9**

A Web site schematic

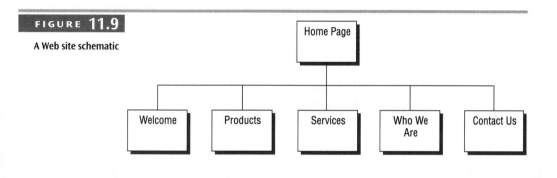

WARNING   Each Web page typically has no more than 10 pages it links to directly. More than ten choices is cumbersome from both a design and user standpoint.

A Web site with a large number of pages has more complex levels of organization. The home page/second-level page relationship is repeated, creating a site map that looks similar to a family tree. A Web site that contains 13 documents might have three levels of organization (see Figure 11.10).

FIGURE **11.10**

A Web site with three levels of organization

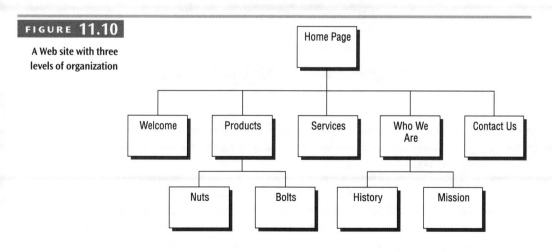

PART

Photoshop and the Web

In the previous example, each second-level page serves as a child to the home page and a parent to the third-level pages that are linked off of it. This pattern can be repeated down to four, five, or more levels, depending on the number of documents in the site.

N O T E   Site maps are primarily created in programs like Microsoft Word, Powerpoint, and specialized Web project management tools, but they can also be created in Photoshop using the program's drawing and type tools.

Navigation

Because Web pages are hyperlinked and allow users to determine their own path through a site, navigation systems are crucial to good user experiences. Navigation can either be text-based or graphical. Common graphical navigation devices include icons, buttons, and menu bars (see Figure 11.11).

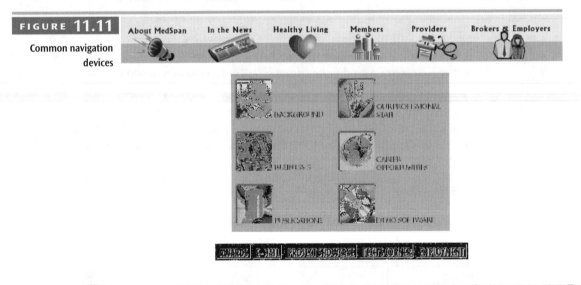

FIGURE 11.11

Common navigation devices

N O T E   Author Edward R. Tufte has written extensively on the subject of information design and visual thinking. Titles include *Envisioning Information* and *The Visual Display of Quantitative Information*.

The task of ensuring clear navigation falls to Web designers. Armed with a site map, a designer sketches out all the areas that a user will be able to jump to from any page on the Web site. These areas typically include the home page, second-level pages, a search engine, and an e-mail link. Figure 11.12 demonstrates a navigation bar that includes all of these main-level navigation options.

FIGURE 11.12

A navigation bar with main navigation options

A Web site with dozens of documents will need second-level navigation options. Second-level navigation is often text-based since each second-level page needs a separate navigation system, and downloading multiple graphical navigation devices can be time consuming. Another reason text-based navigation is advisable is that second-level navigation usually requires frequent updates—documents are often added or removed from a Web site. Figure 11.13 shows a Web page with main and second-level navigation.

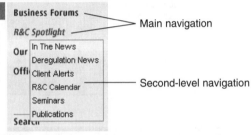

FIGURE 11.13

Mousing over the main level (R&C spotlight) accesses the second-level navigation.

Page Design

The biggest difference between print and the Web is that Web designers have no control over the delivery mechanism. Unlike print, where a designer can specify paper stock and size, Web pages are viewed on a wide range of computers and other electronic devices.

These devices also have limited amounts of space on which to display an area of a Web page. Common print layout techniques such as multiple columns of running text are not relevant in this environment because an entire Web page cannot usually be seen on a computer without moving the page. Figure 11.14 demonstrates this problem.

Web browsers typically provide scroll bars for documents that contain more information than can fit in the area provided by a computer monitor. Scroll bars allow Web designers to create pages of infinite length (see Figure 11.15).

The fact that a Web page is scrollable poses unique challenges to the Web designer. Information such as branding and navigation items are often repeated in a Web page because the user may need to access such information at various locations in the document (see Figure 11.16).

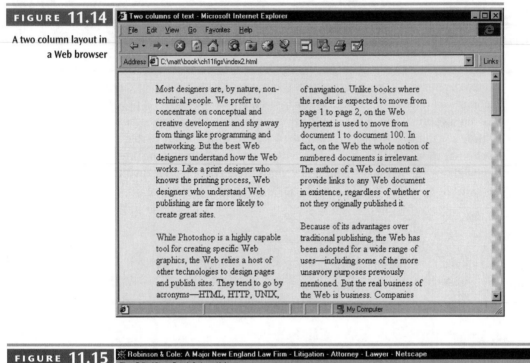

FIGURE 11.14

A two column layout in a Web browser

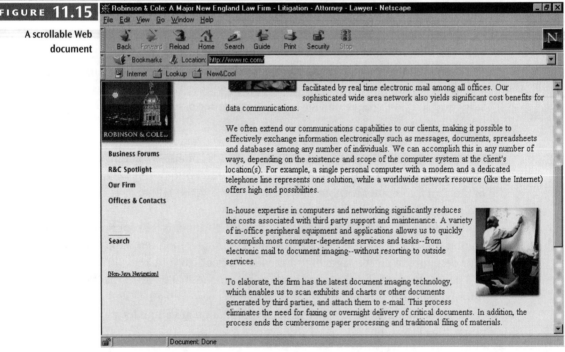

FIGURE 11.15

A scrollable Web document

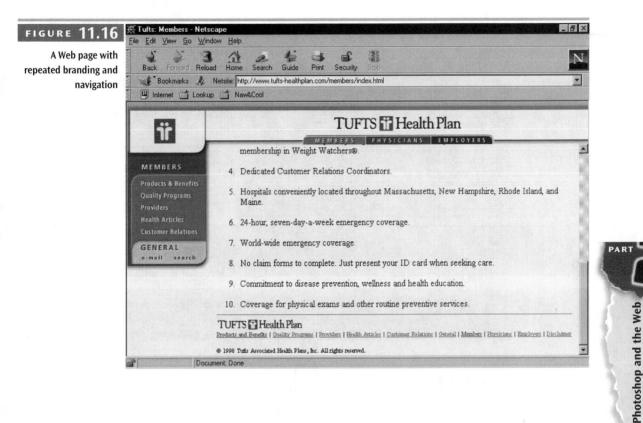

FIGURE 11.16

A Web page with repeated branding and navigation

Publishing

Web sites are published by moving HTML and associated multimedia files onto Web servers. Web servers are typically at a remote location—away from where the site was actually designed.

File Transfer Protocol (FTP) is a standard by which files can be moved, renamed, or deleted on a remote computer. When a designer has completed a Web site and is ready to publish, the files are moved to a Web server with the aid of an FTP program. Applications like WSFTP for Windows (Figure 11.17) and Fetch for the Macintosh are inexpensive shareware programs commonly used by Web designers and publishers.

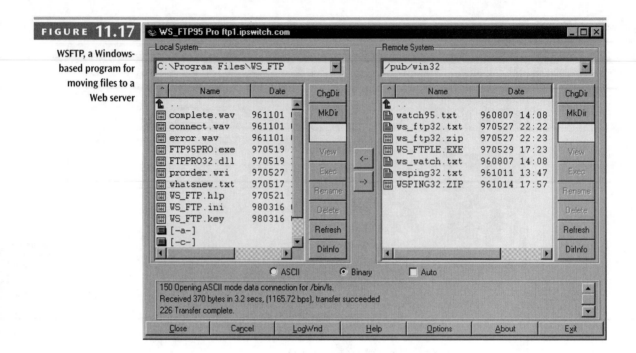

FIGURE 11.17

WSFTP, a Windows-based program for moving files to a Web server

Who Runs the Web?

The Web can be likened to the Frankenstein monster—it's powerful, it scares some people, and it is out of control. It is also a great experiment. Despite the fact that no governmental body provides the regulations and standards that make the Web run, businesses have invested billions of dollars into Web technology. If any given country attempted to regulate technical standards, the fact that the Web is a global entity would limit that country's reach.

For designers, it is important to know what standards to follow when creating sites. More importantly, designers need to know what technologies will be adopted in the future so they can remain educated and employable.

Although the Web is uncontrolled, there are some forces that influence its path. Selected software companies, a working group called The World Wide Web Consortium, or the W3C, and commercial entities that run its search and addressing functions impact how we use the Web.

Browser Software Companies

Because Netscape and Microsoft make the most popular Web browsers, the features they include in their software drive the way users experience the Web. Netscape and

Microsoft are in an intense battle to claim that largest market share, so the companies are constantly providing cutting-edge features that are usually incompatible with the other company's browser.

Browsers from Netscape and Microsoft are both designed in a way that allows other software vendors to provide enhancements, so popular plug-ins manufacturers like Progressive Networks and Macromedia also determine the way we listen to and interact with the Web. Both browsers also support Java, a popular Web programming language invented by Sun Microsystems.

But allowing market forces to drive the development of the medium has both its strengths and weaknesses. Market forces have sped up innovation and provided designers with much better ways to engage their audience. But the market has also splintered audiences with browsers that have incompatible features. Web designers have great browser features they can exploit, but it has become difficult to design enhanced Web sites that function for a wide audience.

Web designers can (and should!) stay current on browser technology by visiting Browserwatch and BrowserWars at the following Web sites:

- `http://www.browserwatch.com`
- `http://www.browserwars.com`

The World Wide Web Consortium

The W3C is an organization that develops and approves standards for Web technologies. The W3C homepage is shown in Figure 11.18. The group is managed by the Laboratory for Computer Science at the Massachusetts Institute of Technology in Boston. In Europe, the W3C is headquartered at the French National Institute for Research in Computing and Automation.

The judgments of the W3C are of particular interest to Web designers because their decisions become the recommended technologies that all new Web browsers tend to support. Browsers can and do support more advanced, custom technologies, but the W3C standards are generally supported across all browsers and computer platforms.

Standards organizations like the W3C can take a long time to approve technologies that are already in popular use. It is often difficult for Web designers to base their designs solely on approved W3C standards. For example, frames—which allow the division of a Web page into independent areas—were used by designers for years before they were formally approved by the W3C.

N O T E Web designers will want to visit the W3C site (`http//www.w3c.org`) on a regular basis to check on the status of pending Web standards and technologies.

FIGURE 11.18

The W3C home page

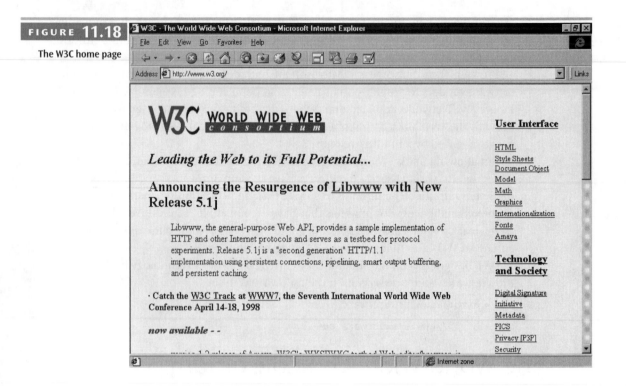

Search Engines

The search engine, more than any other medium, is responsible for directing Web users to the sites they want to visit. Similar to a phone book, a search engine is an exhaustive, searchable listing of the pages that make up the Web. Search engines are powered by sophisticated software that combs the Web for new pages.

Search engine sites provide multiple ways to search for a Web site. The most popular device is the text search where a user keys in a word or series of words that best describes the information that the user is looking for (see Figure 11.19).

Because most people find new Web sites with search engines, it is important for Web developers to register a new site with the engines. As demonstrated in Figure 11.20, registration is a free service that requires a limited amount of information.

While there are hundreds of search engines, less than a dozen are considered major players in the industry. The most popular engines—Yahoo!, Excite, HotBot, and so on—generate revenues from the sale of advertising banners that sit atop their pages.

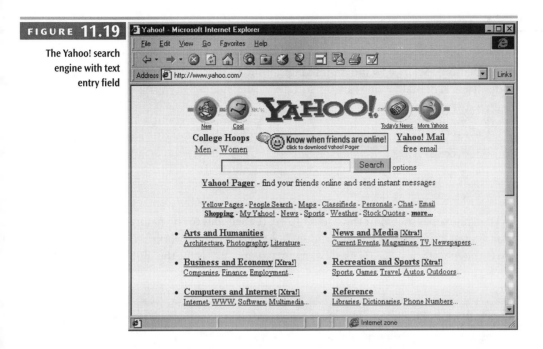

FIGURE 11.19

The Yahoo! search engine with text entry field

FIGURE 11.20

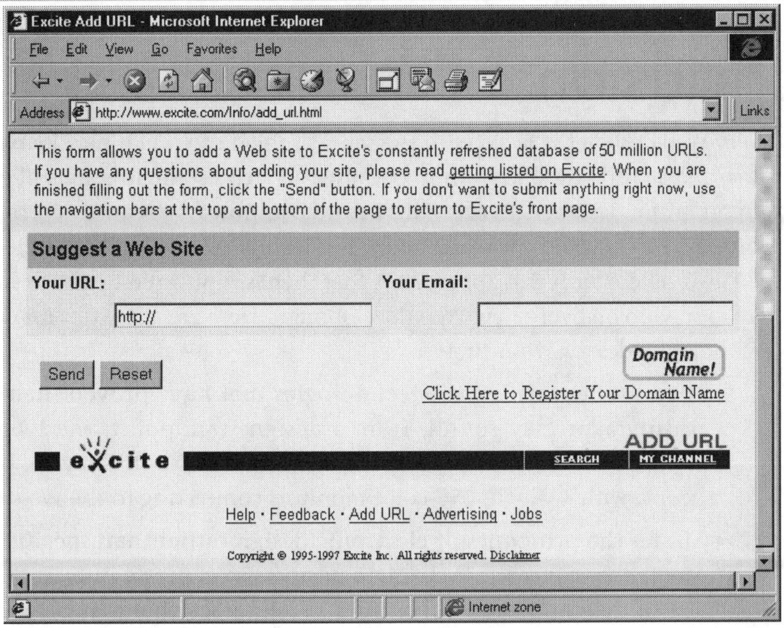

Excite's search engine registration form

InterNIC

InterNIC, a division of Network Solutions, is currently the only company authorized by the National Science Foundation to register Internet domain names in the United States. Typical domain names are

- `coke.com`
- `w3c.org`
- `ibm.com`
- `hud.gov`
- `nike.com`

Domain names include a three letter suffix that alludes to the nature of the site: `.com` is used by commercial organizations, `.net` is used by networks, `.gov` is used by government agencies, `.org` is used by organizations, `.mil` is for the military, and `.edu` is used by educational institutions.

N O T E   For more information about registering a domain name, visit the InterNIC Web site at `http://www.internic.org`.

Conclusion

Every Web designer is faced with the same problem: so much new Web technology to learn and so little time to learn it. Because the Web's standards are still evolving, it is important for designers to stay current and continue to research new trends and technologies. You never know when a new hot technology will reinvent the Web, right?

The problem with this approach is that there simply aren't enough hours in the day to stay up on every new Web development. Here are a few tips for deciding what technologies deserve your time:

- **Spend time learning the technologies that have proven themselves**. As surprising as it may sound, from a design standpoint, the Web has actually changed little over the last half decade. Most sites still have to be designed for people with 15-inch, 256-color monitors connecting to the Web with a modem.

- **Master the principles of electronic design rather than specific technologies.** Media that cover the Web are in business to generate interest and increase the size of their audience. Sometimes a technology that may be portrayed as very important will turn out to be a flop—just ask the "experts" in ActiveX and Push technology.

- **Consider if you have the time, money, and level of interest to become good at a new technology.** How many hours will it take to get familiar with the technology? Does it fit in with your overall skill set? If it involves programming, wouldn't your time be better spent enhancing your existing design skills? Color, layout, typography—now that's the fun stuff!

- **Concentrate on becoming a great interactive multimedia designer.** If you want to start learning how to design for the Web of the future, don't think in terms of specific plug-ins or programming languages. Once high-bandwidth solutions become more widely available, it will be possible to send any type of digital information—full motion video, interactive education, entertainment, and so on—over the Web.

Up Next

Now that you have a general idea of what the Web is all about, it's time to get down to specifics—namely, the technical side of creating Web graphics. So, fire Photoshop back up, and let's start talking about GIFs, JPEGs, PNGs, FPX.

PART

Photoshop and the Web

Mastering the Medium: A Site of Your Own

When I started my Web design career, my skills and familiarity with the medium were limited. I faced a common dilemma: You can't get better without experience, but nobody will hire you without experience. So how do you find ways to help improve your skills? The answer is to invent a project: the development of a Web site of your own.

I used my first Web site as a test bed for HTML and graphic techniques that I was learning at the time. The results weren't always pretty. But in time, my skills matured, and things started to get interesting. As shown in Figure 11.21, at one point I created surreal, 3D navigation devices using Photoshop's Filters and Layers features. These strange objects provided a very unique look, and the Web site won a number of awards.

The Web site also collected e-mail from people who enjoyed the effort I was putting into the pages. I developed a circle of e-mail pals who shared a love for great Web design. Best of all, the site generated clients. What started as a way to learn more about the medium became an effective marketing device.

Figure 11.21 An early iteration of my personal Web site

So what makes for an effective personal Web site? In general, Web designers tend to fall into three categories: information designers, artists, and graphic designers. When you start creating your first site, consider which category you best fit into.

- The *information designer* favors content and navigation over gratuitous graphics, so these people strive to create sites that are clean and user friendly.

- The *artist* is far more visual, and these sites contain challenging—sometimes controversial—imagery.

- Somewhere in between is the utilitarian *graphic designer*. These people represent the majority and promote their services on sites that emphasize type design and professional layouts.

Regardless of the kind of designer, most personal Web sites contain these sections:

- Background information on the designer (education, experience, etc.)

- Description of services

- Portfolio of selected projects

- Client list

- Contact information (e-mail, phone, etc.)

Now that I run an agency and am in the position to hire Web designers, I can't stress enough the importance of a great personal Web site. When I get a resume, I immediately look for the applicant's Web address. If there isn't one, I don't usually read any further. If there is one but the site has bad type or weak layout, there's little chance I'll arrange an interview. But if the site knocks me over with creativity, style, and sensitivity to the medium, I'll often rearrange my schedule so I can meet with the designer as soon as possible.

GRAPHIC FORMATS

Featuring

CHAPTER 12

GRAPHIC FORMATS

If you were designing Web sites three or four years ago, making graphics was pretty simple. Back then, Web browsers supported only one internal graphic file format—GIF—and the biggest decision was how to pronounce it. There were no animations, no streaming video, and certainly no possibility of anything resembling interactive multimedia.

Today, the situation is totally different. Designers now have hundreds of tools and an endless list of emerging technologies. And if they research even a fraction of these technologies, they run the risk of wasting lots of time on something that may never have a practical application. It's enough to make a Web designer wish they were working in print.

Fortunately, one of Photoshop's great strengths is that it has consistently adopted only the features that Web designers truly need. The program has been around so long that Adobe isn't about to add some new file format simply because it's a buzzword. And once Adobe does add a new tool, chances are good that it will be a solid, well-considered enhancement to the program.

This chapter details Photoshop's carefully considered line of Web graphic file formatting tools, as well as some other applications that build upon Photoshop's current capabilities.

Internally Supported Graphics

Unlike HTML, which must be supported by Web browsers, there is no standard graphic format. In fact, the World Wide Web was intentionally designed as an open multimedia space, capable of handling an unlimited number of graphic standards. But in practice, the Web isn't as open as it seems.

While it is possible to attach any graphic file to a Web page, few of the possible formats are supported internally in the browser. This means that while you can attach a postscript file to a Web page and view it with another program, no browser will be able to display the file on the Web page itself.

Today's Web browsers also support a wide array of plug-in–based media. Plug-in technology was developed by Netscape as a way of adding additional capability to a Web browser. Software firms such as Macromedia and Progressive Networks have developed plug-ins that offer interactive games, real-time audio broadcasts, and other cutting edge media.

The problem with plug-in technology is that users must have the appropriate software installed to experience the media. While all of the popular plug-ins are available for download, not everyone is willing to get the software. If a Web site visitor isn't willing to download and install the Shockwave plug-in, there's no way they're going to be able to experience the snazzy Macromedia Director movie you've created.

Fortunately, the manufacturers of Web browsers have settled on a few internally supported graphic formats. Graphics Interchange Format (GIF), Joint Photographic Experts Group (JPEG), and Portable Network Graphics (PNG) are file formats that have been adopted to varying degrees by Netscape and Microsoft. If you create a GIF file and link it into a Web page's HTML code, people will be able to see it without downloading additional software.

N O T E   New in Photoshop 5 is the FlashPix (FPX) image format. Developed by Live Picture, this format requires no special plug-ins or browser upgrades. However, the format requires special Web server software.

With each new version of Photoshop, Adobe has added and upgraded tools for encoding Web graphic formats as they have emerged. The program currently supports GIF, JPEG, and PNG file formats, and provides a number of tools for creating such files. While these file formats lack some of the visual punch of other cutting edge Web technologies, they continue to serve as workhorses and form the backbone of most of the Web page designs created today.

Graphics Interchange Format (GIF)

GIF (pronounced "giff" or "jiff") is the most popular graphic format on the Web. The GIF format was originally invented for use on CompuServe, one of the first commercial online networks. Since it was designed for use on a computer network with low-bandwidth users, GIF proved to be an ideal choice as the first internally supported graphic format for the Web. To this day, the majority of graphics seen on Web pages are GIFs.

Compression

GIF became so popular because of its ability to compress graphic data efficiently. GIF relies on the Lempel-Ziv Welch (LZW) algorithm, a mathematical formula that can transform large files into smaller files that are more suited for the Web. The LZW algorithm works its magic by compressing a series of symbols into a single symbol multiplied by its number of appearances. For example, if 10 black pixels were grouped together in a graphic, file formats without compression would represent the 10 black pixels as 10 symbols. However, GIF notes this repetition by using only two symbols: the number of times the color repeats and the color itself. Instead of 10 elements of data, there are only two (see Figure 12.1).

PART

Photoshop and the Web

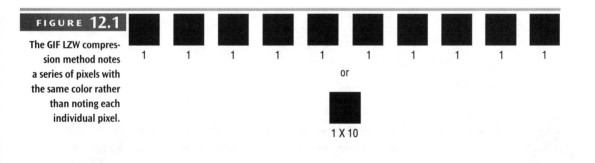

FIGURE 12.1

The GIF LZW compression method notes a series of pixels with the same color rather than noting each individual pixel.

1   1   1   1   1   1   1   1   1   1

or

1 X 10

N O T E   LZW compression is called a "lossless" data format because, although the data is being compacted, the decompressed graphic looks exactly the same as the original file.

Indexed Color Mode

The GIF format is limited to a 256-color palette. This means that no matter how many colors a file contains, it will need to slim down to 256 colors or less if it wants to become a GIF. The reason for this limitation goes back to the fact that the GIF standard was designed for low-bandwidth network situations. Since every color that is included in a graphic is additional data, fewer colors mean smaller file sizes and shorter downloads. Photoshop has provided Indexed Color mode as a way of automatically removing colors from a graphic.

Converting to Indexed Color Mode

To save a graphic as a GIF, convert the image from RGB mode to Indexed Color mode by doing the following:

1. Select Image ➤ Mode ➤ Indexed Color from the Menu Bar to view the Indexed Color dialog.

![Indexed Color dialog box showing Palette: Web, Color Depth: Other, Colors: 216, Dither: None, Color Matching: Faster selected, Preview checked]

2. Select Web from the Palette drop-down menu.

3. From Color Matching, select either Faster or Best.

4. Click OK.

N O T E   As we will learn in Chapter 13, the Web is standardized on 216 specific colors. Use Photoshop's Web palette in the creation of all GIFs destined for use on the Web.

Dithering

When two or more colors are placed closely together in certain patterns, the human eye tends to blend the colors naturally into a single hue. Photoshop takes advantage of this process by using its Dithering feature to simulate colors that may not be available in a limited color palette. Since GIF can save no more than 256 colors, dithering can be useful for simulating color in graphics that contain a wide range of hues.

Whether you want to use the Dither option depends on the type of graphic you are converting. If the graphic has been designed with only a few dozen colors, there is usually no need to apply the Dither option. However, if your graphic contains subtle shading or a wide variety of colors variations, dithering is a must.

Figure 12.2 demonstrates the advantages of using dithering on a graphic that is comprised of many values. While both graphics have been converted to 256 colors, the file on the left has not implemented dithering and is very coarse. The file on the right has been processed with Photoshop's Dithering feature and is more natural.

FIGURE 12.2

Non-dithered vs. dithered

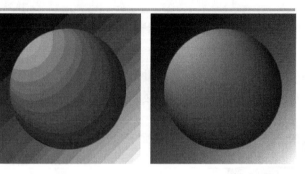

WARNING Graphics with a wide tonal range that don't have dithering applied can develop harsh transitions called banding.

Dithering an Image

To apply Photoshop's Dithering effect to an image, open an image and do the following:

1. From the Menu Bar, select Image ➤ Mode ➤ Indexed Color. The Indexed Color dialog appears.
2. Choose Web from the Palette drop-down menu.
3. Select Options ➤ Dither ➤ Diffusion.
4. In Color Matching, select either Faster or Best.
5. Select Preserve Exact Colors.
6. Click OK.

The image will now be mapped to the 216 browser-safe color palette. Any colors in the original image that weren't in the 216 palette will be simulated with a pattern of browser-safe colors.

Interlacing

When a graphic is downloaded from the Web, it usually loads from top to bottom. Interlacing is an alternate effect whereby different parts of a graphic will unveil simultaneously.

As shown in Figure 12.3, an interlaced GIF is saved line by line in a series of steps. Starting from the top of the image and first line of pixels, an interlaced GIF saves every eighth line. Then, starting from the fourth line, every eighth line down is saved. Ultimately, all of the lines of pixels in the image are saved in this fashion.

When the image is downloaded to a Web browser, it will unveil in a similar manner. As different portions of the image load simultaneously, our eyes can piece together what the file represents well before the whole image has downloaded (see Figure 12.4).

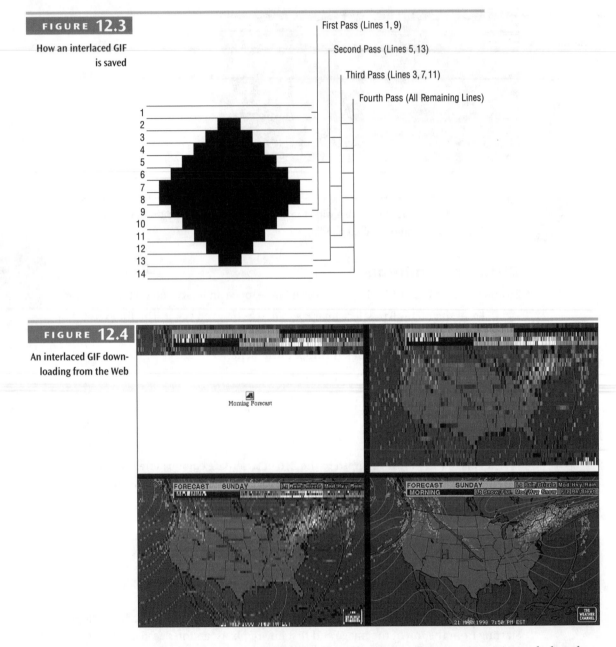

FIGURE **12.3**

How an interlaced GIF
is saved

First Pass (Lines 1, 9)

Second Pass (Lines 5,13)

Third Pass (Lines 3, 7, 11)

Fourth Pass (All Remaining Lines)

FIGURE **12.4**

An interlaced GIF down-
loading from the Web

Interlacing serves two purposes. First, if a person can recognize an image before the
entire graphic has downloaded, the viewer can move on to reading other information
on the page. This is particularly important for people who are operating with very little

bandwidth. Second, the interlacing effect can serve as limited entertainment that helps engage the viewer as the rest of the graphic downloads.

NOTE Only consider applying interlacing to graphics over 10K in size. If a graphic is very small, it will load so rapidly that the interlacing effect will go unnoticed.

Applying Interlacing to a GIF

To create an interlaced GIF, convert a graphic to Indexed Color mode and follow these steps:

1. Select File ➤ Save As from the Menu Bar. This will bring up the Save As dialog. Make sure the Save Thumbnail checkbox is not selected in order to reduce file size.

2. From the Save As drop-down menu, select the CompuServe GIF file format and click Save. This will bring up the GIF89a Options dialog.

3. From the Row Order options, select the Interlaced radio button.

4. Click OK and save the file with the .gif file extension.

The GIF will now gradually render itself as it is downloaded in a modern Web browser.

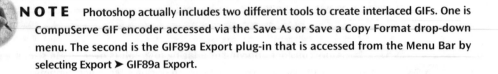

N O T E   Photoshop actually includes two different tools to create interlaced GIFs. One is CompuServe GIF encoder accessed via the Save As or Save a Copy Format drop-down menu. The second is the GIF89a Export plug-in that is accessed from the Menu Bar by selecting Export ➤ GIF89a Export.

Transparency

The Transparency effect is how you make one or more colors in a graphic "invisible," allowing other underlying graphics to show through. Why would you need to create a graphic with transparent colors? The most common reason is that all Web graphics are confined to a rectilinear shape. It is not possible to save a circle or irregularly shaped object without also including the space around it.

GIF's Transparency effect is a way to solve that problem. For example, in Figure 12.5 we have a sphere placed above a patterned background image. The graphic has no transparency effect, and the area surrounding the sphere is black. Clearly, the sphere is not integrated into the overall design.

FIGURE 12.5

An opaque graphic on a patterned background

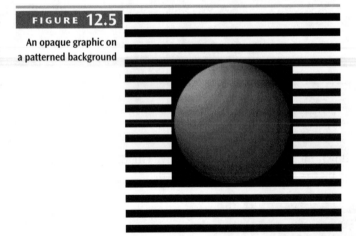

Another problem with the Web is that most Web browsers do not support absolute positioning. If a Web page has a dramatic background image and a designer places a graphic on top of that image, there is no way to predict exactly where that top image will end up. The end result is a background and graphic combination that doesn't line up properly (see Figure 12.6).

FIGURE 12.6

A misaligned Web graphic and background

Instead of including some of the background image in the graphic, a better approach is to put the sphere on a solid color and make the color transparent. The final effect looks much more realistic (see Figure 12.7).

FIGURE 12.7

A transparent graphic on a graphic background

Applying the Transparency Effect

Once you have designed a Web graphic and converted it to Indexed Color mode, you're ready to apply a Transparency effect.

1. Select File ➤ Export ➤ GIF89a Export. The GIF89a Export dialog will appear and provide a number of options.

PART

Photoshop and the Web

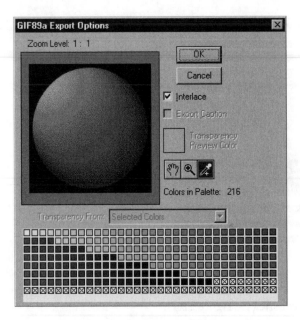

2. Use the Hand tool in the Zoom Level window to move the graphic around and find the color that you would like to make transparent (see Figure 12.8).

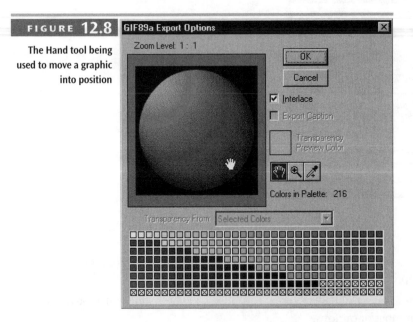

FIGURE **12.8**

The Hand tool being used to move a graphic into position

3. As depicted in Figure 12.9, use the Magnifying Glass tool to zoom in or zoom out on certain areas of the graphic. To zoom out, hold down the Alt key on a PC. On a Mac, hold down the Option key.

FIGURE **12.9**

The Magnifying Glass
tool being used to zoom
in on a particular
portion of an image

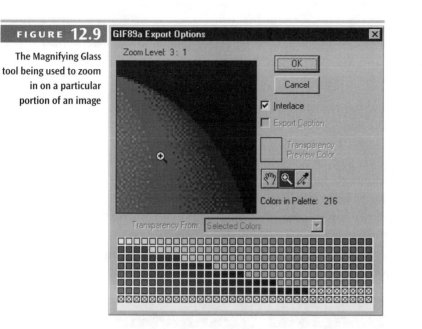

4. Select the Eyedropper tool and click on the color(s) in the graphic that you would like to make transparent (see Figure 12.10).

FIGURE **12.10**

The Eyedropper tool
being used to make
a particular color
transparent

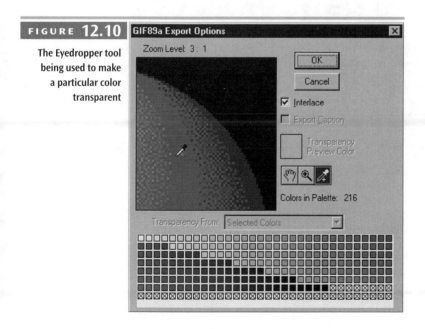

PART

Photoshop and the Web

TIP   Choose your transparent color(s) carefully. If even a small amount of selected color is being used in an area you didn't expect, it will be made transparent and make your graphic look like it is full of pinholes.

5. Alternatively, you can use the Eyedropper to select colors to be transparent from the palette at the bottom of the GIF89a Export dialog. The palette also serves as an indicator for which colors will become transparent.

6. To switch a color back to its original non-transparent state, select the Eyedropper tool. On the PC, hold down the Ctrl key. On the Mac, press the Apple key. The plus sign on the Eyedropper tool will become a minus sign. Click on the appropriate colors, either in the Zoom Level window or in the palette, to make them non-transparent.

7. Every transparent color will be indicated as gray. To change the indicator color, click the Transparency Index Color window. This will launch Photoshop's Color Picker dialog from which you can modify the color.

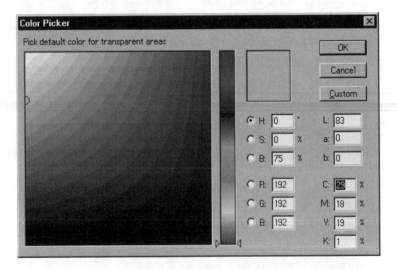

8. Once you have selected the appropriate colors to make transparent, click OK and save the file.

Upon viewing the graphic in a Web browser, any color you have selected for transparency will be invisible. Any background color or graphic behind the image will show through the transparent areas of the graphic.

Halos

One of the pitfalls of using the Transparency tool is that it can create an effect called *halos*. Photoshop applies anti-aliasing to smooth the edges of objects as they are drawn. For example, if a dark blue circle is drawn on a white background, Photoshop will create intermediate colors, in this case lighter blues, between the edges of the circle and the background (see Figure 12.11).

PART

FIGURE 12.11

Photoshop's anti-aliasing technique

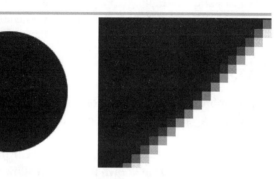

Photoshop and the Web

While this smoothing effect makes Photoshop graphics looks great, it can play havoc with graphics that have transparent backgrounds. When such images are put on the Web and placed on top of patterns or other colors, the anti-aliasing "fringe" becomes apparent. Figure 12.12 shows a black circle on a black background. Ideally, the result should be a completely black screen. But in this case, the halo creates an outline of the circle.

FIGURE 12.12

The halo effect

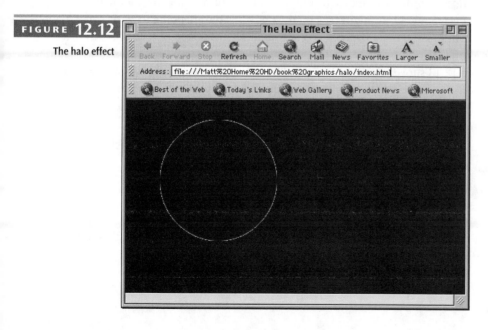

While halos can never be totally eliminated, there are a couple of preventative steps you can take. First, choose a transparency color that is as close as possible in hue and value to the color or pattern that the graphic will be sitting on. If a Web background image is a brick wall, select a dark red for the transparency color. Photoshop will create intermediate steps from the edge of the object to the dark red color that will be much harder to see once the object is placed on the brick wall background.

The second step is to pick background patterns that have as little contrast as possible. Patterns like black and white checkerboard are especially hard to deal with. In general, most Web designers stay away from full-screen, patterned background images to avoid problems with halos.

GIF Animation

If you've spent more than five minutes on the Web, you've surely experienced an animated GIF. Annoying advertising banners, spinning globes, silly cartoons—they're all examples of animated GIF technology.

But how did the Web get so animated? When the GIF file format was created by CompuServe, it included a little-known feature that allowed designers to store multiple images in a single GIF. These images play in sequence, much like an animated cartoon.

A designer can specify the length of time that passes between the loading of each image. If the time is short, the animation will speed up, and if it is long, the animation will slow down.

Creating a GIF Animation

The starting point in creating a GIF animation is to conceive of an idea for an animated effect. Some ideas might be a bouncing ball, a bird flapping its wings, or a logo fading in and out. Once a concept is established, the next step is to create the object to be animated.

Figure 12.13 shows a logo designed in Photoshop. The concept was that the black logo would emerge from the darkness, be illuminated by a white light, and then fade back into darkness.

FIGURE 12.13

A logo developed in Photoshop

A backlighting effect was applied to create the desired effect and the file was saved as a GIF, shown in Figure 12.14.

FIGURE 12.14

A logo with a
backlighting effect

The backlighting effect was adjusted to create some intermediate steps between pure darkness and full brightness. These images were also saved as GIFs (see Figure 12.15).

FIGURE 12.15

Three intermediate
steps

T I P   The number of frames in a GIF animation has a significant effect on the final file size of the animated GIF. Try to be as concise as possible in communicating the idea without ruining the illusion of motion.

At this point, Photoshop hits a brick wall as an animation tool. The application is currently incapable of actually animating the GIF files. Animators have to rely on separate GIF animation programs to get the job done. An excellent PC application called GIF Movie Gear is included on the CD-ROM that comes with this book. Mac users can use the GifBuilder program that is also included on the CD-ROM.

N O T E   ImageReady, a new product from Adobe, also allows you to create animations.

GIF Movie Gear

GIF Movie Gear is a fantastic tool for constructing GIF animations. The program is especially adept at creating very small files and is the best GIF animation tool currently available for the PC. The GIF Movie Gear interface is divided into four areas: the menu bar, the toolbars, the animation view, and the status bar.

The menu bar contains all of the program's major commands. As Figure 12.16 demonstrates, the animation view has been populated with the frames in the logo animation by using the File ➤ Insert Frame command from the menu bar.

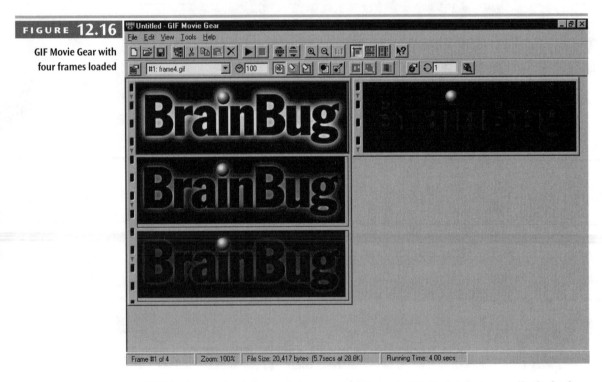

FIGURE 12.16

GIF Movie Gear with four frames loaded

GIF Movie Gear's uppermost toolbar contains a myriad of functions, all of which can be deciphered by holding the mouse over each icon. Most of these functions are icon-based shortcuts of the main menu options.

The lower toolbar provides information specific to the current GIF animation being created and the individual frame that is being modified.

The final part of the interface is the status bar. The status bar provides both the total file size of the current animation and the length of time it will run.

Creating an Animated GIF with GIF Movie Gear

Launch the GIF Movie Gear application and do the following:

1. Load each frame of the animation using the File ➤ Insert Frame command.

2. Click on each frame and set the interframe delay in the Edit ➤ Frame Properties dialog.

3. Confirm that the animation is running as intended by selecting the Show Animation Preview command (the forward arrow in the top toolbar).

4. Select File ➤ Save to save the file as an animated GIF.

TIP   GIF Movie Gear's online help system provides additional information about file size optimization and color palette management. Select Help ➤ Contents from the main menu.

GifBuilder

GifBuilder is a tool for constructing GIF animations on the Macintosh. The program was one of the first developed for creating animated GIFs, and it remains the most powerful and capable GIF animation tool for the Mac OS.

GifBuilder's interface is divided into the main menu and two windows. The main menu offers many options, including the ability to adjust pixel depth, interlacing, transparency, interframe delay, and looping. GifBuilder's interface is divided into two areas that include the Frames window and the Animation window. The Frames window provides text-based information about each frame and the Animation window displays the animation as it is being constructed.

In Figure 12.17, the four logo frames created in Photoshop have been loaded into GifBuilder. The Frames window provides information on each frame, including the size (in pixels), the position of the upper-left corner of each graphic, and the delay before the next frame will load.

PART

Photoshop and the Web

FIGURE 12.17

The GifBuilder
interface with four
frames loaded

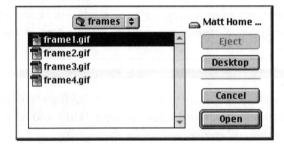

4 frames	Length: 0.40 s		Size: 365×115		
Name	Size	Position	Disp.	Delay	Transp.
frame1.gif	365×115	(0; 0)	N	10	–
frame2.gif	360×110	(0; 0)	N	10	–
frame3.gif	360×110	(0; 0)	N	10	–
frame4.gif	364×115	(0; 0)	N	10	–

Creating an Animated GIF with GifBuilder

Launch GifBuilder and follow these steps:

1. Load each frame of the animation using the File ➤ Add Frame command.

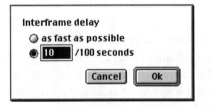

2. Click on each frame in the Frames window and select Options ➤ Interframe Delay from the main menu to set the delay.

3. Confirm that the animation is running as intended by selecting Animation ➤ Start from the main menu.

4. Select File ➤ Save to save the file as an animated GIF.

TIP   GifBuilder offers additional information about its advanced capabilities in the Documentation file included inside the main GifBuilder directory.

Joint Photographic Experts Group (JPEG)

The Joint Photographic Experts Group (JPEG—pronounced "jay-peg") is a compression standard that was developed for shrinking the file size of continuous tone images. It is best applied to photographs or graphics with complicated shading and lighting effects. Common uses of the JPEG format on the Web include product shots, 3D-rendered environments, and subtly shaded graphics.

Compression

JPEG compresses an image by saving a complete black and white version of it and most of its color information. Since not all of the color information is retained, JPEG is called a *lossy* format. This lossy nature of JPEG is usually seen, especially in highly compressed files, as a fuzzy or noisy patchwork of pixels (see Figure 12.18).

FIGURE 12.18

Detail of JPEG's noisy compression

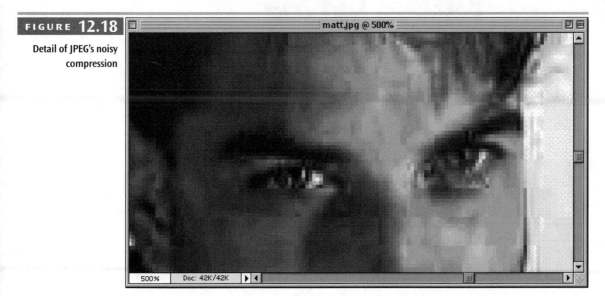

Unlike the GIF compression algorithm that analyzes files line by line, JPEG breaks the image into zones of similar color. Thus, using the JPEG format for stark graphics that have large areas of the same color usually offers poor results. In such situations, GIF is a better alternative and compresses files much better than JPEG (see Figure 12.19).

FIGURE **12.19**

JPEG vs. GIF in line art scenario

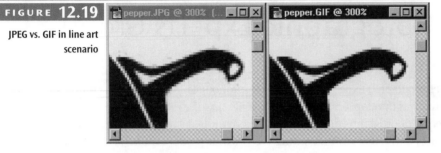

However, JPEG shines as a compression method from both a file size and quality standpoint when it is applied to graphics that contain a wide range of tonal values. Figure 12.20 demonstrates how subtle values are retained much better with the JPEG format.

FIGURE **12.20**

JPEG vs. GIF in wide tonal range scenario

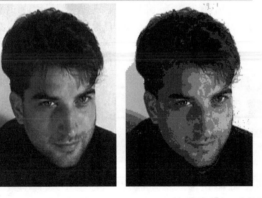

WARNING   Always edit work in the original native Photoshop file and not from subsequent JPEGs. Even the highest quality setting in Photoshop's JPEG encoder creates a lossy image that is unsuitable for additional editing.

The Photoshop JPEG Encoder

The Photoshop JPEG Encoder allows you to set image and format options when you convert a graphic into a JPEG. The controls for adjusting Photoshop's JPEG Encoder are accessed via the JPEG Options dialog.

The upper portion of the dialog is dedicated to adjusting the Image Options via the Quality setting. Zero is the lowest quality and 10 is the highest. As indicated on the controls, a lower quality setting results in a smaller file, and a higher quality setting results in a larger file. Figure 12.21 demonstrates the relative difference in file size based on two settings.

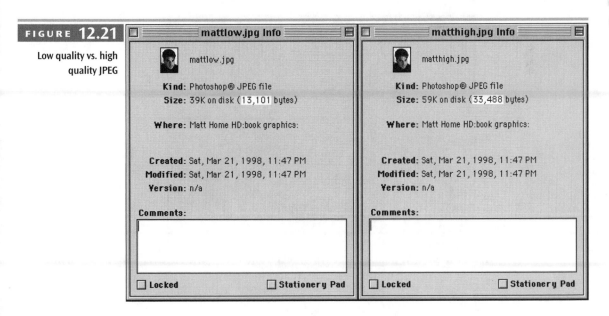

FIGURE 12.21

Low quality vs. high quality JPEG

TIP   To check a file size in Windows, right-click on the image and select **Properties**. On the Mac, click once on the image and select **File ➤ Get Info**. In both dialogs, be sure to refer to the figure in parentheses—this is the exact file size.

The bottom portion of the JPEG Options dialog provides formatting options. The Baseline Optimized feature provides enhanced color quality and offers slightly smaller file size compared to the Baseline ('Standard') option. The Progressive option creates an effect similar to interlacing, discussed earlier in the chapter.

The final option in the JPEG Options dialog is the Save Paths command. Since Web designers only work from native Photoshop files and use JPEG solely for the creation of Web graphics, there is no need to select this option.

TIP   Unlike GIFs, JPEGs cannot be saved in Indexed Color mode. Instead, save JPEGs in RGB color mode.

Creating a JPEG

To create a JPEG, follow these steps:

1. Open a document in RGB mode and select File ➤ Save As from the Menu Bar. The Save As dialog appears.

Save As	? ✕
Save in: 📁 graphics ▼ ⬆ 🔲 ▦ ▤	

File name: matt.jpg   Save

Save As: JPEG (*.JPG;*.JPE)   ▼   Cancel

☐ Save Thumbnail   ☑ Use Lower Case Extension

2. In the Save As dialog, select the JPEG format from the Save As drop-down menu and click OK. The JPEG Options dialog appears.

JPEG Options

Image Options
Quality: 10 Maximum
small file   large file

OK
Cancel

Format Options
○ Baseline ("Standard")
◉ Baseline Optimized
○ Progressive
Scans: 3

3. In the Image Options area, adjust the quality to a setting that is appropriate for your image. Quality settings from 3 to 5 strike a balance between good quality and small file size.

4. Select Baseline Optimized from the Format Options area.

5. Turn off the Save Paths option if it is activated.

6. Click OK and save the graphic with the .jpg file extension.

N O T E   It is best to experiment with different levels of compression for each JPEG and arrive at a setting that balances quality and file size.

Progressive JPEGs

One of the features of Photoshop's JPEG Encoder is the ability to create progressive files. Progressive JPEGs are similar to interlaced GIFs in that they affect the way a JPEG appears as it is downloaded. Rather than load from top to bottom, progressive JPEGs download different areas of the graphic at the same time. This provides the viewer with an overall sense of what is contained in the image before the entire JPEG is completely downloaded.

Photoshop's JPEG Options dialog offers a Progressive option in the Format Options area. The Progressive option provides a Scans setting that can be set from 3 to 5. The selection reflects the successive number of steps the file will render as it is downloaded. For example, Scans set to 3 will create a JPEG that downloads in three steps, while the 5 setting will download in five.

W A R N I N G   While saving a JPEG with Photoshop's Progressive setting sometimes results in the smallest file size compared to Baseline and Baseline Optimized, the progressive JPEG standard is only supported by recent Web browsers.

Creating a Progressive JPEG

To create a progressive JPEG, follow these steps:

1. Open a document in RGB mode and select File ➤ Save As from the Menu Bar.

2. In the Save As dialog, select the JPEG format from the Save As drop-down menu and click OK.

3. Select Progressive from the Format Options area and indicate the number of Scans.

4. Click OK and save the graphic with the .jpg file extension.

JPEG Animation

Unlike the GIF format, JPEG does not allow the inclusion of more than one image into a file. Thus, JPEG animation is not widely implemented on the Web. If there is need to run a sequence of JPEGs in the same place on a Web page, designers can use a script or downloadable application written in Java. But Java can take a good deal of time to initialize and run on slower computers. In addition, not all Web browsers can make use of Java. While recent versions of the Netscape and Microsoft browsers do support the Java standard, older browsers, especially those from the commercial online service America Online, do not.

So while GIF may not always provide the best image quality, it is far more reliable as an animation format.

Portable Network Graphics (PNG)

In 1994, Unisys, the inventor of the GIF compression method, announced that they would be demanding licensing fees from developers of software that supported the GIF format. The potential cost associated with using GIF, combined with JPEG's lossy nature, led to a grassroots effort to develop a new graphic format. The proposed format would be patent free and improve upon the GIF and JPEG formats.

The result of this effort is called Portable Network Graphics (PNG—pronounced "ping"). Despite the fact that implementation of PNG on the Web still remains limited, Photoshop has provided the basic tools for encoding files to PNG format.

However, the PNG specification includes some truly spectacular capabilities such as automatic cross-platform color adjustment and variable transparency effects that have yet to be included in Photoshop's PNG Encoder. Adobe is expected to add these capabilities over time if the popularity of the format grows.

Compression

PNG is said to offer better compression than GIF, with savings ranging from 10 to 30 percent. However, like all compressed data formats, such savings are dependent on the quality of the encoder. Photoshop's PNG Encoder typically creates slightly larger PNG files than GIF files (see Figure 12.22).

FIGURE 12.22

PNG vs. GIF and respective file sizes

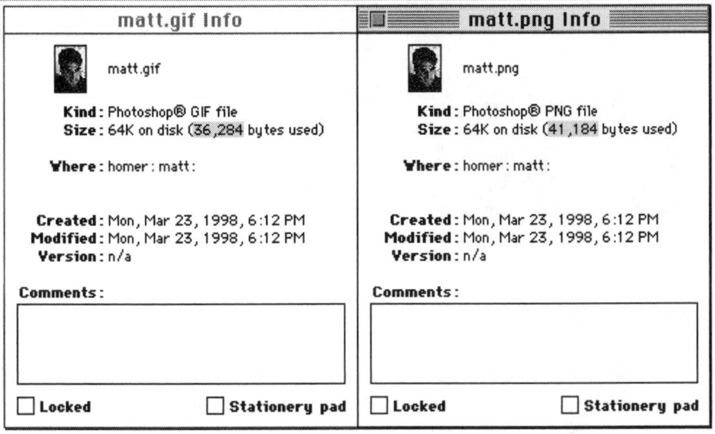

Like GIF, PNG is a lossless format, meaning that whatever color data was in the original file will be present after the image is decoded in a Web browser. But unlike GIF, PNG is not limited to a 256-color palette—PNG can create files from both RGB and Indexed Color mode source graphics.

PNG is indeed a lossless format, and as such creates RGB-based graphics that are many times larger than JPEGs. Figure 12.23 demonstrates differences in file size for a typical RGB-based graphic.

FIGURE 12.23

PNG vs. JPEG and respective file sizes

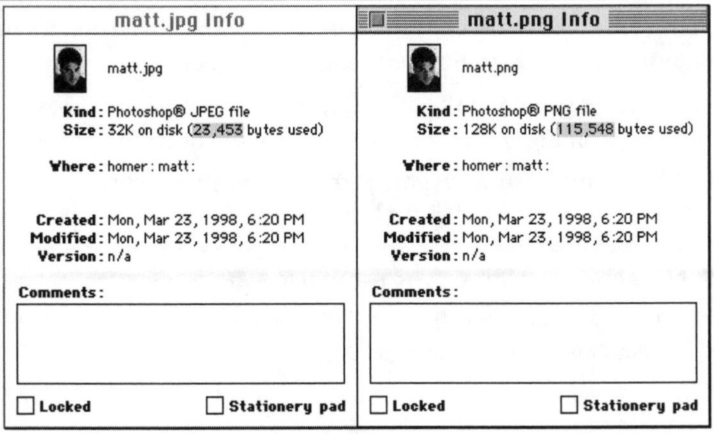

Currently, Photoshop provides two basic kinds of tools in the PNG Encoder interface: Interlacing and Compression.

```
┌─ PNG Options ──────────────────────── ✕ ─┐
│                                           │
│  ┌─ Interlace ──────┐    ┌────────────┐   │
│  │                  │    │     OK     │   │
│  │   ⦿ None         │    └────────────┘   │
│  │                  │    ┌────────────┐   │
│  │   ○ Adam7        │    │   Cancel   │   │
│  │                  │    └────────────┘   │
│  └──────────────────┘                     │
│  ┌─ Filter ─────────┐                     │
│  │                  │                     │
│  │   ⦿ None         │                     │
│  │                  │                     │
│  │   ○ Sub          │                     │
│  │                  │                     │
│  │   ○ Up           │                     │
│  │                  │                     │
│  │   ○ Average      │                     │
│  │                  │                     │
│  │   ○ Paeth        │                     │
│  │                  │                     │
│  │   ○ Adaptive     │                     │
│  │                  │                     │
│  └──────────────────┘                     │
└───────────────────────────────────────────┘
```

Interlacing can be turned off (None) or on (Adam7). Compression can be specified in the Filter area of the PNG Options dialog via six different compression options: None, Sub, Up, Average, Paeth, and Adaptive. Each of these techniques compresses data in slightly different ways, but the overall file sizes end up being about the same.

Creating a PNG

To create a PNG, follow these steps:

1. Open a document in either RGB or Indexed Color mode and select File ➤ Save As from the Menu Bar.

2. In the Save As dialog, select the PNG format from the Save As drop-down menu and click OK. This will launch the PNG Options dialog.

3. In the Interlace section of the dialog, select None if you don't want the image to interlace. If you do want interlacing, select Adam7.

4. In the Filter section of the dialog, select None if you don't want the image to be specially compressed. If you do, try one of the other five options.

5. Click OK and save the graphic with the .png file extension.

WARNING   At this time, very few Web browsers can make use of PNG as an internally supported graphic format. Only Microsoft Internet Explorer 4.0 or higher can currently display PNG files on a Web page.

FlashPix (FPX)

FlashPix first surfaced in 1994 as IVUE, a proprietary graphics format for Live Picture's graphics editing program. In 1995, Kodak, Microsoft, Hewlett Packard, and others teamed up with Live Picture to modify IVUE into a standard imaging architecture that would allow complex photographs to be manipulated extremely rapidly without the need for super-fast equipment. While the format's use is relatively new, hundreds of products now support it—from digital cameras to scanners to Photoshop 5. FlashPix is designed to support a variety of applications, from printing to the Web, on "legacy" (meaning older) PCs running on as little as 8MB of RAM, with much better performance for viewing image detail and editing high-resolution images.

Now FlashPix is a built-in file format in Photoshop—just like GIF, JPEG, and PNG. But like PNG, it's still not widely implemented on the Web. However, FlashPix is a standard endorsed by the Digital Imaging Group (DIG), which includes the major players in digital imaging, such as Kodak, Microsoft, Adobe, and HP. All the key DIG players are using FlashPix in some way.

Quality with Speed

Imagine you took a beautiful aerial picture of the city of Boston, Massachusetts. If you scan in that image at 600 dpi, it would be extremely large and take forever to download, right? Not if you save it as a FlashPix file.

In a FlashPix file, each resolution is subdivided into square tiles. This allows applications to select the appropriate resolution a user needs for a selected procedure and to access directly the specific areas of an image needed for the operation being performed. No longer do applications have to process the entire image in order to view a small section, nor process a high-resolution image to produce a low-resolution display.

Edits are applied to high-resolution images only when necessary—usually when users want high-quality output, have clicked the print button, and are done interacting with their image. An edit, layout choice, or other use of an image is stored as a small script separate from the image data itself. The script and image data are wrapped inside a structured storage container. To display or print the edited version, a FlashPix-optimized application applies the changes described in the script to the appropriate resolution of the original image data. So, in the FlashPix architecture, people can use and modify an image in any number of ways, but store the original high-resolution image data in only one place. This capability really provides a breakthrough in how you can use images on the Web.

Photoshop is not a FlashPix-optimized program, and you can't use it to its full potential. However, you can open and save in the FlashPix format. When saving a FlashPix image in Photoshop, you have the option of no compression or full JPEG compression from levels 1 to 10; level 10 being the highest. Level 8 insures decent compression and excellent detail.

WARNING   Never turn an image less than 600 dpi into a FlashPix file.

When you save an image in FlashPix format, it creates a set of images at several resolutions and then arranges them hierarchically. The Digital Imaging Group, who created the format, explains the format as a pyramid, with the highest resolution image at the bottom and the lowest at the top. When an application opens the image into a browser, it displays the appropriate resolution for the current size of the browser window at that time.

The best part about a FlashPix image is that if the user zooms in, the pixels outside the area displayed do not have to be kept in the computer's working memory. This allows users to modify FlashPix images using relatively little RAM.

Creating an FPX File

To create an FPX file, follow these steps:

1. Open a document in RGB mode (or open and convert if it's in Indexed Color mode) and select File ➤ Save As from the Menu Bar.

2. In the Save As dialog, select the FPX format from the Save As drop-down menu and click OK. This will launch the FlashPix Options dialog.

![FlashPix Options dialog box with Encoding set to JPEG, Quality set to 6 High, a slider from "small file" to "large file", and OK and Cancel buttons.]

3. At this point, you are given two choices from the Encoding drop-down menu. You can either not compress it at all, or use JPEG compression from levels 1 through 10. Compression isn't entirely important unless you have limited room on your server. Click OK.

 TIP   Users don't have to download the FPX file in its entirety—that's why it's such a great file format. Don't bother with compression unless absolutely necessary.

Viewing FlashPix Images

When FlashPix was first released, you needed a browser plug-in from Live Picture to view graphics saved in the format. Now, Live Picture offers both a Java applet and Image Server option. These options let the Web designer set up the FlashPix file so it appears in the user's browser as if it was a simple image map. Every time the user clicks on a certain section, Image Server or an applet calls up that portion of the image.

Image Server is great because it makes the FlashPix format much more usable. If a Web user doesn't have to go get a plug-in, chances are good they'll stick around a site longer. But Image Server is not an inexpensive piece of software, and you must find someone who is willing to buy, install, and support the software on a Web server.

N O T E   For more information on Image Server and other Live Picture software products, visit the Web site at `http://www.livepicture.com`.

Conclusion

The PNG standard promises some much-needed enhancements to internally supported graphics. But it will take time for Web browsers to implement this format. There are currently two to three versions of Microsoft Internet Explorer and Netscape Navigator in use, and none supports the full PNG standard. Even after PNG-capable browsers become available, it may take years for the majority of Web users to discard their old browsers and adopt the new versions.

Because the FlashPix format is server-dependent, it makes using the format a non-issue for your Web audience—they don't need a plug-in or Java applet to see the images. However, *because* the FlashPix format is server-dependent, you need to find a Web hosting environment that is using the technology. Right now, there are very few.

So despite the growth of the Web over the last half-decade, in most cases you still only have two choices: GIF and JPEG. GIF remains the most useful Web graphic format, while JPEG offers advantages in specific situations.

Up Next

Now that you've learned everything you wanted to know about Web graphic formats, it's time to move on to the intricacies of Web color. If you think that having a background in print—Pantone swatch books, press checks, etc.—will be of help, think again. As we'll see in the next chapter, putting colors on computers is an entirely different kind of art.

Mastering the Medium: The Great Platform Debate

My agency is a place of constant debate, and it has nothing to do with great philosophical issues of our time or even the latest design styles. Instead, these talented folks spend their energy extolling the virtues of their computer platform of choice, either the Macintosh or the PC.

Until recently, this debate was a moot point because only a small percentage of Web designers even considered using a PC for development. Sure, a PC was fine for occasionally taking a look at how most of the world sees a Web site, but design with one? Never!

Recently, things have begun to change, although most of the Photoshop Masters profiled in this book continue to develop on the Macintosh platform. The reasons why the PC has made some inroads vary, but they include the following:

- "So many people look at Web sites on a PC. It will be easier to develop on the same platform."
- "The new browser technology is always available on the PC platform first. I want to develop on a platform where I can mess around with technology like DHTML months before the Mac users."
- "Everything else in my office is a PC and our MIS guy hates Macs."
- "I heard Apple wasn't doing too well. Why should I invest in technology from a company that won't be around next year?"

However, there are tradeoffs when switching from Mac to the PC. They include these:

- Mac fonts tend to be in EPS format. On the PC, they need to be True Type. How can you get around this? You have to buy the True Type versions or convert them all manually using a program like Macromedia Fontographer, which is expensive if you don't already own a copy.
- You will need to buy all new software at full price, including Photoshop. This can be costly.
- You can't open a Photoshop file created on the Mac unless it has a .psd file extension. This is no big deal—you can quickly change the filename. But this can be a pain if you have lots of files that were created on the Mac with no PC filenames.
- Managing fonts on the PC, compared to using a Mac with a utility like Suitcase, can be more difficult.

Recently I became a cross-platform user after being dedicated to the Macintosh for nearly a decade. While the first few weeks on the PC were challenging, I now work on both platforms equally. Photoshop, except in some very minor ways, is the exact same program on both types of computers.

For me, there is very little difference between the two platforms, and I use them interchangeably. Most of the screen shots for this book were done on the PC, but this is due to technical reasons unrelated to the platform. Many of the graphics were originally done on the Mac.

All things being equal, and when it comes to Photoshop most things are, the decision to use one platform over another comes down to a preference between the Mac and Windows user interface. Do you like the Start button or the happy Mac icon? How about arcane disk error messages or chimes of death?

Either way, it's difficult to make a bad choice these days.

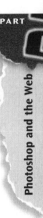

PART

Photoshop and the Web

WEB COLOR

Featuring

WEB COLOR

If you're making the transition from being a print designer to a Web designer, you may think that dealing with color will be easier on the Web. In print, the colors on the computer screen never match what ultimately comes off the printing press. Colors specified from a printed swatch book are usually faded and weak compared to what is displayed on a monitor. It can all be very frustrating.

But after a few attempts at designing Web sites, you may begin to miss the relative certainty of color printing. Web clients may call you and complain that a Web site's graphics are too dark—despite the fact that the graphics looked fine on *your* computer. Other clients may report strange color shifts in a Web site's graphics during viewing.

Without knowing it, you've stumbled into Web color's idiosyncrasies and the much larger issue of how color is projected onto computer monitors. This chapter unravels many Web color mysteries and provides hard won strategies for creating graphics with color that stands up across browsers, operating systems, and computers.

Understanding Light

OK, time for a quick science lesson. Before discussing how color works on a computer, we need to understand the basic properties of light and the difference between additive and subtractive color.

Light is transmitted via electromagnetic particles called photons. Photons vibrate in a range of frequencies and interact with the materials around us. Some of these materials absorb nearly all of the photons that strike them. With nearly all photons absorbed, the materials reflect no color and are seen as being black. Coal is an example of such a material. Other types of materials tend not to absorb photons and instead reflect the energy back into our eyes. These particular materials are seen as white (see Figure 13.1).

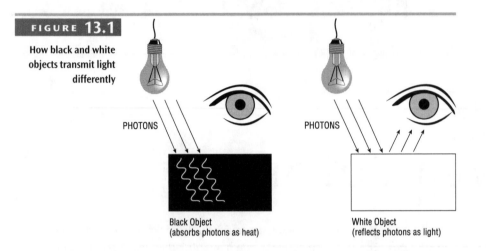

FIGURE **13.1**

How black and white objects transmit light differently

PHOTONS

PHOTONS

Black Object
(absorbs photons as heat)

White Object
(reflects photons as light)

In between black and white are materials that reflect only certain kinds of photons. A red apple absorbs all of the photons except the ones that we see as red. These reflected photons vibrate at a particular frequency that our eyes and brain equate with red. All of the objects around us are selectively absorbing different colors and reflecting back what remains. This is what is meant by subtractive color.

Our first, hands-on experience with color is usually of the subtractive nature. Crayons, colored pencils, and finger paint are all examples of mediums that remove color. Combining red, yellow, and blue paint, for example, tends to result in a black color. A dark color is one where all the bases have been covered and nearly all the light that strikes the object is absorbed.

Additive color works in the opposite manner. If you combine red, green, and blue light, the result is a beam of white light. The light coming from the sun is seen as white because it is a mixture of many different colors of light. This tendency for light to be additive is the same regardless of the source—televisions, computer monitors, and laptops all project images using additive color. For artists and designers who are used to working with paint and ink—subtractive color—the world of additive color requires different ways of thinking.

Color Management Systems

The combination of computer hardware and software that projects additive color onto a monitor is called a *color management system*. They all work in the same general way, but each color management system renders colors somewhat differently.

Many of the problems that Macintosh-based Web designers have with color can be traced back to the fact that the Macintosh has a different color management system than the PC. As a result, a Macintosh with an Apple monitor tends to display color brighter and lighter than a PC. A yellow color on a Mac may look orange on a PC.

WARNING With 90 percent of the world currently viewing the Web on a PC, Macintosh Photoshop users who are designing for the Web should view their work on both platforms to ensure that colors are being portrayed correctly.

The first color management systems could only display a handful of colors. As recently as a few years ago, Microsoft was designing their online service for the worst case scenario of users with computers capable of displaying only 16 colors. The developer of the first popular Web browser, Netscape, set the worst case scenario at 256 colors. To this day, many computers, including the majority of laptops, still cannot display more than 256 colors at one time.

Bit Depth

The actual way computer color is referred to is *bit depth*. A monitor displaying up to 256 colors is said to be in 8-bit color mode. In the early days of computing, computers had 1-bit monitors and each pixel was either on or off. Currently, computers are capable of operating in 24-bit mode or higher—more than 16 million colors!

Table 13.1 details each bit setting.

TABLE **13.1** BIT SETTINGS AND NUMBER OF COLORS	
Bit Setting	**Number of Colors**
1-bit	2 colors
2-bit	4 colors
3-bit	8 colors
4-bit	16 colors
5-bit	32 colors
6-bit	64 colors
7-bit	128 colors
8-bit	256 colors
15-bit	32,768 colors
16-bit	65,536 colors
24-bit	16,777,216 colors +

Changing Bit Depth

Changing bit depth on a PC or Macintosh is a straightforward process. In Windows, do the following:

1. Access Display Properties by right-clicking on the desktop.

2. Select the Settings menu and adjust your bit depth by clicking on the Color Palette drop-down menu.

On the Macintosh, do the following:

1. Access the Monitors control panel inside the System folder.

2. In the upper window, scroll down the list of bit depths and select the one you would like to use.

Browser-Safe Color

If a Web designer includes more colors in a graphic than a computer is capable of displaying, the machine will try to compensate. Often the computer's color management system will try to substitute with the closest available alternatives. But the system doesn't always make the best choice, and sometimes the results can be downright ugly. *Palette flash* is when a system becomes overwhelmed and renders graphics with shockingly inappropriate colors. If you've ever been browsing the Web and have had your graphics suddenly become weirdly colorized, you've experienced palette flash.

Color management systems usually reserve at least 40 colors for the computer's system software. Common examples are the platinum gray color that a Macintosh uses for dialogs and scroll bars and the navy blue that Microsoft uses for document title bars. With 40 colors spoken for in a 256-color, or 8-bit system, only 216 colors remain for applications like Web browsers. And, 216 is precisely the number of colors that Web designers have to work with.

In a rare show of standardization, both Microsoft and Netscape have adopted the *same* palette of 216 colors for use with their Web browsers. However, the palette was developed on a purely mathematical basis. Consequently, the palette has an inordinate number of blues and greens and not enough reds (shown in the color insert). Additionally, most of the colors are far too dark to be used as a background color on which body copy would be placed.

The 216-color palette clearly has its limitations, and Web designers might be justified in discarding the palette and working with whatever colors they desired. But not using the palette increases the odds that your Web site won't be seen as intended. With more than a half a dozen different browser versions in use today and the number of incompatibilities between them growing, the 216-color palette serves as one of the few standards designers can depend on.

Loading the 216 Palette

With version 5, Photoshop has become more Web color friendly and includes a copy of the 216 palette with the program. To load the palette, do the following:

1. Select Window ➤ Show Swatches.

2. Off the Swatches palette, click on the right arrow to view the Swatches menu.

3. Select Replace Swatches to replace the current swatch.

4. From the Adobe Photoshop 5 directory, open Goodies/Color Palettes and double-click on `Web Safe Colors`.

5. Click Open.

The 216 palette will now be loaded into the Swatches palette.

Using the 216 Palette

To begin working on a new Web graphic with the 216 palette loaded into the Swatches palette, do the following:

1. Select the Eyedropper tool in the Toolbar.

2. As shown in Figure 13.2, click on the color you would like to use from the Swatches palette.

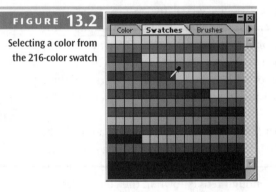

FIGURE **13.2**

Selecting a color from
the 216-color swatch

3. Select a tool from the Toolbar and apply the color to your graphic.

N O T E   When designing in Photoshop, be sure to set your desktop color to a medium gray. Color is relative and anything other than medium gray will improperly influence your color choices.

Using Filters and Effects

When you use Filters and other Photoshop effects like anti-aliasing, the file you are working on will inevitably grow to include colors that aren't browser-safe. It is important to convert these offending colors back to the 216 palette when you are ready to save the file as a GIF. To do so, follow these steps:

1. Create a graphic in Photoshop using the 216 palette.

2. Apply a variety of filters and effects.

3. Select Image ➤ Mode ➤ Indexed Color from the Menu Bar.

4. In the Indexed Color dialog, select Web from the Palette drop-down menu.

```
Indexed Color                                    [X]
  ┌─────────────────────────────────────┐
  │  Palette:  Web                    ▼  │    ┌──────────┐
  │                                      │    │    OK    │
  │  Color Depth:  Other              ▼  │    └──────────┘
  │                                      │    ┌──────────┐
  │  Colors:  216                        │    │  Cancel  │
  └─────────────────────────────────────┘    └──────────┘
  ┌─ Options ───────────────────────────┐    ☑ Preview
  │  Dither:  Diffusion               ▼  │
  │  Color Matching:  ○ Faster  ◉ Best   │
  │             ☑ Preserve Exact Colors  │
  └─────────────────────────────────────┘
```

5. Under Options, select Diffusion from the Dither drop-down menu.

6. Click OK.

Dithering is a technique employed by Photoshop to approximate colors that are not part of the browser-safe palette. Not using the dithering feature will result in graphics with harsh transitions.

NOTE   To learn about Photoshop's Dither option, refer to Chapter 12.

Beyond the 216 Palette

Despite the fact that the 216 palette is limited, clever designers have devised ways to extend the palette. There are also times when the 216 palette cannot be adhered to, specifically when using the JPEG file format.

Simulating Other Colors

Great ideas are often stolen, and I swiped this one from the queen of Web color, Lynda Weinman. Lynda is the author of the book *Coloring Web Graphics*, an invaluable resource on the subject. In it she discusses dithering different 216 colors to create colors that appear to be something other than the 216 variety.

As described in Chapter 12, dithering is the process by which pixels are arranged in patterns to simulate other colors. This technique can be used by designers to create synthetic, browser-safe colors.

To create a "new" color from the 216 palette, do the following:

1. Load the 216 palette into the Swatches palette, as described earlier in this chapter.

2. Create a file that is 20 pixels high by 20 pixels wide.

3. As depicted in Figure 13.3, use the Pencil tool to draw a checkerboard pattern using two similar colors from the 216 palette.

FIGURE **13.3**

A close-up of two different 216 colors being painted in a checkerboard pattern

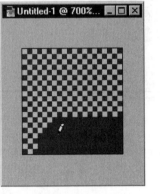

When the image is complete and viewed at normal size, the pixels will begin to mix into a single color. You can use this method to match a particular Pantone color with no 216 equivalent or simply when you are uninspired by the standard Web color choices.

For examples of additional simulated colors, see the color insert of this book.

The JPEG Format

As detailed in Chapter 12, the two most popular graphic formats used on the Web are GIF and JPEG. When it comes to flat color artwork and line art illustrations, GIF is the ideal choice. The format compresses areas of similar color extremely well and is perfect for such graphics as spot illustrations, menu bars, and buttons.

JPEG, on the other hand, is best applied to photo-based artwork or graphics with subtle shading and lighting effects. But when it comes to the 216 palette, the JPEG file format is a renegade. JPEG is unable to save specific colors and creates approximations of the colors used in a graphic during compression. Even if you use only browser-safe colors in the creation of a graphic, saving the file in JPEG format will tweak the colors enough to make them unsafe for the browser.

Despite the fact that JPEG bucks the 216 palette, it is still a widely used Web graphic format. While 256 color systems cannot render many of the colors in a JPEG, the format's compression method generates visual patterns that are seemingly random and very difficult to detect. So even though a 256-color computer can't render the exact greens and blues in a landscape photo, the overall visual effect of the color substitutions is hard for most people to notice. In fact, in very low-color hardware situations—when there are only 16 colors—JPEG images often hold up better than GIFs because they are better suited to extreme color substitutions.

Specifying Color with HTML

In Chapter 16, you will learn to create Web page layouts with HTML and graphics. To apply color to non-graphic elements such as text, links, and pages, color must be specified either by name or with special numerical codes.

Colors by Name

With HTML, you can assign colors to non-graphic elements by name. There are well over 100 such names (brown, green, hot pink, and so on), but only 10 are actually browser-safe colors:

- Black
- White
- Aqua
- Blue
- Cyan
- Fuchsia
- Lime
- Magenta
- Red
- Yellow

WARNING   Not all browsers support the specification of Web colors by name, especially older, non-IE browsers.

Colors by Number

The other, more reliable way to specify color with HTML is with special numerical codes referred to as *hexadecimal color*. Hexadecimal color is so named because it contains six values: two for red, two for green, and two for blue.

While Photoshop is capable of providing RGB values, at this point in time it cannot offer a hexadecimal equivalent. To convert a browser-safe color from RGB to hexadecimal values, do the following:

1. Load the Web Safe Colors palette into the Swatches palette.

2. Use the Eyedropper tool to select the color you would like to convert.

3. Select Window ➤ Show Color from the Menu Bar to display the Color palette.

4. Locate the RGB color values on the Color palette and use the following conversion chart to construct the hexadecimal equivalent for red, green, and blue:

RGB value	Hex value
0	00
51	33
102	66
153	99
204	CC
255	FF

A bright blue browser-safe color that has an RGB value of 51, 0, and 204 would have the hexadecimal equivalent of 3300CC. In HTML, hexadecimal colors are set off from the rest of the text with a pound sign. Thus, the bright blue color would be noted as #3300CC.

You may notice that all of the browser-safe colors have an RGB value of either 0, 51, 102, 153, 204, or 255 and that all of the hexadecimal values are either 00, 33, 66, 99, CC, or FF. This is because all of the browser-safe colors are built from combinations of 0%, 20%, 40%, 60%, 80%, and 100% of red, green, and blue. The entire palette of browser-safe colors was derived from this simple formula.

T I P   There are lots of RGB/hexadecimal converter applications available, but once you know the six simple conversions, there's no reason to use these programs. Learn to "speak" hexadecimal and you'll have an idea of what color is being specified just by looking at the HTML.

Color for Television

The Web is no longer being viewed just on computers. Devices like WebTV, which displays Web sites on ordinary televisions, are becoming more common in living rooms. Unfortunately for the designer, televisions have their own set of idiosyncrasies with regard to color.

The primary issue for Web designers is that a number of the 216 browser-safe colors are actually illegal to use in broadcast television. The Web color named Yellow exceeds the legal amplitude for a television signal and should not be used. Ultimately, only 163 of the 216 browser-safe colors can be used in television applications. The following browser-safe hexadecimal color values can be used.

FF	CC	99	66	33	00
FF3366	CC0033	990033	660033	330033	000099
FF6699	CC3366	993366	660066	330066	000066
FF0066	CC0066	990066	663366	330099	000033
FF3399	CC6699	990099	660099	3300CC	0033FF
FF99CC	CC3399	993399	6600CC	3300FF	0033CC
FF0099	CC0099	996699	663399	3333FF	003399
FF66CC	CC00CC	9900CC	6600FF	3333CC	0066FF
FF33CC	CC33CC	9933CC	6633CC	333399	0066CC
FF00CC	CC66CC	9900FF	6633FF	333366	003366
FF00FF	CC99CC	9933FF	6666FF	3366FF	0099FF
FF33FF	CC00FF	9966CC	6666CC	3366CC	006699
FF66FF	CC33FF	9966FF	666699	3399FF	0099CC
FF99FF	CC66FF	9999FF	6699FF	336699	009999
FFCCFF	CC99FF	9999CC	6699CC	3399CC	006666
FF9966	CCCCFF	99CCFF	66CCCC	33CCCC	003333
FF6633	CCCC33	99CCCC	669999	339999	009966
FF3300	CCCC66	99CC99	66CC99	336666	00CC66
FF3333	CCCC99	99CC66	66CC66	33CC99	006633
FF6666	CC9900	99CC33	669966	339966	009933
FF9999	CC9933	99CC00	66CC33	33CC66	00CC33
FFCCCC	CC6600	999900	66CC00	33CC33	00CC00
FFFFFF	CC9966	999933	669933	339933	009900
	CC6633	999966	669900	336633	006600
	CC3300	996600	666600	33CC00	003300
	CC3333	996633	666633	339900	000000
	CC6666	993300	663300	336600	
	CC9999	990000	660000	330000	
	CCCCCC	993333	663333	330000	
		996666	666666	333333	
		999999			

The decision to use only 163 of the possible 216 colors should be based on the Web site's intended audience. If you are trying to reach the widest possible audience, it may be worthwhile to use the 163-color palette. But given that devices like WebTV are currently used by less than one percent of the Web viewing audience, it may be some time before the 163-palette is used on a regular basis.

Colors and File Size

On the Web, it is important to create files that are as small as possible to limit the amount of time a page takes to download. There are two ways to reduce file size with color. The first involves using fewer colors in composing a graphic. The second technique involves reducing the library of colors that the file uses to render the graphic.

Palette Reduction

Since every color in a graphic is additional information, using fewer colors in a graphic will result in smaller file sizes. When designers are creating an image for the Web, they should carefully consider the number of different colors that are being used. Of course, limiting the number of colors in a graphic will sometimes reduce the quality of the image. So designers must strike a balance between using the fewest colors possible and retaining the highest possible image quality.

CLUTS

Another way to cut down the file size of a graphic is to reduce the number of colors in the file's Color Lookup Table (CLUT). CLUTs are invisible files attached to GIFs; they provide the file with a library of colors from which the image is rendered. However, the more colors in the CLUT, the bigger the file will be. You can see the actual colors that make up a CLUT by opening a GIF and selecting the Swatches palette (see Figure 13.4).

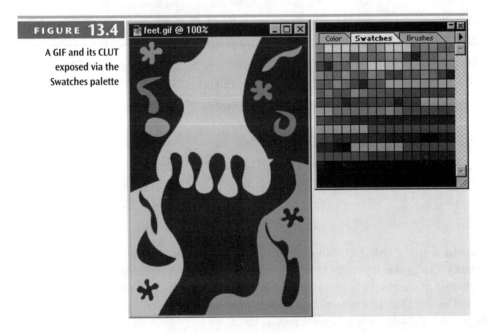

FIGURE 13.4

A GIF and its CLUT exposed via the Swatches palette

In Figure 13.5, the basic file information for two identical black-and-white graphics is displayed. The first file includes a 216-color CLUT, and the second includes a 2-color CLUT that contains only black and white. Look at the difference in file size! The file on the right will download far more quickly than the graphic on the left simply because its CLUT has been optimized to include only the colors that are used in the image.

FIGURE 13.5

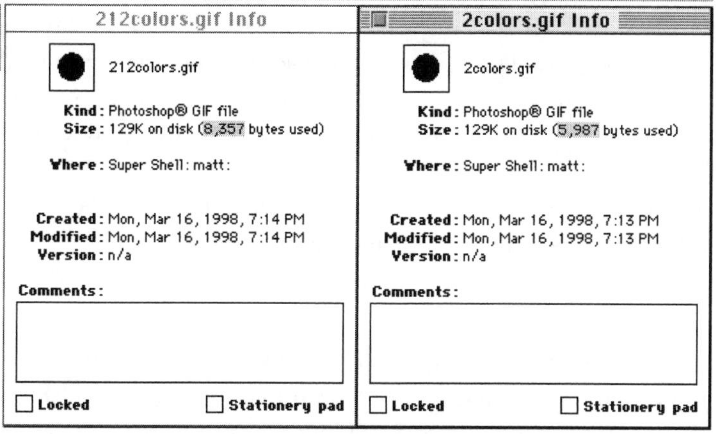

GIF with 216-color CLUT vs. GIF with 2-color CLUT

PART

Photoshop and the Web

Optimizing CLUTS

Unfortunately, when Photoshop creates a GIF with the Web color palette, it includes all 216 colors in the CLUT, regardless of the number of colors that are used in the graphic. Fortunately, there is a workaround:

1. Create a file in RGB mode and switch it to Indexed Color mode by selecting Image ➤ Mode ➤ Indexed Color.

2. Convert the file using the Web option from the Palette drop-down menu.

3. Click OK.

4. Convert the file to RGB mode by selecting Image ➤ Mode ➤ RGB.

5. Switch the file back to Indexed Color mode by selecting Image ➤ Mode ➤ Indexed Color.

6 Convert the file using the Exact option from the Palette drop-down menu.

7. Click OK.

8. Save the image as a GIF.

This technique can often shave thousands of bits off a file. A savings of one or two kilobytes may not seem like a lot, but on a page heavy with graphics, it makes for a significant improvement in the download time.

Tips for Designing with Color

The scope of this chapter is limited to the technical issues associated with using color on the Web. The subject of actually designing with color is much larger and deserving of its own tome. Nonetheless, here are helpful tips on choosing colors for Web designs:

- If a Web site design isn't working, consider using fewer colors. Make the site revolve around a very limited palette of colors. In design, less can indeed be more.

- Long passages of light text on a dark background can be very hard to read. Consider using dark text on a light background in such situations. Beyond white, the 216 palette provides a few colors that are light enough to be used as Web page background colors.

- A Web site's body text doesn't always have to be black. Try a dark blue or green color for the text if it's in keeping with the overall design.

- Photographs on a Web site don't necessarily have to be in full color. Think about tinting them or adjusting their saturation. Such treatments can make images taken by different photographers appear to be part of a single style.

- If you want an animation to blend into a Web page, consider using black or white as the background color. Other colors can be harder to match, especially if the animation is being created in a 3D program.

Conclusion

We usually think of Web design in terms of style and flash, but usability is an equally important issue. Studies indicate that users will wait no longer than eight seconds for significant portions of a Web page to be downloaded—any longer and they move on to another site.

Dealing with color on the Web is an issue of usability. If a GIF contains non-216 colors, it will be less usable than a GIF that adopts the Web Safe Colors palette. If a graphic contains more colors than is absolutely necessary, it will take longer to download and make for a less usable Web site.

Now that the program includes the 216 palette, Photoshop Web designers have the tools at their disposal to meet the Web's color standards.

Up Next

You're hundreds of pages into this book, but have you given any thought to the individual letterforms that make up each printed page? How about the Web—have you ever noticed how some pages just seem easier to read? These questions have to do with the oft-overlooked subject of typography, and it's the focus of the next chapter.

Mastering the Medium: A Good Place to Work

These days, almost everyone needs a Web designer. Companies are paying good salaries for people with even limited experience, and the most talented Web designers are writing their own tickets. Here's a look at some of the different kinds of companies that are in the market for designers:

Web design boutiques   Since the mid-90s, hundreds of Web shops have sprouted up across the country. In the past, most of the Web designers employed at these shops were nothing more than HTML programmers who knew how to operate a graphics application. Recently, such low-end shops have begun to disappear while higher-end design shops have solidified their place in the market.

Advertising agencies   Many traditional agencies have formed internal Web design shops to round out their line of services. However, agencies that don't totally buy into the medium—especially in the account services area—end up with unprofitable Web departments. It's usually just a matter of time before these departments are eliminated. On the other hand, the biggest ad agencies have lucrative clients with money to spend on Web services. As long as account executives can handle the work, even modestly talented agency shops can be profitable.

Online publishers   Newspapers, magazines, and broadcast companies all tend to publish information on the Web. In addition, there are the new media companies like search engines, city guides, and auction sites that have design needs. Many early online publishing ventures have failed, but companies like Yahoo! and ebay have become very successful.

Corporations   Whether it's healthcare, high tech, or insurance, large corporations have made significant investments in the Web. The largest companies usually have dozens of sites to maintain, both internal and external. The biggest challenge corporate developers face is overcoming politics and getting multiple departments to agree on a Web publishing plan.

All employers can be broken down into two groups: startups and established companies. Startups are the cool places to work. They're best suited for people who enjoy flexibility and an informal work environment. When looking at an opportunity with a startup, it's often a good idea to inquire about the company's financing. A good salary will mean nothing if the owner can't make payroll. Also, startups are usually weak in management and process. On the plus side, startups provide the potential for great personal growth.

Established companies, on the other hand, are the safe choice. Employees will always get their paycheck and the benefits are good. Corporations also have highly refined management structures and policies. But you'll need to learn how to deal with office politics. Corporations are also more boring than startups. However, if you have a family, the security of a big company can be very attractive.

If you tend to be very independent and enjoy working from home, then a freelance career is worth considering. Freelancers can design in their pajamas and work whenever they want, as long as their clients get quality work that is on time. But make no mistake, a freelancer is running a business, and they must get and keep clients.

Being a freelancer also means having to deal with things like bookkeeping, accounting, and—worst of all—collecting on past due accounts. The life of a freelancer is sometimes lonely, but the lack of office politics and bad coffee can be very attractive. The most successful freelancers tend to be agency veterans or former corporate designers. Either way, these people have a robust network that provides them with a steady supply of billable design work.

Whatever type of position you take, it is very important to have people available to you who you can learn from. This does not mean that there must be a senior Web designer present—it can be anyone from a great interactive programmer to a marketing guru. If you're a freelancer, you can participate in professional organizations. The point is to surround yourself with people who can help you grow professionally and expand your skills. In the long run, such support is far more important than salary or benefits, because without it you will become isolated and your value in the market will decrease.

chapter 14

GRAPHIC
TYPE

Featuring

GRAPHIC TYPE

ype is a complex aspect of design, so much so that some designers are completely dedicated to its study, examination, creation, and artistry. Lifetimes are spent learning this subtle art. And while the profession of typography lacks the profile of other design fields, if you get good enough at type design you might just have a font named after you someday.

Most designers don't design their own fonts, but designers are often judged by their ability to work with existing typefaces. Typography is a major element in any design, and specifying inappropriate fonts or using them in a klutzy way is a sure sign that the designer is not at the top of their field.

While working with type on the Web is more limiting, good type design is still possible. In fact, it's usually what sets the great Web designers apart from the rest of the pack. These designers understand how to combine regular HTML text with stylish text graphics created in Photoshop.

This chapter will introduce you to basic typographic concepts. Later in the chapter, we'll apply those concepts when we specify type with Photoshop to create graphic type files. Finally, we'll discuss resources for creating special type effects.

The Anatomy of Type

Much like human beings, type comes in all shapes and sizes. Type can be skinny or fat, upright or bent over. Type belongs to specific families with particular characteristics. Also like people, type works best when it's given an appropriate amount of space in which to exist. The following section details each of these characteristics and their importance in working with type.

Fonts, Families, and Faces

The word *font* is actually a carry-over from the days of the printing press. It is used interchangeably these days with *typeface*.

For the purposes of Web design, type is grouped by family and face. *Type family* refers to a specific grouping of type. As with human families, each group shares attributes. Type families group faces by specific kinds of features (see Figure 14.1).

Common, generic families include the following:

Serif   Typefaces with strokes

Sans-Serif   Rounded faces with no strokes

Monospaced   Each letter takes up the same space as another

Script   Type resembles handwriting

Decorative   Type has special decorative features such as dots, strokes, and other designs

---

FIGURE 14.1

Examples of type families

Serif
Sans-Serif
Monospaced
Script
Decorative

A *typeface* refers to type within a family (see Figure 14.2). Common faces within the families discussed here include the following:

Serif   Times, Century Schoolbook, Garamond

Sans-Serif   Helvetica, Arial, Verdana

Monospaced   Courier

Script   Signature, Nuptial

Decorative   Whimsy, Party, Bergell

N O T E   For additional information on type families and faces, see Chapter 17, which discusses the use of type in terms of Cascading Style Sheets.

FIGURE 14.2

Examples of typefaces

Times New Roman is a Serif Font

Helvetica is a Sans-Serif Font

Courier is a Monospaced Font

Boulevard is a Script Font

WILLOW IS A DECORATIVE FONT

Type Form

Typefaces can have *form*. Form includes weight, width, and posture. Form specifically relates to the shape and direction in which a given typeface is presented.

Type Weight

As with families and individuals, some typefaces are dark and heavy, others light and slender. Still others are of "average" build, appearing to have an overall average weight and appearance. Type *weight* influences the way a given face will appear.

Roman   If you belong to the average weight class and you're a typeface, you'd be described as *Roman*. Roman type is simplistic and unadorned. These days, especially on computers, Roman is often referred to as "normal."

Times Roman: Simplistic & Unadorned

Bold   This weight is used to emphasize information within body text. However, it is more customary to use an italic type posture for such purposes. Below is an example of Times face in bold.

Times Bold

Light   Slender, delicate type is referred to as *light*. Light typefaces carry less power than Roman or bold forms, but they can be perfect when a subtle, simple look is called for. Below is a light version and bold version of the same Copperplate face. Note the difference in presentation between the two forms.

COPPERPLATE LIGHT
COPPERPLATE BOLD

Type Width

Typefaces can have a variety of widths—the actual space the face takes up along the horizontal axis.

PART

Photoshop and the Web

Condensed   Also referred to as *compressed*, a condensed form is one where the type-face is *smaller* in width than its Roman counterpart. Shown below is the American Typewriter font in standard and condensed forms.

American Typewriter
    Condensed Form

Expanded   Some refer to this width property as *extended*. It is the converse of con-densed. Instead of less horizontal width on the face than a Roman counterpart, the typeface is wider, or extended.

minima
minima expanded

Type Posture

Old movies sometimes portray parents making children walk around with a school-book on their heads. The idea was to ensure optimum posture. For typefaces, posture is the angle at which the type is set.

Italic   One of the more familiar postures, italic, like bold forms, is the proper way to emphasize text on a page. Italic has its historic roots in handwriting.

Times Roman Italic

Oblique   Oblique type forms are a result of the recent electronic method of typesetting. Obliques tend to be somewhat rigid, rather than bending and flexing where necessary. This causes them to be less readable and sometimes rather awkward when compared to the more elegant italic form. Oblique typefaces are predominantly found in the sans-serif category.

Helvetica Oblique

N O T E   Backslanting is type that is angled in the opposite direction as compared to italic type. Most type designers don't use backslanted type since it can be difficult to read.

Proportion

Another consideration when working with typefaces is their size and proportion to one another—and to other elements on a page.

Type is measured in a variety of ways, including *points* and *pixels*. Point measure-ment is based on print measurement, whereas pixel measurement uses a computer's pixel-based technology to interpret point size. Photoshop allows you to set type in either points or pixels, but since you're a Web designer, you'll want to use pixels.

Unless told otherwise, most Web browsers display standard passages of text as 12 point Times New Roman. Smaller type is used for footer and ancillary information, and larger type is used in headers (see Figure 14.3).

Size can help indicate what role the typeface is playing on the page—large type is used for headers, medium type for body text, and small type for notes and less-emphasized information such as copyright notices.

TIP Varying type size on a page is important, but it is also important to keep things consistent. If one header is set in 24 point Bodoni, they all should be.

Orientation

The direction in which your face runs will have a significant impact on how the type is perceived. Direction in type is often referred to as *orientation*. Figure 14.4 shows three types of orientation: vertical, rendered on a shape, and reversed and upside-down.

Horizontal type is more stable, less full of motion, and more legible. Departing from a horizontal orientation should be done with great care.

FIGURE 14.3

HTML-based type

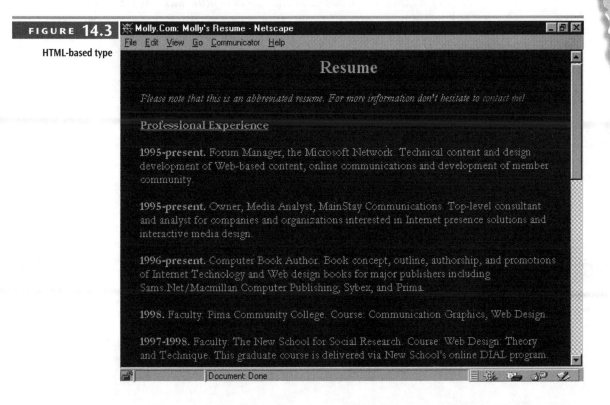

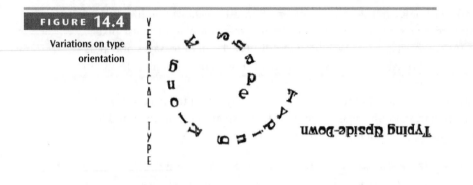

FIGURE **14.4**

Variations on type
orientation

Leading

Typography also concerns itself with the space between lines, which is called *leading*. In her book, *Pagemaker 4: An Easy Desk Reference*, Robin Williams explains:

The term leading is a holdover from the days when all type was cast in metal. Literally, every single letter, space, and punctuation mark was on a separate piece of metal (guess what kind of metal they used). And they had to make a complete set of metal characters for each point size of type. The typesetter lined up all these tiny lead letters and spaces in little rows. Then, between each row of type, he inserted a thin strip of lead to separate them. Leading, therefore, is a term referring to the space between the lines of type.

How close or how far a line is from another can influence readability. In Figure 14.5, I've set 18-point type with leading at 18 points. You'll see that for this typeface (Caslon), the space between the lines appears natural and easy to read.

FIGURE **14.5**

18 point Caslon set with
a leading of 18 points

I loved her most, and thought to set my rest
On her kind nursery. Hence, and avoid my sight!
So be my grave my peace, as here I give
Her father's heart from her!

In Figure 14.6, I've reduced the leading to 10 points, but kept the size of the type steady at 18 points. The text has become unreadable.

FIGURE **14.6**

18 point Caslon set with
a leading of 10 points

I loved her most, and thought to set my rest
On her kind nursery. Hence, and avoid my sight!
So be my grave my peace, as here I give
Her father's heart from her!

Similarly, if I set the leading too far apart, readability is affected. In Figure 14.7, I use the same 18 point typeface at a leading of 30 points.

PART

Photoshop and the Web

FIGURE 14.7

18 point Caslon set with
a leading of 30 points

I loved her most, and thought to set my rest

On her kind nursery. Hence, and avoid my sight!

So be my grave my peace, as here I give

Her father's heart from her!

The effect is interesting, and can be used for shorter bursts of text. However, for body text, avoid leading like this—it causes a strain on the eye, affecting readability.

TIP   For the sake of readability, there should be no more than eight to 12 words in a line of text.

Kerning and Tracking

Kerning is the space between individual letters. Unlike monospaced fonts, where every letter is designed to take up the same amount of space, proportional fonts require kerning pairs so that all of the letters in a word fit together in an elegant manner. The letters that comprise the words in this sentence have been meticulously designed so that they all fit together perfectly.

A good typeface will have the exact amount of distance between as many combinations of letters as possible built into the font. All of this information is contained in what is referred to as a *kerning table*. The quality of a font can often be judged by the number of kerning pairs that the kerning table contains.

Tracking is an adjustment that can be made between letters and words. Figure 14.8 shows an example of a 12 point Helvetica font with normal tracking, then spaced with values of 200 and -200.

FIGURE 14.8

12 point Helvetica type
with three types of
tracking

I loved her most, and thought to set my rest ——————— No tracking

I loved her most, and thought to set my rest— Tracking value of 200

lovedhermost,andthoughttosetmyrest ——————— Tracking value of -200

Like kerning, tracking affects the readability of a passage. While the use of tracking can add visual interest to a page, unusual space values should be restricted to decorative or short bursts of text. Body text requires normal spacing to be attractive and comfortable to the reader.

Color

When it comes to type, color has two different meanings. The first relates to the level of darkness or lightness projected by a large amount of body type. For example, if the type on this page were set in Palatino, the overall effect would be dark. On the other hand, if this page was set in Goudy Old Style, the page would be airy and have a lighter "color." Computer monitors are low-resolution devices with limited ability to render delicate type, so Web body type is usually very dark in color.

The other kind of color is the actual hue that type projects—red, blue, green, black, etc. Adding color to fonts can help give a page distinction. As with size and face, a light touch is important—you don't want to overwhelm your site's visitors with 10 different colors on a page. In fact, sticking to two static colors—one for headers and auxiliary text, and one for body text—is a very safe way to get a bit of color into your design.

On the Web, you can use color for text, text-based headers, links, visited links, and active links. This gives you many opportunities to apply color to text, but it also provides ample opportunity to create ugly pages. Until you know how to work with color, it's best to proceed with caution.

Sometimes the best way to begin to work with color is to limit your palette to shades of gray. Contrast can be used to simulate a *sense* of color. As mentioned earlier in the discussion of type forms, bold, italic, and oblique can be used to create emphasis within a page. Light type is softer and warmer than **bold** type, which literally jumps off the page.

When designing type for a full Web page, many designers will use a darker color for primary headers, and then lighten the color (or change it) as the headers descend. Figure 14.9 shows a Web page with two headers in different shades of gray.

FIGURE 14.9

Gradations of type color in headers

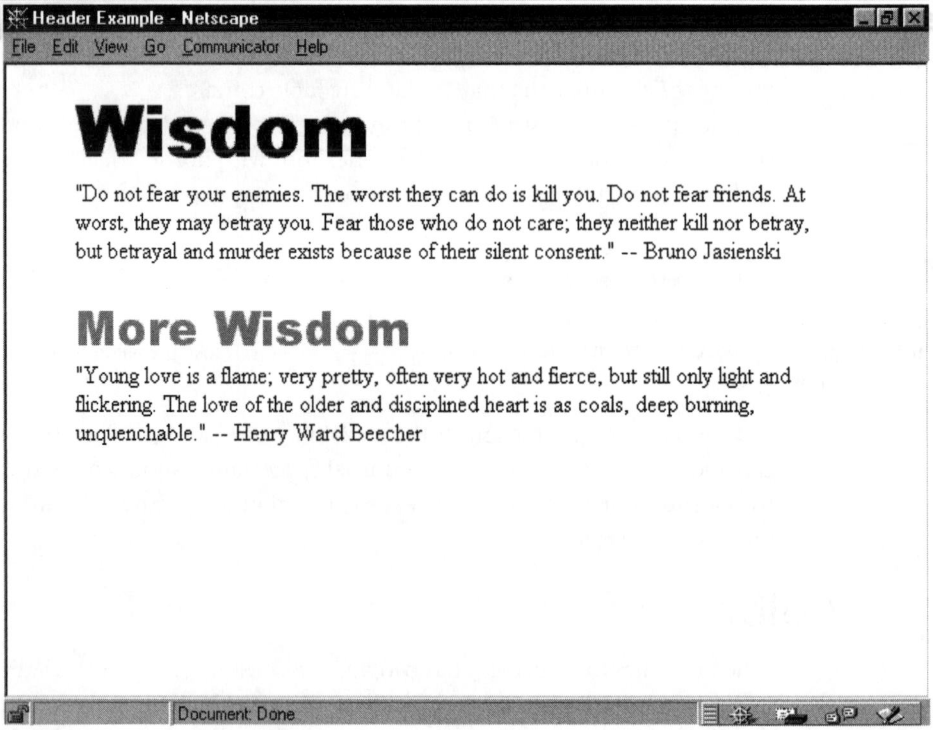

Note that this technique creates visual texture, in addition to demonstrating the emphasis of each individual section: The bolder the header, the more dominant a position the information associated with it commands.

Specifying Type

Choosing typefaces, also known as specifying type, is a critical portion of the Web design process. Rather than being an afterthought, specifying type should be an integral part of the design process. Unfortunately, many aspiring designers make the type selection process much more difficult than it needs to be. In his book *How to Spec Type*, Alex White explains:

> *Having a good understanding of just a few principles (plus the application of common sense) will get you through nearly any type speccing problem, no matter how dissimilar previous problems may appear at first glance.*

If you look at just about any publication, you'll see that there are only two categories of text: body and display. Body type is the text in a book or magazine—the lengthy stuff set at relatively small sizes. Display type is the bigger type that is used for headlines in a newspaper or movie poster.

Body Type

Body type is the meat and potatoes of design. There's usually a lot of it, set at smaller sizes—9 to 12 points. And while most people don't notice the difference between Courier and Helvetica, it does have an impact on the look and feel of a Web page. In print, there are lots of different body faces, but on the Web (at least in 1998) you can only really use about a half dozen. They include

- Times
- Times New Roman
- Arial
- Helvetica
- Courier
- Verdana

Web designers could get pretty bored with only a half dozen fonts to work with, and believe me, they do. I'm hopeful that the two major browser companies will find *one* way to give designers more choice in the fonts they can use.

Display Type

If body type is meat and potatoes, then display type is the waiter claiming how good the food is. Display type is usually set at 16 points and higher and surrounds body type in short bursts of text. There are thousands of display fonts, including

- Comic Sans
- Anvil
- Impact
- Amplifier
- Bodega
- Stencil

Do some of these fonts seem unfamiliar to you? Don't worry, there are so many that it's impossible to know them all. Find some you like and start experimenting with them.

N O T E   My favorite display type foundry? It's T-26, located in Chicago. This company provides the coolest display fonts (not to mention some great music) at very reasonable prices. Visit the Web site at www.t26font.com.

What Is Graphic Type?

On the Web, there are two kinds of type: HTML and graphic. HTML type comprises nearly all of the body type that you see on the Web. This kind of type is specified via the HTML that formats a Web page. Graphic type is used mainly for display type—items such as headers, logos, etc.

The primary advantage of using graphic type over HTML type is control. As we will learn in Chapter 16, HTML provides only the most general type control—the names of the fonts to be used, relative size, etc. Also, HTML type relies on the end-users having the fonts you specify installed on their computers. While there are techniques you can learn to help you manage HTML type (see Chapter 17: *Cascading Style Sheets*), there is still no method that allows the kind of control that you can gain using graphic type.

The downside to graphic type is that graphics take more time to download than HMTL. This can cause problems for your site visitors. Fortunately, most graphic type requires only a few colors and, with the exception of special effects such as typographic edges and shadows, little gradation of light and color. Thus, graphic text tends to download very quickly, and most people don't mind the short wait.

T I P   Most graphic type is saved in the GIF format. As we saw in Chapter 12, GIF is the best format for hard-edged graphics. Since most text qualifies as hard-edged, GIF is clearly the format of choice.

Photoshop's Type Tool

Graphic type is created in Photoshop with the Type tool (see Figure 14.10). There are four variations on the tool (from left to right): regular type, mask type, vertical type, and vertical mask type. You will usually be using regular, horizontal type, which fills the type with the color you have selected and places it on a horizontal axis.

FIGURE 14.10

The Photoshop Toolbar with the Type tool selected

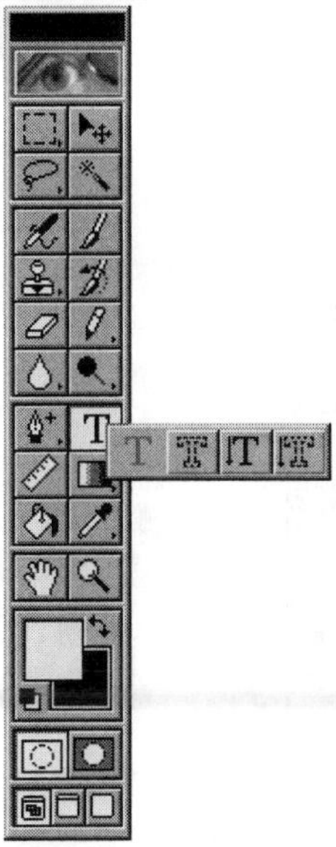

Once you've invoked the tool, a dialog appears with a number of options and boxes (see Figure 14.11). With version 5 of the program, Adobe has significantly upgraded the Type tool. Capabilities now include the following:

Font   Select the typeface you'd like to use.

Size   Select the size you'd like, in points or pixels.

Kerning   Select a positive or negative number to adjust the space between individual letters.

Color   View the actual color of the type you're setting. If you click on the colored rectangle, you'll be presented with the Photoshop Color Picker.

Leading   Set the amount of space between individual lines.

Tracking   Adjust the space between a series of letters and words with a positive or negative number.

TIP   Notice that you can either adjust the Kerning or the Tracking, but not both. If more than one character is selected, you can set tracking. If none are selected, you can only adjust the spacing between the current letter and the next (kerning).

Baseline   Adjust how high or low text sits within its allotted space.

Preview   See how the type you're setting looks in your graphic.

Auto Kern   Automatically restore normal kerning between letters.

Anti-Aliased   Set the automatic type smoother. I recommend that you do this when setting type 12 points or higher.

Rotate   Flip the text that you're setting. Note that this only works with the vertical type tools.

Finally, there's an OK box and a Cancel box. Use these to set or to cancel the type when you've finished setting options.

FIGURE 14.11

The Type Tool dialog

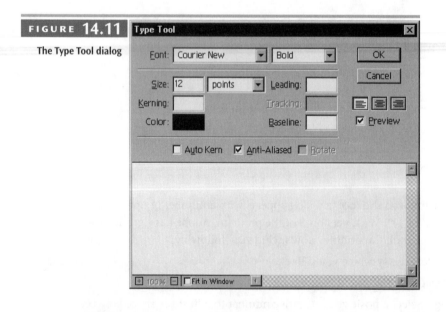

TIP   Have you purchased new fonts and are wondering how to make them available for use with Photoshop? If you're on a Mac, simply drag them into your System folder. On the PC, go to the Start menu and choose Settings ➤ Control Panel and select the Fonts control panel. Select File ➤ Install New Font to load the fonts into your computer.

Setting Type

Setting type involves three steps: creating a work area, setting the actual type, and moving the type to its final location.

To create a work area, follow these steps:

1. Select File ➤ New. The New dialog will open.

2. In the Width and Height text boxes, add the measurements of your work area in pixels.

3. In the Resolution text box, type **72** (the standard Web resolution).

4. From the Mode drop-down list, select RGB.

5. Select an option in the Contents area. I like to set this to White as it creates a cleaner background on which to set type.

6. Click OK. Your workspace will appear. You'll want to size and place it in the Photoshop work area to your own comfort and tastes.

Figure 14.12 shows the New dialog. I've set it up for a 300×50 pixel workspace, 72 dpi resolution, RGB mode, and a white content. This workspace is going to be used for a graphic type page header.

FIGURE 14.12

Creating a workspace for a page header

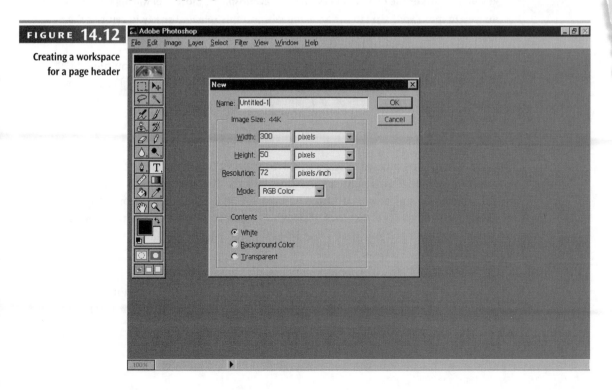

Now you'll want to actually set the type. Follow these steps:

1. Select the Type tool.

2. Click the Type tool cursor in the workspace. This will open the Type Tool dialog.

3. Make all of your font selections. If you have Preview selected, you will see the type appear in the workspace as you type.

4. Click OK.

At this point, you'll want to move the type to the exact place you want it to appear. Follow these steps:

1. Select the Move tool.

2. Click the Move tool on the type.

3. Hold the mouse button down and drag until the type is where you want it.

4. Release the mouse button.

Your type is set!

 TIP If you'd like to move your type without deselecting the Type tool, press the Ctrl key in Windows or the Command key on the Macintosh. The Move tool will appear, allowing you to move your type to the area you wish. Simply release the key to return to the Type tool.

At this point, you should consider saving the file as a native Photoshop file (PSD). This allows you to return to the initial file to add additional color, special effects, or change the placement of the type at a later time.

Editing Type

Veteran users will be pleased to learn that Photoshop's Text tool can edit text that has been previously set. That's right, a graphic text menu that you created months ago with Photoshop 5 can now be updated without creating the new text from scratch!

Every time you use the Text tool, Photoshop creates a new layer. You will notice by looking at the Layers palette that a text layer is noted with a special "T" icon (see Figure 14.13).

To edit previously set type, follow these steps:

1. Select Window ➤ Show Layers and double-click on the "T" icon in the Layers palette.

2. Use the Type Tool dialog to edit the text.

3. Click OK.

Once you set text on a layer, it is impossible to use other tools on that layer (Pencil, Paintbrush, etc.) until the layer has been rendered into a bitmap image. To render a text layer, select Layer ➤ Type ➤ Render Layer from the Menu Bar. The "T" icon will no longer be visible on the layer of type.

WARNING   Once a text layer has been rendered, the text can no longer be edited in the Type Tool dialog. For more about this feature, see Chapter 7.

FIGURE 14.13

The special text layer feature

[Layers panel showing: Normal, Opacity: 100 %, Preserve Transparency, "yum" text layer with T icon, Layer 1]

Anti-Aliasing

Because graphic type is set in pixels, there tends to be a squaring of any curved line. This is what creates the jagged edges that you can usually see when people have not anti-aliased their type (see Figure 14.14).

FIGURE 14.14

Type without anti-aliasing applied

Untitled-1 @ 100% (Jaggies,RGB)

Jaggies

Anti-aliasing is an important effect that will help you keep your graphic type looking smooth and readable. By invoking the Anti-Aliased feature, Photoshop will smooth out type by applying intermediate colors around the edges. While this effect adds more colors to a graphic, the file size increases by only a small amount.

NOTE   Anti-aliasing is best applied to type that is 12 points or larger. Smaller type usually becomes too blurry to read with anti-aliasing applied.

Let's step through and reset the type shown in Figure 14.14 to anti-aliased type.

1. Create a workspace by following steps 1 through 6 in the earlier section, "Setting Type." I've created a space 595 pixels wide by 100 pixels high. My content is set to White as I know I'm going to want a white background.

2. Select the Type tool.

3. In the Type Tool dialog, select a typeface. I've chosen QuickType Condensed; if you don't have this font, choose Helvetica or Arial.

4. Set the size. Mine is set to 40 points.

5. To anti-alias your text, simply be sure that the Anti-Aliased checkbox is selected.

![Type Tool dialog box showing Font: Anvilregular, Regular; Size: 110 points; Leading: blank; Kerning: 0; Tracking: 0; Color: black; Baseline: 0; OK and Cancel buttons; Preview checkbox checked; Auto Kern unchecked, Anti-Aliased checked, Rotate unchecked. Preview shows the text "No Jaggies". Bottom shows 100% and Fit in Window.]

6. Type your text into the large type box.

7. Click OK.

No jagged edges! Now compare Figures 14.14 and 14.15 to see how anti-aliasing effectively improves the look of type.

FIGURE 14.15

Anti-aliasing applied

Untitled-1 @ 100% (No Jaggies,RGB)

No Jaggies

N O T E Want to know more about anti-aliasing? See Chapter 4.

Leading Adjustment

As mentioned earlier in the chapter, leading is the vertical space between individual lines of type. Typically, the amount of space between each line of text is 2 points larger than the size of the type. So, if you've set your type at 10 points, your default leading is going to be 12.

There are times, however, when you'll want to make the type fit a little more tightly, or spread the lines out. To do this, you can adjust the leading using a numeric value.

W A R N I N G Lines of type that are too close or too spread out can cause readability problems.

The quote shown in Figure 14.16 is taken from Shakespeare's Romeo and Juliet. I've set the type in 12 point Times, with default leading—I left the Type Tool Leading box blank.

PART

Photoshop and the Web

FIGURE **14.16**

Normal leading

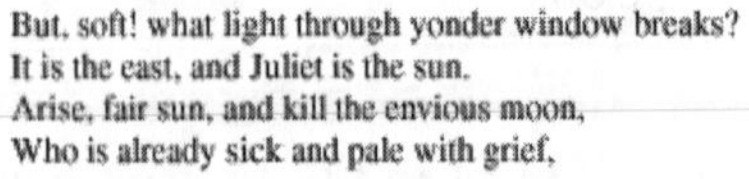

But, soft! what light through yonder window breaks?
It is the east, and Juliet is the sun.
Arise, fair sun, and kill the envious moon,
Who is already sick and pale with grief,

To set the type with tighter leading, follow these steps:

1. Create a workspace 300 pixels wide by 200 pixels high, giving you plenty of space to work in. I used white and set the type in black.

2. Select the Type tool.

3. Click the Type tool cursor in your workspace. The Type Tool dialog will appear.

4. Select the Times typeface (or Times New Roman if you don't have Times).

5. Set the size to 12 points.

6. Set the leading to 10.

7. Type in some text, hitting the Return/Enter key between lines.

8. Click OK.

Your work should match Figure 14.17. This is tight leading. Again, it can be used for nice special effects, but only in small bursts.

FIGURE **14.17**

Tight leading

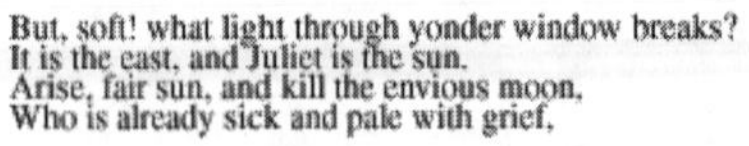

But, soft! what light through yonder window breaks?
It is the east, and Juliet is the sun.
Arise, fair sun, and kill the envious moon,
Who is already sick and pale with grief,

Now let's try it with more space between each line. Follow these steps:

1. Create another workspace 300 pixels wide by 200 pixels high.

2. Select the Type tool and click in the workspace to open the Type Tool dialog.

3. Choose the Times or Times Roman typeface.

4. Set the size to 12 points.

5. This time, set the leading to 20.

6. Type in some text and hit the Return/Enter key between lines.

7. Click OK.

Figure 14.18 shows how different type looks with wider settings. There are times when you will want to use leading to achieve a variety of stylish typographic material, but for body text or wherever readability is a major issue, definitely stick closer to the defaults.

FIGURE 14.18

Wide leading

But, soft! what light through yonder window breaks?

It is the east, and Juliet is the sun.

Arise, fair sun, and kill the envious moon,

Who is already sick and pale with grief.

NOTE Always save your original files in the native Photoshop format (PSD). If you're ready to save your file for use on the Web, see Chapter 12 about saving a file to GIF format.

Kerning Type

As described earlier in the chapter, kerning is the spacing between individual letters. For the typographically inclined, it's an important part of setting type, but there are no methods available to kern HTML type. Cascading Style Sheets, which were supposed to answer a lot of type concerns for Web designers, still have no technique available for kerning.

However, thanks to Photoshop's upgraded Type tool, kerning can now be easily accomplished when creating graphic type. To manually kern some type, do the following:

1. Select the Type tool and click in the workspace to open the Type Tool dialog.

2. Uncheck the Auto Kern option if it is selected. This will make the Kerning option active.

3. In the large type box, implant the cursor between two letters.

4. In the Kerning field, enter a positive or negative number.

5. Click OK.

TIP Ultimately, you will find it much more convenient to adjust kerning by using the keyboard equivalents. On the PC, press Alt+→ or Alt+← to move 20 increments at a time. Pressing Alt+Shift will make a 100-increment adjustment. On the Mac, use the Option and Option+Apple keys in conjunction with the forward and back arrows.

Photoshop's Auto Kern can act as an undo option. To undo manual kerning, do the following:

1. Double-click on the Type layer to open the Type Tool dialog.

2. Implant the cursor between two manually kerned letters or highlight a whole series of letters.

3. Place a check in the Auto Kern checkbox.

WARNING   While you do have one level of undo available at all times, the History function is not accessible while working in the Type Tool dialog.

Tracking Type

With version 5, Photoshop also provides a new type option: tracking. Whereas kerning is for adjusting the space between letters, tracking is used to make universal changes to both letter and word spacing.

In Figure 14.19, Romeo is quoted using unspecified (default) tracking.

FIGURE **14.19**

Standard tracking

By a name
I know not how to tell thee who I am:
My name, dear saint, is hateful to myself,
Because it is an enemy to thee;
Had I it written, I would tear the word.

To tighten the spacing between the letters, follow these steps:

1. Create a workspace as you did in prior exercises.
2. Select the Type tool and open the Type Tool dialog.
3. Choose Helvetica (or Arial if you don't have Helvetica).
4. Set the type at 12 points.
5. In the Tracking box, type in –100 (negative 1).
6. Click OK.

You'll see in Figure 14.20 that there is now no space between each individual letter within a word. In fact, there's negative space. Again, this is a neat technique but one to be used only periodically—you're far more likely to manually kern certain pairs of letters than to space out an entire passage.

FIGURE **14.20**

Negative value tracking

By a name
I know not how to tell thee who I am:
My name, dear saint, is hateful to myself,
Because it is an enemy to thee;
Had I it written, I would tear the word.

To widen the spacing, follow the same steps:

1. Create your workspace.
2. Select the Type tool and open the Type Tool dialog.
3. Choose Helvetica or Arial for your typeface.

4. Choose 12 point type.

5. In the Tracking field, type in **500**.

6. Click OK.

Wow! Look at the difference shown in Figure 14.21.

FIGURE **14.21**

Wide tracking

```
By  a  name
I  know  not  how  to  tell  thee  who  I  am:
My  name,  dear  saint,  is  hateful  to  myself,
Because  it  is  an  enemy  to  thee;
Had  I  it  written,  I  would  tear  the  word.
```

In the last few years, unconventional uses of tracking have been applied to display type in youth culture magazines like Bikini and Raygun, and even some mainstream publications and Web sites are now using the technique.

Advanced Type Effects

As detailed in Chapter 7, Photoshop 5 now includes a tremendous feature called Layer Effects that allows you to quickly create type that is shadowed, highlighted, beveled and embossed.

N O T E   See Chapter 7 for much more information about the Layer Effects feature.

There is also an infinite range of special effects that can be applied to graphic type with Photoshop's Filters feature. To see an example of text that was shaded using Photoshop's Lighting Effects feature and learn more about what filters can do, see Chapter 8.

T I P   Text layers must be converted to regular, bitmapped layers in order to be used with filters.

Third-Party Type Effects

Third-party Photoshop plug-ins are available for creating type effects. Because the range of third-party software is constantly expanding, it's best to check in with these vendors on a regular basis:

- Adobe Plug-In Source keeps a list of third-party plug-ins that will help you find compatible software to use with Photoshop (http://www.pluginsource.com).

PART

Photoshop and the Web

• DesktopPublishing.com™ is a great site that serves a wide range of design needs. Be sure to visit the Web Designer's Paradise as well as typography sections for helpful information (http://www.desktoppublishing.com/).

WARNING   Drop shadows are a subtle gradation of color. But the GIF file format is not well suited for subtle changes in color, so your Web graphic will inevitably degrade during the conversion process.

Vector Type

Not all type-based graphics are created with Photoshop. In fact, most logos and other print-based artwork exist as Encapsulated PostScript (EPS) files created in programs like Adobe Illustrator, which records artwork as a series of numbers and formulas—also known as vector files. Despite their differences, both Photoshop and Illustrator are capable of opening a number of shared formats.

To open an Illustrator-created logo or graphic in Photoshop, do the following:

1. Select File ➤ Open from the Menu Bar.

2. Locate the file you want to open and click OK.

3. In the Rasterize Generic EPS Format dialog, select a width, height, resolution, and mode for the image.

4. Select Anti-aliased to smooth the image. Choose Constrain Proportions if you are altering the size of the image and want to maintain current proportions.

Rasterize Generic EPS Format	☒
Image Size: 472K	
Width: 6.354 inches	OK
Height: 4.884 inches	Cancel
Resolution: 72 pixels/inch	
Mode: RGB Color	
☑ Anti-aliased ☑ Constrain Proportions	

5. Click OK.

Now you can work on an EPS file that was originally created in Adobe Illustrator.

Conclusion

Some day you may not need Photoshop to create great-looking type. The practice of creating individual Web graphics that contain nothing more than stylized letters will be totally outdated. Why go to that kind of trouble when you can simply tell a browser what you want the user to see?

New technology such as Microsoft's Web Embedding Font Tool (WEFT) is offering a peek at such a future. WEFT creates font files that are automatically downloaded to users, providing them with exactly the fonts the designer intended for them to see. Combined with Cascading Style Sheets, such typography can be precisely specified and positioned on a page.

But this scenario still exists in the future, perhaps as much as three to five years away—or more. Most people are still using older browsers that don't do any of this neat stuff, and even the new ones don't support basic typesetting features like kerning and anti-aliasing.

Until these things change, designers will continue to create little bits of text in Photoshop to insure that their Web pages are typographically refined.

Up Next

Having learned the ins and outs of creating graphical type, we'll tackle all of the other kinds of graphics you might want to put on a Web page. Backgrounds, menus, ad banners—if it's a graphic and part of a Web page, we'll be creating it.

Mastering the Medium: Resources at the Ready

Whether you're working for a large company or as a freelancer, every Web designer requires certain resources to perform their job. It's important to invest in the right things—if you blow your budget on lots of gadgets, you may not have the money for the really important stuff.

The first thing a Web designer needs is a computer. Regardless of whether you buy a PC or a Macintosh, it is important that the computer have sufficient RAM and hard drive capacity. However, the performance required for most Web design work is modest compared to the needs of print designers. Web designers can find suitable machines for under $2500.

After you have a computer, you'll need software. Photoshop is probably the first and most expensive piece of software you'll need, but after that you'll also need an HTML editor, GIF animation program, RGB/hexadecimal color conversion tool, image mapping software, and FTP program so you can move a Web site to a Web server. Fortunately, all of these programs can be found on the CD-ROM and at the *Mastering Photoshop 5 for the Web* companion Web site (see Appendix F).

Web designers frequently need to include scanned images in a Web site, so purchasing a flatbed scanner is usually a must. The Web requires only low resolution images, so it isn't necessary to buy a high-end scanner. As long as the device has a decent resolution and captures in full color, any good quality scanner will do the trick.

Speaking of digitizing, one piece of hardware that often proves unnecessary is a digital camera. Unless you're adding new photos to a Web site on a regular basis, it is far cheaper to use a traditional camera and digitize the images with a scanner.

Some people collect dolls, others collect baseball cards. If you're a designer, you probably collect fonts. Fonts add style to a document, but they can also be the genesis of a great design concept. Some of my favorite display fonts come from a type foundry called T26 in Chicago. You can visit them on the Web at http://www.t26-font.com.

It's midnight and you need a picture of a sunflower for a Web site that's due tomorrow. Where can you find one? On the Web, of course. Online stock photography houses like Photodisc (http://www.photodisc.com) provide tremendous selection and around-the-clock service.

Ultimately, the most critical hardware you'll ever own is the tape, Zip, Jaz, or external hard drive that you use to back up your data. Someday all of the information on your computer—every graphic, e-mail, and letter—may become lost forever due to a malfunction. Play it safe and back up your files every day.

COLOR REFERENCE

This special color section is a reference to Photoshop's key color tools and features.

In the first section you will find Color Tutorials. These illustrate the various color tools available in Photoshop.

Directly following these tutorials, you will find a four-page Web safe palette. The palette includes the hexadecimal and RGB values for each of the 216 Web safe colors. This palette was designed by Amy Burnham for Molly E. Holzschlag's *Web by Design*. Examples of hybrid-safe colors are included after the palette.

There's also a look at the portfolios of some of the best Photoshop Web designers working today, and even a peek at the special companion Web site to this book, which can be found at http://www.straznitskas.com.

COLOR TUTORIALS

These tutorials provide a colorful look at Photoshop tools and techniques. Culled from the 18 chapters and the appendix, many of these figures include illustrations that were created in Photoshop. For more information about drawing hard-edged illustrations like the ones depicted, see Chapter 5.

1. Workspace

The Photoshop workspace provides a Menu Bar, Toolbar, image window, and a series of palettes. Windows users also have a Status Bar running along the very bottom of the space.

2. Hand Tool

The Hand tool is used to adjust the portion of an image that is viewed.

3. Navigator Palette

The Navigator palette provides a proportionally accurate thumbnail and a way to position a graphic in the image window.

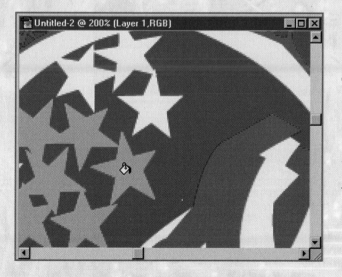

4. Paint Bucket

The Paint Bucket tool is used to fill in large areas of similar color.

5. History Brush

Using the History Brush in combination with the Impressionist feature to paint back a portion of an image and create a special effect.

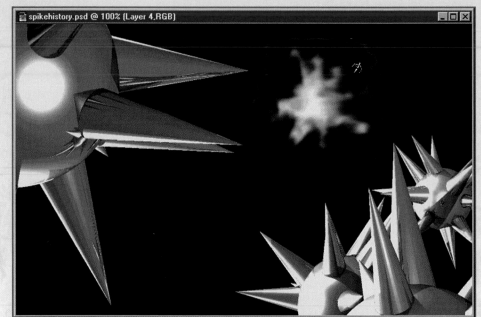

6. Color Palette, RGB

The Color palette is adjusted via the RGB settings, in this case generating a bright green color.

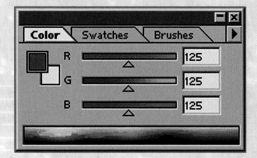

7. Color Palette, Gray

The Color palette can be used to create gray values as well.

8.
Foreground Color

The foreground color (blue) is applied with the painting and drawing tools— in this case the Paintbrush.

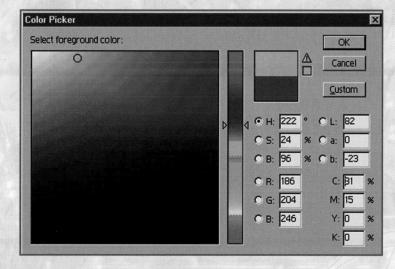

9. Color Picker

The Color Picker's color indicator window with a new and current color indicated.

10. **Linear Gradient Tool**

The Linear Gradient tool produces transitions of color along a straight path.

Untitled-1 @ 100% (RGB)

11. **Radial Gradient Tool**

The Radial Gradient tool creates spherical transitions between two or more colors.

Untitled-1 @ 100% (RGB)

12. **Angle Gradient Tool**

The Angle Gradient tool creates a spectrum of color from dark to light, set in a specified angle.

Untitled-1 @ 100% (RGB)

13. Reflected Gradient Tool

The Reflected Gradient tool creates an effect similar to what happens when light strikes a reflective object.

14. Diamond Gradient Tool

The Diamond Gradient tool applies a four-sided, diamond-shaped gradation to an image.

15. Paths

A stylized, hard-edged illustration created in Photoshop using the Paths feature.

16. Channels

An image with three color channels and a composite RGB channel (Photo courtesy of Auriea Harvey).

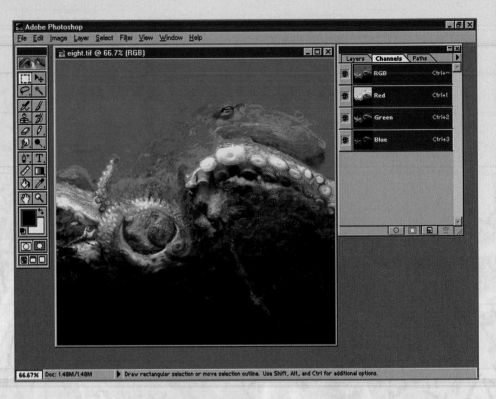

17. Layers

A graphic built using Photoshop's Layers feature.

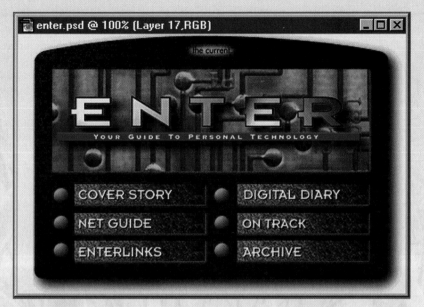

enter.psd @ 100% (Layer 17,RGB)

the current

E N T E R

YOUR GUIDE TO PERSONAL TECHNOLOGY

COVER STORY · DIGITAL DIARY
NET GUIDE · ON TRACK
ENTERLINKS · ARCHIVE

18. Add Noise

A highly stylized Web graphic with a texture created with the Add Noise filter.

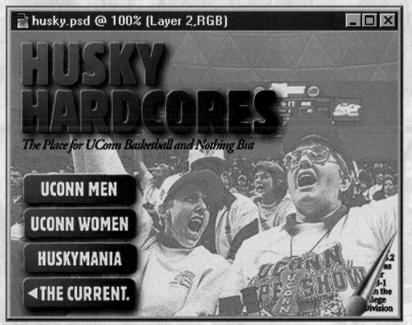

husky.psd @ 100% (Layer 2,RGB)

HUSKY HARDCORES

The Place for UConn Basketball and Nothing But

UCONN MEN

UCONN WOMEN

HUSKYMANIA

◄ THE CURRENT.

19. Lighting Effects

A Web site interface with realistically shaded type and buttons created with the Lighting Effects filter.

20. Blizzard Image Effects

A photograph with the Blizzard Image Effects action applied to the image.

21. Browser-Safe Colors

The Web is standardized on these specific 216 colors which can be loaded into the Swatches palette and used in making graphics.

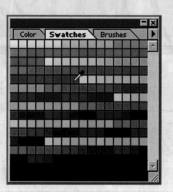

22. Simulating Color

Drawing a checkerboard pattern with two of the 216 browser-safe Web colors is used to simulate a new color.

23. CLUT

A GIF's Color Look-up Table (CLUT) is exposed by selecting the Swatches palette.

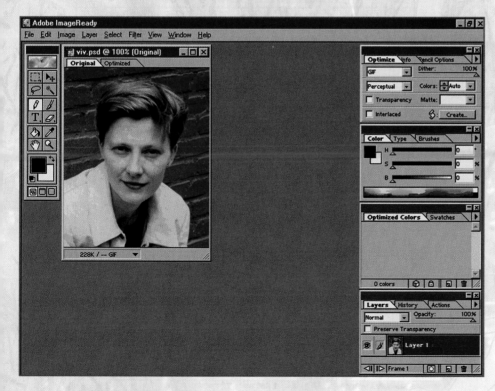

24. ImageReady Workspace

The Adobe Image-Ready workspace.

25. Video Capture

Video capture programs like Adobe Premiere are used to digitize video media like VCR and Hi-8 tapes.

26. Video Editing

Individual frames can then be exported to Photoshop for editing.

27. Rulers and Guides

Rulers and Guides can be used to define a precise selection area.

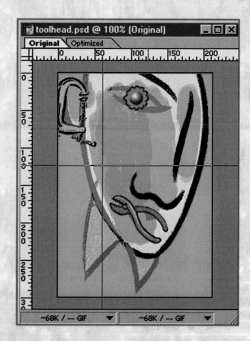

28. ImageReady

ImageReady's Rulers and Guides can be used together to slice a Web graphic into individual elements that fit perfectly together.

THE COLOR SAFE PALETTE

990033 R: 153 G: 000 B: 051	**FF3366** R: 255 G: 051 B: 102	**CC0033** R: 204 G: 000 B: 051	**FF0033** R: 255 G: 000 B: 051	**FF9999** R: 255 G: 153 B: 153	**CC3366** R: 204 G: 051 B: 102
FFCCFF R: 255 G: 204 B: 255	**CC6699** R: 204 G: 102 B: 153	**993366** R: 153 G: 051 B: 102	**660033** R: 102 G: 000 B: 051	**CC3399** R: 204 G: 051 B: 153	**FF99CC** R: 255 G: 153 B: 204
FF66CC R: 255 G: 102 B: 204	**FF99FF** R: 255 G: 153 B: 255	**FF6699** R: 255 G: 102 B: 153	**CC0066** R: 204 G: 000 B: 102	**FF0066** R: 255 G: 000 B: 102	**FF3399** R: 255 G: 051 B: 153
FF0099 R: 255 G: 000 B: 153	**FF33CC** R: 255 G: 051 B: 204	**FF00CC** R: 255 G: 000 B: 204	**FF66FF** R: 255 G: 102 B: 255	**FF33FF** R: 255 G: 051 B: 255	**FF00FF** R: 255 G: 000 B: 255
CC0099 R: 204 G: 000 B: 153	**990066** R: 153 G: 000 B: 102	**CC66CC** R: 204 G: 102 B: 204	**CC33CC** R: 204 G: 051 B: 204	**CC99FF** R: 204 G: 153 B: 255	**CC66FF** R: 204 G: 102 B: 255
CC33FF R: 204 G: 051 B: 255	**993399** R: 153 G: 051 B: 153	**CC00CC** R: 204 G: 000 B: 204	**CC00FF** R: 204 G: 000 B: 255	**9900CC** R: 153 G: 000 B: 204	**990099** R: 153 G: 000 B: 153
CC99CC R: 204 G: 153 B: 204	**996699** R: 153 G: 102 B: 153	**663366** R: 102 G: 051 B: 102	**660099** R: 102 G: 000 B: 153	**9933CC** R: 153 G: 051 B: 204	**660066** R: 102 G: 000 B: 102
9900FF R: 153 G: 000 B: 255	**9933FF** R: 153 G: 051 B: 255	**9966CC** R: 153 G: 102 B: 204	**330033** R: 051 G: 000 B: 051	**663399** R: 102 G: 051 B: 153	**6633CC** R: 102 G: 051 B: 204
6600CC R: 102 G: 000 B: 204	**9966FF** R: 153 G: 102 B: 255	**330066** R: 051 G: 000 B: 102	**6600FF** R: 102 G: 000 B: 255	**6633FF** R: 102 G: 051 B: 255	**CCCCFF** R: 204 G: 204 B: 255

Used with permission from *Web by Design* by Molly E. Holzschlag. Designed by Amy Burnham.

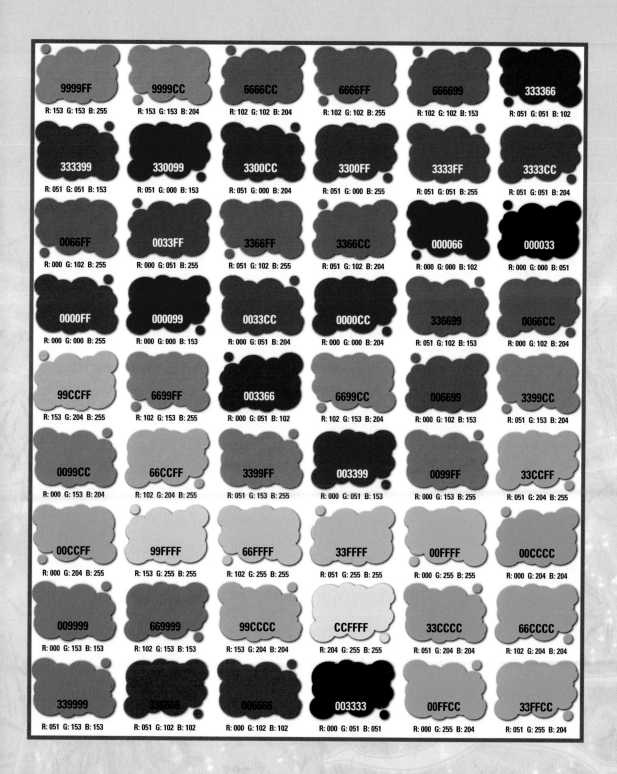

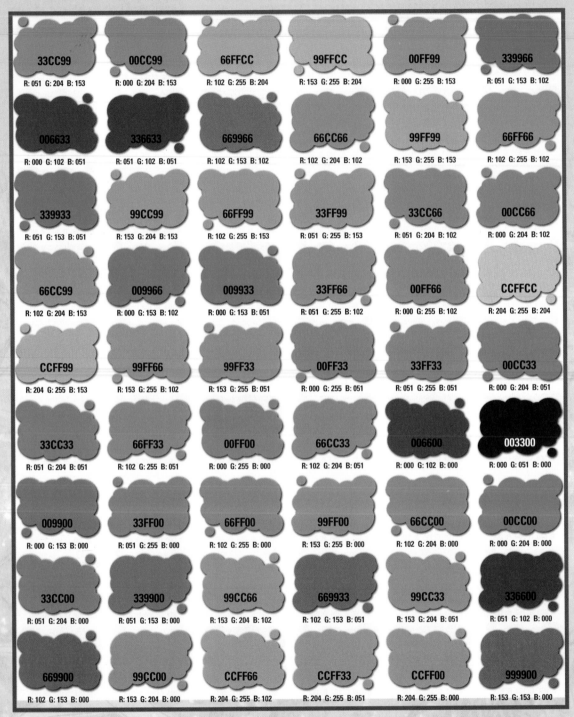

33CC99 R: 051 G: 204 B: 153	**00CC99** R: 000 G: 204 B: 153	**66FFCC** R: 102 G: 255 B: 204	**99FFCC** R: 153 G: 255 B: 204	**00FF99** R: 000 G: 255 B: 153	**339966** R: 051 G: 153 B: 102
006633 R: 000 G: 102 B: 051	**336633** R: 051 G: 102 B: 051	**669966** R: 102 G: 153 B: 102	**66CC66** R: 102 G: 204 B: 102	**99FF99** R: 153 G: 255 B: 153	**66FF66** R: 102 G: 255 B: 102
339933 R: 051 G: 153 B: 051	**99CC99** R: 153 G: 204 B: 153	**66FF99** R: 102 G: 255 B: 153	**33FF99** R: 051 G: 255 B: 153	**33CC66** R: 051 G: 204 B: 102	**00CC66** R: 000 G: 204 B: 102
66CC99 R: 102 G: 204 B: 153	**009966** R: 000 G: 153 B: 102	**009933** R: 000 G: 153 B: 051	**33FF66** R: 051 G: 255 B: 102	**00FF66** R: 000 G: 255 B: 102	**CCFFCC** R: 204 G: 255 B: 204
CCFF99 R: 204 G: 255 B: 153	**99FF66** R: 153 G: 255 B: 102	**99FF33** R: 153 G: 255 B: 051	**00FF33** R: 000 G: 255 B: 051	**33FF33** R: 051 G: 255 B: 051	**00CC33** R: 000 G: 204 B: 051
33CC33 R: 051 G: 204 B: 051	**66FF33** R: 102 G: 255 B: 051	**00FF00** R: 000 G: 255 B: 000	**66CC33** R: 102 G: 204 B: 051	**006600** R: 000 G: 102 B: 000	**003300** R: 000 G: 051 B: 000
009900 R: 000 G: 153 B: 000	**33FF00** R: 051 G: 255 B: 000	**66FF00** R: 102 G: 255 B: 000	**99FF00** R: 153 G: 255 B: 000	**66CC00** R: 102 G: 204 B: 000	**00CC00** R: 000 G: 204 B: 000
33CC00 R: 051 G: 204 B: 000	**339900** R: 051 G: 153 B: 000	**99CC66** R: 153 G: 204 B: 102	**669933** R: 102 G: 153 B: 051	**99CC33** R: 153 G: 204 B: 051	**336600** R: 051 G: 102 B: 000
669900 R: 102 G: 153 B: 000	**99CC00** R: 153 G: 204 B: 000	**CCFF66** R: 204 G: 255 B: 102	**CCFF33** R: 204 G: 255 B: 051	**CCFF00** R: 204 G: 255 B: 000	**999900** R: 153 G: 153 B: 000

CCCC00	CCCC33	333300	666600	999933	CCCC66
R: 204 G: 204 B: 000	R: 204 G: 204 B: 051	R: 051 G: 051 B: 000	R: 102 G: 102 B: 000	R: 153 G: 153 B: 051	R: 204 G: 204 B: 102
666633	999966	CCCC99	FFFFCC	FFFF99	FFFF66
R: 102 G: 102 B: 051	R: 153 G: 153 B: 102	R: 204 G: 204 B: 153	R: 255 G: 255 B: 204	R: 255 G: 255 B: 153	R: 255 G: 255 B: 102
FFFF33	FFFF00	FFCC00	FFCC66	FFCC33	CC9933
R: 255 G: 255 B: 051	R: 255 G: 255 B: 000	R: 255 G: 204 B: 000	R: 255 G: 204 B: 102	R: 255 G: 204 B: 051	R: 204 G: 153 B: 051
996600	CC9900	FF9900	CC6600	993300	CC6633
R: 153 G: 102 B: 000	R: 204 G: 153 B: 000	R: 255 G: 153 B: 000	R: 204 G: 102 B: 000	R: 153 G: 051 B: 000	R: 204 G: 102 B: 051
663300	FF9966	FF6633	FF9933	FF6600	CC3300
R: 102 G: 051 B: 000	R: 255 G: 153 B: 102	R: 255 G: 102 B: 051	R: 255 G: 153 B: 051	R: 255 G: 102 B: 000	R: 204 G: 051 B: 000
996633	330000	663333	996666	CC9999	993333
R: 153 G: 102 B: 051	R: 051 G: 000 B: 000	R: 102 G: 051 B: 051	R: 153 G: 102 B: 102	R: 204 G: 153 B: 153	R: 153 G: 051 B: 051
CC6666	FFCCCC	FF3333	CC3333	FF6666	660000
R: 204 G: 102 B: 102	R: 255 G: 204 B: 204	R: 255 G: 051 B: 051	R: 204 G: 051 B: 051	R: 255 G: 102 B: 102	R: 102 G: 000 B: 000
990000	CC0000	FF0000	FF3300	CC9966	FFCC99
R: 153 G: 000 B: 000	R: 204 G: 000 B: 000	R: 255 G: 000 B: 000	R: 255 G: 051 B: 000	R: 204 G: 153 B: 102	R: 255 G: 204 B: 153
FFFFFF	CCCCCC	999999	6C6666	333333	000000
R: 255 G: 255 B: 255	R: 204 G: 204 B: 204	R: 153 G: 153 B: 153	R: 102 G: 102 B: 102	R: 051 G: 051 B: 051	R: 000 G: 000 B: 000

HYBRID-SAFE BROWSER COLORS

Using checkerboard patterns of color derived from the 216 palette, Web designers can create a swatch of color that appears to be a non-216 color. Here are four examples.

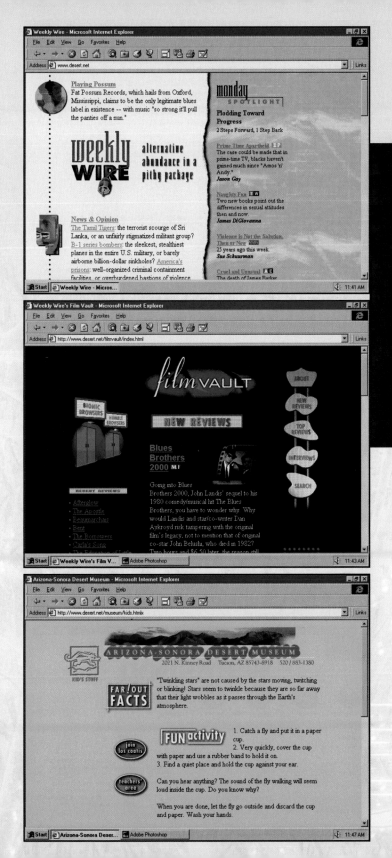

Amy Burnham

Amy is Art Director for DesertNet, an online publisher of alternative newspapers located in Tucson, Arizona. See Chapter 1.

Craig Kosak

From Microsoft headquarters in Seattle, Washington, Craig architects the look and feel of the company's top Web sites. See Chapter 2.

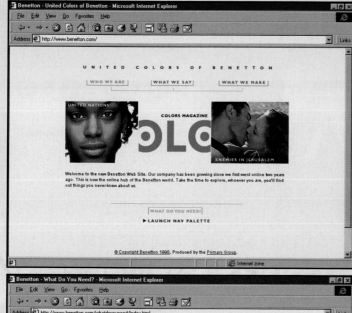

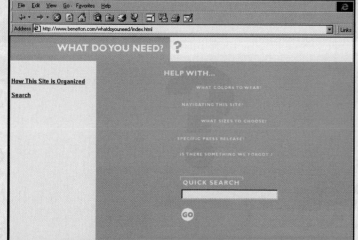

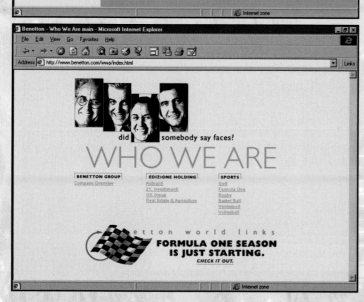

Heather Champp

Heather Champp is a New York-based designer and well-known Web personality. See Chapter 3.

Eric Eaton, Anna McMillan, and Sabine Messner

Based in San Francisco, Eric, Anna, and Sabine form the design team behind the Hotwired family of Web sites—including Webmonkey, RGB Gallery, and Hotbot. See Chapter 4.

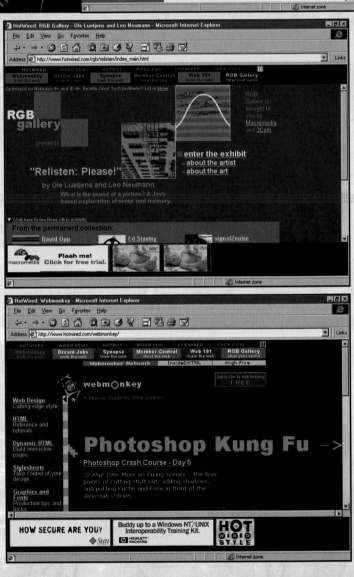

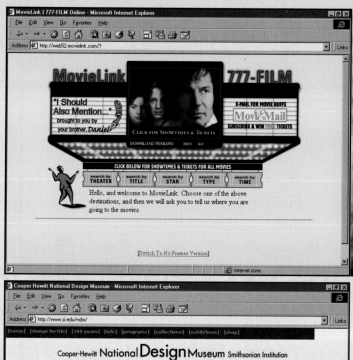

Elisabeth Roxby

Elisabeth is a freelance Web designer working and living in New York City. See Chapter 5.

Irene Fazio

Irene is Art Director for BrainBug, an interactive agency in Hartford, Connecticut. See Chapter 6.

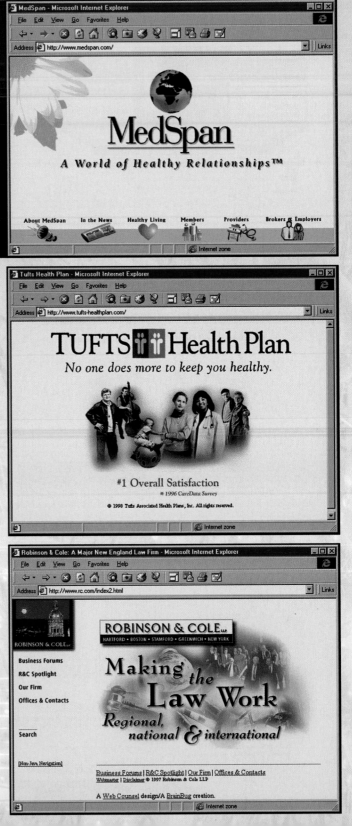

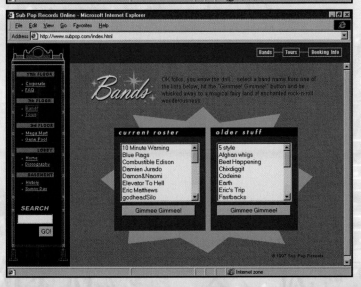

Joe Walker

Joe Walker is a freelance Web designer living and working in Seattle, Washington. See Chapter 6.

Auriea Harvey

Auriea Harvey is the

New York-based creative

force behind Entropy8.

See Chapter 7.

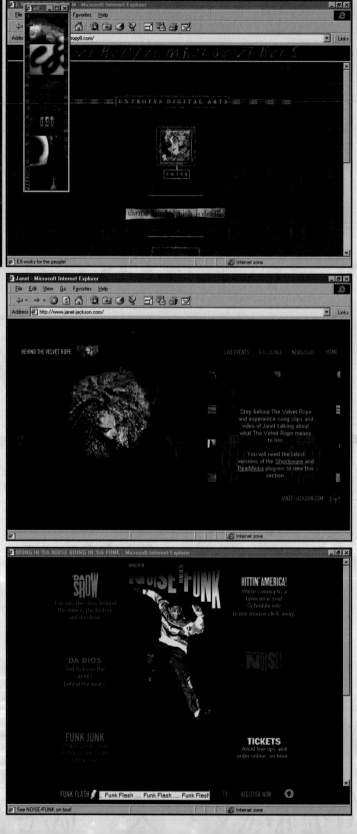

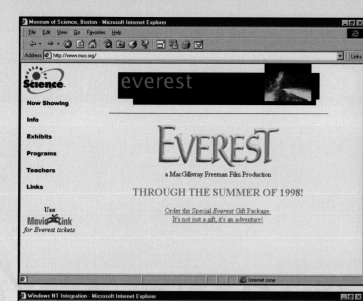

Alisha and Claudio Vera

Alisha and Claudio own and operate Black Bean Studios, a Web shop in Boston, Massachusetts. See Chapter 8.

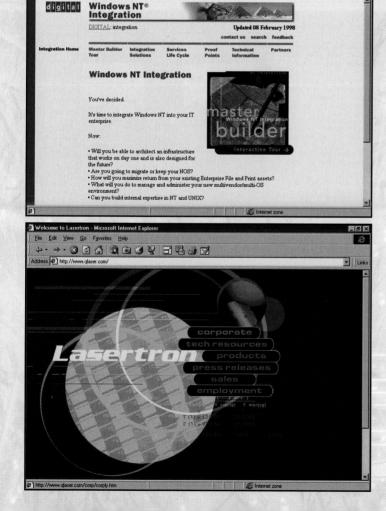

Vivian Selbo

Vivian is a conceptual Web artist living and working in New York City. See Chapter 9.

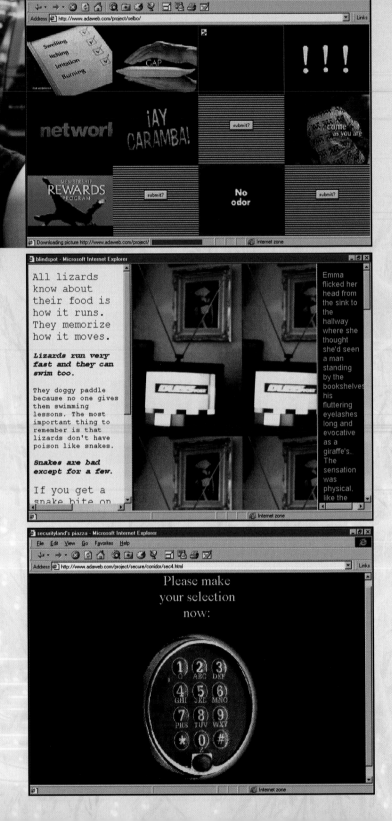

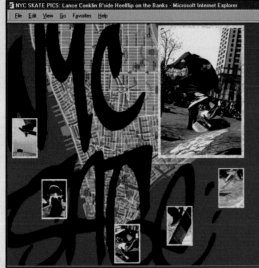

Peter Guagenti

Peter is Creative Director for Cybersight, an interactive agency headquartered in Portland, Oregon. See Chapter 10.

STRAZNITSKAS.COM

straznitskas.com *is a Web site developed specially by the author for readers of Mastering Photoshop 5 for the Web. With a look that is very reminiscent of the Photoshop interface, the site provides additional tips, links to all of the software mentioned in this book, working examples of the DHTML effects, and much more. You can visit the site at* http://www.straznitskas.com.

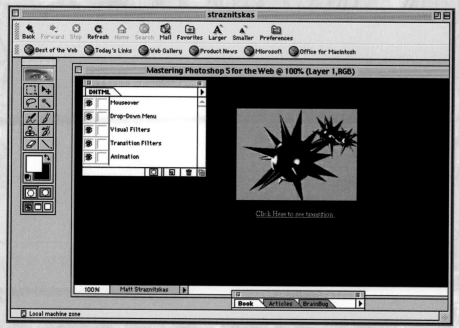

chapter 15

WEB GRAPHICS

Featuring

WEB GRAPHICS

 his is the one you've been waiting for. After working through 14 chapters—dealing with everything from channels and masks to GIFs and JPEGs—you're now ready to start creating some real Web graphics.

As you may have inferred from the preceding chapters, a Web page is not one large, single graphic. Instead, it is a mosaic of smaller, individual graphics and computer-generated type held together with HTML.

This chapter covers all of the types of graphics that comprise a typical Web page. Keep in mind that not all of the graphics mentioned need to be included on every Web page you design. Make your graphic choices based on a design's underlying theme or concept and you'll be in good shape.

Background Graphics

Using graphics to create backgrounds is a great way to add style to your pages. However, if you're going to use them, use them well. The Web is filled with graphic backgrounds that are cliché, or that clash with the design. Background graphics should serve the overall design, not detract from it.

Backgrounds can be in either GIF or JPEG format, depending on what kind of image you use. Be sure to use the graphic processing skills that you learned in Chapter 12 when designing background images. With careful optimization, you can create very complex background designs that take up little memory. Generally speaking, your backgrounds should be *less than* 20 kilobytes. On the Web, smaller is definitely better.

WARNING   Background graphics should never be transparent. It's also a good idea to avoid interlaced GIFs or progressive JPEGs. Stick to standard, noninterlaced GIFs or JPEGs for maximum background stability.

There are two main background styles: square tile and margin-style tile strip. Each style has subsets, and you will learn to work with a variety of functional as well as decorative graphic types.

Square Tiles

Strictly speaking, all backgrounds are tiles. Whether they take the form of a square or a rectangle, they literally *tile* into the available background space.

Using square tiles, you can create a pattern or wallpaper effect. Tiles should typically be 100 pixels by 100 pixels, although you will find occasion to make them larger, or perhaps smaller. The 100×100 guideline is a good one to follow in most instances of square tiling.

If you have a visible border around your tile, or a single image centered on the tile, you will end up showing the world that your background tiles are repeated (see Figure 15.1). While this effect may be desirous to your design, be aware that it is usually considered amateurish.

FIGURE 15.1

Repeated tile with visible borders

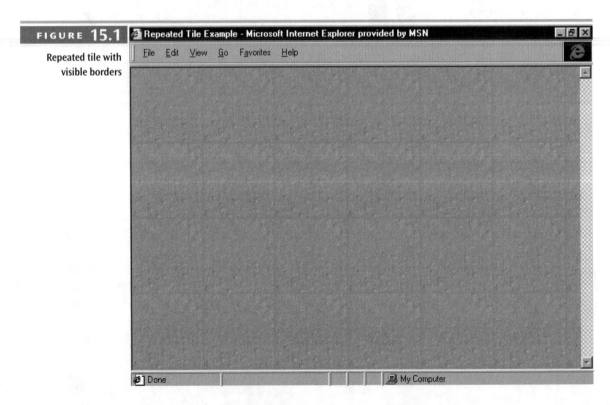

For professional results, you'll want to create a tile that is *seamless*. Seamless tiles create a visual effect much like wallpaper on a wall. The design is consistent and smooth.

Seamless Tiles

Seamless tiles often require a fine hand. The objective is to make the tiles appear continuous. You must anticipate how the tiles will fit together, and use advanced drawing techniques to ensure that a tile appears seamless. Figure 15.2 shows a seamless background tile, and Figure 15.3 shows the wallpaper-style results on an actual page.

WARNING A background tile should be appropriate in both dimensional size and kilobytes. Remember that the larger the file, the longer the load time.

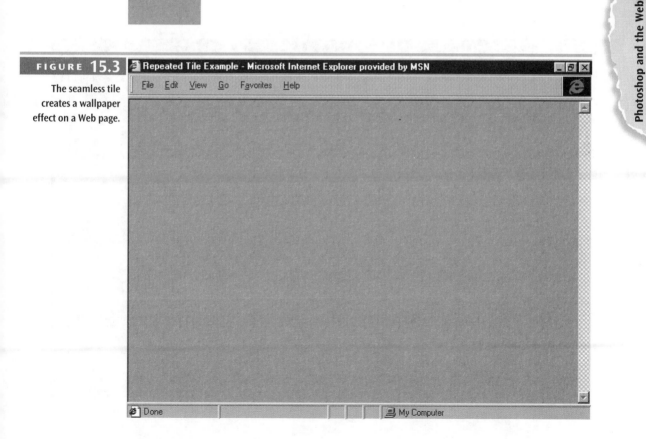

FIGURE 15.2

A seamless tile

FIGURE 15.3

The seamless tile creates a wallpaper effect on a Web page.

PART

Photoshop and the Web

N O T E   ImageReady, a new Web graphics processing program from Adobe, provides another way to create background tiles. See Appendix A for more information about ImageReady and the technique.

Whether you create your own pattern or use textures found in stock collections, you need to choose something from which to make a tile. Once you've chosen your background pattern, open up Photoshop and follow these steps:

1. Open your pattern—it could be anything from a graphic you created, something you scanned in, or a photo or texture purchased from a stock photo house.

2. From the Menu Bar, choose Select ➤ All, then Edit ➤ Define Pattern.

3. Create a large workspace file of approximately 400×400 pixels and Select Edit ➤ Fill ➤ Pattern to fill the area with your pattern.

Now you'll see how your pattern tiles look *before* you make any modifications. In Figure 15.4, you'll see some seams and repetitions that are distracting.

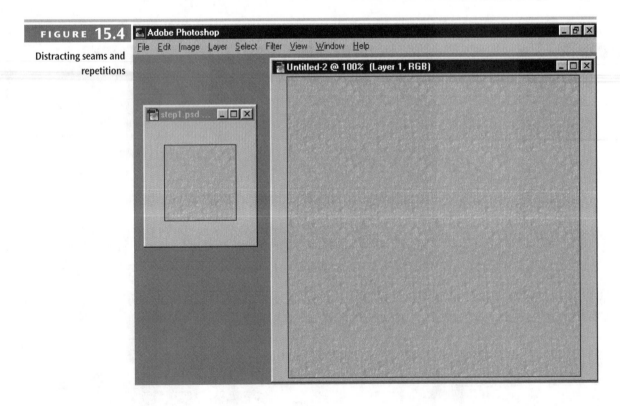

FIGURE 15.4

Distracting seams and repetitions

To hone in on the seams:

1. Select your pattern document.

2. Select Filter ➤ Other ➤ Offset.

3. In the Offset dialog, put half of the dimensions into the horizontal and vertical input boxes. For example, if your pattern is 100×100, enter 50 and 50 respectively.

4. Be sure to check Wrap Around.

5. Click OK.

This will offset your pattern so that you can see where the seams or repetitions are located.

To smooth the seams:

1. Select the Rubber Stamp tool from the Toolbar.

2. Press Alt+Click on a smooth area of your pattern.

3. Now use the Rubber Stamp tool to smooth out the pattern.

You can test your progress by selecting and defining your pattern and filling the large workspace with it. Eventually, you'll get a smooth look you're happy with (see Figure 15.5).

You can also smooth patterns by working in small areas using the Blur tool, or by cutting and pasting areas of the pattern over seams. These techniques all take patience, but if you work at it, you'll become more skilled at the process and learn to create attractive, seamless patterns with ease.

An important concern regarding background design is readability. Your background shouldn't interfere with a visitor's ability to read the text that will be placed on top of it. Be sure to fully test your design with the chosen text and link colors to ensure that both the esthetic look of the tile and the clarity of any text remain intact.

N O T E   For more information on specifying text and link colors, see Chapter 16.

PART

Photoshop and the Web

FIGURE 15.5

Smooth results

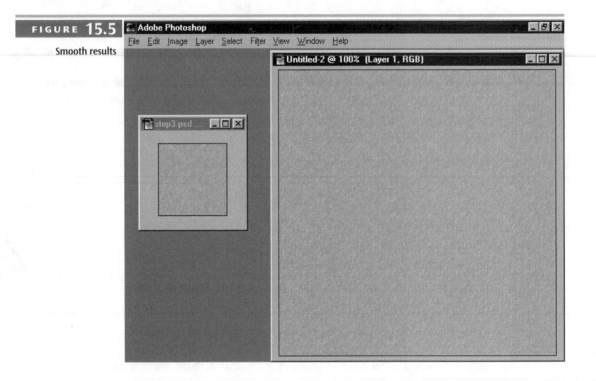

Margin Backgrounds

Margin backgrounds are extremely popular on the Web. The margin field can be made up of a flat color (see Figure 15.6) or a texture or design (see Figure 15.7). The text field can also be a flat color (see Figure 15.8) or a texture (see Figure 15.9). These combinations add a lot of visual interest to a site.

Margin backgrounds can either be decorative or functional. Decorative margins are used to create color and texture splashes, fills, or bleeds. Functional margins use the margin area for both decorative and practical purposes, such as the implementation of links, text information, buttons, or a combination thereof.

The major concern with margin backgrounds is size. Because all backgrounds are loaded in a repeat pattern, you must understand how this pattern affects the design you're creating. Vertical repetition can work to your advantage because you can keep the tile thin and use the vertical repeat to create the pattern. If a margin background's width is too short, however, it will repeat at inconvenient points along the horizontal axis in your design. Furthermore, this repetition causes problems at a variety of resolutions.

N O T E   Background graphics tile into all of the browser's available space but do not force scroll bars to appear.

FIGURE 15.6

A margin background
with flat color

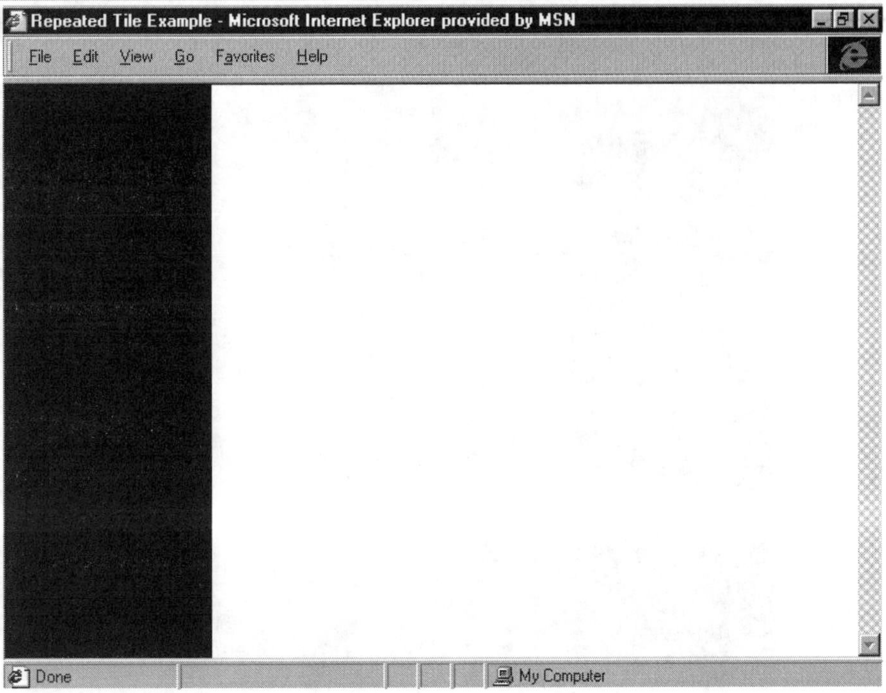

FIGURE 15.7

A margin background
with a textured
margin field

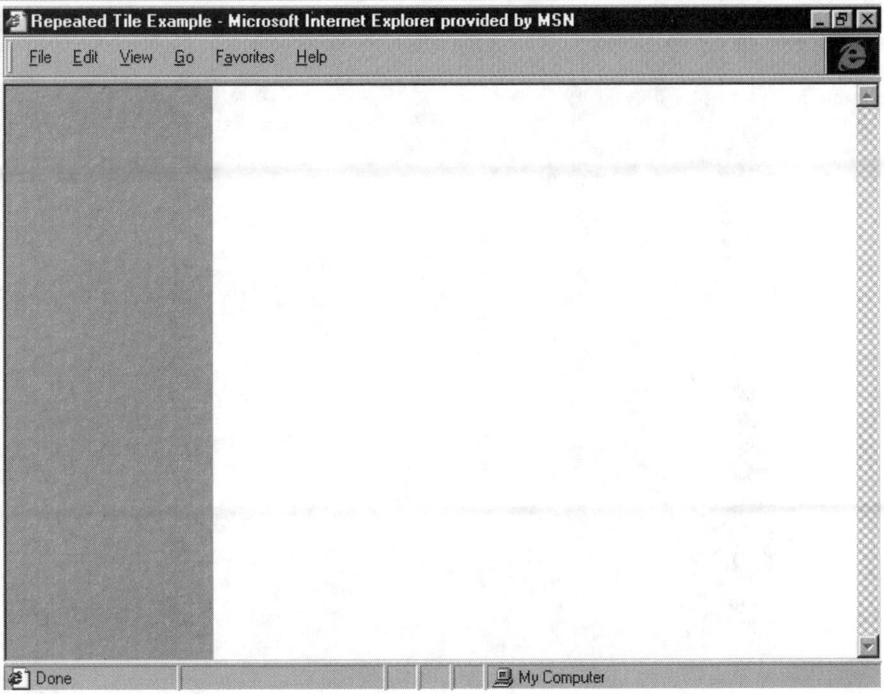

FIGURE 15.8

A margin background with both texture and flat color

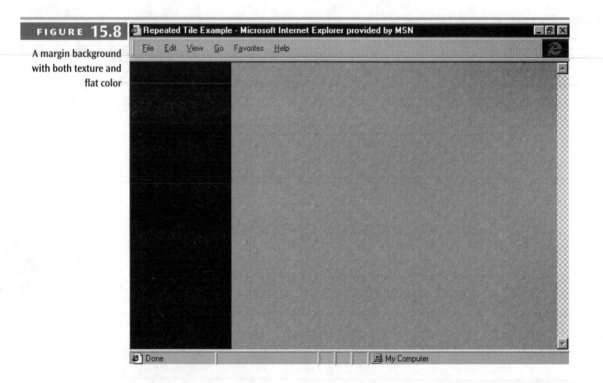

FIGURE 15.9

A margin background with texture in both areas

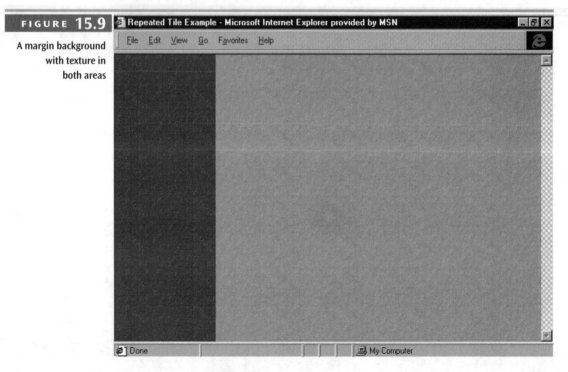

If I create a tile that is 640 pixels in width, and I'm viewing on a screen that has a 640×480 resolution, I'll see the background that I created without running the risk of it repeating on the horizontal axis. But what happens when I view the same page at an 800×600 resolution or higher? The tile repeats (see Figure 15.10).

FIGURE 15.10

A background that isn't wide enough risks being repeated at a higher resolution.

Designers remedy this by designing vertical tiles at an average of 1200 pixels in width. Your height can vary to accommodate the design. The suggested height is at least 20-30 pixels, because some older browsers have trouble with backgrounds that are very short.

Top margin designs work in a similar fashion, but the repeat axis problem occurs in reverse. If you don't make the tile long enough to fit the page, the top margin will repeat (see Figure 15.11). Therefore, top margin backgrounds should be long—as long as you need for a given page. The width can be kept short, however, as the tiling mechanism will fill the page appropriately (see Figure 15.12).

WARNING Test your Web page backgrounds on as many computers and browsers as possible. You'll be surprised how often text and graphics will move around in different environments and ruin your background effect.

PART

Photoshop and the Web

FIGURE 15.11

A vertical tile repeating on the horizontal axis

FIGURE 15.12

The desired effect of a top-margin tile

Making a Decorative Margin

Decorative margins use a pattern within the margin (see Figure 15.13).

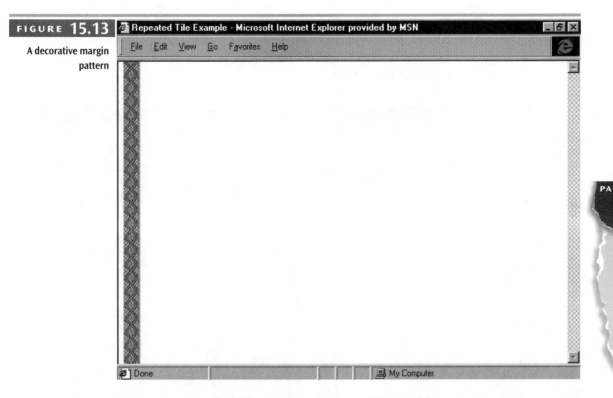

FIGURE 15.13

A decorative margin pattern

Just as square tiles repeat and require smoothing, you'll need to ensure that your tile is smooth along the edges. Open Photoshop and follow these steps:

1. Create a new file, with dimensions 1200 pixels wide by 50 pixels high.

2. Fill the file with the color or pattern you want.

3. Make a new layer and add the decorative pattern to the section desired. In my example, I've added a decorative strip to the left.

4. Use the offset technique described under "Seamless Tiles" earlier in the chapter to ensure that the horizontal edges of the decorative layer are smooth.

5. Flatten the image.

6. Optimize it accordingly (GIF or JPEG, depending upon the type of design and colors).

Functional Margins

Essentially, a functional margin is similar to a decorative margin, except that you must have enough room for content as well as ensure that any pattern you use does not interfere with the text or graphics that will go on top of it.

To build a functional margin, follow the same steps for creating a decorative margin in the previous section. Remember, however, that a functional margin will typically be wider (see Figure 15.14).

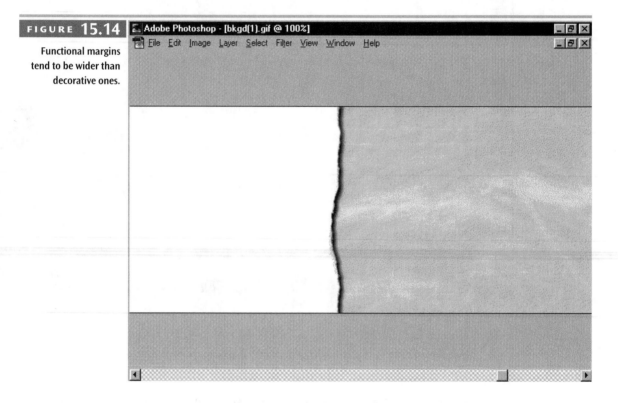

FIGURE 15.14

Functional margins tend to be wider than decorative ones.

Full Background Design (Watermarks)

Sometimes you'll want to use full-size images as a background. In these instances, you'll have to determine how to handle repetition—people with very large monitors might see the image repeat down the page depending on how large you make it. Unless it's at least 800 pixels deep by 1200 pixels wide, many people will be able to see it repeat. Another concern with full backgrounds is file size. Logically, the larger the file's dimensions, the bigger the file will be in terms of kilobytes. However, if designed and optimized properly, the file sizes can remain within acceptable limits and the effects can be quite interesting (see Figures 15.15 and 15.16).

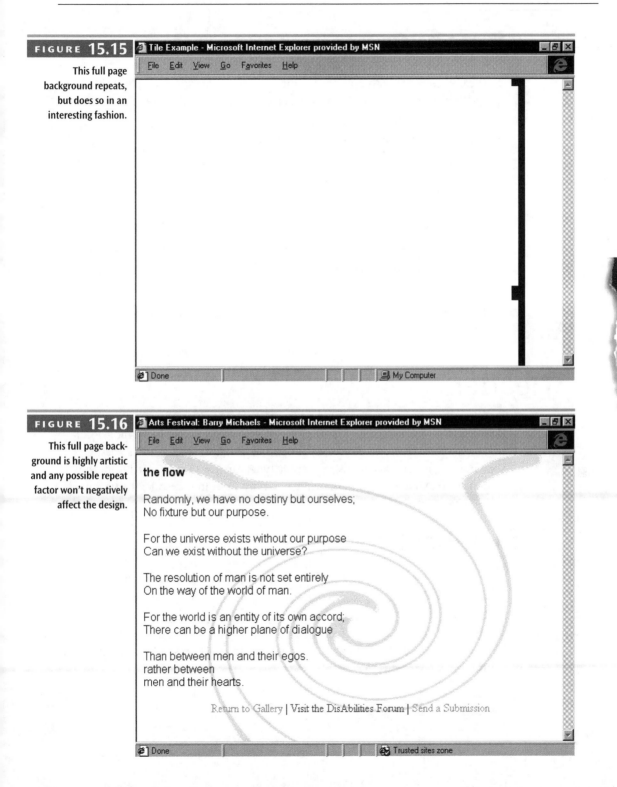

FIGURE 15.15

This full page background repeats, but does so in an interesting fashion.

FIGURE 15.16

This full page background is highly artistic and any possible repeat factor won't negatively affect the design.

Making a Watermark

To make a watermark, open Photoshop and follow these steps:

1. Create a new file with appropriate dimensions, preparing for an 800×600 average, but keeping in mind that visitors will be viewing the site at 640×480 and higher resolutions.

2. Fill the file with your Web-safe background color.

3. Make a new layer.

4. Add your watermark to the new layer.

5. Use the opacity slider to adjust image for the best visual advantage.

6. Save the file.

Typically, watermarks are best saved as JPEGs. If you only have a few areas of solid color, however, you will do well with GIFs.

 WARNING   Older Web browsers do not support JPEG files as a background image format.

Headers

Using graphical headers is a nice departure from tired HTML-based text headers. You can add logo-graphic material, control your choice of fonts (see Chapter 14 for more information on graphic type), and use colors, patterns, and light sources as you so desire.

Shown below is a flat header using graphic type. Already I've departed from the limitations of HTML-based text, and while you only see it in grayscale, the type uses several colors and variations.

Flat Header

Next, I've added a pattern to the header. As a result, it's now more interesting.

Textured Text

But there's still more I can do with it. Now I've added a drop shadow, which adds a little fun to the look.

Compare these headers to the plain HTML header shown below, and you can easily see why graphic headers are so attractive to designers.

Plain Ol' HTML Header

Building a Standard Header

Headers for most Web sites measure approximately 350×50 pixels, although this will vary greatly depending upon your look and feel. However, for the sake of clarity, we'll stick to the standard size. Don't be afraid to experiment, though, and use a variety of sizes and even vertical versus horizontal headers. Just keep good design sense in mind!

To build a standard header, follow these steps:

1. In Photoshop, select File ➤ New.
2. Set the dimensions for 350×50.
3. Fill the background with a Web-safe color.
4. Set your text with the Type tool (see Chapter 14).

Buttons

Buttons, like headers, help add color, style, and interest to your Web pages. Buttons can be a combination of images, logo-graphic material, and type. In the following exercises, we'll work with type, but you should feel free to experiment with a variety of graphic material.

Creating a Flat Button

Flat buttons are very similar to standard headers, except that their size is obviously going to be different! We'll work with buttons that are 100×25 pixels in dimension. Follow these steps:

1. Select File ➤ New.
2. Prepare a file 100×25 pixels in size.
3. Fill the first layer with the Web-safe background color appropriate to your Web page's design.
4. Make another layer.
5. Select your type with the Type tool.
6. Set the type.

PART

Photoshop and the Web

If you like the results, save the image as a Web graphic (see below).

Home

Add texture and shadows just as you would with standard headers.

Making Buttons for Mouseover Applications

These days, mouseover applications using JavaScript or DHTML are popular and easy-to-create enhancements to Web sites. One of the most common methods of creating dynamic movement is by using a *mouseover*, which forces a graphic to change as the mouse passes over it.

One of the most elegant designs is the change of text color on mouseover. To create this effect, you will be required to have two different buttons for each button option, one that will be the standard, or static button, and the other button being the mouse-over button.

Where many people go astray with mouseover buttons is that they initially create two separate buttons and try to match up the location of the text by hand. This is quite imperfect, and will cause inconsistencies in the way the mouseover state appears.

To create duplicate buttons with different text colors, you'll take advantage of Photoshop's Layers feature. Follow these steps:

1. Select File ➤ New to make a new file. Button dimensions tend to be no bigger than 100 pixels wide and 30 pixels tall.

2. Fill the background with your Web-safe color.

3. Select the Text tool and set your type using your static color.

4. Select Layer ➤ Type ➤ Render Layer to rasterize the type.

5. Copy the text layer.

6. Select the new text layer.

7. Fill with the mouseover color.

8. Save the file in PSD format so it will be available for further modification.

To generate the static button, follow these steps:

1. Open the Photoshop file that contains your button.

2. Hide the mouseover layer (see Figure 15.17).

3. Convert the image to Indexed Color mode.

4. Select File ➤ Export ➤ GIF89 to export this file as a GIF89.

5. Save it with a name that identifies it as the static button, such as `b-off.gif`.

FIGURE 15.17

Hiding the
mouseover layer

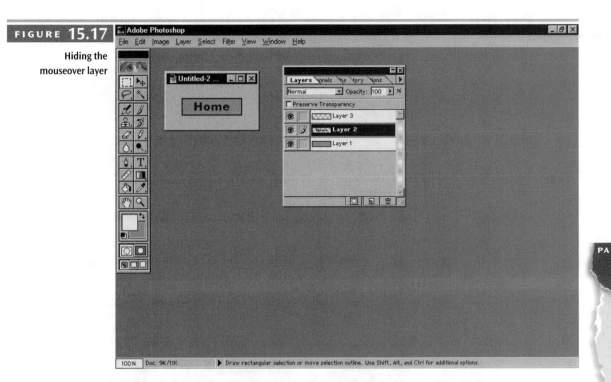

To generate the mouseover button, follow these steps:

1. Return to the Photoshop file.

2. Turn your static color off.

3. Unhide the mouseover layer (see Figure 15.18).

4. Convert the image to Indexed Color mode.

5. Select File ➤ Export ➤ GIF89 to export this file as a GIF89.

6. Save the file with an appropriate name, such as b-on.gif.

N O T E   See Chapter 18 for a script that will make your mouseover graphics come to life!

N O T E   Photoshop 5's new Bevel and Emboss feature (Layer ➤ Effects ➤ Bevel and Emboss) provides a convenient way to create beveled buttons. Also, several pre-prepared beveling actions are available in Photoshop (see Chapter 9).

PART

Photoshop and the Web

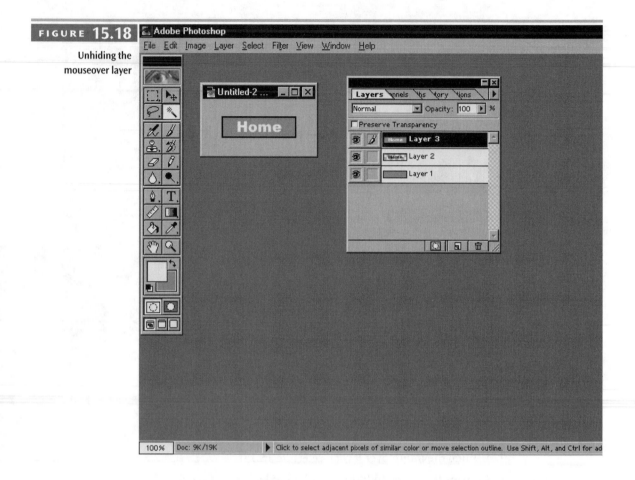

FIGURE **15.18**

Unhiding the
mouseover layer

Image Maps

In Chapter 16, I will discuss how to arrange text and graphics with HTML to create interactive Web pages. One of these interactive devices is called an image map. *Image maps* are images that are broken down into sections and made "hot." In other words, each section is linked to a separate Web page.

Photoshop comes in handy when you are drawing or selecting map files to make into an image map and to optimize the mapped image. However, the actual act of mapping is much more easily accomplished using one of the many inexpensive mapping utilities available.

When creating image maps, first select an image that lends itself to mapping. Ideally, this means something that has very specific sections to it, as shown in Figure 15.19. Image maps are often the graphic-type variety, as in Figure 15.20.

FIGURE 15.19

This image has specific areas that make it a good choice for mapping.

FIGURE 15.20

Maps are often comprised of graphic type.

In either case, the individual areas must be noted by coordinates so the server will know what page to present when a user clicks through the map. Your mapping tool will generate the coordinates for you. On the PC, I like to use MapEdit (which is included on the CD-ROM that comes with this book). On the Macintosh, WebMap is a popular image mapping program and is available from `http://www.webmap.com/`. Many of the WYSIWYG HTML editors mentioned in Chapter 16 provide built-in image mapping, and ImageReady, the new Web graphics tool from Adobe, also provides a way to create image maps using Layers.

Figure 15.21 shows my image in the mapping interface.

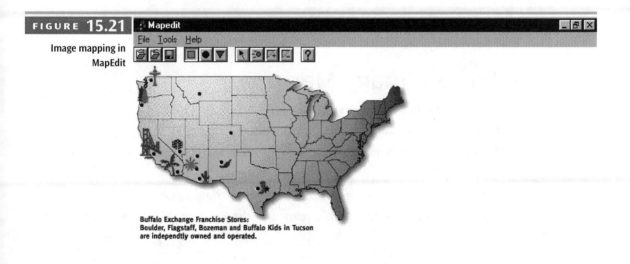

FIGURE 15.21

Image mapping in MapEdit

Here's a look at the resulting syntax:

```
<map name="Map">
<area shape="polygon"
coords="15,9,51,9,51,34,35,34,26,37,18,37,9,31,3,15,16,18,15,10"
href="wa.htm">
<area shape="polygon"
coords="7,66,34,66,34,91,66,120,71,129,67,133,69,150,51,151,45,132,29,124,29
,122,6,80,7,68" href="ca.htm">
<area shape="polygon"
coords="68,115,74,130,71,132,70,152,94,151,102,151,102,107,73,107,71,113,68,
113" href="az.htm">
<area shape="polygon"
coords="105,107,105,151,108,151,108,157,150,157,152,106,105,106"
href="nm.htm">
<area shape="polygon"
coords="36,66,70,66,70,104,68,108,65,112,65,115,35,89,36,68" href="nv.htm">
<area shape="polygon"
coords="155,110,161,110,161,125,185,131,198,133,199,154,202,153,201,162,158,
159,180,193,168,190,153,163,155,163,151,150,132,162,122,159,154,150,154,110"
href="tx.htm">
<area shape="polygon" coords="52,36,53,63,6,63,10,33,19,41,50,36"
href="or.htm">
<area shape="rect" coords="104,75,157,105" href="co.htm">
<area shape="polygon"
coords="59,15,135,15,135,46,92,48,90,52,79,53,73,43,68,42,70,35,59,25"
href="mt.htm">
</map>
```

In this case, each area that links to a page has its coordinates provided. Note that the polygon shape requires a lot of coordinates.

Building an Image Map

To build an image map, follow these steps:

1. Select the image you want to map using Photoshop.

2. Make any adjustments such as cropping, filtering, and adding decorative elements.

3. Save the file and move to your mapping program.

4. Define the areas you want mapped using the program's tools.

5. Generate the coordinates and save them in the associated HTML file.

6. Save and close the graphic file.

7. Reopen the file in Photoshop and apply optimization techniques to the file.

Once you put the file into the HTML for your Web page, and as long as the coordinates and appropriate syntax within the image source are intact, you will have a fully functioning image map!

Photos and Illustrations

Photos and illustrations add visual information to a Web page. The trick with these kinds of images is to enhance the overall design rather than detract from it. Sometimes you'll want to use a standard photo or illustration, but other times applying a graphic edge to your material will be in order.

In Figure 15.22, I've used a photograph that is set flat on the page. Figure 15.23 shows the same photograph with an edge effect applied.

FIGURE 15.22

A photograph set in a Web page with no enhancements

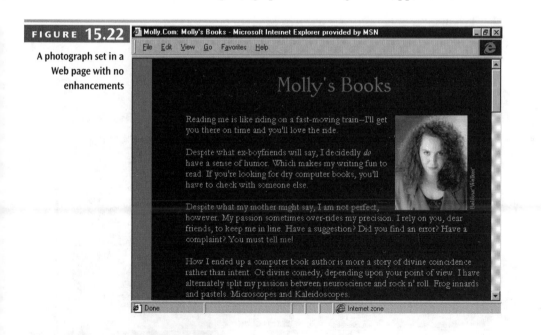

FIGURE 15.23

The same photograph with an edge effect

Adding a Special Effect to a Photo

For this exercise, I used a filter from the Auto F/X Photographic Edges collection. This collection is quite expensive, but you can find less expensive and even free edge effect filters on the Web.

1. Open the photo or illustration to which you'd like to add a special effect in Photoshop.

2. Prior to adding the edge effect, be sure you've repaired any spot problems and cropped the graphic appropriately.

3. Once you are satisfied with your photo's look, select Filter ➤ Auto F/X ➤ Photographic Edges.

4. The Auto F/X Photographic Edges dialog will appear (see Figure 15.24).

5. Choose your effects.

6. Adjust the look of the edge.

7. Click Apply.

Auto F/X will apply the edges for a nice-looking final result!

FIGURE 15.24

Choosing effects in the Photographic Edges dialog

Advertising Banners

As mentioned in Chapter 11, search engines and other content-driven Web sites tend to rely on ad banners to support themselves. Thus, designers are often asked by clients to create ad banners that will grab attention and drive visitors to a particular Web site. Ad banners are also used as "house ads" to promote other areas or happenings within a Web site.

Advertising banners on the Internet typically adhere to a specific dimension of 468×60 pixels (see Figure 15.25). The only time it's a good idea to deviate from this convention is when a particular content provider has unique requirements (see Figure 15.26).

FIGURE 15.25

A standard-size ad banner, 468×60

FIGURE 15.26

A nonstandard-size ad banner, 375×50

PART

Photoshop and the Web

Banners should also follow some of these guidelines:

- Banners should be GIF or JPEG files. Some companies use other technologies as well, such as Java or Shockwave.
- Banners should be fairly small in file size. Eight kilobytes is a good maximum for GIFs or JPEGs.
- Animated GIFs—a popular method of getting inviting, active information into a banner—should be no more than 12 kilobytes maximum. Images should not "loop" more than three times.

Again, individual content providers may have their own requirements. Be sure to contact your provider's sales rep for a list of exact specifications.

Creating a Standard Advertising Banner

To create a standard advertising banner, be sure to follow the guidelines in the prior section. Then follow these steps:

1. Select File ➤ New.
2. Create a file that is 468×60 pixels.
3. Select Edit ➤ Fill and fill with the Web-safe color of your choice.
4. Add type or images as appropriate.
5. Flatten, save, and optimize the banner.

Your banner is ready for prime time!

Conclusion

Now that you've seen the different kinds of Web graphics that are commonly created, you may think Photoshop is overloaded with features for such work. In many cases, this is true—a Web designer will seldom use half the tools that Photoshop provides. Like graphic type, you *should* be able to tell a browser that you want a striped background image or rounded navigation button.

On the other hand, it's doubtful that browser manufacturers will ever provide a range of built-in graphics options that will satisfy designers. Just imagine the kind of canned background textures a programmer might make available to us!

The issue of choice is the reason why Photoshop is so popular with Web designers. It may provide far more features than a typical Web designer will need, but at least it provides them all. It's far better to let designers choose their tools than to have programmers choose for them.

Up Next

Congratulations, you've finished Part II of this book! If completion of Part I represented a Bachelors degree, then completion of Part II marks a Masters degree. Now it's time to learn about using HTML, Cascading Style Sheets, and Dynamic HTML so you can put your Photoshop graphics to use in actual Web pages.

Mastering the Medium:
The Business of Being in Business

At some point in their professional lives, many Web designers will either work full or part time as a freelancer. A freelancer is an independent contractor who tends to work from a home-based office. With the advent of inexpensive computer technology, freelancing has become a very popular way for designers to maintain a full or partial income.

The life of a freelancer can be very attractive, especially the flexible hours and casual dress. But new freelancers are sometimes unprepared for the duties associated with running a business. Here are a few issues:

Marketing/PR   For a young freelancer with few industry contacts, developing a client base is critical. Artists and designers tend to be introverts, but this is no time to be a shrinking violet. Get your face in front of people and use techniques like phone calls, e-mail, direct mail, and Web sites to stay in touch.

Timesheets   Most people hate paperwork, but it is essential for Web designers to keep a record of all time put into a job—including time spent with a client in meetings, on the phone, and so on. Without such records, it is impossible to know whether or not you're losing money on a job. Plus, if you have a dispute with a client over billing, timesheets provide the only physical evidence of the time that was put into a job.

Expenses   Be sure to keep a tally of all out-of-pocket expenses that you put into a job. For example, if a client prefers to see color prints of a Web site as it is being developed, this expense should be billed back to the client at cost. Other examples include overnight delivery and long-distance travel. Expenses usually not billed back to the client include phone calls, faxes, and car mileage.

Bookkeeping   Whether you use pencil and paper or programs like Quickbooks or Peachtree, you must keep track of all of the money flowing in and out of your business. On a month-by-month basis, track what you billed out, what you actually received, and how much you spent on hardware, software, and other controllable expenses. Only by doing this can you determine how much you're *actually* making being in business for yourself.

Taxes   Unlike bookkeeping, taxes are not a do-it-yourself activity. Find a good local accountant who prefers to work with small businesses and hire them once a year to do your taxes. It will be the best money you'll ever spend. Also, be sure to save all of your receipts. If the IRS ever comes knocking, you'll need them.

Collections   Designers tend to be nice people who will kill themselves to make the client happy. Unfortunately, in business, nice people can finish last—especially when it comes to getting paid. Sometimes clients can't or won't pay their bills, and they tend to not pay those who are the easiest to put off. Do yourself a favor and befriend a good lawyer. After you've sent multiple invoices to no avail, you'll be glad you know someone who can make an effective collection call.

Beyond the duties of being in business, it is important for freelancers to have their own space, even if that space is in their home. Find a work area with a door. Not only is a door important so you can maintain a quiet work environment, but a door can also be shut when you're done working for the day/night. One of the problems with working from home is that it's very hard to leave your work at the office. If your work area is out of sight, it will create some definition between working and living.

Finally, it is critical for freelance Web designers to find support and community to combat the job's biggest drawback: loneliness. Without regular human contact, the normal ups and downs of running your own business can seem worse than they really are. Do yourself a favor and schedule some time to spend with others.

PART

Photoshop and the Web

WEB PAGE DESIGN

HTML

Featuring

HTML

If you've been reading this book from beginning to end, by now you know how to use Photoshop to create all sorts of Web graphics—everything from colorful menu buttons to eye-catching animations. But how do you bring them all together to form an actual Web page? At least for now, the answer is with Hypertext Markup Language (HTML).

As I discussed in Chapter 11, HTML was intended to describe the structure of a Web document, not the layout of a page. But where there's a will there's a way, and crafty Web designers have come up with tricks and workarounds for creating attractive layouts with HTML.

In this chapter, I'll show you how to conceptualize a Web page design with Photoshop. I'll also cover some of the tools that can make a designer's foray into coding a little easier. Finally, I'll delve into the basics of HTML and make some of the layout ideas a reality with tables and frames.

Designing Web Pages

So what does it take to become a great Web page designer? Some people say it takes creativity, but the real answer is time: time to learn what great design is and how to create effective layouts despite HTML's limitations.

Every designer has their own approach to designing Web pages, but they all start by visualizing some ideas, either in their mind or on paper. After they have some rough concepts defined, the designer fires up the computer and refines their sketches with a tool like Photoshop.

Good Thinking

During the initial stages of Web page design, you can benefit by shutting your computer off. Why? Because tools like Photoshop make us lazy. The program's ability to create stunning graphic effects often blinds us to the fact that we really haven't solved a design problem. Instead, we've created pretty images that have done nothing to organize Web-site content or provide good user experiences.

Before you can solve a design problem, you need to identify it. Begin by thinking about the following questions:

- What is the nature of the Web site you are creating? Are you trying to entertain people with games and multimedia or present mainly textual information—company health benefits, product listings, and so on?

- What company or organization are you creating the Web site for and what is their brand identity? Is it a national chain of yogurt stores or a non-profit organization? What are their colors, fonts, and other graphic standards?

- What are the main areas of the Web site that people will need access to from every page? How will second-, third-, or fourth-level pages be accessed?

Putting It on Paper

As soon as you've got a sense of the design problem you're trying to solve, get out some paper and begin sketching some design ideas. In Figure 16.1, I've presented a few rough ideas of what a Web page might look like. Since this site contains a great deal of information, I came up with some clean designs that provide clear navigation to the major portions of the site.

Photoshop as a Layout Tool

Once you've identified a design problem and sketched some ideas, it's time to fire up the computer and take the concepts to the next level. Photoshop is the best tool for this because a page you develop with the program can later comprise the actual graphics used on the Web. The large, single file can be edited into individual graphics and exported for use in Web pages—a great time-saver!

Based on my loose sketches, I used Photoshop to create the file depicted in Figure 16.2.

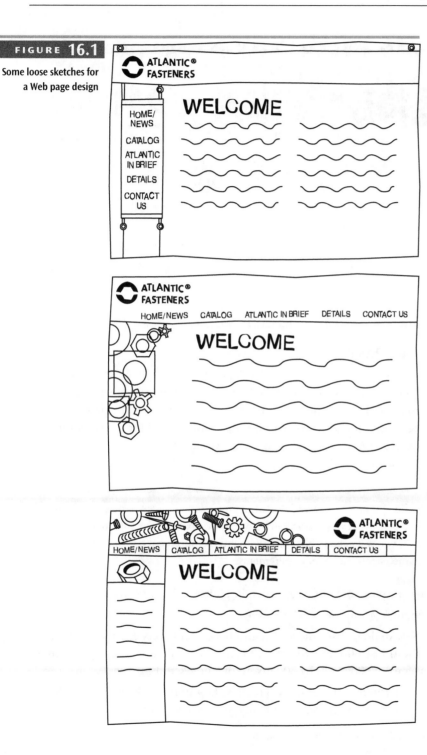

FIGURE 16.1

Some loose sketches for
a Web page design

FIGURE **16.2**

The layout for the Web
page created in
Photoshop

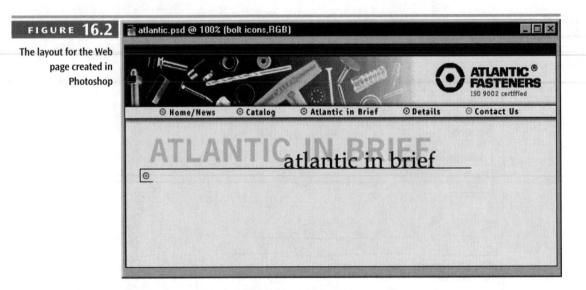

Now we'll cover some of the steps it takes to create such a design in Photoshop.

Creating the Page

The first step is to launch Photoshop and create a new file. As I mentioned in Chapter 1, most Web designers create pages that are no larger than 600 pixels wide by 300 pixels deep in order to accommodate the smallest computer monitors and the worst resolutions. Designing to this dimension will create a page with no scrolling on either the horizontal or vertical axes. While your page length can certainly vary, it's wise to keep to the 600-pixel width to avoid unstable design.

N O T E   How long should a Web page be? Most professionals recommend using approximately three screens. That would give you between 300 pixels and about 1,000 pixels per page. Obviously, you will need to be flexible with this measurement depending upon your audience and the page's particular requirements.

To create a workspace for your page design in Photoshop, follow these steps:

1. Open Photoshop, and select File ➤ New.

2. In the New dialog, enter the width and height in pixels. Remember that the width should be 600, but the length can vary. In Figure 16.2, I've created a working area of 600 pixels by 300 pixels for a non-scrolling page.

3. Be sure that you're working in RGB (you will optimize individual graphics later on), using a transparent page, and that you are set at 72 dpi.

Now you're ready to add color and images.

Using Layers

As you learned in Chapter 7, Layers are perhaps the most powerful aspect of Photoshop because you can have absolute control over each part of a design. Remember to create a new layer for each part of your page.

Here's how to build a page using layers:

1. Select Layer ➤ New ➤ Layer.

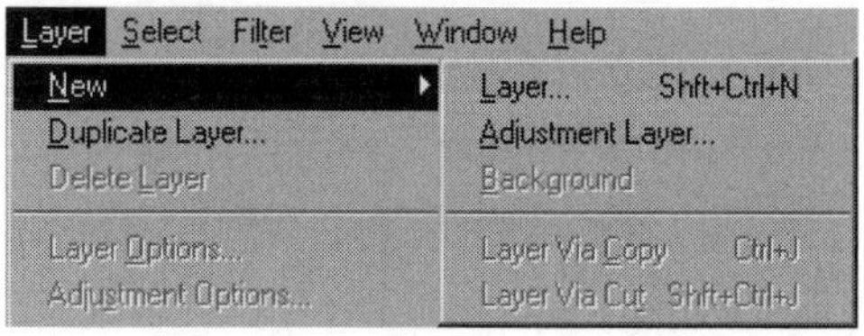

2. Select your background color using the Eyedropper tool—it's in the lower part of the Toolbar next to the Paintbucket.

3. Choose Edit ➤ Fill, and fill the layer with a browser-safe color selection. In this case, I'm using white. Make sure you select Foreground and uncheck the Transparency box in the Fill dialog.

Next I'll add the logo (see Figure 16.3) to the page.

FIGURE 16.3

The logo to be used on the Web page

4. Create a new layer, following the directions in step 1.

5. Open the logo file. Choose Image ➤ Image Size, and appropriately size your logo to the space using the Image Size dialog.

6. Choose Select ➤ All.

7. Choose Edit ➤ Copy.

8. Move to your new layer on the workspace.

9. Choose Edit ➤ Paste and paste your image onto the layer.

10. Now select the Move tool and move the image where you want it (see Figure 16.4).

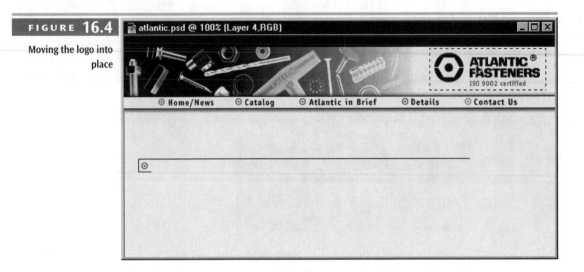

FIGURE 16.4

Moving the logo into place

Now I'm going to add a text header:

11. Select the Text tool and click on your workspace to bring up the Type Tool dialog. This will automatically create a new layer for you.

12. Now choose your typeface, size, leading, and spacing. In most cases you'll want to be sure you have the Anti-aliased checkbox checked.

13. Click OK.

14. Using the Move tool, place the text where you want it (see Figure 16.5).

FIGURE 16.5

Moving the text header
into place

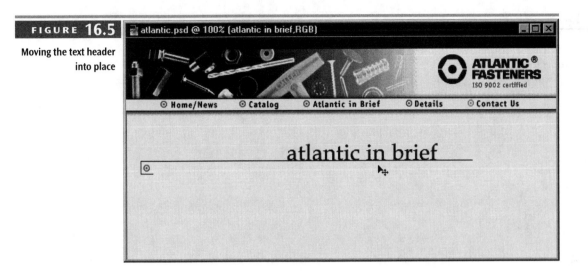

Obviously, we didn't cover every step that went into the creation of this graphic, but by now you can probably figure out how it was done. Imagery was scanned in and placed at the top of the page. Other icons and text elements were inserted into the image on separate layers.

You can anticipate body text by creating individual layers with the paragraphs you'll want to use, but in most cases you'll be relying on HTML to create that text. Default body text is typically 12 point Times on the PC and 12 point Geneva on the Macintosh.

Exporting Files

When creating actual Web pages, it isn't practical to save entire 600×300 images as Web graphics—the time it would take to download these bulky graphics would be unworkable. Instead, Web designers must strategically chop up their Photoshop layout into smaller pieces and then align those graphics with HTML.

When you're ready to make individual graphics out of the layered files you've created, do this:

1. Open your PSD file.

2. Determine what portion of the image you're going to save and turn off all the unnecessary layers. In Figure 16.6, I've turned off everything but the graphics and text for the page header.

3. Use the Rectangular Marquee tool to select the smallest possible area around the header without clipping off any parts of the header (see Figure 16.7).

4. Select Image ➤ Crop to crop the image.

5. As detailed in Chapter 12, convert the image to Indexed Color mode and save the file as a GIF.

Now the GIF can be used in an HTML Web page layout.

PART

Web Page Design

FIGURE 16.6
The file with just the
page header layers
activated

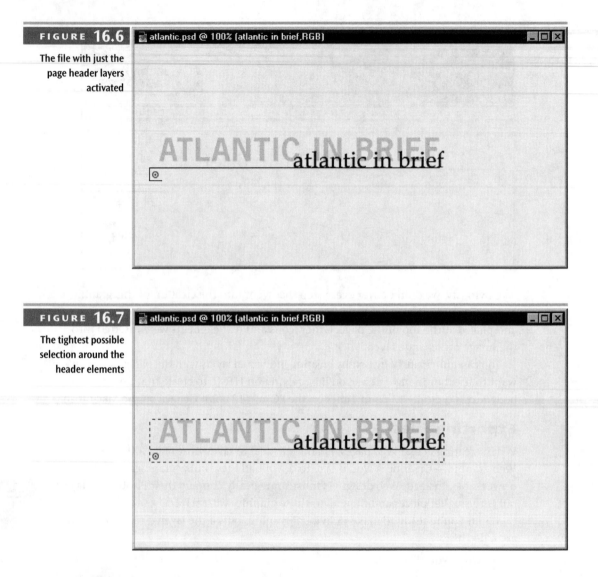

FIGURE 16.7
The tightest possible
selection around the
header elements

TIP When saving cropped graphics, it's a good idea to jot down the height and width of the images. As you'll learn later in the chapter, specifying the height and width of an image in HTML is very important.

HTML Tools

There are three primary methods of generating HTML. The text, or ASCII, editor is the most rudimentary, but it offers skilled coders tremendous control over their pages. The HTML editing environment is a middle-range solution, offering a text-based interface with power tools for creating HTML. The What-You-See-Is-What-You-Get (WYSIWYG) editor is completely graphical, but offers much less control over the code generated.

Text Editors

Old school coders will insist that the best way to create HTML documents is the simplest: by hand with text editors. There are many advantages to the pure text environment. First and foremost, text environments demand that you actually learn HTML! Text editors force you to become a knowledgeable coder—eventually you'll know every tag by heart. The other advantage is that you'll never be at the mercy of a software program. You'll know what you're doing and why you're doing it.

Another significant advantage is that troubleshooting is a breeze when you're familiar with what everything means. You can identify trouble spots with ease instead of muddling through fat code produced by a weighty interface.

The better you know HTML, the more creative you can be with it, too. Most software programs are confined to a specific method of doing things—and this method may not always be the most effective or flexible. Software programs are also limited by HTML version releases and can only keep up with so much information. Knowing code always gives you the edge in terms of what new tricks you choose to add to your HTML repertoire.

Finally, when you know HTML, you can take it anywhere. Whether you end up working within a software package or simply pull up that plain text editor, *you* are the versatile power tool!

So where do you find a text editor? Chances are, you've already got one—all computer platforms ship with a native editor. For people working on the PC platform, there are a number of editors that can be used to create HTML documents. Windows Notepad in both the 3.1 and 95 versions is a favorite among text-coding fans (see Figure 16.8). The Macintosh OS comes with a text editor called SimpleText that can be used for programming HTML.

PART

Web Page Design

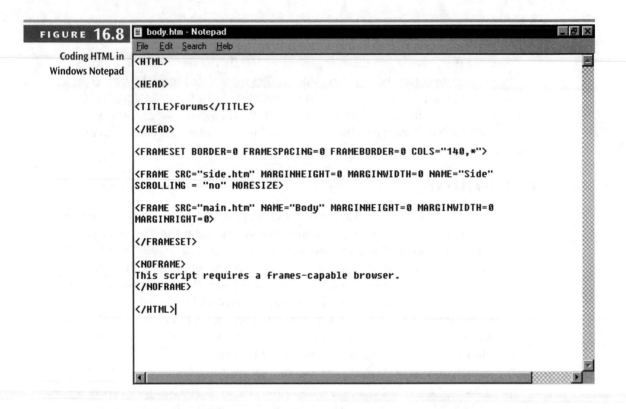

FIGURE 16.8

Coding HTML in
Windows Notepad

```
body.htm - Notepad
File   Edit   Search   Help

<HTML>

<HEAD>

<TITLE>Forums</TITLE>

</HEAD>

<FRAMESET BORDER=0 FRAMESPACING=0 FRAMEBORDER=0 COLS="140,*">

<FRAME SRC="side.htm" MARGINHEIGHT=0 MARGINWIDTH=0 NAME="Side"
SCROLLING = "no" NORESIZE>

<FRAME SRC="main.htm" NAME="Body" MARGINHEIGHT=0 MARGINWIDTH=0
MARGINRIGHT=0>

</FRAMESET>

<NOFRAME>
This script requires a frames-capable browser.
</NOFRAME>

</HTML>
```

HTML Editors

As the name suggests, HTML editors are text editors that have been optimized for working with HTML. These editors are a few steps away from plain-text editors, but many miles away from WYSIWYG (What-You-See-Is-What-You-Get) editors. All of the advantages I've ascribed to text editors exist in HTML editors. By the time you get to the more complex WYSIWYG editors, those advantages are lost.

HTML editors are essentially text editors with enhancements such as toolbars for automatic tag insertion, image wizards that automatically size an image and create the width and height values, and tag color-coding to help you navigate your HTML page. Other features typically include spell checkers and HTML syntax verification software. Perhaps one of the most powerful features of HTML editing environments is that you can update hundreds of pages of code automatically.

Editing environments for the PC are abundant and include Allaire HomeSite (see Figure 16.9), which can be found in demo form at http://www.allaire.com/, HotDog Pro, available from http://www.sausage.com/, and HTML Assistant Pro, which you can check out at http://www.brooknorth.com/pro97.html.

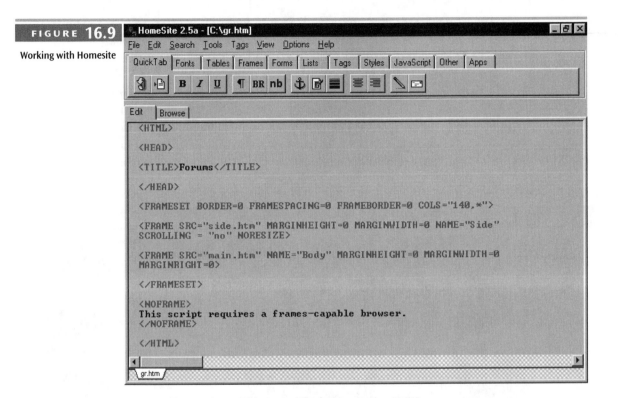

FIGURE 16.9

Working with Homesite

Favorite Macintosh editing environments include BBEdit by Bare Bones Software (http://www.bbedit.com); HTML Edit, offering pop-up menus for standard HTML tags, as well as supporting tables and forms (http://dragon.acadiau.ca/~giles/); and PageSpinner, available for demonstration download at http://www.algonet.se/~optima/pagespinner.html.

What You See: Not Always What You Get

With graphical user interfaces (GUIs) that require no knowledge of HTML, WYSIWYG editors are extremely popular. However, most professional coders find them unsatisfactory.

Individual circumstances will determine whether WYSIWYG editors are for you. In many cases you may not have a choice—the company you work for will require you to use a certain brand of software that takes advantage of the unique features of a given WYSIWYG package.

Use them if you must, but I encourage you to learn how to code HTML before you work with WYSIWYG. The lack of control you will experience and the extraneous or "fat" code generated by such programs will only confuse you if you don't have a strong grasp of HTML fundamentals.

PART

Web Page Design

The PC market is filling up fast with a wide range of WYSIWYG editors. The most well known include Microsoft FrontPage (http://www.microsoft.com/frontpage/), Claris HomePage (http://www.claris.com/), and NetObjects Fusion (http://www.netobjects.com).

A recent entrant into the market is Macromedia's Dreamweaver (http://www.macromedia.com), which is one of the best WYSIWYG editors around. Dreamweaver creates clean code and has lots of useful options, including the ability to code Cascading Style Sheets and DHTML. Dreamweaver also provides a text editor environment so you can switch back and forth between WYSIWYG and text editor mode (see Figure 16.10).

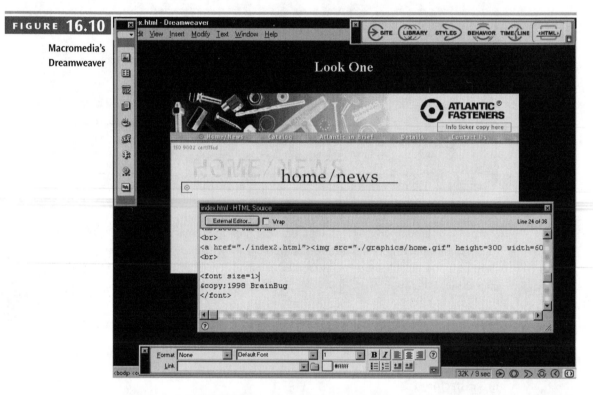

FIGURE 16.10

Macromedia's
Dreamweaver

Macintosh WYSIWYGs are becoming very popular, which may be due to the many desktop publishers who are familiar with WYSIWYG layout programs such as Quark. Macintosh editors include Adobe Pagemill (http://www.adobe.com), which offers integration with other programs within the Adobe suite. Many designers use Pagemill, although it carries the limitations that all other WYSIWYG software packages do. Microsoft FrontPage for Macintosh is another popular choice among non-designers (http://www.microsoft.com/frontpage/). Macromedia Dreamweaver is also available for the Mac.

The Best Tool

Which type of HTML tool should you choose? That depends on your HTML skills and your need for control. The HTML editor tends to be the best environment for most coding jobs because it includes numerous power tools that help you work more efficiently. Text editors are good for working in a pinch—quickly making a spelling change to an existing HTML document, and so on. Most designers would do well to stay away from WYSIWYG editors until they've learned basic HTML and can clean up the mess that some of these programs leave behind.

HTML Basics

Popular opinion states that HTML is not rocket science, that the language is logical and simple.

This opinion is somewhat true. Basic HTML is very accessible to most people because it uses sensible easy-to-learn syntax. However, the more you use HTML as a layout tool, you will find that the language becomes more complex. This complexity is further demonstrated in the additions being made to HTML, such as inline scripting and dynamic commands.

Because the thrust of this book is how to use Photoshop for the Web, and not how to become an all around HTML coder, I'll only explain the tags necessary for creating graphically based Web page layouts.

The First Rule

The First Rule of HTML is to close what you open. This refers to the fact that most HTML tags require an open-tag statement, and a corresponding closing-tag statement, as follows:

```
<html>
</html>
```

As with all rules, this one has some exceptions. But despite the exceptions, you can count on HTML to be fairly consistent. One way to demonstrate this consistency is by taking a look at HTML's main components:

Tag An HTML tag is the component that commands a Web browser to perform a given function such as creating a paragraph or denoting an image. In most cases, tags must first be opened and then closed after that function is complete. There are plenty of exceptions to this rule, however, as you will see as we study HTML in more detail.

PART

Web Page Design

Attribute (or argument)   An HTML attribute modifies a tag. For example, I can align a paragraph or an image within the tag.

Value   Values are ascribed to attributes, and they will qualify the modification. For example, if I use an align attribute on a tag, I can provide a value to that attribute. Values can be literal, such as left or right, or they can be numeric, as in the case of image width and height, where the value relates to the dimensions of the image in pixels.

Basic Page Formatting

All HTML pages are formatted using specific tags that indicate the page's nature, its head section, body section, and title. The tags you must always use on a standard HTML page are as follows:

\<html\> . . . \</html\>   The beginning \<html\> and ending \<html\> tags announce to the browser that an HTML page is about to begin or end.

\<head\> . . . \</head\>   The \<head\> tag includes header information such as titles, special commands, and script data.

\<title\> . . . \</title\>   Title tags allow you to name your page. This information will be displayed in the browser's title bar. While, theoretically, you can get by without this tag, I don't advise it! Name your pages appropriately—titles help visitors identify where they are in a given site.

```
<title>Welcome To My Page!</title>
```

\<body\> . . . \</body\>   The \<body\> tag determines the basic attributes of a page, including the background color and/or graphic to be used, and the text color variables. Whatever goes in between these tags is going to appear in the visible field of your Web browser.

A standard HTML page structure looks like this:

```
<html>
<head>
<title>Welcome To My Page!</title>
</head>
<body>

</body>
</html>
```

Looks pretty simple, doesn't it? Well, it is! The basic elements of an HTML page are very logical, and you should have no trouble remembering the basic structure of any page. Start here and you've created a stable foundation for sure coding success.

Paragraphs and Breaks

Once you've created the basic structure of a page, you'll want to add text information. Simply type your paragraphs into the body section of a tag.

This is the paragraph tag: <p>. It has two standard uses. The first is to place a single <p> at the end of a paragraph, which will command a carriage return and one line space, as follows:

```
Here is a sample paragraph of text.
HTML coders can select from two
methods to control paragraph formatting.
This is one of the methods.
<p>
```

You'll notice in the above example, there is no closing </p> tag. However, paragraphs in HTML can also be coded using the standard open/close method:

```
<p>
Here is a sample paragraph of text.
HTML coders can select from two
methods to control paragraph formatting.
This is the other method.
</p>
```

This is a line break: <br>. No additional lines are added after the break. This tag is helpful when formatting text that requires you to break a line, such as in an address:

```
Clutter Unlimited<br>
P.O. Box 000<br>
Anywhere, Anyplace<br>
```

With these simple tags, you can create a complete text document in HTML! Figure 16.11 shows the code as viewed in the HomeSite interface, and Figure 16.12 shows the results in Netscape 4.0.

TIP In HTML, type is specified with the <font> tag. To set a passage of text at a medium size Helvetica, the tag would be <font face="helvetica" size=3> with a </font> tag at the end of the passage of text. For smaller type, set the size tag to 1 or 2; for bigger type, set it to 4 or 5.

TIP To view a Web page that you've just created on your computer, fire up your browser and select File ➤ Open, Open Page, or Open File (it's different depending on your browser and platform). Click through the dialog until you find the HTML file you want to view.

PART

Web Page Design

FIGURE 16.11

Working with HTML code

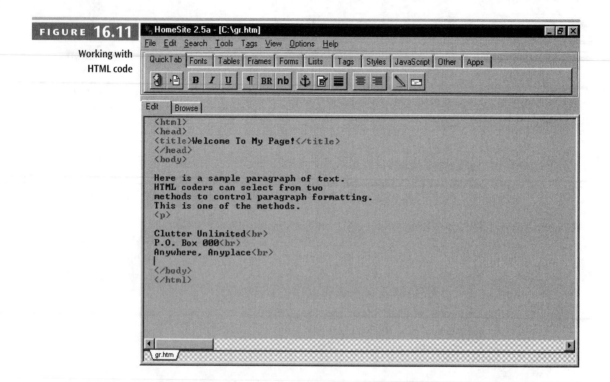

FIGURE 16.12

The HTML example in Netscape 4.0

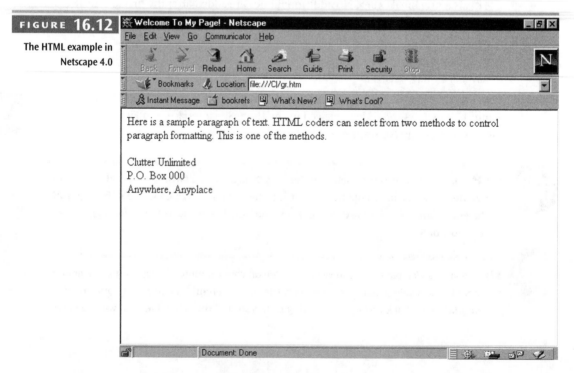

Linking

Linking is what makes the Web go 'round! Links are created in HTML by using the anchor tag, <a>. You must also include a reference attribute, href, and a closing </a> tag, as follows:

```
<a href="link.htm">Here's a link to another page.</a>
```

Not only can you link from page to page, but you can link within a page as well. I refer to these two forms of linking as *standard linking* and *intra-page linking* respectively.

Standard Linking

To link to another page, you must be certain that your reference links to that page. There are several methods to do this:

Absolute Linking   This method requires that you use a complete URL in the reference. Use absolute linking when you are linking to a page that resides on another server:

```
<a href="http://www.sybex.com">Visit the Sybex Web site</a>
```

Relative Linking   When you are linking to a page that resides on your own server, you can link to it without using an absolute URL. If I'm linking from my welcome page to my contact page—and both pages reside in the same directory—the code on my welcome page will look like this:

```
<a href="contact.htm">Go to the Contact Page</a>
```

But what if the page resides in another directory? For example, I want to link to a column in my Articles directory. I'm going to have to define that directory. Here's how the code will appear:

```
<a href="articles/column1.htm">Read My Column on Online Databases!</a>
```

If I want to link back up to the root directory from a subdirectory, I can use the standard ../, which denotes root:

```
<a href="../contact.htm">Back to the Contact Page</a>
```

Intra-Page Linking

Not only can you link to other pages, but you can link to points, called *targets*, within a single HTML page. This is done by naming a particular section of text (or a graphic, object, or other medium) and then referencing that target. At the top of the page you might have a series of link selections that reach down farther into the page. An example would be

```
<a href="#selection3">The Third Rule can be found here</a>
```

The target would appear like this:

```
<a name="selection3">The Third Rule:</a>
```

Click on the first link, and you will end up at the target, as demonstrated in Figures 16.13 and 16.14.

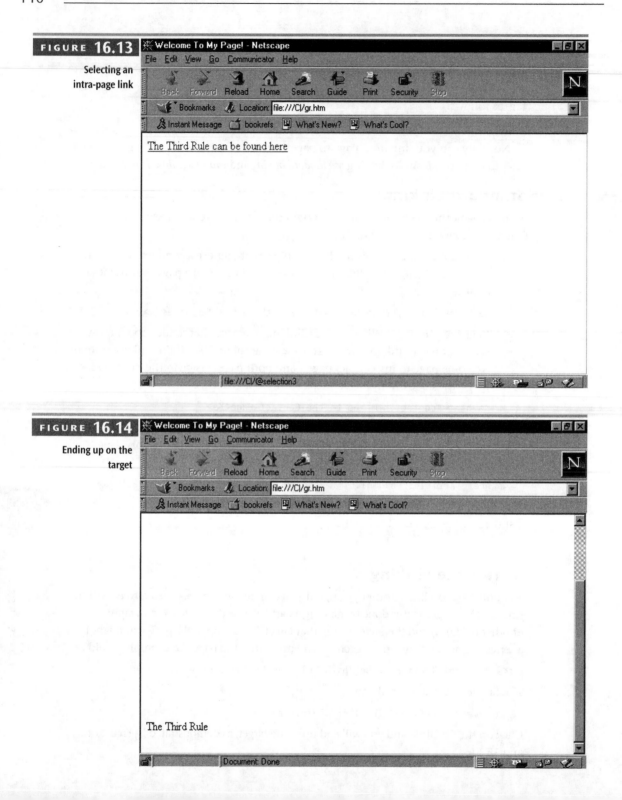

FIGURE 16.13

Selecting an
intra-page link

FIGURE 16.14

Ending up on the
target

Adding Images

Images make a page visually appealing, and the image tag is one you'll be using regularly. Image tags are an exception to the first rule—they don't require a closing tag, but they do have a number of important attributes. I'm including the attributes that I think are important for you in the context of this book.

Image tags are made up of the image tag, `<img>`, and the image source, `src`:

```
<img src="bird.gif">
```

As long as the image `bird.gif` is in the same directory as the HTML page that is calling it, this is all the code *requires* to make that picture render. However, I highly recommend you include the following attributes in *every* image tag you code:

`width="x"`   This defines the width of the image.

`height="x"`   This is the image's height.

`border="x"`   The value of *x* in this case determines how much of a border the browser will draw around an image. In most cases, your border value will equal anything other than "0."

`alt="x"`   The `alt` attribute allows you to provide a description of the image. This is very helpful for people who turn off their images, and for those individuals who are using text-only browsers.

Adding the information to the earlier image example will result in this code:

```
<img src="bird.gif" width="150" height="150" border="0" alt="A photo of a bird">
```

When you define width, height, and border, your browser can prepare the layout for that image in advance. This can improve the speed at which a browser draws the page.

WARNING   Images residing in a Graphics subdirectory need to be properly referred to in the image tag. If the graphic `bird.gif` is sitting in the Graphics subdirectory, the proper link would be `<imgsrc="./graphics/bird.gif">`. Otherwise, the image will not display.

HTML Layout Techniques

The Photoshop layer exercise earlier in this chapter can use simple HTML as its backbone. However, as your designs become more complex, you'll need supportive techniques.

Tables are the primary answer to layout control. They provide significant control over the placement of graphics, creation of adequate white space, and general page structure. Frames come in at a close second, offering up interface options such as static navigation. This section will help you get started using both tables and frames.

N O T E   Looking for more information on layout design? Try Molly E. Holzschlag's *Web by Design*: *The Complete Guide* (Sybex, 1998).

Tables

To prepare you to use tables to lay out the pages you've developed in Photoshop, I'm going to introduce you to the basic table tags. Then, I'll show you the attributes you can use for greater control.

The three table tags necessary to create a table are listed here:

<table> . . . </table>   This tag determines the beginning of a table within an HTML document.

<tr> . . . </tr>   This is the table row tag and it determines rows—the left-to-right, horizontal space within a table.

<td> . . . </td>   The table data tag defines individual table cells. The table cell tag and the information contained therein determine the columnar structure of a table.

T I P   All text and graphics are placed inside the <td> tags.

Here is a simple table built with the three preceding tags:

```
<table>
<tr>
<td>
This is my first table cell.
</td>
<td>
And this is my second table cell.
</td>
</tr>
<tr>
<td>
```

```
This is the first table cell in the second table row.
</td>
<td>
And this is the second table in the second table row.
</td>
</tr>
</table>
```

Figure 16.15 shows how this code appears when viewed in the Internet Explorer browser.

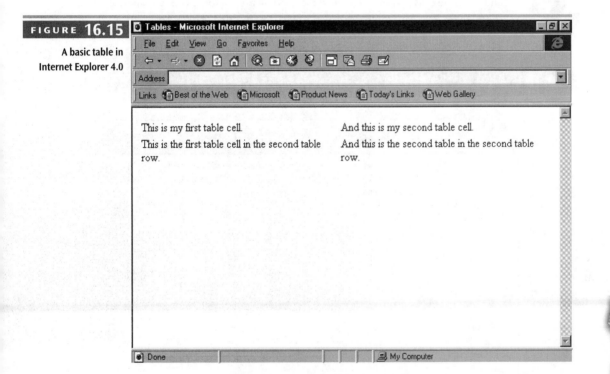

FIGURE **16.15**

A basic table in
Internet Explorer 4.0

When designing your Web layouts in Photoshop, it is important to think about how your designs can be broken up into logical columns and rows. When you look at the visible grid in Figure 16.16, think about how a page layout might be broken up into different sections and placed into the table.

There are times when you're going to want a lot more flexibility than what is demonstrated in Figure 16.16. Tables afford you this by giving you a variety of attributes per tag.

Table tag attributes include these:

align=x   Align tables on a page with this attribute. The *x* is a variable to be replaced with left or right. Because browsers default alignment to the left, and

PART

Web Page Design

it's commonplace to center tables using other tags, the only really effective use of this attribute is when you want an entire table placed to the far right of the browser field.

border=x   The *x* variable is to be replaced with a value from 0 on up. This value defines the width of the visual border around the table. For the purposes of laying out pages, this value will usually be set to 0.

T I P   Want to see the way the table is controlling your layout? Set the border value to 1 and the table cells and rows will draw the grid you are creating. This is a handy method of checking to see if your table is most effectively interpreting your layout.

FIGURE 16.16

The visible grid

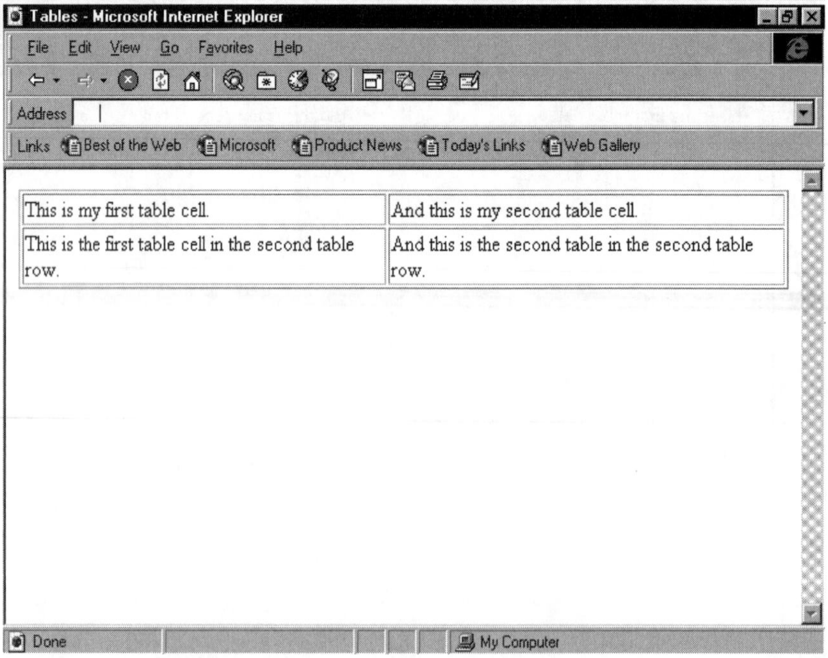

This is my first table cell.	And this is my second table cell.
This is the first table cell in the second table row.	And this is the second table in the second table row.

cellspacing=x   This defines the amount of space between each individual table cell (in other words, between visual columns). The *x* requires a value from 0 on up. This helps you gain white space between items you might place within a cell.

cellpadding=x   This attribute calls for the space around the edges of each cell within the table—its padding. Again, use this attribute to create white space.

TIP Another way to adjust the spacing in a table is to insert a graphic "shim"—also called a spacer—into the <td> tag. These are 1 pixel by 1 pixel transparent GIFs that are manually stretched with the height and width tags.

width=x% or width=x To define the width of a table, you can choose to use a number that relates to the percentage of browser space you wish to span, or a specific numeral that will be translated into pixel widths. Setting the table width is extremely important. Going over the 595-pixel width maximum could cause your page to scroll horizontally at 640×480 resolution. I highly recommend using a pixel-width value rather than a percentage to fix your design as much as possible.

TIP If you'd like to center your table on the page, I recommend using the <div> tag along with an alignment attribute such as <div align=center>. The opening tag and attribute is placed before your table; after you've closed the table, close the division with </div>.

Here's a look at a table with table tag attributes at work:

```
<table align="right" border="1" cellspacing="10" cellpadding="10"
width="595">
<tr>
<td>
This is my first table cell.
</td>
<td>
And this is my second table cell.
</td>
</tr>
<tr>
<td>
This is the first table cell in the second table row.
</td>
<td>
And this is the second table in the second table row.
</td>
</tr>
</table>
```

Figure 16.17 demonstrates the attributes in action. Compare this figure to the previous one to see the control that becomes available when using attributes.

PART

Web Page Design

FIGURE 16.17

Table attributes in
action

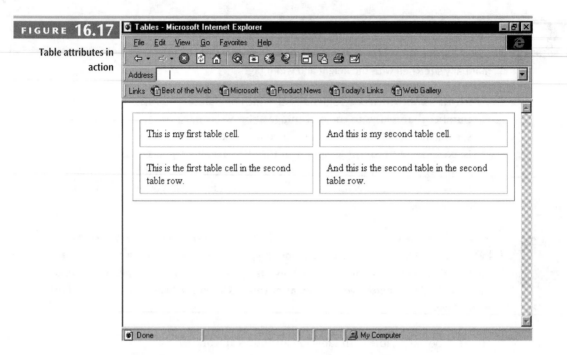

Attributes for table rows do exist, but are rarely used. You gain ultimate control
working with table cells. Alignment attributes are as follows:

align=x   Where the x variable will be left, right, or middle. When you use
this attribute within a table cell, the data inside the cell will align with the
literal value you assign to the attribute. In other words, a left value will left-
justify the cell's contents, the middle value will center the cell's contents, and a
right value will justify the cell's contents to the right of the cell. Here's a look
at how the align attribute in a table cell works (I've set the border at 1 so you
can see the table's structure):

```
<table align="right" border="1" cellspacing="10" cellpadding="10"
width="595">
<tr>
<td align="right">
This is my first table cell.
</td>
<td>
And this is my second table cell.
</td>
</tr>
<tr>
<td>
```

```
This is the first table cell in the second table row.
</td>
<td align="right">
And this is the second table in the second table row.
</td>
</tr>
</table>
```

You'll notice in Figure 16.18 that the first table cell in the first row and the second table cell in the second row align the internal text to the right.

valign=x   Where *x* is top, middle, or bottom. The vertical alignment of a table cell will place the cell's contents at the top, middle, or bottom of the cell.

Here's how you use the valign attribute:

```
<table align="right" border="0" cellspacing="10" cellpadding="10"
width="595">
<tr>
<td valign="top" align="right">
This is my first table cell.
</td>
<td valign="middle">
And this is my second table cell.
</td>
</tr>
<tr>
<td valign="top">
This is the first table cell in the second table row.
</td>
<td valign="bottom" align="right">
And this is the second table in the second table row.
</td>
</tr>
</table>
```

In this instance, the first table cell in the first row and the first table cell in the second row are vertically aligned to the top. The second table cell in the first row is vertically aligned to the middle, and the second table cell in the second row is bottom aligned.

colspan=x   Where *x* is the number of columns, colspan refers to the number of columns the cell you are working with will span (see Figure 16.19).

PART

3

Web Page Design

FIGURE 16.18

Alignment within
table cells

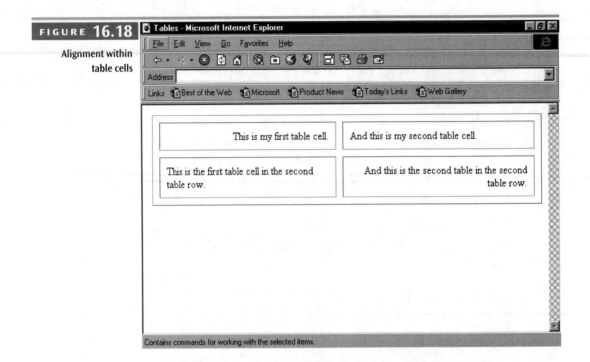

FIGURE 16.19

The colspan attribute
in action

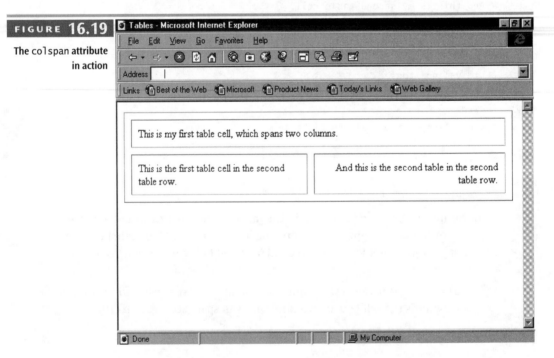

Here's what the `colspan` attribute looks like in action:

```
<table border="1" cellspacing="10" cellpadding="10" width="595">
<tr>
<td colspan="2">
This is my first table cell, which spans two columns.
</td>
</tr>
<tr>
<td>
This is the first table cell in the second table row.
</td>
<td align="right">
And this is the second table in the second table row.
</td>
</tr>
</table>
```

rowspan=x Where *x* is the number of rows, rowspan refers to the number of rows the cell stretches (see Figure 16.20).

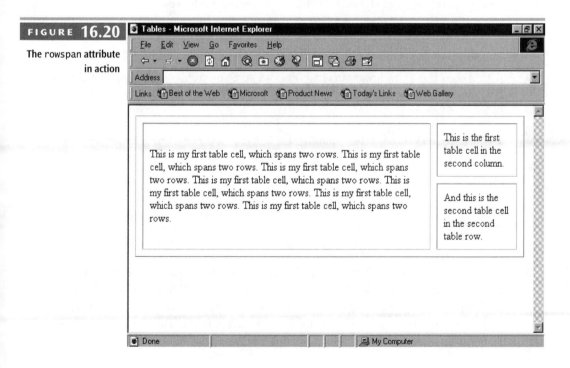

FIGURE 16.20

The rowspan attribute in action

PART

Web Page Design

And finally, here's how the rowspan tag is used:

```
<table border="1" cellspacing="10" cellpadding="10" width="595">
<tr>
<td rowspan="2">
This is my first table cell, which spans two rows.
This is my first table cell, which spans two rows.
This is my first table cell, which spans two rows.
This is my first table cell, which spans two rows.
This is my first table cell, which spans two rows.
This is my first table cell, which spans two rows.
This is my first table cell, which spans two rows.
</td>
<td>
This is the first table cell in the second column.
</td>
</tr>
<tr>
<td>
And this is the second table cell in the second table row.
</td>
</tr>
</table>
```

Using the colspan and rowspan attributes can give you tremendous power over lay-out, allowing for multicolumn design and better control over your pages.

TIP   Once you get comfortable putting text into tables, try inserting graphics with the IMG SRC tag. This is how most Web page layouts are composed.

Frames

Frames are especially helpful to designers when a portion or several portions of a page are designed as stationary elements. An instance where frames are particularly useful is in navigation, which is usually fixed to the left or right, and sometimes at the bot-tom or top. In Figure 16.21, you may notice how the browser's right scroll bar extends only part way up the page—a visual clue that the navigation at the top of the page is sitting in a separate frame.

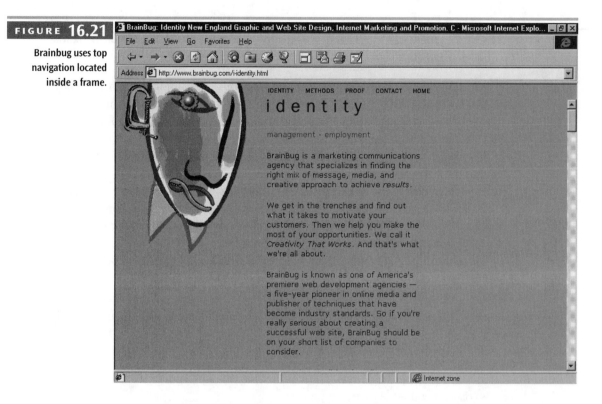

FIGURE 16.21

Brainbug uses top
navigation located
inside a frame.

Creating a basic framed page requires at least three separate pages of HTML. You need the *frameset*, the unseen page of HTML code that controls the layout and function of the frames. Then, you'll need an individual page of code for each individual frame. So, if the most basic framed page has two visible pages, there are a total of three HTML pages; if a framed page has three visible pages, there are four pages; and so forth. There will always be an unseen frameset page.

The Frameset

In the frameset, you'll argue primarily for the rows and/or columns you wish to create, and the HTML pages that will fill those rows or columns. This is done using two major tags.

<frameset>   This tag is for the frame, and its basic arguments define rows and columns. The frameset information is closed with a corresponding </frameset> tag.

<frame>   This tag argues individual frames within the frameset. This includes the location of the HTML document required to fill the frame, using src=x (where x is the relative or absolute URL to the location of the HTML page).

N O T E   The <frame> tag has no counterpart </frame> tag. All the information for individual frames is placed within the tag, and it is considered closed at the right angle bracket (>).

Much like tables, frames are built by creating a grid of columns and rows. Tables can be complex with the spanning of columns and rows. With tables, horizontal and vertical reference points are the responsibility of the coder. Frames are more simplistic. A column is an overtly vertical control, a row a horizontal one.

The syntax is equally clear. Rows are rows, columns are cols. Both columns and rows can be defined in terms of pixels or percentages. For example, cols="220, *" calls for a left column with a *width* of 220 pixels, and the right column, called by the asterisk, will be the remainder of the available viewing space. To add more columns, simply define each one in turn. For example, if you want to create four columns of equal percent, the syntax would read cols="25%,25%,25%,25%".

If you want to create rows, simply change the syntax to rows="220, *", and the result would be a top row with a *height* of 220 pixels. To create four individual rows of equal percent, you would code for rows="25%,25%,25%,25%".

To create combinations of columns and rows, simply stack the values into the appropriate tags and pages of the framed site.

A simple frameset looks like this:

```
<html>

<frameset cols="220, *">

<frame src="leftmenu.htm">
<frame src="welcome.htm">

</frameset>

</html>
```

Of course, you'll have to have the leftmenu.htm and welcome.htm pages available in order to view the page.

Frame Attributes

There are several powerful attributes available to the <frameset> and <frame> tags.

I'll introduce attributes here that are either common to both the Netscape Navigator 3.0 and above and Internet Explorer 3.0 and above browsers, or are required to design for both of them. Then you'll have the opportunity to perform tasks to see them at work.

The following are commonly used attributes for the <frameset> tag.

cols=x   Create columns. The *x* is a variable to be replaced with either a pixel value, a percentage value, or a combination of one of those and an asterisk (*), which creates a *dynamic* or *relative size* frame—the remainder of the framed space.

rows=x   Create rows in the same fashion that the cols attribute is used.

border=x   Used by Netscape Navigator 3.0 and above to control border width. The variable value is set in pixel width.

frameborder=x   Used by Internet Explorer to control border width in pixels. Netscape Navigator 3.0 and above uses the attribute with a yes or no value.

framespacing=x   Used by Internet Explorer to control border width.

Use these tag attributes for individual frame control:

frameborder=x   Control frameborders around individual frames. Netscape Navigator requires a yes or no value, whereas Internet Explorer will look for a numeric pixel-width value.

marginheight=x   Control the height of the frame's margin by entering a value in pixels.

marginwidth=x   Control the width of the frame's margin by entering a value in pixels.

name=x   Name an individual frame. Naming frames permits targeting by links within other HTML pages. Names must begin with a standard letter or numeral.

noresize   Place this handy tag in your string if you don't want your users to manually adjust a frame's height or width sizing.

scrolling=x   Control the appearance of a scrollbar by entering yes, no, or auto. A yes value automatically places a scrollbar in the frame, a no value ensures that no scrollbar ever appears. The auto argument turns the power over to the browser, which will automatically place a scrollbar in a frame should it be required.

src=x   Replace the *x* variable with the relative or absolute URL of the HTML page you wish to place within the frame.

Here's a frameset with a variety of attributes at work:

```
<html>

<frameset cols="220, *">

<frame src="leftmenu.htm" scrolling="no" marginwidth="0" marginheight="0"
name="menu">

<frame src="welcome.htm" scrolling="auto" marginwidth="0" marginheight="0"
name="right" noresize>

</frameset>

</html>
```

Figure 16.22 shows the frame results when viewed in Netscape 4.0.

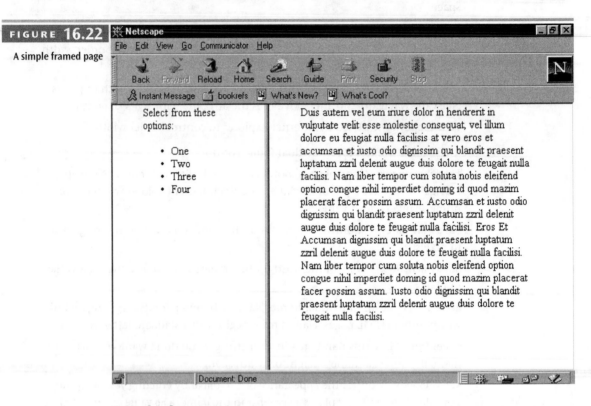

FIGURE **16.22**

A simple framed page

Borderless Frames

Each browser either requires a different attribute to control width, or a different value to control spacing. It looks confusing, but if you stack attributes, you can easily create borderless frames that will be readable by both browsers. This technique results in two legal syntax options:

```
<frameset frameborder="0" framespacing="0" border="0">
```

or

```
<frameset frameborder="no" framespacing="0" border="0">
```

Either one is correct, and it's just a matter of personal preference as to which you'll use. Remember to add your columns and rows to the string in order to create a full range of frameset arguments.

```
<html>

<frameset frameborder=0 framespacing=0 border=0 cols="220, *">

<frame src="leftmenu.htm" marginheight=5 marginwidth=5 noresize
scrolling=auto>
```

```
<frame src="welcome.htm" name=col2 marginheight=15 marginwidth=15 noresize
scrolling=auto>

</frameset>
</html>
```

Voila! No border on the frameset in Figure 16.23.

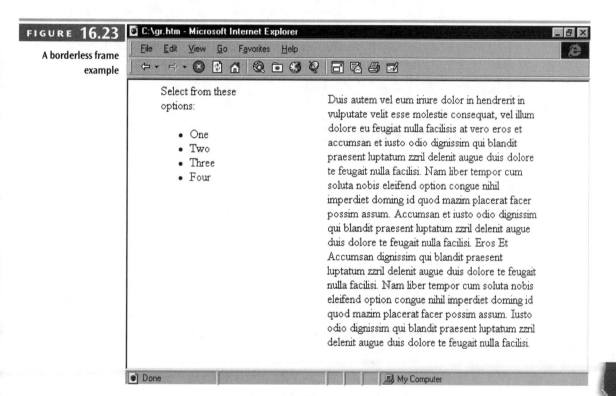

FIGURE **16.23**

A borderless frame
example

Managing HTML and Related Files

When creating a Web site, it is beneficial to give some thought to how you will save, name, structure, and move your files. Why? Because if files aren't saved or named right, your Web site won't function. Also, unless there is an overall structure, other people who work on the site will have a hard time knowing where different graphics and files can be found. Web sites with serpentine directory structures or unstructured naming conventions create great inefficiencies and make simple changes a real chore. Take a look at Figure 16.24—how long might it take to find a particular file in this mess?

PART

Web Page Design

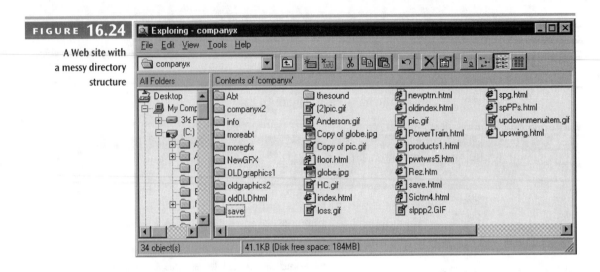

FIGURE **16.24**

A Web site with
a messy directory
structure

Saving Files

Depending on what program you use to write your HTML, you may need to save your file in a certain way so as not to corrupt the HTML you have written. Information that would normally be included by regular word-processing software can make some HTML files unreadable.

The best way to avoid this problem is to save your HTML document using the Save As feature in your text editor. One of the options should be to save As Text, With Line Breaks. Saving your file in this format strips out any word-processor information, preserving only the breaks—also known as returns—between the lines.

WARNING   Just like in Photoshop, you should do file saves as often as possible to avoid losing data in the event of a computer crash.

File Naming Practices

The starting point for a well-organized directory structure begins with filenames. All HTML files must have an `.html` file extension. You will occasionally see the `.htm` variation. This extension is a UNIX convention stipulating that file extensions can't be more than three characters long. Only use this convention if the person running your Web server tells you to do so.

The first page of a site is either called `index.html` or `default.htm` (the Microsoft standard). This is a configuration decision made by the Web host. In order to avoid any possible conflicts, two copies of the same page can be included in the Web root—one called `index.html` and one called `default.htm`.

Filenames are case-sensitive—`contact.html` is different than `Contact.html`, and they must be referenced in HTML code accordingly. If you were to change the name of your `contact.html` file to `Contact.html`, any links in an HTML page to `contact.html` would immediately be broken. The link will be "looking" for a file with an all-lowercase filename.

T I P   Standardize on all lowercase characters for filenames to avoid problems with uppercase and lowercase conflicts.

It is also important to develop file naming conventions that make it easy to find a particular file. I've developed the following standards for very small Web sites:

`index.html`	The home page
`about.html`	Information about a company
`services.html`	The services a company provides
`products.html`	The products a company offers
`contact.html`	The contact page

I've also developed naming conventions for graphics, where "xxxx" is the unique name of the graphic (i.e. `h-news.gif`):

`bg-xxxx.gif`	A background image
`m-xxxx.gif`	A menu graphic
`mb-xxxx.gif`	An individual menu button
`h-xxxx.gif`	A header graphic
`f-xxxx.gif`	A footer graphic
`p-xxxx.jpg`	A picture or photographic element

It isn't necessary to follow these particular conventions—you can make up your own—but whatever ones you use, make sure you stick to them. Otherwise, you'll spend a lot of time looking for header-news.gif instead of news-header.gif.

Directory Structures

Figure 16.25 shows a well-organized directory structure for a medium-sized site—about 50 pages.

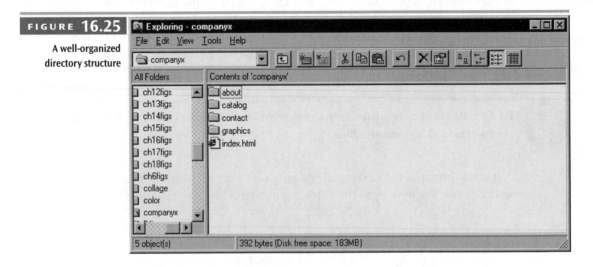

FIGURE **16.25**

A well-organized
directory structure

You'll notice at the root level an `index.html` file and four subdirectories. The `index.html` file is always placed in the root directory and never inside a subdirectory. When you type a domain name like `coke.com` into a browser, the server automatically sends you to the `index.html` file sitting in the root directory. If it isn't present at that level, you won't be able to access the home page unless you can guess Coke's directory structure—an unlikely scenario.

The four subdirectories consist of `about`, `catalog`, `contact`, and `graphics`. As shown in Figure 16.26, inside any of the first three subdirectories you'll find a directory structure that is similar to the root level, except there are lots more files and only one subdirectory (`graphics`).

N O T E   Index files are used in subdirectories as the default file, so if you type **www.companyx.com/about** into a browser, you'll automatically be sent the `index.html` file in the **about** subdirectory. This can be useful in promotional efforts when a company doesn't want to buy or can't get a domain name for a specific campaign.

Directories that contain GIF, JPEG, and other media files are usually called either `graphics`, `images`, or `media`. Again, any name you choose is fine as long as you stay consistent.

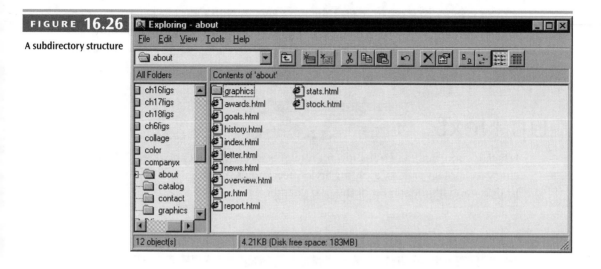

FIGURE 16.26

A subdirectory structure

NOTE   The best directory structure for a Web site is often the site map (see Chapter 11).

Moving Files by FTP

As mentioned in Chapter 11, HTML and other files are typically moved to a Web server via a File Transfer Protocol (FTP) program. WSFTP (Windows) and Fetch (Mac) are both included on the CD-ROM that comes with this book. If you learn how to use these programs, you can move a Web site created on your computer to a Web server anywhere in the world.

When transferring files to and from a Web server, it is very important to set the transfer protocol according to the type of file that is going to be transferred. HTML and all text files are ASCII-based files, and they should be transferred with the ASCII option selected. Graphics, Java Class, and all executable files must be transferred as binary files or they will become corrupted.

Conclusion

Having trouble with all of this HTML stuff? Don't worry, you'll get there. Becoming familiar with HTML can take a few weeks or a few months, depending on the designer. One way to extend your knowledge of tags is to use your Web browser's View Source command. In this way, you can see exactly how your favorite Web sites were constructed.

PART

Web Page Design

Although it's a far cry from creating print layouts with tools like QuarkXPress or PageMaker, manual HTML offers the best chance that your designs will be fully realized. Like driving a car with a standard transmission, hand-coding provides the ultimate control over HTML.

Up Next

HTML is good, but it doesn't allow for total precision in layout and design. Fortunately, a new technology called Cascading Style Sheets holds the promise for more refined Web layouts—and it's the subject of the next chapter.

Mastering the Medium: The Web Design Process

Some people say that talent separates the good Web design shops from the bad, but they're only half-right. The other key to success is having a process by which a site is delivered on time, on budget, and bug free. Most clients understand that the Web is a new medium and everyone is learning as they go, but if a Web shop messes up the development process enough times, it won't be around very long.

Some Web designers and companies have a formalized plan of attack with which they tackle new projects, while others have a more intuitive process that manages to get the job done. Either way, these professionals have figured out a way to get sites into and out of production and keep the client happy. The process tends to include the following steps:

1. **Initial Consultation**   This first step requires that the designer accumulate key information about the project. Facts to be gathered include the target audience for the site, the primary message to be communicated, and the intended Web server platform. Initial consultation typically concludes with the draft of a diagram that notes all of the pages in the site.

2. **Conceptual Development**   At this point, the designer takes all that was learned from the initial consultation and begins to sketch out ideas. Often, these ideas are presented to the client as rough pencil sketches that provide a range of different layout, design, and navigation choices.

3. **Comps**   Upon the client's selection of a preferred concept, the designer moves ahead with the production of color comps (short for "comprehensives"). The static images, typically no more than 600 pixels wide by 300 pixels tall (the full screen size of a small monitor), are most commonly created in a program like Photoshop. The comps are either printed in color and put on black presentation board, or included on a Web page that the client can view.

4. **HTML Layout and Navigation**   Once the comps are approved, designers will chop up the Photoshop graphics into specific pieces (headers, footers, and so on) and use HTML to arrange them into a few functioning Web pages. Navigation is also coded into the page, providing the client with the first real taste of how users will interact with the site.

5. **Graphics Production**   With the final look and feel of the site approved, the designer will proceed to mass produce all the necessary graphics. Saved as GIFs or JPEGs, the directory of graphics will include all of the site's headers, footers, and menus.

6. **Content Flow**   The client's written content is coded and, with all of the graphics in hand, the various sections of the site are systematically assembled.

7. **Testing**   Before the site is delivered to the client, the designer will thoroughly test every Web page and link. With a written list of bugs in hand, the designer will make each repair and cross it off the list.

8. **Delivery**   Upon receipt, the client will often conduct their own testing, with a special focus on typos and other content-related mistakes. After these minor corrections are made, the site is officially launched.

This whole process can take anywhere from one to twelve months to complete, with the average being about four months. Following the launch of a site, measurements are conducted to determine how people are using the site. Over the course of six to twelve months, data is gathered, a site redesign effort is initiated, and the Web design process starts all over again

PART

Web Page Design

CASCADING STYLE SHEETS

Featuring

CASCADING STYLE SHEETS

HTML was originally intended to be a markup language, not a way to describe the physical design of a Web page. Fortunately, Web designers have found ways around HTML's limitations by using tables, frames, and other devices. But shouldn't there be a language that precisely describes the location of all Web page elements? Wouldn't it be great if you could change a font throughout a Web site by just making a single adjustment?

That's the point of Cascading Style Sheets (CSS). They make Web pages look the way you want them to. Plus, CSS makes managing a Web site much easier. A single document can control text formatting throughout an entire Web site, making style alterations a snap.

In this chapter we'll explore CSS in detail, including a look at three types of style-sheet applications: inline, embedded, and linked. We'll conclude with a discussion on how to use CSS to arrange text and graphics on a Web page.

What Are Style Sheets?

Cascading Style Sheets is a standard that refers to several methods of applying style elements to HTML pages. In this case, think of style as any kind of design element, such as typeface, background, text, link colors, margin controls, and placement of objects on a page.

CSS was developed in order to gain a greater level of control over text and graphics. But CSS is a new technology that has some drawbacks. The biggest issue is that, at this time, Web browsers don't fully support CSS. While Microsoft introduced CSS in their Windows 95 3.0 version of IE, there were some bugs with the implementation. Netscape, in a rush to meet the competition, built Navigator 4.0 to be CSS compliant. But bugs abound there as well! Add to this the fact that a minority of Web visitors keep up-to-date with the latest and greatest browser, and the reality of following HTML 4.0's strict standard is still out of reach for most commercial and hobbyist designs.

Nonetheless, style sheets provide a long-awaited solution for many of HTML's limitations. The results are better font control, color management, margin control, and even additional special effects, such as text shadowing.

David Givens, Manager of Internet Publishing for BrainBug, has this to say about his use of CSS:

> *Cascading Style Sheets provides me with a level of consistency, organization, and control during site development that is unattainable with HTML alone. One look at a style sheet informs anyone working on a Web site of many of the design choices that have been made, which makes for a more focused and ultimately satisfying project—especially on a mammoth Web site.*
>
> *Our implementation of CSS has been centered on the increased level of type control it offers—providing a way to streamline the many choices of size, face, style, and color that is given piecemeal by HTML. Where implementing HTML is rather like going through a cafeteria lunch line, the addition of CSS elevates the whole process to that of reading a menu at a fine restaurant.*

The logic and power of style sheets outweighs the current problems with browser support, so it's clear that designers should learn style-sheet concepts and techniques and be at the ready to employ them where necessary.

N O T E   CSS examples in this book are optimized for IE 4.

Methods and Syntax

There are a variety of methods by which style sheets can be applied to an HTML document. Syntax refers to the actual structure of the information contained within a style sheet.

Methods

Here are three methods for applying a style sheet to an HTML document:

Inline   This method allows you to take any HTML tag and add a style to it. Using the inline method gives you maximum control over any aspect of a Web page. Let's say you wanted to control the look and feel of a specific paragraph. You could simply add a `style=x` attribute to the paragraph tag, and the browser would display that paragraph using the style values you've added to the code.

Embedded   Embedding allows you to control a full page of HTML. Using the `<style>` tag, which is placed within the `<head>` section of an HTML page, inserts detailed style attributes that will be applied to the entire page.

Linked (or *External*)   A linked style sheet is a powerful tool that allows you to create master styles that you can apply to an entire site. A main style sheet document is created by a Web designer using the `.css` extension. This document contains the styles you want an entire Web site (a single page or even thousands of pages) to adopt. Any page that links to this document will take on the prescribed styles.

Style Sheet Syntax

Sentences require specific elements, as do mathematical equations. Style sheets are similar to both in that if they do not follow a specified order, or syntax, they might not function properly.

Whatever method you choose to deliver your style to HTML documents, the syntax is going to be similar. Style sheets, like sentences, are made up of very specific parts. These parts include the following:

Selector   A *selector* is the element that will receive the attributes you assign. It can simply be a tag, such as a header, H1, or a paragraph, P. Style sheets allow for advanced selectors, including classes, which are discussed briefly later in the chapter.

Property   A *property* defines a selector. For example, if you have a paragraph as a selector, you can include properties to define that selector. Properties include such things as margins, fonts, and backgrounds. There are many properties in style sheets that you can use to define a selector.

Value   *Values* define properties. Let's say I have a level one header, H1, as my selector, and I've included a type family `type-family` as a property. The typeface that I actually define is the value of that property.

Declaration   Properties and values combine to make up a *declaration*.

Web Page Design

Rule　A selector and a declaration make up a *rule*.

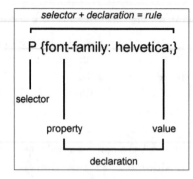

Think of selectors as nouns, properties as verbs, and values as adjectives or adverbs. Following this metaphor, rules can be seen as sentences!

Seem confusing? It can be at first, but like any language, it takes study and practice to become fluent!

Why Cascade?

The term *cascading* is used because multiple styles can be used in an individual HTML page. A style-sheet–compliant browser will follow an order—a cascade—to interpret style information.

This means that I can use all three style types and the browser will interpret the linked, embedded, and inline styles in that order. Even though I might have master styles applied to an entire site, I can control aspects of individual pages with embedded styles, and individual areas within those pages with inline styles.

Another aspect of cascading is *inheritance*. Inheritance dictates that unless I command otherwise, a particular style will be inherited by other influenced aspects of the HTML page. For example, if I command for a specific text color in a <p> tag, all tags within that paragraph will inherit that color unless I state otherwise.

Inline Style

Inline style is applied to any logical HTML tag using the `style` attribute, as follows:

```
<p style="font: 12pt times">
The text in this line will display as 12 point text using the Times font.
</p>
<p style="font: 12pt verdana">
The text in this line will display as 12 point text using the verdana font.
</p>
```

Figure 17.1 shows two lines of text, one with the standard default typeface (Times) for a PC, and one with the Verdana typeface applied.

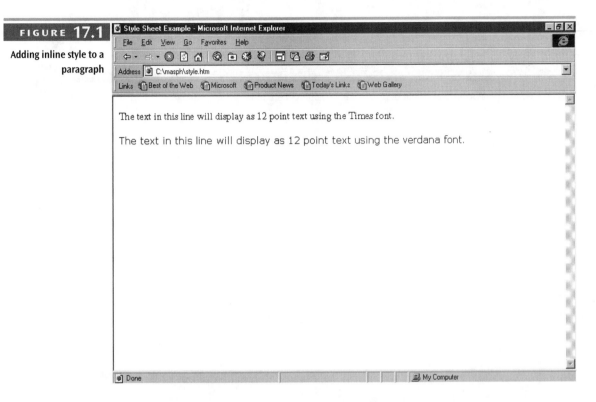

FIGURE 17.1

Adding inline style to a
paragraph

You can add inline style to any HTML tag that makes sense. Such tags include paragraphs, headers, horizontal rules, anchors, and table cells. Each is a logical candidate for inline style.

There are two tags that can help you apply inline style to sections of a page. They are the <div> (division) tag, and the <span> tag.

These tags specify a defined range of text, so everything in between them will adopt the style you wish to use. The only difference between <div> and <span> is that <div> forces a line break, while <span> doesn't. Therefore, you should use <span> to modify the style of any portion of text shorter than a paragraph.

Here's an example of the <div> tag at work:

```
<div style="font-family: Garamond; font-size: 14pt;">All of the text within
this section is 14 point Garamond.
</div>
```

And the <span> tag:

```
<span style="color: #CCCCCC"> this text appears in the color gray, with no
line break after the closing span tag </span> and the rest of the text.
```

Figure 17.2 shows the results.

In general, inline styles are useful, but it's far better to develop standards for an entire Web page or site and then apply them using embedded or linked style sheets.

PART

Web Page Design

FIGURE 17.2

Using the <div> and
<span> tags

Embedded Style

Embedded styles use the <style> tag, placed under the </head> tag and before the
<body> tag in a standard HTML document:

```
<html>
<head>
<title>Embedded Style Sheet Example I</title>
</head>
<style>

BODY {
        background: #FFFFFF;
        color: #000000;
        }
H1 {
        font: 14pt verdana; color: #CCCCCC;
        }
P {
```

```
        font: 12pt times;
        }
A {
        color: #FF0000; text-decoration: none
        }

</style>
```

As you can tell from the example above, the style sheet is beginning to look quite a bit different than standard HTML, but it's not difficult to follow the logic. In this case, the page's body is calling for a background color, a text color, and top, left, and right margin spacing in inches.

Notice how the level one heading, H1, calls for a font using the font's name and a literal point size. This is a prime example of why CSS is so powerful—not only can I choose to control sizing in points, but also in pixels (px), percentage (75%), and centimeters (cm).

Another interesting aspect of this style sheet includes the difference in fonts as defined by the header and paragraph style—they're different in color, indentation, and face. With the advent of style sheets, the days of having an HTML page littered with font tags and non-breaking spaces are limited. Style is handled in a nice, compact fashion.

The anchor tag, A, in the style sheet shows yet another very handy piece of syntax. The `text-decoration: none` string forces underlining to be removed from links, so the results are clean and attractive. Figure 17.3 shows this embedded style example in action.

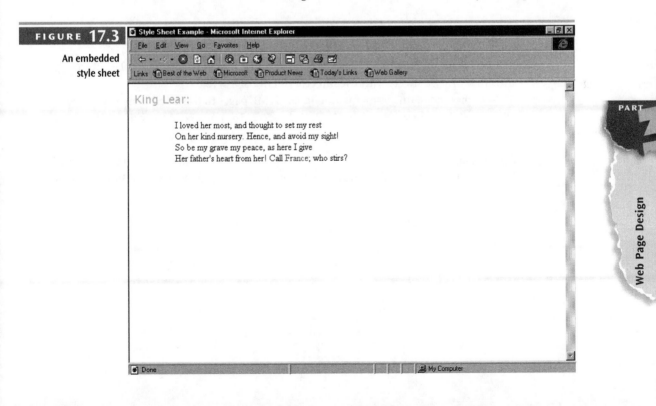

FIGURE 17.3

An embedded style sheet

PART

Web Page Design

Linked Style Sheets

Linked, or *external*, style sheets extend the concept of embedded style. Using the same code as you would with an embedded style sheet, you simply place this information in a separate document. This document is then saved with the file extension of .css. Then, you link to this page all the pages you want to adopt this style.

Here's the syntax for a linked style sheet:

```
<style>

BODY {
        background: #FFFFFF;
        color: #000000;
        }
H1 {
        font-family: helvetica, arial;
        font-size: 24pt;
        color: #0000FF;
        }
P {
        font-family: garamond, times;
        font-size: 14pt;
        }

</style>
```

Now, save this document as a unique file. Name it style-1.css and place it in a directory of style sheets with the directory name of style.

Now proceed to link as many individual HTML pages to this document as you want, using the following syntax, placed below the </title> and above the </head> tag:

```
<link rel=stylesheet href="style-1.css" type="text/css">
```

Any page containing this link will adopt the styles you've called for in style-1.css. You've captured the results using a small sample of information, as shown in Figure 17.4.

FIGURE 17.4

A linked style sheet
example

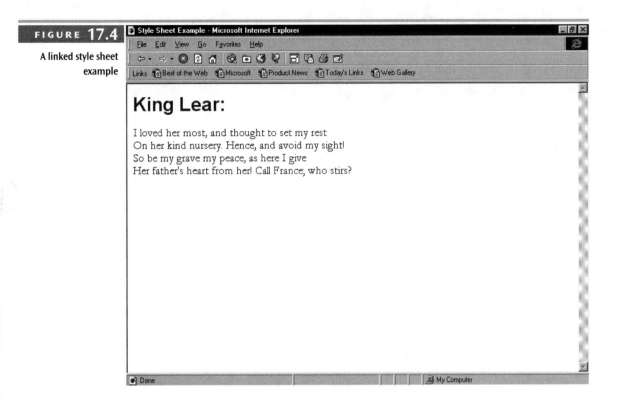

At this point, it's important to remember the cascading concept. If you want to have 10 HTML pages globally affected by this one style sheet, you can. Then, if you want minor adjustments to be made in individual pages, you can either embed more style in that individual page, or use an inline style.

The following page of code is linked to a master style sheet:

```
<html>

<head>

<title>Linked Style Sheet Example</title>

<link rel=stylesheet href="style-1.css" type="text/css">

</head>
```

PART

Web Page Design

```
<body>

<h1>King Lear:</h1>

<p>
I loved her most, and thought to set my rest <br>
On her kind nursery. Hence, and avoid my sight! <br>
So be my grave my peace, as here I give <br>
Her father's heart from her! Call France; who stirs? <br>
call Burgundy. Cornwall and Albany, <br>
With my two daughters' dowers digest this third: <br>
Let pride, which she calls plainness, marry her. <br>
I do invest you jointly with my power, <br>
Pre-eminence, and all the large effects <br>
That troop with majesty. Ourself, by monthly course, <br>
With reservation of an hundred knights, <br>
By you to be sustain'd, shall our abode <br>
Make with you by due turns. Only we still retain <br>
The name, and all the additions to a king; <br>
The sway, revenue, execution of the rest,<br>
Beloved sons, be yours: which to confirm, <br>
This coronet part betwixt you.
</p>

<h1>Kent:</h1>

<p>
Royal Lear,<br>
Whom I have ever honour'd as my king,<br>
Loved as my father, as my master follow'd,<br>
As my great patron thought on in my prayers
</p>

</body>
</html>
```

Figure 17.5 picks up the linked style information.

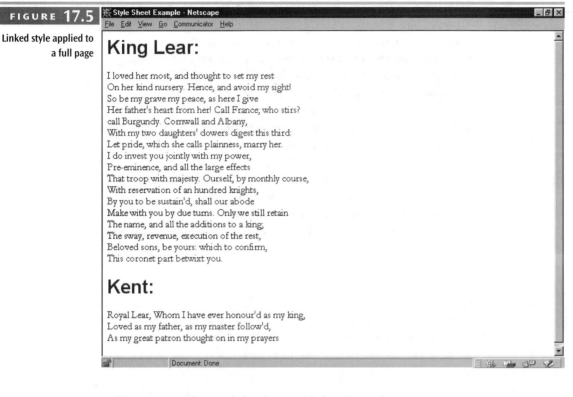

FIGURE **17.5**

Linked style applied to
a full page

Here, some inline style has been added to the code:

```
<html>

<head>

<title>Linked Style Sheet Example</title>

<link rel=stylesheet href="style-1.css" type="text/css">

</head>

<body>

<h1>King Lear:</h1>

<p>
I loved her most, and thought to set my rest <br>
On her kind nursery. Hence, and avoid my sight! <br>
So be my grave my peace, as here I give <br>
Her father's heart from her! Call France; who stirs? <br>
```

```
call <span style="text-decoration: underline">Burgundy, Cornwall and
Albany,</span> <br>
With my two daughters' dowers digest this third: <br>
Let pride, which she calls plainness, marry her. <br>
I do invest you jointly with my power, <br>
Pre-eminence, and all the large effects <br>
That troop with majesty. Ourself, by monthly course, <br>
With reservation of an hundred knights, <br>
By you to be sustain'd, shall our abode <br>
Make with you by due turns. Only we still retain <br>
The name, and all the additions to a king; <br>
The sway, revenue, execution of the rest,<br>
Beloved sons, be yours: which to confirm, <br>
This coronet part <span style="color: #CC9966">betwixt you.</span>
</p>

<h1>Kent:</h1>

<p>
Royal Lear, Whom I have ever honour'd as my king,<br>
Loved as my father, as my master follow'd,<br>
As my great patron thought on in my prayers
</p>

</body>
</html>
```

and you can see the results in Figure 17.6, the cascade in action—with the inline style overpowering the linked style.

WARNING   Be absolutely sure to view your style sheet pages in an appropriate browser—Internet Explorer 3.0 and above, and Netscape 4.0 and above. Otherwise all of your styles might disappear! You should always test your style-sheet–enhanced pages without the style sheet (use an older browser, or just change the name of the style sheet temporarily so the browser can't find it) to make sure they still look acceptable.

If you think about the long sections of text found in a play such as *King Lear*, it's easy to see how linked style sheets can be extremely helpful in terms of applying a singular look and feel to multiple pages with ease. Then, by using embedded or inline style, modifications can be made to individual pages as desired.

FIGURE 17.6

Inline style overpowers
linked style

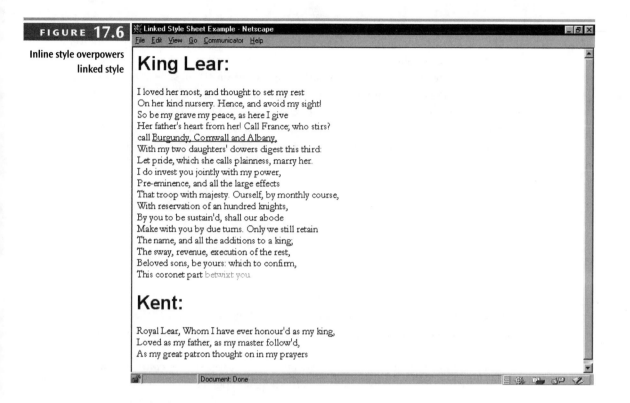

Properties and Values

There are numerous style sheet properties, many more than I can teach in one chapter. But to get you off to a working start, I've included some style sheet properties and values here. Typography and layout are the two most immediate and relevant areas where CSS is useful for designers. In the following sections I'll introduce you to style sheet methods of working with type and to some layout techniques.

You will definitely require more information about style sheets if you find that you are using them regularly in your design work. Up-to-date style sheet resources are available on the Web, and there are quite a number of books that address working with style.

PART

Web Page Design

N O T E   A primary online resource for style sheet information is the World Wide Web Consortium's style sheet section, `http://www.w3C.org/Style/`. In this area, you will find the complete specification and latest information on HTML style sheets. Because Microsoft's Internet Explorer pioneered popular browser support of style sheets, they've accumulated some excellent references on their site, `http://www.microsoft.com/`. Another, general reference that is very helpful is the style sheet section of The Web Developer's Virtual Library, `http://www.wdvl.com/`.

Fonts

One of the most attractive aspects of style sheets is their capacity to call for multiple fonts on a given page without having to use numerous <font> tags. Style sheets allow you, as you've seen, to choose a variety of typefaces and apply them to very specific sections of a page, such as a header number, paragraph, span, or division. Instead of the standard HTML <font> tag, however, you use the style sheet attribute font-family. You can add a variety of attributes along with that font family , or use classes and grouping (discussed later in the chapter) to exercise the power of type through the use of style sheets.

The reality of font support in style sheets is similar to issues encountered when using the <font> tag and its attributes. The specific typeface must be native to the computer viewing your page. As with the <font> tag, style sheets allow you to stack any number of typefaces to maximize the chances that your browser will pick up a typeface you want your audience to see. If they don't have Century Schoolbook, they'll probably have Garamond, and so forth. And while these typefaces have significant differences, their families are similar enough to be considered workable in style sheet design.

N O T E   Chapter 14 offers more on graphic type.

Style Sheet Font Families

Style sheets recognize five font families, attempting to address the major typographical groups:

> **Serif**   Serif faces are faces with letters that begin and end with small crossbars, also called finishing *strokes*. These strokes are said to aid in readability, and therefore serif typefaces are often used for body text. Some examples of serif faces include Times, Garamond, and Century Schoolbook (see Figure 17.7).

PART

Web Page Design

FIGURE **17.7**

An example of a serif typeface

Sans Serif   Sans-serif typefaces tend to be rounded and have no strokes. Common sans-serif typefaces include Optima, Futura, and Arial (see Figure 17.8).

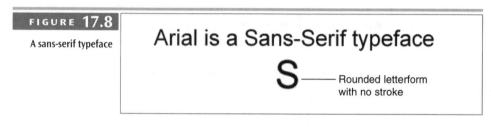

FIGURE **17.8**

A sans-serif typeface

Script   A script face looks similar to cursive or handwriting. A popular script face is Park Avenue, shown in Figure 17.9.

FIGURE **17.9**

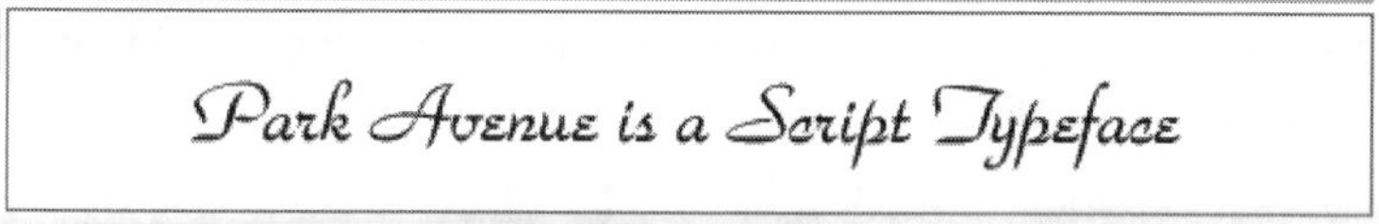

Park Avenue is a script typeface.

Park Avenue is a Script Typeface

Monospace   These faces look like they were typed on a typewriter. They are called monospace fonts because each letter within the face takes up the same width. This means that a *w*, which is wider in most faces than an *i*, is actually the same width in a monospace font. Courier (see Figure 17.10) is the most common monospace font on both PCs and Macintosh computers.

FIGURE **17.10**

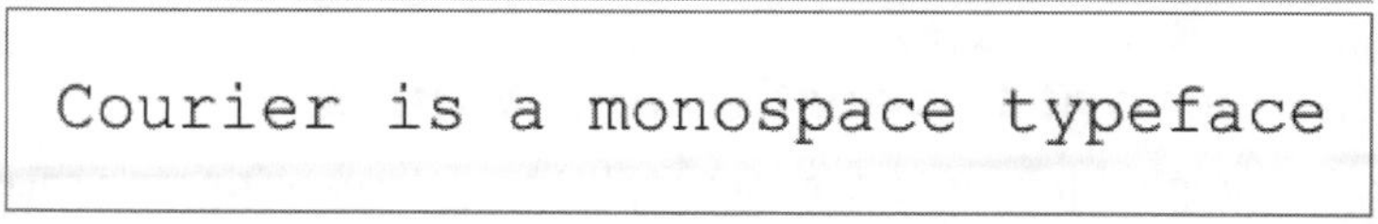

Monospace fonts are also referred to as typewriter fonts.

`Courier is a monospace typeface`

Decorative   Referred to by most typographers as *fantasy* typefaces, the decorative fonts are best used for headers and artistic text rather than body text. Decorative faces include Party and Whimsy, both depicted in Figure 17.11.

FIGURE 17.11

Party and Whimsy are
fantasy fonts.

Party is a fantasy, or decorative typeface

As is Whimsy

N O T E   For more information about font families and typography in general, see Chapter 14.

You can apply a series of font names to any logical HTML tag using the inline, embedded, and linked methods of style sheets.

Here's an inline example:

```
<p style="font-family: party, whimsy, fantasy">
We're having a party!
</p>
```

As you can see, I've specified the appropriate family name. If the browser cannot find the first two fonts installed on the viewer's computer, it will find the first fantasy font it can and use that.

N O T E   As mentioned in Chapter 14, there is a danger in using specialized fonts such as those in the fantasy family. If a user doesn't have the fantasy font installed, the browser will default to an installed font—usually something totally inappropriate. However, the new Web Embedding Font Tool (WEFT) from Microsoft addresses this issue, at least when using a newer version of the IE browser. For more information, visit the Microsoft typography site at http://www.microsoft.com/typography.

Defining Font Properties and Values

There is a range of properties you can apply to typefaces using style sheets, and an admirable selection of values you can apply to those properties. I'll focus on the most immediate and familiar here so you can get started using them in your designs.

As with standard HTML fonts, there are properties to control size and color. Unlike HTML fonts, you can also control the weight and style of a typeface, as well as line height, or *leading*, which is the measurement between individual lines of set type. Furthermore, the available methods to control font size far exceed anything that standard HTML has to offer.

Color Style sheets rely on standard browser color techniques. In other words, you will use hexadecimal (and preferably browser-safe) colors for optimal results. You can add color, like all style properties, to any reasonable HTML tag inline, in an embedded style sheet, or a linked style sheet option.

NOTE For more information about hexadecimal color, see Chapter 13.

This inline example applies font face and color to a paragraph:

```
<p style="font: arial, helvetica, sans-serif; color: #CCCCCC">
"We are an intelligent species and the use of our intelligence quite
properly gives us pleasure. In this respect the brain is like a
muscle. When it is in use we feel very good. Understanding is joyous." -
Carl Sagan, 1979
</p>
```

This paragraph will appear in gray when viewed through a browser that supports style sheets (see Figure 17.12).

Here's an example of color use with an embedded or linked style sheet:

```
<style>

BODY {
        background: #000000;
        }
H1 {
        font-family: helvetica, arial, sans-serif; color: #CCCCCC;
        }
P {
        font-family: garamond, times, serif;
        color: #FFFFFF;
        }

</style>
```

In this instance, the body has a black background with white text. The H1 header is gray, and the paragraph text is white (see Figure 17.13).

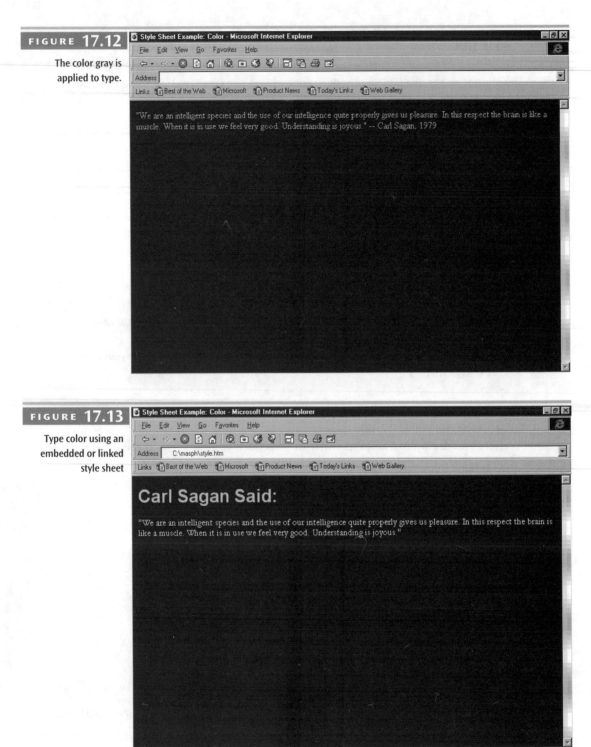

FIGURE 17.12

The color gray is
applied to type.

FIGURE 17.13

Type color using an
embedded or linked
style sheet

Weight Weight refers to the thickness of a typeface. The Arial face, for example, has variations in weight, including black (a very heavy face), bold, light, and so forth.

TIP Since typefaces have different variants, unless you are absolutely sure that your visitor has a specific typeface, it's generally wise to apply a value that is going to be available to all typefaces you are using in a declaration. There's really only one standard weight available to most every typeface, and that's bold!

Here's an example of weight applied inline:

```
<p style="font-family: arial, helvetica, sans-serif; font-weight: bold;
color=#CCCCCC;"> "We are an intelligent species and the use of our
intelligence quite properly gives us pleasure. In this respect the brain is
like a muscle. When it is in use we feel very good. Understanding is
joyous." - Carl Sagan, 1979
</p>
```

In Figure 17.14, you can see how the bold weight is applied to the paragraph.

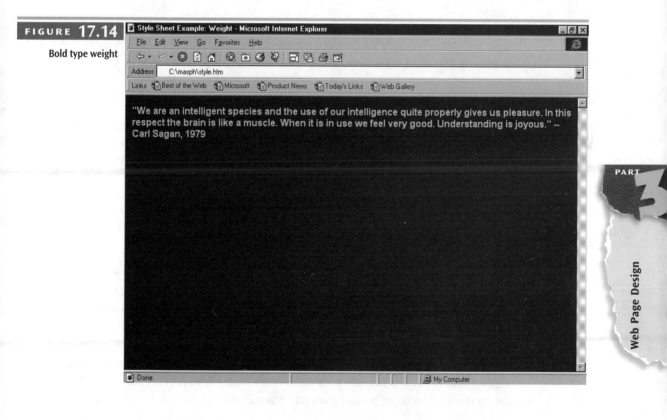

FIGURE 17.14

Bold type weight

You can also apply weight to an embedded or linked sheet:

```
<style>
```

```
BODY {
        background: #000000;
        color: #FFFFFF;
        }
H1 {
        font-family: helvetica, arial, sans-serif;
        font-weight: bold;
        color: #CCCCCC;
        }
P {
        font-family: garamond, times, serif;
        }
```

```
</style>
```

Style   In this context, style refers to the slant of a given typeface. There are two styles, *italic* and *oblique*. As with weight variations, oblique is a rare option and should be used cautiously. However, italic is available in almost every typeface, so you're pretty safe using it.

Inline style will look like this:

```
<p style="font-family: century schoolbook, times, serif; font-style:
italic;"> "We are an intelligent species and the use of our intelligence
quite properly gives us pleasure. In this respect the brain is like a
muscle. When it is in use we feel very good. Understanding is joyous." -
Carl Sagan, 1979
</p>
```

Figure 17.15 shows the italicized results.

 T I P   Italics and bold should be used sparingly. Their function in typography is *emphasis*. Typically, you will want to avoid using bold or italics for long sections of body text.

Size   Type size in style sheets can be defined using points, pixels, inches, centimeters, millimeters, and picas. For Web designers, points or pixels are the most natural choice, although this will depend upon your preferences. I stick with points because this is the measurement I use when setting graphical type for the Web.

FIGURE 17.15

Italicized type

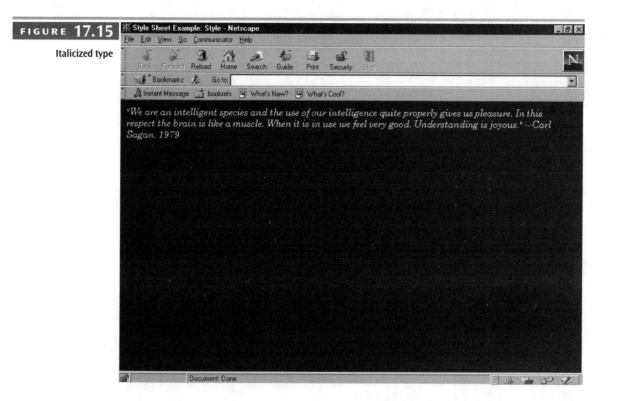

WARNING While the concept of so many size options is exciting, using measurements other than points can cause serious problems. One of these is the no-print phenomenon found when pixels are used as a measurement rather than points. While the type will appear in style sheet browsers (such as Internet Explorer 3.0 and above, and Netscape 4.0 and above), type defined in pixels may not print! For the sake of stability and consistency, I recommend using points as a measurement when setting type using style sheets.

Here's an example of inline style setting the size of the typeface in points:

```
<p style="font-family: century schoolbook, times, serif; font-size: 24pt;
font-style: italic;"> "We are an intelligent species and the use of our
intelligence quite properly gives us pleasure. In this respect the brain is
like a muscle. When it is in use we feel very good. Understanding is
joyous." - Carl Sagan, 1979
</p>
```

PART

Web Page Design

and here's an embedded or linked example:

```
<style>
```

```
BODY {
        background: #000000;
        color: #FFFFFF;
        }
H1 {
        font-family: helvetica, arial, sans-serif;
        font-size: 14pt;
        font-weight: bold;
        color: #CCCCCC;
        }
P {
        font-family: century schoolbook, times, serif;
        font-size: 12pt;
        font-style: italic;
    }
```

```
</style>
```

I recommend that you play around with measurement options just to get the hang of it and become familiar with them. But, remember, using measurements other than points can cause problems.

Other Type Considerations

Several other type options are good to be aware of, including these:

Text-decoration This option is useful for turning link underlining off—simply set text-decoration to none. Underline, italic, and strikethrough values are also supported.

Line-height Also known as leading, line-height sets the height of each line of text—essentially this value is the space in between each line.

Background This option places a color or image behind text, either with a color or a url(address) where address points to a background image tile. Note that this can be assigned not only to the <body> tag, but to any tag or span of text to highlight an area on a page.

Layout Overview

Style sheets promise a future of very complete layout control. However, until browser technology supports all of the existing and planned style sheet properties and values, and the public is regularly using these browsers, the use of style sheets for layout purposes is limited.

The importance of supplying you with this information is to demonstrate the evolution of HTML in terms of design and control. Style sheets offer that control, and when their use becomes realistic, you'll have the knowledge at your fingertips.

Style sheets can help you with layout by providing you with a variety of alignment options and margin control. Alignment of text can be most simply controlled with the text-align property. Values include left, right, center, and justify.

The following style sheet shows text alignment and how it affects each paragraph:

```
<p style="text-align: justify">
"And don't tell me God works in mysterious ways", Yossarian continued
"There's nothing mysterious about it, He's not working at all. He's playing.
</p>

<p style="text-align: right">
Or else He's forgotten all about us. That's the kind of God you people talk
about, a country bumpkin, a clumsy, bungling, brainless, conceited, uncouth
hayseed.
</p>

<p style="text-align: left">
Good God, how much reverence can you have for a Supreme Being who finds it
necessary to include such phenomena as phlegm and tooth decay in His divine
system of Creation?
</p>

<p style="text-align: center">
What in the world was running through that warped, evil, scatalogical mind
of His when He robbed old people of the power to control their bowel
movements? Why in the world did He ever create pain?" - Joseph Heller, from
Catch 22.
</p>
```

Figure 17.16 shows the alignment differences of each paragraph.

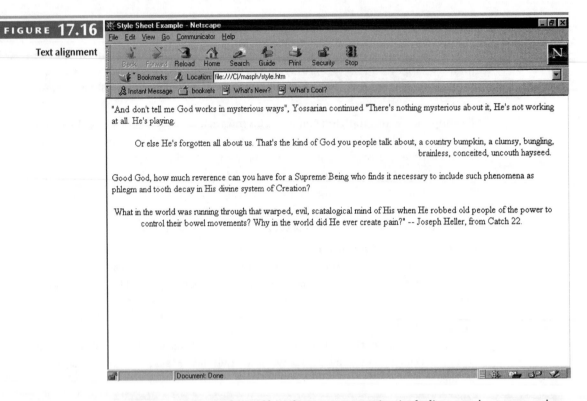

FIGURE 17.16

Text alignment

Margin control uses four self-explanatory properties, including margin-top, margin-bottom, margin-left, and margin-right. These properties can be applied, as with all CSS properties, to any logical selector. Typically, the BODY and P (paragraph) selectors will be naturals for margin controls.

As with font measurement values, you can use a number of measurement systems for margin control. Pixels, points, centimeters, inches, and percentages are all logical and legal value types. I prefer to stick to pixels, because standard HTML layout and design is usually measured in pixels.

NOTE   CSS allows for negative values for margin properties, so the designer can overlap areas of a page's design, which is a powerful feature with no existing relative in standard HTML. However, browser support is still sketchy regarding negative values, and they should be used with care.

Here's an example of a style sheet using margin controls:

```
<style>
BODY {
        background: #000000;
        color: #FFFFFF;
```

```
      margin-top: 100px;
      margin-left; 100px;
      }
P {

      font-family: century schoolbook, times, serif;
      font-size: 12pt;
      }

</style>
```

Figure 17.17 shows the results.

One of the most powerful capabilites of CSS is the ability to absolutely position elements on a Web page. Not only can text and graphics be precisely set off from the left and top sides of a Web browser, but these elements can also be layered on top of one another.

In Figure 17.18, a square and rectangle have been positioned on a Web page. Note that this is not one single graphic—the square and rectangle are separate GIFs with the order in which they appear explicitly set in the source code.

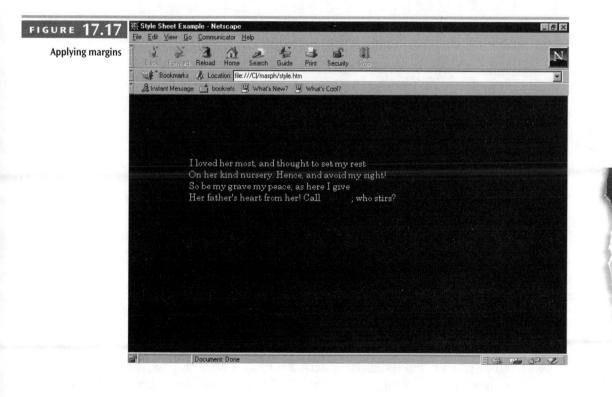

FIGURE 17.17

Applying margins

PART

Web Page Design

FIGURE **17.18**

Precise positioning
and layering of two
elements with CSS

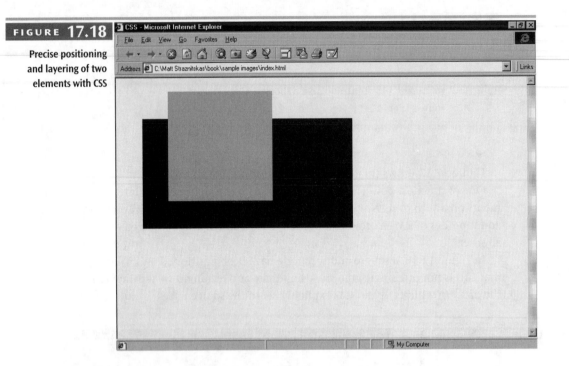

And here's the HTML and CSS that make it happen:

```
<HTML>
<HEAD>
<TITLE>CSS</TITLE>
</HEAD>
<BODY BGCOLOR="#FFFFFF">

<div id="rectangle" style="position:absolute; left:50px; top:75px">
<img src="rectangle.gif" width="400" height="200">
</div>

<div id="square" style="position:absolute; left:100px; top:25px">
<img src="square.gif" width="200" height="200">
</div>

</BODY>
</HTML>
```

Note that by simply putting the square after the rectangle, the square sits in front of the rectangle on the Web page. When you begin to think about the possibilities of mixing graphics and text together in layouts that are precisely positioned and layered, the power of CSS becomes clear. Figure 17.19 displays some layout experiments found on the Microsoft Typography Web site (http://www.microsoft.com/typography) that use CSS and embedded fonts. It is important to note that these pages contain *no GIFs or JPEGs*—everything is either a typeface or a symbol font.

FIGURE 17.19

Unique Web page layouts using CSS and embedded fonts

PART

Web Page Design

Class and Grouping

Two other interesting aspects of style sheets include class and grouping. Class refers to ways of breaking down your style rules into very precise pieces. Whenever you want some of the text on your pages to look different than the other text, you can create what amounts to a custom-built HTML tag. Each type of specially formatted text you define is called a *style class*.

For example, suppose you wanted two different kinds of H1 headings in your document. You would create a style class for each one by putting the following code in the style sheet:

```
<style>
H1.serif {
        font: 24pt Century Schoolbook
            }
H1.sans {
        font: 18pt Arial
            }
</style>
```

To choose between the two style classes in an HTML page, you would use the class attribute, as follows.

```
<h1 class="serif">Wisdom</h1>
"Do not fear your enemies. The worst they can do is kill you. Do not fear
friends. At worst, they may betray you. Fear those who do not care; they
neither kill nor betray, but betrayal and murder exists because of their
silent consent." - Bruno Jasienski

<h1 class=sans>More Wisdom</h1>
"Young love is a flame; very pretty, often very hot and fierce, but still
only light and flickering. The love of the older and disciplined heart is as
coals, deep burning, unquenchable." - Henry Ward Beecher
```

The word "Wisdom" appears in 24-point Bergell to people whose browsers support style sheets (and whose computers have the Bergell font installed!), while the words "More Wisdom" appear in the 18-point Arial font. You'll also see that the text in between defaults to Times, because I haven't made a rule for it anywhere (see Figure 17.20). Therefore, the browser selects its own default body font.

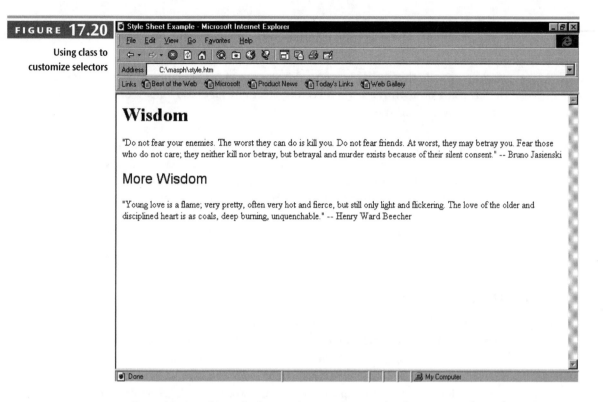

FIGURE 17.20

Using class to
customize selectors

Grouping is achieved when style properties and values are condensed, resulting in tighter rules. Consider the following class example:

```
P.1 {
        font: arial;
        font-size: 12pt;
        line-height: 14pt
        }
```

This means that all paragraphs with the class of "1" will show up as a 12 point Arial font with a line height of 14 points. If I apply grouping to this class, I end up with the following results:

```
P.1 {font: 12pt/14pt arial}
```

The design will be the same, either way. Notice, however, that I place the font size first, the line height after the forward slash, and then the name of the font. Grouping requires a specific syntactical order to work properly.

PART

Web Page Design

Tools for CSS

I am a strong proponent of knowing how to write HTML by hand, but some pages of CSS—especially those with very complex arrangements of graphics and text—are better off being done with a WYSIWYG tool. It simply takes too long to put some pages of complex CSS together by hand.

With the development of programs like Macromedia Dreamweaver (`http://www.dreamweaver.com`), designers finally have some usable tools for doing complex coding. Since most CSS tools are new, it is important to stay current on industry developments. Unlike Quark and Pagemaker, tools such as Dreamweaver are brand new to the market and may end up being outclassed by other applications.

All of this is not to say that the basics of CSS shouldn't be second nature to most Web designers. No matter how good the tool, there will always be times when you'll need to roll up your sleeves and tinker with code.

Conclusion

While this chapter veers away from the study of Photoshop, it is critical that you learn about CSS. As style sheets become more accessible to designers, much of the Web design work currently being done with Photoshop will be done with style sheets instead. However, that's not to say that learning Photoshop is a waste of time. Working through basic design principles in Photoshop will assist you in working with CSS-based layouts.

There is certainly some frustration when you set out to learn a method, particularly one as complex as style sheets, only to find yourself waiting until the technology catches up with the technique. Still, I am certain you'll not only be ahead of the game because of your early exposure to these techniques, but ultimately you'll be more competitive as a professional. Most importantly, you will feel satisfaction knowing that you have more than one option when approaching a Web design project.

Up Next

Get out your pocket protector and slide rule, because we're about to enter the fun yet technical world of Dynamic HTML (DHTML). More than just some new tags, DHTML is a whole new way to create interactive pages. Best of all, these visual effects won't make your users wait forever for the pages to download.

Mastering the Medium: Clients from Hell

If for some reason this book were being written for marketing managers rather than designers, then this section would be called "Designers from Hell." It's common for designers to have problems with clients, but it's just as common for clients to have problems with designers. The underlying issue is that designers and clients have different goals. Designers are usually interested in

Being stylish   There's nothing a designer hates worse than being asked to design with overused typefaces or tired color schemes. Doing work that is fresh and unique is essential.

Making a name for themselves   It's important for designers to carve out an identity for themselves. Designers hope to have the respect of their peers and some claim to fame, whether it's being great with type or knowing the latest animation software.

Doing important work   A project doesn't have to be for a big company to make a designer take an interest, but it must have the potential to be something special. Designers are looking for clients who have a compelling vision for their products or services.

On the other hand, clients are focused on

Increasing sales   The whole point of marketing is ultimately to make more money. Sometimes the best way to accomplish this is through artful Web sites, but sometimes it means designing garish, animated banner ads. Clients will generally do whatever it takes to increase market share and profits.

Improving brand recognition   Most companies are constantly trying to improve the visibility of their brand. One way to do this is to maintain a consistent look to all of their materials. If the company logo is red, it's imperative that the logo remains red on the Web.

Keeping a job/getting a better job   Everyone wants to succeed, and the primary way you get raises and promotions in business is to have your management feel that you are doing a good job. If management demands a Web site by the end of the month, that employee will be motivated to put deadlines before quality.

Beyond the normal designer/client goal conflicts, there do exist true Clients from Hell. These companies tend to have one or all of the following characteristics:

No experience   Some clients don't have experience in assembling effective marketing teams. Sometimes the team is a large group of managers with little Web experience, while other times everything must be run by a President or CEO who has never used a computer. This problem is found most frequently in small to mid-size companies.

No content The production of a Web site often relies on the client providing written content for the site. Clients can often be very tardy with this deliverable—weeks, months, or even years! If you don't get paid until the job is done, you may never end up getting payment from these clients.

No payment Speaking of payment, there are actually some clients who never pay their bills. In my experience, about 1% of all billings show up as bad debt on the general ledger.

It's often difficult to tell when you've got a Client from Hell on your hands until it's too late. However, veteran designers in your area can point out possible Clients from Hell and help you avoid them.

DYNAMIC HTML

Featuring

CHAPTER 18

DYNAMIC HTML

A s discussed in Chapter 17, the advent of Cascading Style Sheets (CSS) means that many of the design limitations associated with HTML have been overcome. But neither HTML nor CSS is capable of true multimedia feats. Sure, you can use animated GIFs and plug-ins to create Web page animation and interactivity, but these technologies have drawbacks.

Enter Dynamic HTML (DHTML). As the name suggests, DHTML improves on HTML by making Web page elements such as text and graphics interactive and dynamic. Best of all, DHTML Web pages download in a heartbeat.

Software companies such as Microsoft and Netscape have recently released Web browsers that support DHTML. Designers now have a slew of new interactive effects at their disposal, including the ability to choreograph text and graphics into animated, television-like presentations.

This chapter offers insight on DHTML and some useful code to make DHTML effects work. If you don't know how to write scripts, don't worry—you can copy some of the code here and put it into your Web pages. The important thing is to start thinking *dynamically*.

What Is DHTML?

More than anything else, DHTML is a marketing term. There's nothing wrong with marketing terms, but in order to understand DHTML, it is important to know about its components.

DHTML effects are accomplished using three technologies: HTML, CSS, and scripting. While each of these technologies has been around for some time, they are being used together now and providing designers with the opportunity to create Web pages that look and interact better than ever before.

HTML

As discussed in Chapter 16, HTML is the markup language used to create Web pages. HTML serves as the backbone for DHTML effects. If you don't know how to create HTML documents, go back to Chapter 16 before you attempt these DHTML effects.

Cascading Style Sheets

As described in Chapter 17, the CSS standard includes the ability to position graphic elements precisely on a Web page. Such elements must be set off from the rest of the Web page using <span> or <div> tags. The following passage states that the graphic called bug.gif is to be positioned 200 pixels from the left margin and 50 pixels from the top margin on the Web page (see Figure 18.1).

```
<div id="bug" style="position:absolute; left:200px; top:50px">
<img src="graphics/bug.gif" width="132" height="100">
</div>
```

Scripting

With CSS, each item on a Web page can not only be positioned exactly, but it can also be made available for special actions and properties. These properties are controlled through scripting. Scripting makes Web page elements dynamic—buttons that press down, text that disappears, and images that fly across the screen.

DHTML can be accomplished with two scripting languages: VBScript and JavaScript. VBScript stands for Visual Basic Scripting and is a simplified version of Microsoft's Visual Basic programming language. JavaScript is the scripting version of Sun Microsystem's Java programming language.

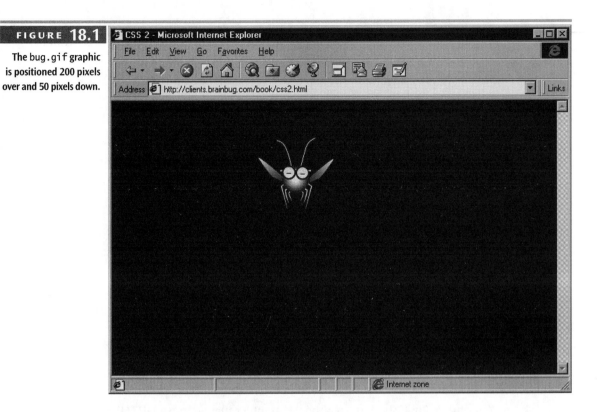

FIGURE 18.1

The bug.gif graphic
is positioned 200 pixels
over and 50 pixels down.

Andy Weatherwax, an accomplished DHTML designer, offers the following advice
on choosing a scripting language.

*Although either scripting language can be used to create DHTML, JavaScript
provides the most versatility because it is currently supported by both Netscape's and Microsoft's browsers. Also, the syntax of JavaScript is similar to
that of Java and C++, familiar languages to many Web developers.*

*Microsoft and Netscape support JavaScript, but they are at different stages of
implementation. Use caution when authoring cross-platform DHTML. If you
are authoring for a specific browser, as in intranet development, the choice
becomes one of personal preference. Some Web developers use a combination
of JavaScript and VBScript to make their sites dynamic.*

Writing scripts is an endeavor that's more demanding than composing HTML. On
the other hand, scripting is not nearly as complex as actual programming language
since it doesn't involve compiling code.

PART

Web Page Design

TIP   Creating DHTML effects does not necessarily mean that you have to write scripts. Later in this chapter you'll learn two ways to avoid having to write code.

DHTML and IE 4

DHTML is accomplished with HTML, CSS, and scripting, but what you can actually do with DHTML is defined by the components included in a Web browser. For example, IE 4 contains built-in visual and transition filters. Web designers need only refer to these filters by name or number to invoke them in a script.

Because DHTML is implemented differently in both IE and Netscape, it is important to determine an intended browser application and version before writing any DHTML. All of the DHTML examples in this book are intended for the Windows version of the IE 4 Web browser.

WARNING   The Macintosh version of IE 4 doesn't support DHTML at this time.

How Does Photoshop Fit In?

You can use Photoshop for creating the graphics that go into a DHTML effect. For example, if you want to create a series of interactive buttons, the first thing you'll need to do is fire up Photoshop, design some buttons, and create every possible state—on or off for each button. In my example, I have three buttons, so there are four possible states. The first version will be all of the buttons in their inactive states. The second, third, and fourth versions will be each of the buttons activated (see Figure 18.2). In this case, the activated state turns on a small light inside the button.

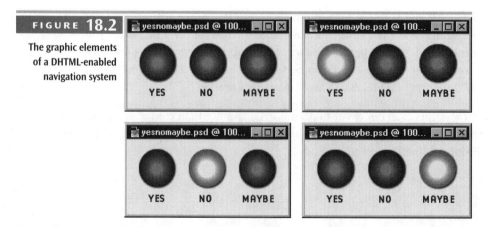

FIGURE 18.2

The graphic elements of a DHTML-enabled navigation system

Photoshop is also a good place to simulate DHTML effects. To envision what an interactive or animated effect might look like, try creating the various graphic components in Photoshop and then turn different layers on and off. In this way, you can simulate what the state changes or movement might look like.

Interactive Navigation

For years, Web designers have had to jump through hoops to create simple interactive effects. Buttons that change color or menus that drop down from the side of a page had to be created with complex Java applications. DHTML addresses these needs with compact passages of code that are quick to download.

Mouseovers

A button that changes its appearance based on user input is one of the most popular interactive effects on the Web. Why do we like it so much? Probably because it reminds us of the tactile nature of buttons and switches in the real world. Whatever the reason, DHTML is a big help in creating these simple effects.

Creating an Interactive Menu Button

Figure 18.3 depicts a typical menu button. The graphic on the left is the button in its normal state, and the graphic on the right is the button in its activated state. The two graphic states were created in Photoshop and saved as separate GIFs.

FIGURE **18.3**

A simple button in inactive and active states

To put our button on a Web page and make it interactive with DHTML, we need to write some code. This page starts like other HTML document:

```
<html>
<head>
<title>Mouseover Effect</title>
```

Next, the scripting language is specified.

```
<script language = "JavaScript" type="text/javascript">
```

Here comes the tricky stuff. The next bit of text is the script, which is placed in a <script> tag. The script defines the functions that are stored until executed by events on the page. The script says that when the mouse moves over the image, the browser

PART

Web Page Design

is to substitute the active state button. When the mouse moves off of the image, the browser is to use the inactive state button.

```
<!-
    //mouse on images

        if (document.images) {

            img1on = new Image();
            img1on.src = "graphics/button-on.gif";

        //mouse off images

            img1off = new Image();
            img1off.src = "graphics/button-off.gif";


        }

    function imgOn(imgName) {
        if (document.images) {
            document[imgName].src = eval(imgName + "on.src");
        }
    }

    function imgOff(imgName) {
        if (document.images) {
            document[imgName].src = eval(imgName + "off.src");
        }
    }
    // ->
```

At this point, the <script> and <head> tags are closed and the <body> tag is opened. The <bgcolor> tag is used to specify a white background for the Web page.

```
</script>
</head>
<body bgcolor="#ffffff">
```

At this point you can put an image into the page, hyperlink it if desired, and include references to an event—in this case, a mouseover event. Except for the references to the scripts, creating this code isn't much different than creating a hyperlinked graphic with regular HTML.

```
<A HREF = "#"
onMouseOver = "imgOn('img1')"
onMouseOut = "imgOff('img1')">
<img src="graphics/button-heads.gif" width="36" height="35"
name="img1" border=0></a>
```

Now all you have to do is close the <body> and <html> tags.

```
</body>
</html>
```

Having trouble getting everything to work right? Don't worry—scripting can be painstaking work. Forgetting even a comma may cause a script to malfunction. The important thing is to get an understanding of how images are handled in DHTML effects.

Drop-Down Menus

Drop-down menus are great because they stay hidden when they're not in use—a great space-saver on crowded Web pages. In Figure 18.4, you see a menu that is tucked up into the corner of a page until a user mouses over it.

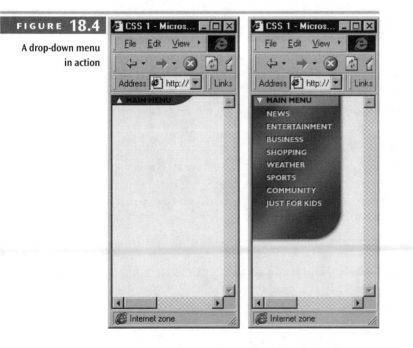

FIGURE 18.4

A drop-down menu in action

PART

Web Page Design

Creating a Drop-Down Menu

Just as in the mouseover example, you start with the basic HTML tags and specify script language.

```
<html>
<head>
<title>Drop Down Menu</title>
<SCRIPT LANGUAGE = "JavaScript">
```

Now add in some JavaScript to make your menu appear or hide depending on the position of the cursor. Also close the necessary tags and set the Web page background color to white.

```
/* Show an object */
function showObject(object) {
    object.visibility = VISIBLE;
}

/* Hide an object */
function hideObject(object) {
    object.visibility = HIDDEN;
}

</SCRIPT>
</head>
<body bgcolor="#ffffff">
```

This example is very similar to the mouseover script in the previous example. In that example, the object you were showing or hiding was an image. In this example, the object is called a *layer* as defined by the <div> tag. A layer can hold any regular HTML elements, such as text or images. As you can see, each <div> tag has an ID attribute, one is called menuUp and the other menuDown. The ID makes everything inside the <div> tag an object.

```
<div id="menuUp" style="position:absolute; left:0px; top:0px; width:400px;
height:100px; z-index:1; visibility: visible">
<A HREF = "#" onMouseOver = "showObject(menuDown)"><img src="graphics/menu-
main-up.jpg" border=0></a>
</div>

<div id="menuDown" style="position:absolute; left:0px; top:0px; width:400px;
height:100px; z-index:1; visibility: hidden">
<A HREF = "#" onMouseOut = "hideObject(menuDown)"><img src="graphics/menu-
main.jpg" border=0></a>
</div>
```

Now you'll define the variables for the visibility of the two layers:

```
<SCRIPT LANGUAGE = "JavaScript">

    var HIDDEN = 'hidden';
    var VISIBLE = 'visible';

    var menuUp = document.all.menuUp.style;
    var menuDown = document.all.menuDown.style;

</SCRIPT>
```

All that's left to do now is close the body and HTML tags.

```
</body>
</html>
```

Filters

There are two kinds of filters in DHTML: visual and transition. Both of the filter effects are very cool, but the visual filters are probably the most useful. Visual filters are things like drop shadows and glows that can be applied to text and graphics. The transition filters create wipes and fades like those used in movies between scenes.

Visual Filters

Microsoft Internet Explorer includes a wide range of visual filters:

- Flip Horizontal
- Flip Vertical
- Gray
- Invert
- Xray
- Alpha
- Blur
- Chroma
- Drop Shadow
- Glow
- Mask
- Shadow
- Wave

Figure 18.5 is an image created in Photoshop. The first graphic has the Drop Shadow filter applied and the second has none.

Visual filters can be chained together, so you can have a graphic that is both glowing and inverted—or any other combination of effects.

 WARNING   Visual filters are a lot of fun to experiment with, but only use them when a Web design or concept warrants. It's best not to overwhelm a design with unnecessary visual effects.

PART

Web Page Design

FIGURE **18.5**

The image on the right has no visual filter applied, while the image on the left has the drop shadow effect applied.

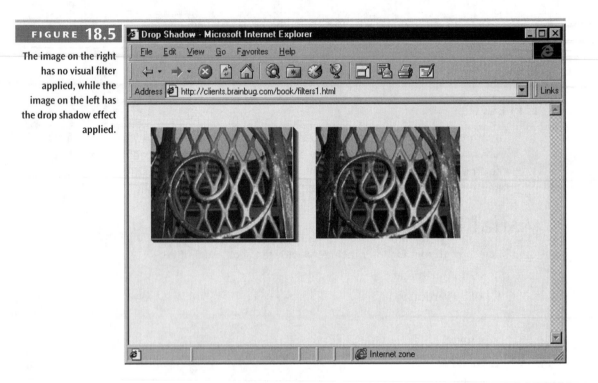

Applying the Drop Shadow Filter

As in the previous DHTML examples, you begin with some HTML.

```
<html>
<head>
<title>Drop Shadow</title>
</head>
<body bgcolor="#ffffff">
```

Now, jump right into wrapping the two images with <div> tags and positioning the graphics with CSS. The first graphic has the color of the shadow specified as black (#000000). The direction of the shadow is set at 135 degrees, resulting in a shadow that is cast from a light source coming from the top-left corner.

```
<DIV ID = "shadow" STYLE = "width: 500; height: 40; position:absolute;
left:30px; top:30px; filter: shadow(color=#000000, direction=135)">
<img src="graphics/3.jpg" width=200 height=150>
</DIV>

<DIV ID = "nohadow" style="position:absolute; left:260px; top:30px">
<img src="graphics/3.jpg" width=200 height=150>
</DIV>
```

Finally, close the remaining HTML tags.

```
</body>
</html>
```

WARNING   Remember, all of the DHTML examples in this chapter were written for the Windows version of IE 4. If the effects are not working in your browser, try using the version of IE that came with this book.

Transition Filters

Transition filters are very useful when you want to present a series of consecutive images in a stylish way. The complete list of transition filters supported by Internet Explorer 4.0 and their corresponding numbers follows. The numbers are used within the script to identify the type of transition.

0. Box In

1. Box Out

2. Circle In

3. Circle Out

4. Wipe Up

5. Wipe Down

6. Wipe Right

7. Wipe Left

8. Vertical Blinds

9. Horizontal Blinds

10. Checker Board Across

11. Checker Board Down

12. Random Dissolve

13. Split Vertical In

14. Split Vertical Out

15. Split Horizontal In

16. Split Horizontal Out

17. Strips Left Down

18. Strips Left

19. Strips Right Down

20. Strips Right Up

21. Random Bars Horizontal

22. Random Bars Vertical

Applying the Random Dissolve Filter to a Photo

With this exercise, you will create a Random Dissolve between two images that have been created in Photoshop (see Figure 18.6).

FIGURE 18.6

A Random Dissolve applied to two images

Begin creating the Random Dissolve by inserting the typical HTML to start the document.

```
<html>
<head>
<title>Random Dissolve</title>
</head>
<body bgcolor="#ffffff">
```

Now define the objects that make up the page. Text and graphics are put inside <div> tags. The text that says, "Click here to see the transition," will initiate the transition effect. Inside the <div> tag named "swap" are the two images that make up the transistion. Note that both images are positioned in the same location on the page.

```
<DIV ID=control1 STYLE="POSITION:absolute;TOP:220;LEFT:45;
visibility:visible">
  <br>
  <A HREF="#"  onclick=TransPhoto()>Click Here to see transition.</a>
</DIV>

<DIV ID="swap" STYLE="POSITION:absolute; WIDTH:200; HEIGHT:150; TOP:20;
LEFT:20; FILTER:revealTrans(Duration=1.0); visibility:visible">
  <IMG ID="photo1" STYLE="Position:absolute; left:20; top:30"
SRC="graphics/1.jpg">
  <IMG ID="photo2" STYLE="Position:absolute;left:20; top: 30"
SRC="graphics/2.jpg">
</DIV>
```

Here's where you insert the script that makes the transition happen. For this effect, you are using VBScript. The script defines all of the actions that will happen in the objects. Note that at the end of this script, the line Transition = 12 is specified. If you would like to use another type of transition, simply change this number to one of the transition filter numbers mentioned in the previous section.

```
<SCRIPT LANGUAGE="VBScript">
dim transDuration
dim TransDirection
dim bTransInProgress

TransDirection = 0
transDuration=2.5

Sub Window_onLoad()
  bTransInProgress = False
End Sub
```

```
sub swap_OnFilterChange()
    bTransInProgress = False
End Sub

Sub TransPhoto()
    if bTransInProgress then Exit Sub
      call swap.filters.item(0).Apply()

    if TransDirection = 1 then
            TransDirection = 2
            photo2.Style.Visibility = ""
            photo1.Style.Visibility = "hidden"
    else
            TransDirection = 1
            photo1.Style.Visibility = ""
            photo2.Style.Visibility = "hidden"
    end if
    swap.filters.item(0).Transition = 12
    swap.filters(0).play(transDuration)
    bTransInProgress = True
End Sub
</SCRIPT>
```

Now close the remaining HTML tags, and the effect will be complete.

```
</body>
</html>
```

Animation

Animation for the Web has been possible for some time using technologies like Flash, Shockwave, ActiveX, Java, and animated GIFs. But each of these technologies has its drawbacks. Flash and Shockwave both require third-party plug-ins. Older computers can have trouble with ActiveX and Java because they are processor intensive, and animated GIFs are limited because they're not interactive and file sizes can be large. With Dynamic HTML, animation can happen anywhere on a Web page and interact fully with all the elements on that page. Figure 18.7 shows a clever use of DHTML. The graphic of a bug is actually a small animated GIF that is moving across the page. So there are two kinds of animation happening at once—character animation accomplished with animated GIF and movement of the GIF along a path via DHTML.

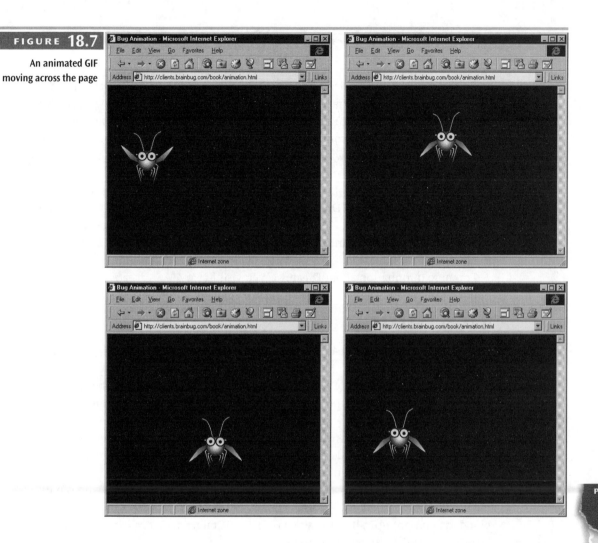

FIGURE **18.7**

An animated GIF
moving across the page

Creating animation with Dynamic HTML is more involved than simple mouseover scripts and is best left to experienced programmers or third-party software products. As I will discuss in the next section, new DHTML authoring products have made creating animation more intuitive and designer-friendly.

PART

Web Page Design

Is There an Easier Way?

After spending some time trying to write scripts, many designers throw up their hands and wonder if there's an easier way. The answer is yes, and there are actually two.

The first way is to collaborate with professional programmers. Web designers are valued for their creative talents, not for their programming skills. As the Web has evolved, skills and positions have become more specialized. Try to find someone who is excited about DHTML, experienced with JavaScript or VBScript, and wants to make your visions a reality.

The other way is to use software that will create the scripts for you. As mentioned in Chapter 17, Macromedia Dreamweaver is an excellent WYSIWYG tool for CSS, and it's equally good for DHTML. This application can be of great help in producing many DHTML effects, especially animation. It even has an option for creating DTHML for Explorer or Navigator.

For more information about Dreamweaver, visit http://www.dreamweaver.com.

Conclusion

From the perspective of Web designers, DHTML is clearly one of the most exciting technologies emerging today. Menus, logos, and images can all be made to respond to the user without using exotic software and annoying installation procedures.

But Microsoft and Netscape have implemented DHTML differently, sometimes so significantly that the pages won't run on the other company's browser. Another issue is that DHTML is only supported by newer versions of Internet Explorer and Navigator (4.0 and higher). At best, older browsers display DHTML pages that are compromised in their layout and organization. At worst, the pages won't load at all.

This situation has lead to a critical decision for designers. For anyone who is building a Web site for the mass consumer market, implementing DHTML may not be the best decision right now. If a Web site has a specific target audience with an up-to-date browser, DHTML becomes more viable.

The long-term advantages of DHTML are so apparent that it seems unlikely the current incompatibilities between browsers will last for long. Hopefully we'll have a DHTML standard that is much more universal. If that's the case, it makes sense for budding Photoshop Masters to begin to harness the power of DHTML and start designing the great Web experiences of tomorrow.

Up Next

Not only have you completed Part III of this book, but you've also completed the main text of *Mastering Photoshop 5 for the Web*. Congratulations! But before you head off into the world with your PhD in Web design, be sure to peruse the appendices. With sections on Adobe's hot new ImageReady product and the companion Web site to this book, you've still got a few things left to learn.

Matt Straznitskas
http://www.brainbug.com
860.418.5787

Mastering the Medium: Be Your Own Brand

The concept of branding has become popular with marketing and design specialists. In most cases, a brand's value is determined by the complete effect that all of a company's communications has on its consumers. Good brands are seen as having a good reputation, and companies spend a lot of time and money to insure that things stay that way.

Recently, it has been suggested that people are also brands and that it is in their interest to carefully consider the ways they are perceived. Of course, there are people who have been doing this for years—Hollywood stars and sports personalities often hire publicity agents to expertly build their brand.

But it's no longer just the rich and famous who have recognized the importance of branding. Managing the way you are perceived is already an important part of everyday business. If you don't think the age of personal branding is already upon us, consider the Internet. Anything you've ever said under your own name in a newsgroup can often be found in a matter of minutes. Unless you've carefully considered every communication you've made, your brand value could depreciate in the minds of people who are important to you.

As our culture becomes more sophisticated and image conscious, businesses will favor job applicants who have mastered the art of building a superior personal brand. Not only will they look for people who haven't done anything to tarnish their brand, they'll also look for people who have raised their value. Here are a few ways that Web designers can enhance their own brand:

Personal Web sites The home page has done more to usher in the age of personal branding than any marketing device ever invented. As detailed in Chapter 11, it is imperative that a Web designer create a site that is reflective of their business objectives.

PART

Web Page Design

Employer/clients   If a Web designer works for a well-known company or has a stable of great clients, the designer will benefit from the association. "If this Web designer is good enough for Microsoft (or any other popular company), then that's good enough for me" is a common refrain among potential employers and clients.

Writing and speaking   Designers tend to toil in anonymity, but some have begun to recognize the value of writing and/or speaking regularly to their industry. Years ago, few people knew David Siegel, the designer of the popular typeface Tekton. But now everyone knows David Siegel, the author of Web design books and lecturer at technology conferences.

If you still don't think personal branding is important, consider how I came to learn about the Photoshop Masters who are profiled in this book. Sure, they're great designers, but how did these dozen or so people get discovered in the first place? They either had (1) a great personal Web site, (2) employment at a well-known company, or (3) articles or books to their credit. Their inclusion in this book has only increased the chances that someone else will want to profile these people in another publication.

The power of personal branding is very real. Because of their adeptness with the Web, designers are in a unique position to talk about it, write about it, and use it to their benefit.

APPENDICES

appendix A

IMAGEREADY

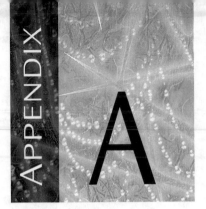

IMAGEREADY

For years, Web designers were second-class citizens when it came to Photoshop. Adobe had invested tremendous resources in making Photoshop the premiere image-editing tool for print, so when the Web came along, much of the program was not of use to Web designers. In recent years, Adobe has added new features to make the creation of Web graphics more convenient, but you still can't use Photoshop to build animations or calculate how long a graphic will take to download.

That's where Adobe's smartly designed ImageReady program comes in. Released as a free tryout version in April of 1998, the application unburdens future versions of Photoshop from having to include animation and other Web-only features.

N O T E For more information about ImageReady, pricing, and available versions for download or sale, visit Adobe on the Web at http://www.adobe.com.

The ImageReady Workspace

The first thing you'll notice about the ImageReady workspace is that it looks a lot like the Photoshop workspace (shown in Figure A.1).

N O T E It is unclear if Adobe intends to keep the cute rubber duck—seen in the Toolbar and as file icons—as the program's logo beyond the 1.0 preview. If you are patient, you can get the development team's position on the matter by viewing the About Adobe ImageReady 1.0 splash screen.

FIGURE A.1

The ImageReady
workspace

ImageReady's Menu Bar contains the same nine items found in Photoshop. There's also a Toolbar, main image window, and a host of palettes. Some of the palettes, such as Layers (shown below), History, and Actions, will seem very familiar.

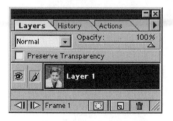

Upon closer inspection, though, you'll begin to see that there are some differences. While there is an Info palette, it contains listings like Hex, a reference to the Hexadecimal color values that were discussed in Chapter 13.

Some palettes are totally new, such as the Type palette, which allows you to change a layer's type without having to go into the Type Tool dialog.

As you begin to delve into each of the nine Menu Bar options, the differences between ImageReady and Photoshop become even more apparent. In the File menu, you'll find new commands such as Save Optimized and Image Info.

New...	Ctrl+N	Exit
Open...	Ctrl+O	
Close	Ctrl+W	
Save Optimized	Ctrl+Alt+S	
Save Optimized As...	Ctrl+Shift+Alt+S	
Save Original	Ctrl+S	
Save Original As...	Ctrl+Shift+S	
Save Copy of Original...		
Revert		
Place Image...		
Import	▶	
Export	▶	
Image Info...	Ctrl+Shift+K	
Preview in	▶	
Jump to	▶	
Preferences	▶	
Recent Files	▶	
Adobe Online...		

By far the biggest physical difference in the two interfaces is the presence of an Animation palette that provides a way to create animated GIFs from layered Photoshop files.

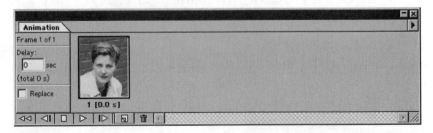

But the most sweeping change is the fact that ImageReady provides you with two distinct ways to view your file. The first is in its Original state, which is the same as working in Photoshop. The other way to view a file is in the Optimized state, which is how the image will look on the Web. Whenever you're in the program, a graphic will have two tabs at the top of the document to allow you to switch between Original and Optimized (see Figure A.2).

This feature is indicative of how ImageReady focuses on the needs of professional Web designers.

FIGURE A.2

A file with Original and Optimized tabs

What It Does

Although ImageReady looks and acts a lot like Photoshop, there are many ImageReady-only features, ranging from on-the-fly file optimization to incredibly convenient ways to chop up and code graphics for the Web.

File Information

To see the kind of on-demand Web file information that ImageReady provides, click on the pop-up menu at the bottom of the current image window (see Figure A.3).

To determine some of this information, ImageReady requires you to click on the Optimized tab at the top of the window whenever you (1) first open the document or (2) make a change to the Original view. Each time you do this, ImageReady will take a moment to generate the compressed version of the file. The program is converting the Optimized version to the Web palette and determining the resulting file size.

T I P   Clicking and dragging the Original or Optimized tab will create another window of the file, allowing you to quickly compare the two versions.

FIGURE **A.3**

The pop-up menu at the bottom of an image window

Color

Selecting the Optimized version of the file creates a selection of colors that can be viewed in the Optimized Colors palette (select Window ➤ Show Optimized Colors from the Menu Bar).

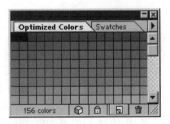

As you move any tool over the image, note that the Info palette (select Window ➤ Show Info) reflects the Hexadecimal color value for each pixel in the image (see Figure A.4).

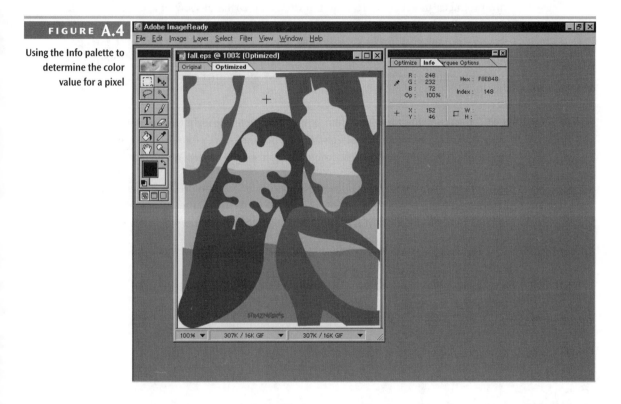

FIGURE A.4

Using the Info palette to
determine the color
value for a pixel

You may notice that some of the values may not be from the 216-color browser-safe palette. To learn more, select Window ➤ Optimize to view the Optimize palette.

The drop-down menu in the upper-left corner provides four file format choices: GIF, JPEG, PNG-8, and PNG-24. Below that is another drop-down menu containing file color palette choices: Perceptual, Adaptive, Web, Mac OS, and Windows. The Perceptual algorithm produces an excellent representation of the Original-view image but uses non-216 colors. To play it safe, select the Web option.

If you would like to specify exactly how many colors you'd like to use in the image, enter a number into the Colors field. The Optimize palette also provides a dithering control. Simply adjust the Dither slider in the upper-right corner of the palette.

TIP   To copy the hexadecimal value of a color in ImageReady and paste it into an HTML file, just use the Eyedropper tool from the Toolbar and select a color from the image. Then use the Edit ➤ Copy Color as HTML command to copy the six-digit number.

Another great color feature in ImageReady is the ability to preview how your image will look on either a PC or a Mac. Select Image ➤ Adjust ➤ Gamma to open the Gamma dialog (shown below), and you can select to temporarily or permanently convert the image to a range of colors that reflects a specific platform.

Slicing

It is very common to use HTML tables to lay out big Web graphics, especially when a large graphic has localized areas of animation. In such cases, the graphic is chopped into smaller pieces and mortised together with HTML. The big pain in using this technique is precisely cropping each piece of the graphic—if you're off by only a pixel, the whole process has to be redone.

To automatically generate the elements of an HTML table-based mosaic, open an image in ImageReady and place guides along areas of the image where you would like it sliced up (see Figure A.5).

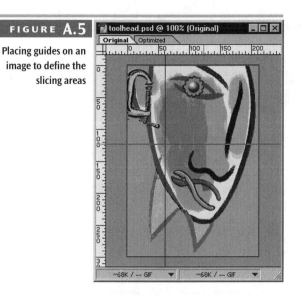

Placing guides on an image to define the slicing areas

Now choose File ➤ Save Optimized, and you will see a Slice Along Guides option at the bottom of the Save As dialog.

Select the option and click Save. Now take a look at the directory in which you saved your file. You will notice multiple images with a unique numbering system (see Figure A.6).

FIGURE A.6

The files generated by using the Slice Along Guides command

Exploring - toolhead

File   Edit   View   Tools   Help

toolhead

All Folders

Contents of 'toolhead'

- inprogress
  - misc
  - sample images
    - filtergfx
    - toolhead
  - submitted
  - sybex template
  - techedits
- BrainBug
- Hbj
- matt
- seminars
- Multimedia Files
- Program Files

toolhead-01-01.gif
toolhead-01-02.gif
toolhead-02-01.gif
toolhead-02-02.gif

4 object(s)   15.3KB (Disk free space: 218MB)

Any file that starts with 01 is from the first row, and 02 files are from the second row. The second series of numbers provides the order in which the images fall, from left to right (see Figure A.7).

FIGURE A.7

The mosaic of images created from the Slice Along Guides command

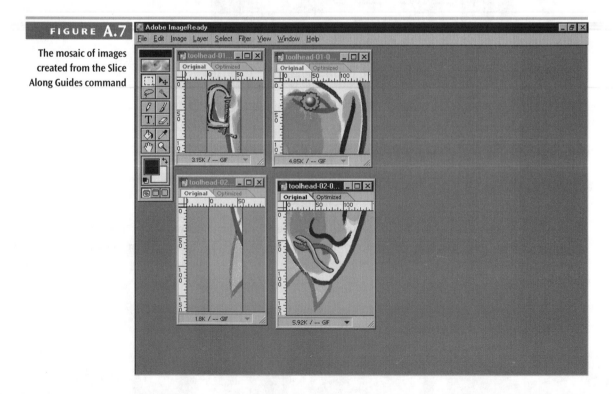

The best part is that ImageReady can also create the source code for the HTML table. Select Image ➤ HTML Slicing, and then Edit ➤ Copy HTML Code. Now paste the text into an HTML file. Based on the previous slicing exercise, Figure A.8 provides the resulting code.

FIGURE A.8

The resulting code from
HTML Slicing/Copy HTML
Code commands

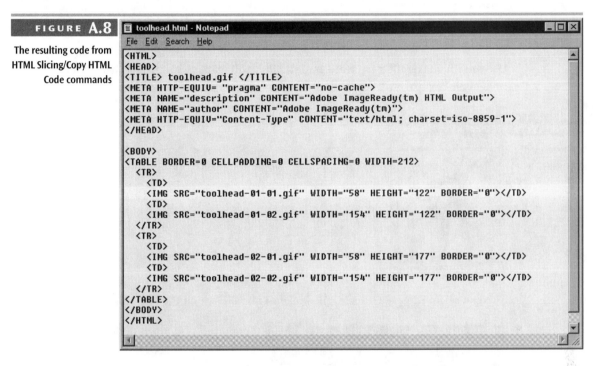

```
toolhead.html - Notepad
File  Edit  Search  Help
<HTML>
<HEAD>
<TITLE> toolhead.gif </TITLE>
<META HTTP-EQUIV= "pragma" CONTENT="no-cache">
<META NAME="description" CONTENT="Adobe ImageReady(tm) HTML Output">
<META NAME="author" CONTENT="Adobe ImageReady(tm)">
<META HTTP-EQUIV="Content-Type" CONTENT="text/html; charset=iso-8859-1">
</HEAD>

<BODY>
<TABLE BORDER=0 CELLPADDING=0 CELLSPACING=0 WIDTH=212>
  <TR>
    <TD>
    <IMG SRC="toolhead-01-01.gif" WIDTH="58" HEIGHT="122" BORDER="0"></TD>
    <TD>
    <IMG SRC="toolhead-01-02.gif" WIDTH="154" HEIGHT="122" BORDER="0"></TD>
  </TR>
  <TR>
    <TD>
    <IMG SRC="toolhead-02-01.gif" WIDTH="58" HEIGHT="177" BORDER="0"></TD>
    <TD>
    <IMG SRC="toolhead-02-02.gif" WIDTH="154" HEIGHT="177" BORDER="0"></TD>
  </TR>
</TABLE>
</BODY>
</HTML>
```

The Slicing feature alone makes ImageReady a must-have program.

Trimming

The ImageReady Trim command (select Image ➤ Trim) provides an easy method for eliminating excess area around a Web graphic. The Trim dialog provides three options.

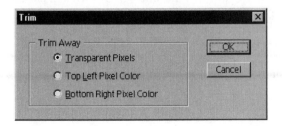

The first option crops away any transparent pixels, leaving just the visible part of the image in the center. The second option samples the pixel color in the upper-left corner and trims away everything that is not that color from around the image. The third option does the exact same thing, but pulls its sample from the bottom-right corner.

Tile Maker

Use the Tile Maker filter to create graphics that will seamlessly repeat as background images on Web pages. To use the filter, open or create a graphic (see Figure A.9).

FIGURE **A.9**

An image to be used as a background graphic in a Web page

Next, select Filter ➤ Other ➤ Tile Maker. This will launch the Tile Maker dialog.

You can either use Blend Edges or Kaleidoscope Tile. In Figure A.10, I have used the Blend Edges option for a more typical background image.

The edges of the graphic are now blended and can be used as a background in a Web page (see Figure A.11).

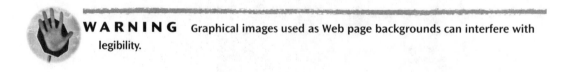

WARNING   Graphical images used as Web page backgrounds can interfere with legibility.

FIGURE A.10

The image with the Tile
Maker filter applied

FIGURE A.11

The tiled background on
a Web page

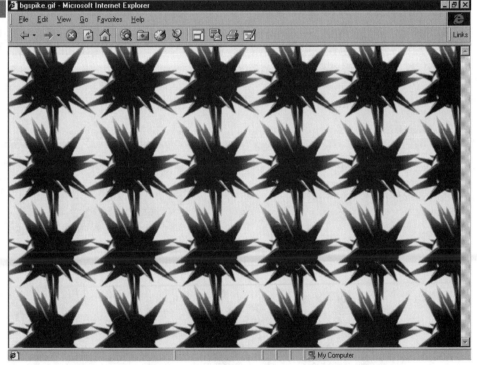

Droplets

If you view the Optimize palette (select Window ➤ Optimize), you will notice that
the palette includes a Create button in the lower-right corner.

This button will put a file (Adobe calls it a *Droplet*) on your computer. Whenever an image is "dropped" onto this file, it will automatically launch ImageReady and be converted to whatever file format and color settings you've selected in the Optimize palette.

Layer Animations

The ImageReady feature that gets all of the headlines is Animation, and not without reason. To get a sense of the power of this feature, select Window ➤ Show Animation to launch the Animation palette. Next, open a layered Photoshop file that you would like to animate, with each of the layers representing a different frame, or cell, in the flick. Figure A.12 displays such a layered file.

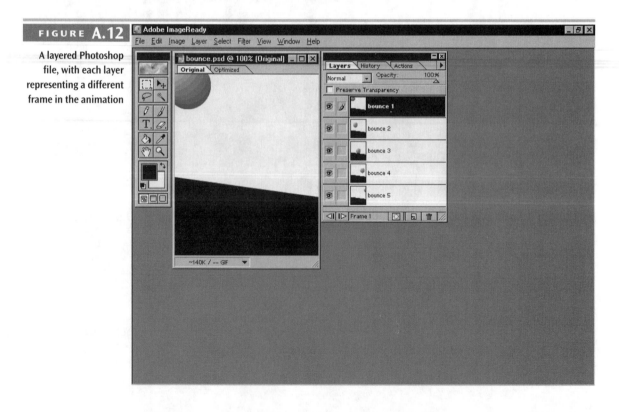

FIGURE A.12

A layered Photoshop file, with each layer representing a different frame in the animation

NOTE For more about creating layered documents in Photoshop, see Chapter 7.

Setting up the animation in ImageReady is a straightforward process of creating a relationship between the frames in the Animation palette and the layers in the Photoshop file. In Figure A.13, I have created five frames by using the New Frame command from the Animation palette menu.

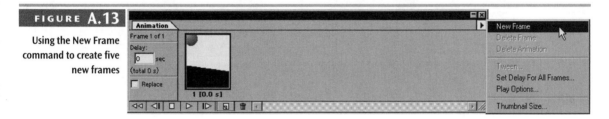

FIGURE A.13

Using the New Frame command to create five new frames

The next step is to click on each frame and associate it with a layer. In Figure A.14, I have made the fifth frame in the animation the fifth layer by making the "bounce 5" layer visible and all of the others invisible.

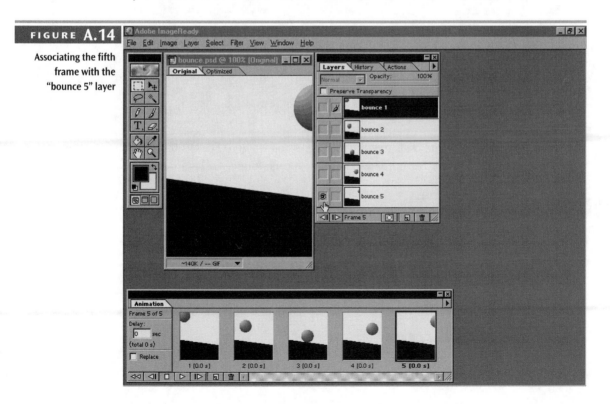

FIGURE A.14

Associating the fifth frame with the "bounce 5" layer

To see what the animation looks like on a Web page, optimize the animation by clicking on the Optimized tab in the image window, then select File ➤ Preview In ➤ *(your browser of choice)*. ImageReady will launch the browser you select and place both the animation and the HTML code on the page (see Figure A.15).

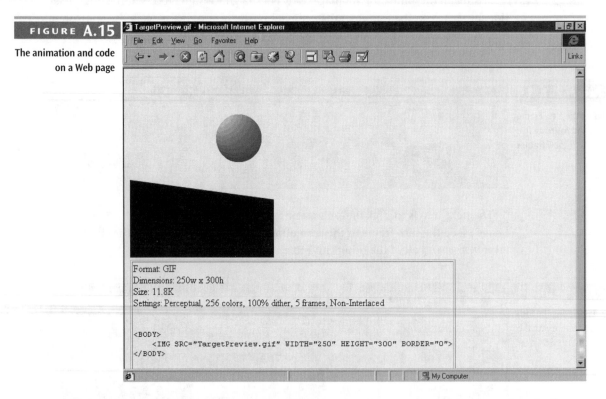

FIGURE A.15

The animation and code on a Web page

If the animation is moving too fast or too slow, you can enter new values in the Delay field on the Animation palette for each frame (see Figure A.16).

FIGURE A.16

Changing the Delay value for a frame in the animation

TIP   The interframe delay can be set globally by selecting Set Frame Delay from the Animation palette menu.

You can also specify the number of times the animation will loop (Forever, Once, or any number of Times) on a Web page. Select Play Options from the Animation palette menu and choose the appropriate option from the Play Options dialog.

And There's More

I've covered some of the important features of the program, but here's a quick look at a few more:

Tween   The Animation palette menu includes the ability to "tween" frames, allowing you to automatically create in-between frames to adjust movement and/or opacity.

Image Maps   Through the Layer Options dialog, you can use individual layers to create an image map for use in HTML.

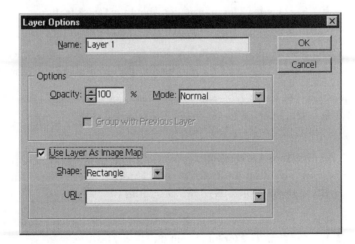

NOTE   For more about image maps, see Chapter 15.

HTML   With the File ➤ Export ➤ Save As HTML command, you can generate an HTML document that includes image width, height, and alt tag information.

 T I P   To define an alt tag, select File ➤ Image Info.

What It Doesn't Do

Currently, Adobe is positioning ImageReady as a Web graphics processing program, *not* a Web graphics development environment. Here are a few of the features that ImageReady 1.0 lacks when compared to Photoshop:

Paths   Paths offer similar capabilities as drawing programs like Adobe Illustrator and Macromedia Freehand. The feature and its ability to create precise selections isn't present in ImageReady.

 N O T E   See Chapter 5 for more about the Paths feature.

Adjustment Layers   Likewise, adjustment layers are not part of ImageReady, so you can't conveniently tinker with an image's overall coloring.

 N O T E   See Chapter 7 for information about the Layers feature.

Selection Tools   ImageReady does have most of the Marquee tools and a Lasso, but it doesn't have a Crop, Polygonal Lasso, or Magnetic Lasso tool.

N O T E   See Chapter 4 for info about the Selection tools.

History Brush   While ImageReady includes Photoshop's History palette as a way of providing multiple levels of Undo, it doesn't have the History Brush for painting back portions of previous edits.

 N O T E   See Chapter 2 for info about the History feature.

Filters   Many filters available in Photoshop are not present in ImageReady, including all of the Noise filters, Lighting Effects, and 3D Transform.

N O T E   See Chapter 8 for more about Photoshop's filters.

Even as a Web graphics processing program, ImageReady currently has a couple of notable omissions when compared to Photoshop:

FlashPix   You cannot save files to the FlashPix format.

N O T E   See Chapter 12 for more about the FlashPix format.

Digimarc   The Digimarc filter, used to invisibly encode graphics with copyright information, is not available in ImageReady. However, ImageReady can identify the strength of a copyright watermark in the pop-up menu on the lower bar of the image window (see Figure A.17).

FIGURE A.17

Selecting the Watermark
Strength option

NOTE   See Chapter 8 for more about the Digimarc filter.

Whither Photoshop?

ImageReady is a very promising application, and you could probably create most Web graphics with this one program. However, at this time, ImageReady doesn't include advanced tools like Paths, Lighting Effects, or a History Brush. Given this, it's going to take time to see if ImageReady gains a foothold like Photoshop has in the Web design community.

However, I believe that the tremendous success of the Web has made it impossible for one application to serve both print and Web designers. Splitting Photoshop into two applications—one for print and one for Web—makes a lot of sense. This way, everyone gets what they need without the overhead of unnecessary features.

The release of ImageReady doesn't mean the end for Photoshop, nor does it mean that all the time you've spent learning the program has been wasted. To the contrary, if some critical features are added and ImageReady becomes the Web design application of the future, it will be a breeze for experienced Photoshop users to make the switch.

THE MENU BAR

THE MENU BAR

The Photoshop Menu Bar provides nine main options: File, Edit, Image, Layer, Select, Filter, Window, View, and Help. Each option contains a host of additional options that will either open a submenu, launch a dialog, or carry out a command. Items off each main Menu Bar option may be grayed out (disabled), indicating they are unavailable or not applicable, based on the file that is currently open.

File

The File menu contains commands that relate to opening, closing, and saving files, as well as access to features that apply to the entire document, such as page setup, preferences, and color settings.

New   The New command opens the new dialog. Use it when creating a new document.

Open   The Open command opens an existing file. It will access the open dialog, allowing you to locate and select the file you wish to open. Photoshop lets you open images in a variety of formats. Images in file formats such as Adobe Illustrator will be *rasterized*—converted to bitmap form—as they are being opened.

Open As (Windows)   The Open As command specifies the format in which to open a file. Macintosh users can select the desired format from the Open dialog.

Close   The Close command closes the currently active image. If all changes to the image have been saved, the image closes when you select this menu option. If you have not saved changes, you will have the option to do so before closing the image.

Save   The Save option saves an image. For images that haven't been saved before, the Save command will prompt you to name the file and select the destination directory. For previously saved images, the Save command will automatically save the latest changes to the current file.

Save As   This option allows you to save an image under a new filename.

Save a Copy   This option saves a copy of a file under a different name, or in a new folder. When editing images, it is always a good idea to save copies of the image before making changes that can't be undone, such as color correcting, flattening, or translating to a different file format.

New...	Ctrl+N
Open...	Ctrl+O
Open As...	Alt+Ctrl+O
Close	Ctrl+W
Save	Ctrl+S
Save As...	Shft+Ctrl+S
Save a Copy...	Alt+Ctrl+S
Revert	
Place...	
Import	▶
Export	▶
Automate	▶
File Info...	
Page Setup...	Shft+Ctrl+P
Print...	Ctrl+P
Preferences	▶
Color Settings	▶
Adobe Online...	
1 C:\...\Gac27.tif	
2 C:\...\Gac26.tif	
3 C:\...\Gac25.tif	
4 C:\...\Gac24.tif	
Exit	Ctrl+Q

N O T E   See Chapter 1 for more information about creating and saving new files.

Revert   The Revert command comes in handy if you have made unsaved changes to a file and would like to return to the most recently saved version.

Place   The Place command allows you to import an EPS graphic (like those created with Adobe Illustrator) into a new layer on an existing Photoshop image. The place command will automatically rasterize the image.

Import   The Import command allows you to open files saved in formats that use plug-in import modules. The Import menu item has a submenu, which provides access to the Quick Edit feature, as well as a list of any plug-ins that have been installed.

N O T E   Plug-ins are software modules that allow you to access graphics from third-party input devices, such as a scanner or video camera. Whenever you install a new device, you must also install the manufacturer's plug-in into the Plug-ins' Import/Export folder. Photoshop supports the current TWAIN, TWAIN32, and TWAIN_32 standards for scanning. For more information about digitizing, see Chapter 10.

Export   Just as the Import commands are used to import files saved in other formats using plug-ins, the Export command is used to export files to other formats using plug-ins. The Export menu item has a submenu where all installed plug-ins will be displayed. When using Photoshop for Web development, you will use the GIF89a Export command for any GIF files that have transparent areas.

Automate   Similar to some of the batch processing capabilities found in Equilibrium's popular Debabelizer application, Photoshop now provides five automated features: Batch, Conditional Mode Change, Contact Sheet, Fit Image, and Multi-Page PDF to PSD. Batch lets you take actions and automatically applies them on a large amount of files. Contact Sheet allows you to choose a directory and create a contact sheet out of all the images in it. Fit Image takes a series of images and allows you to resize them. Multi-Page PDF to PSD lets you take a large PDF and convert it to a PSD file.

N O T E   See Chapter 9 for more about automating your Photoshop processes with Actions.

File Info   The File Info feature is included for users who will be submitting original images to organizations such as newspapers or wire services. It allows you to identify and categorize your image in a standard format that is included in the image's binary code. The information is not visible in the image itself, but can be viewed with Photoshop or other special software.

You can add information about each file regarding captions, keywords, categories, credits, origin, copyright, and Web site address (see the dialog on the next page). This feature may grow in popularity with Web users who want to copyright their work or automatically link the graphic to a URL.

File Info

Section: Caption

Caption:

Caption Writer:

Headline:

Special Instructions:

OK
Cancel
Prev
Next
Load...
Save...
Append

In Windows, you can save this information to Photoshop, JPEG, and TIFF files. On the Mac, you can save File Info to all formats.

TIP   Another way to embed a copyright notice in your file is using the Filter ➤ Digimarc command.

Page Setup   The Page Setup dialog is used to enter output definitions prior to printing an image. The exact appearance of the dialog varies depending on which printer you are using, and not all options are available for all printers.

Print   The Print command is most commonly used to output the active image to a printer. As with the Page Setup command, the options available will be defined by the print driver you have installed.

Preferences   Preferences allow users to adjust the many variables that control how programs work within Photoshop to best suit their needs.

NOTE   See Appendix E for more information about Photoshop's Preferences settings.

Color Settings   This menu item contains options for Monitor Setup, Printing Inks Setup, Separation Setup, and Separation Tables. Each is related to either controlling the colors as they appear on your monitor or controlling the conversion of RGB colors to CMYK output values. As these options apply primarily to professionally printed output, they are of limited use to Web designers.

Adobe Online   This item provides dynamically updated information about Photoshop.

N O T E   The Adobe Online feature requires a connection to the Internet.

Exit/Quit   The Exit command closes Photoshop in Windows. Macintosh people use the Quit command for the same purpose. On either platform, you will be prompted whether or not to save any open, unsaved images before closing the program.

Edit

The Edit menu is generally used for duplicating or moving active selections to a new location or document. Many of the commands such as Cut, Copy, and Paste behave exactly as they do within the operating system.

Undo	Ctrl+Z
Cut	Ctrl+X
Copy	Ctrl+C
Copy Merged	Shft+Ctrl+C
Paste	Ctrl+V
Paste Into	Shft+Ctrl+V
Clear	
Fill...	
Stroke...	
Free Transform	Ctrl+T
Transform	▶
Define Pattern	
Purge	▶

Undo   The Undo command is invaluable for reversing the last applied command. Unlike some other applications, Photoshop provides only one level of Undo.

N O T E   See Chapter 2 for a far more powerful way to undo image edits.

Cut   The Cut command removes a selection from an image and places it on the Clipboard. The Clipboard is used by many applications as a temporary holding file. The cut image is usually placed in a new location or document with the Paste command.

Copy   The Copy command copies a selection and places the copy on the Clipboard. Unlike the Cut command, Copy only copies the selection and doesn't delete it.

Copy Merged   The Copy Merged command allows you to copy a selection from all visible layers and place the copy on the Clipboard. However, when you paste the selection into a new layer or document, the copied layers will have been merged into a single layer.

Paste   The Paste command pastes the contents of the Clipboard in another location of the same image, or into a new layer in another image.

N O T E   For more information about cutting, copying, and pasting, see Chapter 4.

Paste Into   The Paste Into command pastes the contents of the Clipboard inside an active selection. Photoshop then converts the selection into a layer mask for the pasted contents. This gives you the option to move or edit the pasted image—separately from the active selection area—before merging the two layers.

Clear   The Clear command deletes a selection. Using Backspace (Windows) or Delete (Macintosh) will have the same effect. When the selection area is cleared on any layer except the background layer, it will be filled with the foreground color. On the background layer, it is filled with the background color.

Fill   The Fill command is used to fill a selection or layer with a color (foreground, background, white, black or 50% gray), a pattern, or a snapshot. The Fill command is sometimes used to restore selected areas of an image after changes are made. More often, it is used as a way to fill a selection quickly with a particular color.

Stroke   The Stroke command creates a border of specified width around a selection or layer, using the foreground color. When used on a selection area, it creates a border. When used on type, it creates an outline.

Free Transform   The Free Transform command is used to manipulate a selection or layer. When you select Free Transform, a box with handles will display around the active selection or layer. By using the handles you can scale, rotate, flip, distort, or skew the image. Each of these commands is also available on the Transform submenu.

Transform   The Transform command has a submenu listing various commands available to manipulate the active selection or layer.

N O T E   The Free Transform and Transform commands are covered in Chapter 4.

Define Pattern   The Define Pattern command creates patterns that can then be used by the Fill command. When you install Photoshop, several patterns are loaded onto your computer.

Take Snapshot   The Take Snapshot command takes a snapshot of the active layer and puts it in a holding file for later use.

Take Merged Snapshot   The Take Merged Snapshot command takes a snapshot of all visible layers and puts it in a holding file for later use.

Purge   The Purge command displays a submenu with five purging options: Undo, Clipboard, Pattern, Histories, and All. When working on memory-intensive digitized images, the holding files used by these commands can compromise the performance of your computer. The Purge command allows you to free up memory by clearing the holding files when you no longer need them.

Image

The Image menu includes commands used to change the shape or size of an image, as well as make color adjustments. There are many approaches to color correcting in Photoshop. Some of these options are used to adjust color for printing and are therefore not applicable to Web design. Of the 11 options on the Mode menu, you are likely to use only RGB and Indexed Color for Web graphics.

```
Mode              ▶
Adjust            ▶

Duplicate...
Apply Image...
Calculations...

Image Size...
Canvas Size...
Crop

Rotate Canvas     ▶

Histogram...

Trap...
```

Mode   Photoshop can use a variety of color modes for displaying, printing, and storing images. These modes are based on color models (standards for describing color). For Web publishing, you will use the RGB (red, green, blue) color mode, which assigns an intensity value for each color channel of each pixel and is based on the RGB color model. This is the standard color model used by video monitors and is also the default mode for Photoshop. When a graphic is ready to be converted to Web format (GIF), the mode is changed to Indexed Color.

NOTE See Chapters 3 and 12 for more information about color modes and Web graphic formats.

Adjust The Adjust menu item displays a submenu filled with a wide selection of options to make color corrections on an image. These commands are used to adjust the tones and colors of scanned images, or to generate special effects by remapping existing pixel values to new ones.

NOTE Chapter 3 provides information as to which of the Adjust options are useful in Web design.

Duplicate The Duplicate command is useful when you want to experiment with changes to an image. Using the Duplicate Image dialog, you can create a copy of the image in a holding file. The copy can either be flattened (merging layers) or left separate (duplicate). You can make changes to the duplicate image while maintaining the ability to compare the changes with the original.

Apply Image The Apply Image command is used to apply single or composite channels to the active layer of the foreground image. It is primarily used to blend multiple images.

Calculations The Calculations command is similar to the Apply Image command in that they are both used to blend channels of the pixels in the exact same location on the image. However, the Calculations command accesses the Calculations dialog, which allows you to use two source documents to blend into either document.

Image Size The Image Size command accesses the Image Size dialog, which is used to change the dimensions (height and width) of an image, as well as to change the print dimensions and resolution. When preparing graphics for the Web, it is useful to be able to specify the image size in terms of pixels, while maintaining control over the resolution of the image.

Canvas Size The Canvas Size command accesses a dialog that is used to change the image height and width without affecting resolution. When the size of an image is increased, additional canvas space will be added around the image. When the canvas size is decreased, a warning will be displayed that part of the image will be removed to meet the new dimensions.

Crop The Crop command deletes all information outside of a rectangular selection area. The width and height of the image will be reset based on the new dimensions, but the resolution will remain the same.

Rotate Canvas   The Rotate Canvas command rotates an entire image. A submenu offers six options for rotating, from fixed degrees to custom angles.

NOTE   For more information about altering canvas size and orientation, see Chapter 10.

Histogram   The Histogram command evaluates the tonal values of an image. Refer to it periodically while making color corrections. You can't make changes to the image using this command.

Trap   This command only applies to CMYK images used in print. This feature is not applicable to Web design.

Layer

The Layers feature sets Photoshop apart from other image editing applications. Layers allow you to organize the various parts of an image on separate, transparent layers. If you've ever seen an old-fashioned camera-ready mechanical for a color page, you'd know that graphic artists have been using layers to produce artistic effects for a long time.

New	▶
Duplicate Layer...	
Delete Layer	
Layer Options...	
Adjustment Options...	
Effects	▶
Type	▶
Add Layer Mask	▶
Enable Layer Mask	
Group with Previous	Ctrl+G
Ungroup	Shft+Ctrl+G
Arrange	▶
Align To Selection	▶
Distribute Linked	▶
Merge Down	Ctrl+E
Merge Visible	Shft+Ctrl+E
Flatten Image	
Matting	▶

New   The New command adds a new layer to an image. The New menu item has a submenu, which offers four types of layers that can be added.

Duplicate Layer   The Duplicate Layer command creates a copy of the active layer. By using the Duplicate Layer dialog, you can specify if the new layer is to be added to the same image or to a different image.

Delete Layer   The Delete Layer command deletes the active layer. It can only be used on images that have more than one layer.

Layer Options   Use Layer Options to change the characteristics of an image or adjustment layer. You can change the name, create a layer group, or blend with an underlying layer. When selected, the Layer Options dialog will display.

Adjustment Options   Similar to Layer Options, Adjustment Options opens the Adjust dialog, allowing you to make changes to the characteristics of the adjustment layer.

Effects   These special effects can be used on both type and regular layers. Effects are attached to a layer and are applied to everything on the layer.

Type   In Photoshop 5, type is editable until it is rendered with this command.

Add Layer Mask   Add Layer Mask is only available for use on an image layer (not the background layer). It is used to create an extra channel consisting of a mask of the contents of the active layer.

Enable Layer Mask   The Enable Layer Mask command turns on or off the effects of the mask, without discarding it. Toggling this command allows you to compare the before and after effects of the mask.

Group with Previous   The Group with Previous/Group Linked command is used to create clipping groups. A clipping group uses the contents of one layer to mask the contents of another.

Ungroup   The Ungroup command is used to ungroup all layers from a clipping group, select any layer in the group (except the top layer), and select Ungroup.

Arrange   The Arrange command changes the order of the layers in an image. The command is only applicable to multiple layered images. When selected, a submenu will display the various options. You can also move layers by dragging them in the Layers palette.

Align Linked   Using the currently targeted layer as a reference, this command aligns any linked layers. The six choices include: Top, Vertical Center, Bottom, Left, Horizontal Center, and Right.

Distribute Linked   Much like the Align Linked command, Distribute Linked allows you to globally arrange series of linked layers. However, in this case the reference point is the overall dimensions of the canvas. Like Align Linked, the six choices include: Top, Vertical Center, Bottom, Left, Horizontal Center, and Right.

NOTE   The Align Linked and Distribute Linked commands are helpful in arranging header graphics or any other type of Web graphic with numerous elements on different layers. See Chapter 15 for more information about the kinds of graphics that make up a Web page.

Merge Layers   Merge Layers merges one or more layers into one layer. Depending on the status of the active layer (whether it is part of a clipping group or linked to other layers), the command will display differently. Layers are frequently merged to simplify editing or to reduce the file size.

Merge Visible   The Merge Visible command merges all visible layers into the bottom-most visible layer, regardless of which layer is currently active.

Flatten Image   The Flatten Image command converts all visible layers into a single background layer. Flattening an image can reduce the file size dramatically. It is also required prior to saving an image in any format other than native Photoshop.

Matting   The Matting commands are used to help clean up the edges of a pasted object. When you place an object into an image, sometimes the pixels around the edge of the selection still reflect the original background color.

NOTE   See Chapter 7 for a thorough discussion of the Layers feature.

Select

The Select menu contains commands to create selections within an image. You will often want to move one object within an image, or make changes to one area of an image at a time, and selections highlight the area of the image on which you want to perform commands.

All	Ctrl+A
Deselect	Ctrl+D
Reselect	Shft+Ctrl+D
Inverse	Shft+Ctrl+I
Color Range...	
Feather...	Alt+Ctrl+D
Modify	▶
Grow	
Similar	
Transform Selection	
Load Selection...	
Save Selection...	

All The All command selects the entire contents of an image.

Deselect As the name indicates, this command deactivates a selection.

Reselect This command reactivates the most recent selection.

Inverse The Inverse command inverts the active selection. It is useful when you want to make a change to an area outside an object.

Color Range The Color Range command creates a selection based on color, rather than shape. It is a useful command when selecting an unusual shape, like a person's hair, or water. It can be applied to an entire image or a selection area. By sampling the color of the image and adding or subtracting colors from the color range in the Color Range dialog, you can control the pixels included in the selection.

Feather The Feather command softens the edges of a selection. It is used to blend the contents of a selection with the pixels surrounding the edge of the selection, making the selection less harsh. The feather radius, which you define in the Feather Selection dialog, controls the size of the area affected by the command.

Modify The Modify commands change the shape of an active selection mathematically, pixel by pixel. They will not take color into account when modifying a selection. When selected, a submenu displays the available options.

Grow The Grow command increases a selected area by including a wider range of similar colors, near the active selection. Unless your active selection is surrounded by areas of contrasting color, the command can have unpredictable results. The range of additional color selected is based on the Tolerance value entered on the Magic Wand Options palette.

Similar Like the Grow command, the Similar command increases a selection based on increasing the range of similar colors. However, the Similar command will include similar colors from the entire image, not just adjacent to the active selection. It is useful if you want to select one color or range of colors from an entire image.

Transform Selection This command allows you to change the height, width, and orientation of a selection. Note that the command only affects the selection area, not the pixels that are in the selection.

Load Selection Load Selection creates a new selection based on a previously saved selection, such as a mask or image layer. You can load a selection from within the same image or from another image, provided the two images have exactly the same dimensions. When selected, the load selection dialog will display a list of available options. The channels available for use as a selection will depend on the active layer.

Save Selection   Once complete, selections can be saved as channels within a document. Save Selection allows you to use the selection again as a mask for your image. If you have spent some time selecting a specific area of the image, it is a good idea to save the selection so you won't have to recreate it later. When you choose this command, the Save Selection dialog will display. You can choose to save the selection in the current image, or in another open image, provided the two images have exactly the same dimensions.

N O T E   See Chapter 4 for an in-depth look at working with selections.

Filter

The Filter menu contains a wide selection of filters that can be used as both production or artistic effects. Considering that filters can be applied in combination, the range of visual effects you can achieve is astounding.

Last Filter	Ctrl+F
Fade...	Shft+Ctrl+F
Artistic	▶
Blur	▶
Brush Strokes	▶
Distort	▶
Noise	▶
Pixelate	▶
Render	▶
Sharpen	▶
Sketch	▶
Stylize	▶
Texture	▶
Video	▶
Other	▶
Digimarc	▶

Last Filter   The Last Filter command applies the last filter used. It will duplicate the previously selected settings.

Fade   The Fade command reduces or fades the effect of a filter or color adjustment. It must be applied immediately after a filter is applied. The Fade dialog allows you to adjust the mode and opacity of the blend. The effect achieved is similar to applying the filter effect on an adjustment layer and using the layer opacity and blending modes to adjust.

Artistic   The Artistic filters are used to emulate traditional artistic techniques such as those associated with painting, drawing, and photography.

Blur   The Blur filters soften an image by reducing areas of high color contrast. At low settings they can reduce the graininess of an image or reduce contrast. At higher settings they can produce shadows or motion effects.

Brush Strokes   The Brush Strokes filters are similar to the Artistic filters. These filters include the ability to add color, detail, or texture to the image.

Distort   The Distort filters create special effects by changing the position of existing pixels, without changing their color. These can be effective when trying to create 3D effects or reflections.

Noise   Noise filters can blend a selection into a background more effectively. Noise filters can also create textures.

Pixelate   The Pixelate filters distort the colors in an image by altering small groups of similarly colored pixels into a solid group of color. They are primarily used to create artistic effects.

Render   The Render filters add new patterns in an image by either placing new detail over an image or by altering the existing image. The result achieved with the filters is a wide range of special lighting effects.

Sharpen   The opposite of the Blur filters, the Sharpen filters add focus and detail to an image by increasing the color difference in similar adjacent pixels. They can be very effective if you're trying to sharpen an out-of-focus photograph.

Sketch   Sketch emulates the artist's hand-drawn effects. Sketch filters retain little detail or color from the original image.

Stylize   The Stylize filters offer everything from natural effects like Wind to more mechanical processes like Emboss and Extrude.

Texture   The Texture filters add texture to an image. Texture filters can emulate canvas and work well in combination with the Artistic filters.

Video   Video filters are available for editing images captured from video or processing images destined for video or television.

Other   This menu includes some specialized filters that do not fit nicely into the other categories. Among these filters is a Custom option that allows for the creation of new filters.

Digimarc   The Digimarc filter allows you to embed and read invisible copyright information. Digimarc was invented as a way of protecting images from being used without permission and is helpful in protecting Web graphics.

N O T E   To learn all about filters, see Chapter 8.

View

The View menu includes several commands that can change how an image is viewed on the screen.

New View	
Preview	▶
Gamut Warning	Shft+Ctrl+Y
Zoom In	Ctrl++
Zoom Out	Ctrl+-
Fit on Screen	Ctrl+0
Actual Pixels	Alt+Ctrl+0
Print Size	
Hide Edges	
Hide Path	
Show Rulers	
Show Guides	
✓ Snap To Guides	Shft+Ctrl+;
Lock Guides	Alt+Ctrl+;
Clear Guides	
Show Grid	
✓ Snap To Grid	Shft+Ctrl+"

New View   This command allows you to create a reference window for the active image. It allows you to concentrate on a specific area of the image in one view, while keeping an eye on the overall image in the other. It creates a new display window only, not a copy of the image. Changes made in one view will be reflected in the other.

Preview   This command applies specifically to print images that will be converted to CMYK mode. It is not applicable to RGB-mode images and Web designers.

Gamut Warning   This command applies specifically to print images that will be converted to CMYK mode. It is not applicable to RGB-mode images and Web designers.

Zoom In   This command has the same effect as clicking on an image with the Zoom tool. It enlarges the view of the image without changing the image size.

Zoom Out   The reverse of Zoom In, Zoom Out reduces the view of the image without changing the image size.

N O T E   See Chapter 2 for more information about moving around an image.

Fit on Screen   The Fit on Screen command displays the image at the largest possible size.

Actual Pixels   The Actual Pixels command reverts to the default viewing size for an image. When viewed in this mode, the image's pixels are matched in size to your monitor's pixels.

Print Size   The Print Size command lets you view an image at its actual printed size, regardless of its resolution. This command is not useful to Web designers.

Hide/Show Edges   The Hide/Show Edges command will either display or hide the outline of a current selection. Selections are indicated by a moving dashed line—often referred to as "marching ants."

Hide/Show Path   Similar to Hide/Show Edges, this command will either display or hide a path (a selection created with the Pen tool).

Hide/Show Rulers   The Hide/Show Rulers command will either display or hide the horizontal and vertical rulers.

Hide/Show Guides   The Hide/Show Guides command will either display or hide guides. It does not delete guides.

Snap to Guides   Snap to Guides should be selected when you are working with guides and want items to automatically align or "snap to" a guide when placing them in an image.

Lock Guides   The Lock Guides command should be applied after guides have been placed on an image, to prevent accidentally moving them. Selecting this command again will have the effect of unlocking the guides.

Clear Guides   Clear Guides removes all guides.

Hide/Show Grid   Hide/Show Grid displays or hides a grid on top of your image.

Snap to Grid   The Snap to Grid command should be selected when you are working with grids and want items to automatically align or "snap to" a grid when placing them in an image.

N O T E   For more information about rulers, guides, and grids, see Chapter 10.

Window

While the View menu contains commands that affect your image display, the Window menu contains commands that affect your workspace display. The Windows and Macintosh Window menus differ only in that the Windows version offers Cascade, Tile, Arrange Windows, and Close All commands. The remainder of the Window menu is the same across both platforms.

```
Cascade
Tile
Arrange Icons
Close All

Hide Tools

Show Navigator
Show Info
Show Options

Show Color
Show Swatches
Show Brushes

Show Layers
Show Channels
Show Paths

Show History
Show Actions

Hide Status Bar

✓ 1 Untitled-1 @ 100% (Layer 1,RGB)
```

Cascade   The Cascade command displays open image windows stacked and cascading from the top left to the bottom right of the screen.

Tile   The Tile command displays open image windows side by side.

Arrange Icons   The Arrange Icons command lines up the display of minimized image windows.

Close All   Close All closes all open image windows. A warning will display if changes have been made to the images without saving them.

Hide/Show Options   The middle of the Window menu includes commands used to toggle between display or hide commands for palette groups, as well as to control which palette is viewed on top (similar to clicking on that palette's tab).

Open Images   A list of the currently open images appears at the bottom of the Window menu. The active window will be displayed with a checkmark beside it. You can change the active window by selecting the appropriate image.

Help

Photoshop's Online Help system provides much of the same information provided in the user guide. The Windows and Macintosh versions of the Help menu are somewhat different, but the basic functionality is the same.

```
Contents                    F1
Search for Help on...
Keyboard
How to Use Help

About Photoshop...
About Plug-in                 ▶

Export Transparent Image...
Resize Image...
```

About Balloon Help (Macintosh)   Provides information about the Mac's Balloon Help system.

Show/Hide Balloons (Macintosh)   Turns the Balloon Help system on and off.

Contents/Help Contents   Contents allows you to access Online Help in Windows. Help Contents accesses Online Help on the Macintosh.

Search for Help On (Windows)   This command is used to access an index or word search for the Online Help manual.

Keyboard (Windows)   The Keyboard command is used to access a guide to keyboard shortcuts for the Toolbar and palettes. Many of the commands and tools can be accessed by keyboard commands. Some tools have additional options when used in combination with keyboard commands. You'll find the guide to keyboard shortcuts useful when you're trying to track down a keyboard equivalent.

How to Use Help (Windows)   This process steps you through the various options to find help. You can access the contents, index, or search facilities from this menu item.

About Photoshop (Windows)   The About Photoshop command displays your Photoshop license agreement.

About Plug-in (Windows)   The About Plug-in command displays license agreements for various plug-ins that Photoshop uses.

Export Transparent Image   This command launches a helpful Wizard that instructs you on how to create and export a transparent image.

Resize Image   This command launches a helpful Wizard that allows people who have a limited knowledge of Photoshop to resize their image for Web or print.

appendix C

THE PHOTOSHOP TOOLBAR

THE PHOTOSHOP TOOLBAR

Photoshop's Toolbar is divided into seven distinct areas. The first four areas are individual image-editing tools. A small triangle to the right of a tool icon indicates the presence of a submenu that offers additional tools. The last three areas of the Toolbar allow selection of foreground/background colors, editing modes, and screen display options.

Group One

The first group of tools are used to select or move a portion of an image. Depending on the size of the area you are selecting or moving, you will most likely want to adjust how the image is viewed with the tools in Group Four.

N O T E   Refer to Chapter 4 for more about the selection tools.

Marquee Tool

 The Marquee tool offers five different formats: Rectangular, Elliptical, Single Row, Single Column, and Crop. Each format is used to select or crop an area of an image. As you click and drag, the boundary of the selection will appear as moving dashed lines (sometimes called "marching ants").

Move Tool

 The Move tool moves an area of an image. You can move selections within an image or between different images.

Lasso Tool

 The Lasso offers three different types of tools: Lasso, Polygon Lasso, and Magnetic Lasso. Each is used to select an area of an image by drawing an outline around it. By using additional keyboard commands with either format, you can switch between freehand and straight-edged outlines.

Magic Wand Tool

 The Magic Wand tool selects an area of an image based on its color. By adjusting the tolerance range of your selection, you can control how large an area will be selected. When selecting a consistently colored object, you don't have to outline it with the Lasso.

Group Two

The second group of tools is primarily used to apply or manually manipulate color in an image. As you click and drag one of the tools over an image, the underlying pixels of the image will be changed, based on the options selected for that tool.

NOTE   See Chapters 1 and 2 for much more about all of the painting and image editing tools.

Airbrush Tool

 The Airbrush tool is used to apply color in a soft or feathered stroke. Similar to an actual airbrush, this tool is useful for creating shadows, highlights, or graffiti painting.

Paintbrush Tool

 The Paintbrush tool is used to apply color in a uniform width with either soft or hard edges. The stroke can vary dramatically in terms of color application depending on the options you select. The Paintbrush tool is useful for image editing, blending colors, and creating special effects.

Rubber Stamp Tool

 The Rubber Stamp tool copies the pixels in one part of an image for application in another part of an image. The Rubber Stamp can touch up an image, remove an unwanted portion or object, or duplicate part of an image.

History Brush Tool

 Used in conjunction with the History palette, the History Brush paints back previous image edits.

Eraser Tool

 The Eraser tool either applies the background color or converts underlying pixels to full transparency (no color). As a result, it appears to erase the underlying image. It is useful for refining the edges of an image.

Line Tool

 Similar to the Paintbrush, the Line tool applies color in a uniform width. The Pencil tool, a freehand version of the Line tool, is also located under the Line tool.

Blur Tool

 The Blur tool provides three options: Blur, Sharpen, and Smudge. Each alters the focus of a selected area of an image. While not as precise as the blurring and sharpening filters, these tools allow you to selectively affect a specific area of an image.

Dodge Tool

 The Dodge tool provides three toning options: Dodge, Burn, and Sponge. These functions were derived from the traditional photography techniques of increasing or decreasing exposure on specific areas of an image during developing, allowing modification to the tone and saturation of the selected area. By decreasing light during exposure (dodging) you can effectively lighten an area on the image. By increasing light (burning-in), you can darken areas of an image. The Sponge tool alters saturation on Grayscale images.

Group Three

The third group of tools is wide ranging and includes a sophisticated selection/drawing tool, a text tool, a drawing tool, and color blend, fill, and selection tools.

Pen Tool

 The Pen tool offers seven options: Pen, Magnetic Pen, Freeform Pen, Direct Select, Add Anchor Point, Delete Anchor Point, and Convert Point. These tools make precision selections using smooth-edged paths, similar to Adobe Illustrator's drawing tools. Not only can you edit the location of each point, but you can also manipulate the shape of the line connecting them.

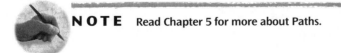 **N O T E**   **Read Chapter 5 for more about Paths.**

Type Tool

The Type tool provides standard Type and Type Mask options for both vertical and horizontal text. While each option works with an image in the shape of type, they all have very different purposes. The Type tool paints text onto an image, while the Outline Type tool creates selections in the shape of various letterforms.

 N O T E   Find out much more about the Type tool in Chapter 14.

Measure Tool

 Used in conjunction with the Info palette, the Measure tool ascertains the distance between two points in your image.

Gradient Tool

The Gradient tool creates a color fade from the foreground color to the background color within the confines of a selection, or across the entire image. The Gradient tool is often used to create a special effect for a Web background image. The Gradient tool includes Linear Gradient, Radial Gradient, Angle Gradient, Reflected Gradient, and Diamond Gradient.

 N O T E   Good Gradient tool info resides in Chapter 3.

Paint Bucket Tool

 The Paint Bucket tool fills similarly colored areas of an image with a foreground color. The size of the area depends on the tool's tolerance setting.

 N O T E   Learn more about the Paint Bucket in Chapter 3.

Eyedropper Tool

 The Eyedropper tool selects a new foreground or background color from an existing image. Like the Line tool, it is very straightforward but highly useful in creating Web graphics.

 N O T E Find out more about the Eyedropper in Chapter 3.

Group Four

The fourth group of tools provides the ability to change how an image is viewed in order to make image editing more convenient. None of these tools alters the image itself.

 N O T E More info about these tools can be found in Chapter 2.

Hand Tool

 The Hand tool scrolls to a particular area of an image. It repositions the image within the viewing window to allow you to focus on a particular area.

Zoom Tool

 The Zoom tool increases or decreases the magnification of an image, allowing you to view an image at different sizes.

Foreground Color/Background Color Indicator

The Foreground Color/Background Color indicator represents the current colors selected for any foreground or background color applications.

The upper-left square indicates the foreground color, while the bottom-right square indicates the background color. A quick click on either color square will give you access to the Color Picker, a tool that lets you select a new color. There are two additional icons included on the Foreground Color/Background Color indicator:

Switch Colors Icon   Located in the upper-right corner, this icon is used to reverse the current foreground and background colors.

Default Colors Icon   Located in the lower-left corner, this icon is used to return to the default settings: black foreground and white background.

N O T E   Look to Chapter 3 for more mention of the Foreground Color/Background Color indicator.

Editing Modes

There are two modes for editing an image: Standard or Quick Mask.

Standard   The Standard mode is used for all normal image editing.

Quick Mask   The Quick Mask mode is used for creating and editing temporary masks. A mask is used to isolate a part of your image to protect it from changes being made to the surrounding areas. When you select Quick Mask, you can use the active selection or make a new selection to create your mask.

N O T E   Find out more about masks in Chapter 6.

Screen Display Options

There are three window controls available along the bottom of the Toolbar. They do not alter images in any way—they merely control how image windows in Photoshop are displayed.

Standard Screen Mode   This is the default screen. It displays the image in a standard window with a title bar at the top and scroll bars on the sides. The Menu Bar displays at the top of the screen. This is the only mode that allows you to view the taskbar or multiple images on your desktop.

Full Screen Mode with Menu Bar   Used to display the image in a standard window but without title bars, scroll bars, or ruler. This mode allows for a larger viewing area, which may be helpful when working with large images.

Full Screen Mode   Used to display the image in a full screen mode against a solid black background. The Menu Bar is not displayed. This mode is used primarily for previewing images without background distractions or color influences.

appendix D

PALETTES

PALETTES

hotoshop provides 12 individual palettes: Tools, Navigator, Info, Options, Color, Swatches, Brushes, Layers, Channels, Paths, History, and Actions. Palettes are accessed off the Window option on the Menu Bar and are organized into palette groups. These groups can be reorganized to suit your personal preferences.

Tools Palette

The Tools palette, also known as the Toolbar, contains all of Photoshop's tools (Paintbrush, Pencil, Selection, and so on).

N O T E   See Appendix C for more information about the Toolbar.

Navigator Palette

The Navigator palette provides access to the zoom and repositioning tools that allow you to easily access different portions of an image.

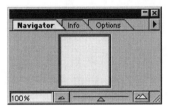

N O T E   Navigate to Chapter 2 for the ins and out of the Navigator palette.

Info Palette

The Info palette provides five types of information: location of the mouse pointer (regardless of the tool selected), the RGB color value of the pixel beneath the pointer, the CMYK color value of the pixel beneath the pointer, the width and height of a given selection, and (when using the Measure tool) the angle and distance of the measurement being made. It provides information only, and no changes can be made to the image with the palette.

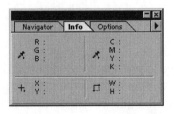

N O T E   Get the info on the Info palette in Chapter 4.

Options Palette

Most of the tools in the Toolbar have an Options palette associated with them. For example, if the Marquee tool is selected, the Marquee Options palette will become active.

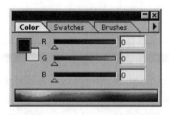

Color Palette

The Color palette is one of several tools that you can use to select a color. Use it to define colors by setting specific numeric values, moving the sliders, or selecting a color from the color bar.

NOTE   See Chapter 3 for more on the Color palette.

Swatches Palette

The Swatches palette displays a series of predefined blocks of color you can use to select a new color. The palette can include the default Photoshop swatches, custom swatches you have loaded, or new swatches you have saved.

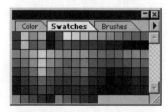

N O T E   More info about the Swatches palette and the 216 palette can be found in Chapter 13.

Brushes Palette

The Brushes palette contains different brush shapes that you can use with the painting tools. You can also define your own brush shapes or load a previously saved set of brushes.

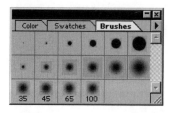

N O T E   Chapter 1 is bristling with info on the Brushes palette.

Layers Palette

A popular feature, the Layers palette displays all the layers in the active image from top to bottom. The background or last layer will appear at the bottom of the list. With the Layers palette, you can rearrange, link, group, hide, or display layers in the active image.

N O T E   Look to Chapter 7 for much more info on Layers.

Channels Palette

The Channels palette provides options for adding, deleting, duplicating, splitting, and merging all of the channels within an image.

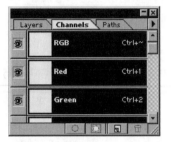

N O T E   Chapter 6 is chock full of information about the Channels feature.

Paths Palette

The Paths palette contains tools for saving and adjusting paths. You can use them with the Pen tool when creating or editing paths. The palette also offers options for reordering and renaming a path.

N O T E   The path to understanding Paths begins in Chapter 5.

History Palette

The History palette is Photoshop's powerful and automatic reversing tool, providing multiple levels of Undo.

N O T E   Get the facts about the History palette in Chapter 2.

Actions Palette

The Actions palette allows you to create a prerecorded series of commands and apply them to one or more images. There are six prerecorded actions installed with Photoshop. While they may not all be useful, they will provide good examples of what actions can do. Unlike the other palettes whose options complement or duplicate commands found on the Menu Bar or Toolbar, the Actions palette is the only place to create actions.

N O T E   To get in on the Actions, see Chapter 9.

appendix E
PREFERENCES

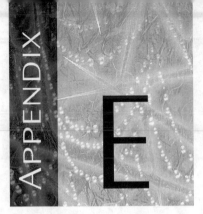

PREFERENCES

ccessed via Photoshop's Menu Bar (File ➤ Preferences), Preferences provide dozens of ways to customize the program's operation. Changes to Preferences settings typically take effect the next time the program is launched.

General

The General Preferences dialog offers a variety of preference settings. You can choose the Color Picker you will use, export the Clipboard to other applications, and reset the locations of palettes in the Photoshop workspace to the manufacturer's default. Other options include short Pantone names (rarely used by Web designers), anti-alias PostScript, tool tips, alert sounds, and dynamic color sliders.

Saving Files

The Saving Files Preferences dialog provides options for saving image previews, file extensions, and file compatibility. The Append File Extension option can be helpful when creating native Photoshop files on the Mac in a cross-platform environment.

Display & Cursors

The Display & Cursors Preferences dialog provides display options that control how images are seen on your monitor. The lower portion of the dialog is dedicated to cursor options and can be very helpful in painting.

NOTE   See Chapter 1 for more information about setting cursor preferences.

Transparency & Gamut

The Transparency & Gamut Preferences dialog offers grid size options, grid colors, and gamut warnings. The gamut warnings are for print use and aren't relevant to Web design.

Units & Rulers

The Units & Rulers Preferences options are of great use to Web designers. Units should be set to pixels for Web design. Column Size should be set to points with Point/Pica size set to PostScript (72 points/inch).

Guides & Grid

The Guides & Grid Preferences dialog is useful for setting the style, colors, and spacing of guides and grids. The default settings for guides are solid lines of light blue.

NOTE   See Chapter 10 for more information about using guides and the grid.

Plug-Ins & Scratch Disks

The Plug-Ins & Scratch Disks Preferences dialog provides technical options for setting the location of the Plug-Ins folder and the location of up to four scratch disks. Scratch disks are used by Photoshop when there is not enough computer memory to perform a task. By default, Photoshop uses the disk that the application is installed on for the first scratch disk. Advanced Photoshop print designers often designate a dedicated drive for use as the first scratch disk. Web graphics are designed at much lower resolution than print and rely less on scratch disks, although new features like History make additional scratch disk demands.

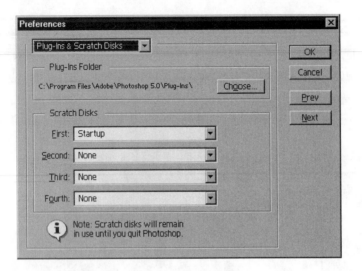

Image Cache

The Image Cache Preferences dialog provides options for the speed at which the program will redraw images. Redrawing typically occurs when you scroll through an image. The dialog provides Cache Settings from 1 to 8. The higher the number is set, the faster the program will redraw the image. The default setting is 4 and should be sufficient for most situations.

Because the way memory is allocated in Windows is different than on the Macintosh, Windows Photoshop users also have the option of setting the total percentage of RAM that the program will use. The default setting is 50% and should be sufficient for most users.

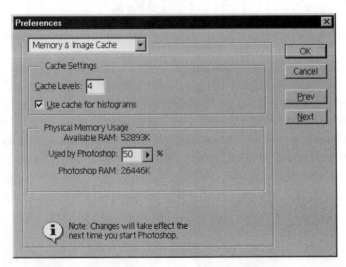

STRAZNITSKAS.COM

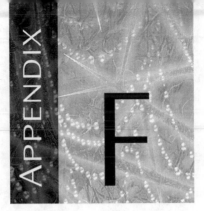

STRAZNITSKAS.COM

In addition to the CD-ROM that comes with this tome, a companion Web site has been developed that provides important resources for readers of *Mastering Photoshop 5 for the Web*. The site provides additional tips, links to all of the software mentioned in this book, working examples of the DHTML effects (you'll need IE 4 for those), and much more.

N O T E   Sure, the domain name may be hard to remember, but it was one of the few that were still available—`straz.com` was taken, and the person who owns `matt.com` wanted $50,000 for it.

The Straznitskas Workspace

The first thing you'll notice about the Straznitskas workspace is that it looks a lot like the Photoshop workspace (shown in Figure F.1).

I've always loved a good concept, and it was too hard to pass up the opportunity of building a Web site about Photoshop that looked and acted like Photoshop. The workspace is divided into three main areas: the Toolbar, image window, and palette.

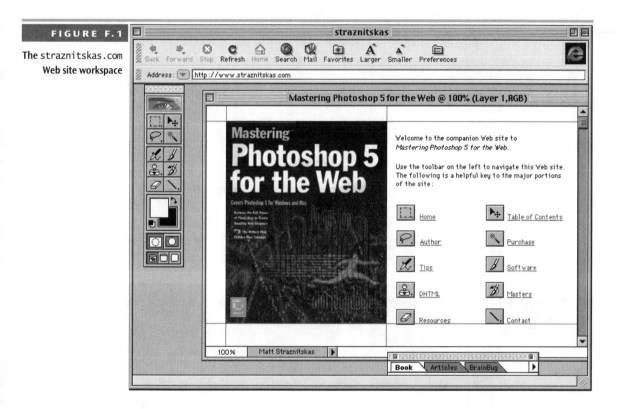

The Toolbar

Frankly, the Toolbar is unintuitive—none of the icons really reflect what's in each area of the site. But my attempts to create alternate icons weren't in keeping with the look I was going after, so I decided to rely on the intelligence of my site's audience to figure it out.

NOTE The Toolbar's interactivity is achieved by overlaying gray versions of the buttons with Java script. It doesn't act exactly like the Photoshop Toolbar, but I had to make some sacrifices for the sake of the site's users. In this case, simply mousing over each icon makes it darken, helping to reinforce which tools actually do something.

The first group of tools provides features for learning more about the book, the author, and how to buy it. Experienced users of this book, particularly those who haven't lost their copy, will have little need for these four tools.

 Home   Launches the home page. This is the default page when you enter the site.

 TOC   Provides you with this book's table of contents.

 Author   Provides some information about myself.

 Purchase   Launches the online bookstore where you can buy another copy of this book.

 T I P   Click on the eye graphic at the very top of the Toolbar to view some additional information about the site.

The second group of tools are more valuable to current users of this book:

 Tips   Provides additional nuggets of info about Photoshop and the Web.

 Software   Provides links to all of the software mentioned in this book (and more!).

 DHTML   Offers working demos of the DHTML examples discussed in Chapter 18.

 Masters   Gives you additional information on the 14 designers profiled in this book.

 Resources   Provides a list of resources—everything from typeface vendors to favorite online design sites.

 Contact   Provides a way for site users to reach the author.

 N O T E   Feel free to e-mail any comments you have. I appreciate feedback on how this book worked for you.

The Image Window

This is where all of the site's content gets placed. Via the magic of HTML-based frames (see Chapter 16), I was able to create an image window that closely resembles the functionality of Photoshop.

TIP To view the code that positions each of the four frames, visit the straznitskas.com Web site and select the View Source command in your browser.

Due to the nature of HTML, I was unable to make the title bar center over the image window. Instead, I created a very wide background image that precisely aligns above the image window. I did the same for the bar that appears below the window (see Figure F.2).

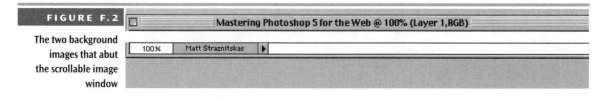

FIGURE F.2

The two background images that abut the scrollable image window

The Palette

For me, the palette was the graphic touch that completed the site and made it a little more special. The palette provides three options:

Book The straznitskas.com book site—you are here.

Articles A link to many of the technology columns that I have penned for business and news publications.

BrainBug A link to my interactive agency.

Conclusion

I've had the idea for a Web site that uses a software application as an interface for a long time, and I'm glad this book gave me the chance to realize it. I hope this appendix also demonstrated to you that good concepts are the starting point for good Web sites—and all design for that matter.

HTML REFERENCE

HTML REFERENCE

This complete HTML reference includes relevant tags and attributes for Web designers. It has been arranged alphabetically for convenient reference.

HTML Tags and Attributes

Tags	Attributes	Description
<!-- ... -->		SGML comment
<!DOCTYPE>		Public declaration
	HTML PUBLIC...	DTD conformance
<A>...</A>		Anchor
	ACCESSKEY=	Keyboard shortcut
	CHARSET=	Character encoding of link
	CLASS= ID= STYLE= TITLE=	Class(es), unique ID, style information, title
	COORDS=	Object coordinates of anchor
	DIR= LANG=	Text direction and language ID
	HREF=	Hypertext link
	NAME=	Name of hypertext link
	REL=	Forward link type
	REV=	Reverse link type
	SHAPE="rect | circle | poly | default"	Object shape of described anchor
	TABINDEX=	Explicit tabbing order
	TARGET=	Target frame name for rendering
	[events]	Core intrinsic events

Tags	Attributes	Description
<ACRONYM>...</ACRONYM>		Acronym content
	CLASS= ID= STYLE= TITLE=	Class(es), unique ID, style information, title
	DIR= LANG=	Text direction and language ID
	[events]	Core intrinsic events
<ADDRESS>...</ADDRESS>		Address content
	CLASS= ID= STYLE= TITLE=	Class(es), unique ID, style information, title
	DIR= LANG=	Text direction and language ID
	[events]	Core intrinsic events
<APPLET>...</APPLET>		Java applet
	ALIGN=	Alignment of applet
	ALT=	Alternate text description
	CODE=	Java applet name
	CODEBASE=	Location of applet
	DOWNLOAD=	Order of applet download
	HEIGHT=	Height of object
	HSPACE=	Horizontal space
	NAME=	Name of applet
	VSPACE=	Vertical space
	WIDTH=	Width of object
<AREA>		Client-side image map area description
	ALT=	Alternate text description
	COORDS=	Coordinates
	HREF=	Hypertext link
	NOHREF	No hypertext link
	SHAPE="rect | circle | poly | default"	Shape of described area
	TABINDEX=	Explicit tabbing order
	TARGET=	Target frame name for rendering
	[events]	Core intrinsic events
<B>...</B>		Bold text
	CLASS= ID= STYLE= TITLE=	Class(es), unique ID, style information, title
	DIR= LANG=	Text direction and language ID
	[events]	Core intrinsic events
<BASE>		Base URL
	HREF=	Hypertext link
	TARGET=	Target frame name for rendering
<BASEFONT>		Font setting for document
	COLOR=	Color of basefont
	FACE=	Typeface of basefont
	SIZE=	Size of basefont
<BDO>		Bi-directional override
	DIR=	Text direction required
	LANG=	Language ID

Tags	Attributes	Description
<BGSOUND>		Background sound
	LOOP=	Number of times sound repeats
	SRC=	Address of sound file
<BIG>...</BIG>		Big text
	CLASS= ID= STYLE= TITLE=	Class(es), unique ID, style information, title
	DIR= LANG=	Text direction and language ID
	[events]	Core intrinsic events
<BLOCKQUOTE>...</BLOCKQUOTE>		Block quote
	CLASS= ID= STYLE= TITLE=	Class(es), unique ID, style information, title
	DIR= LANG=	Text direction and language ID
	[events]	Core intrinsic events
<BODY>...</BODY>		Body of document
	ALINK=	Active link color
	BACKGROUND=	Location of background image
	BGCOLOR=	Background color
	CLASS= ID= STYLE= TITLE=	Class(es), unique ID, style information, title
	DIR= LANG=	Text direction and language ID
	LEFTMARGIN=	Create left margin
	LINK=	Link color
	TEXT=	Text color
	TOPMARGIN=	Create top margin
	VLINK=	Visited link color
	[events] onload, onunload	Core intrinsic events
 		Break
	CLASS= ID= STYLE= TITLE=	Class(es), unique ID, style information, title
	CLEAR=	Fixes text beside or below image
<BUTTON>...</BUTTON>		Form button
	CLASS= ID= STYLE= TITLE=	Class(es), unique ID, style information, title
	DIR= LANG=	Text direction and language ID
	DISABLED	Disables button
	NAME=	Name of button
	TABINDEX=	Explicit tabbing order
	TYPE=	Type of button
	VALUE=	Action desired
	[events] onfocus, onblur	Core intrinsic events
<CAPTION>...</CAPTION>		Table caption
	ALIGN=	Alignment of table caption
	CLASS= ID= STYLE= TITLE=	Class(es), unique ID, style information, title
	DIR= LANG=	Text direction and language ID
	VALIGN=	Vertical alignment
	[events]	Core intrinsic events

Tags	Attributes	Description
`<CENTER>...</CENTER>`		Centers text
	CLASS= ID= STYLE= TITLE=	Class(es), unique ID, style information, title
	DIR= LANG=	Text direction and language ID
	[events]	Core intrinsic events
`<CITE>...</CITE>`		Citation content
	CLASS= ID= STYLE= TITLE=	Class(es), unique ID, style information, title
	DIR= LANG=	Text direction and language ID
	[events]	Core intrinsic events
`<CODE>...</CODE>`		Code content
	CLASS= ID= STYLE= TITLE=	Class(es), unique ID, style information, title
	DIR= LANG=	Text direction and language ID
	[events]	Core intrinsic events
`<COL>...</COL>`		Column
	ALIGN=	Alignment of column
	CLASS= ID= STYLE= TITLE=	Class(es), unique ID, style information, title
	DIR= LANG=	Text direction and language ID
	SPAN=	Number of columns spanned
	VALIGN=	Vertical alignment
	WIDTH=	Width of column
	[events]	Core intrinsic events
`<COLGROUP>`		Column grouping
	ALIGN=	Alignment of column grouping
	CLASS= ID= STYLE= TITLE=	Class(es), unique ID, style information, title
	SPAN=	Number of column groupings spanned
	VALIGN=	Vertical alignment
	WIDTH=	Width of column grouping
`<DD>`		Definition data
	ALIGN=	Alignment of data
	CLASS= ID= STYLE= TITLE=	Class(es), unique ID, style information, title
	DIR= LANG=	Text direction and language ID
	[events]	Core intrinsic events
`<DEL>...</DEL>`		Deleted text
	CITE=	Change data
	CLASS= ID= STYLE= TITLE=	Class(es), unique ID, style information, title
	DATETIME=	ISO change date
	DIR= LANG=	Text direction and language ID
	[events]	Core intrinsic events
`<DFN>...<DFN>`		Definition content
	CLASS= ID= STYLE= TITLE=	Class(es), unique ID, style information, title
	DIR= LANG=	Text direction and language ID
	[events]	Core intrinsic events

Tags	Attributes	Description
<DIR>...<DIR>		Directory list
	CLASS= ID= STYLE= TITLE=	Class(es), unique ID, style information, title
	COMPACT	Compact representation
	DIR= LANG=	Text direction and language ID
	[events]	Core intrinsic events
<DIV>		Document division
	ALIGN=	Alignment of text section
	CLASS= ID= STYLE= TITLE=	Class(es), unique ID, style information, title
	DIR= LANG=	Text direction and language ID
	[events]	Core intrinsic events
<DL>...</DL>		Definition list
	ALIGN=	Alignment of list
	CLASS= ID= STYLE= TITLE=	Class(es), unique ID, style information, title
	CLEAR=	Clears list
	COMPACT	Compact representation
	DIR= LANG=	Text direction and language ID
	[events]	Core intrinsic events
<DT>		Definition term
	ALIGN=	Alignment of term
	CLASS= ID= STYLE= TITLE=	Class(es), unique ID, style information, title
	DIR= LANG=	Text direction and language ID
	[events]	Core intrinsic events
<EM>...</EM>		Emphasized text
	CLASS= ID= STYLE= TITLE=	Class(es), unique ID, style information, title
	DIR= LANG=	Text direction and language ID
	[events]	Core intrinsic events
<EMBED>...</EMBED>		Embedded object
	ALIGN=	Alignment of object
	HEIGHT=	Height of object
	HIDDEN=	Hides object
	PALETTE=	Sets color palette
	PLUGINSPAGE=	Sets plug-ins source link
	SRC=	Location of object source
	WIDTH=	Width of object
	[events]	Core intrinsic events
<FIELDSET>...</FIELDSET>		Form fieldset
	CLASS= ID= STYLE= TITLE=	Class(es), unique ID, style information, title
	DIR= LANG=	Text direction and language ID
	[events]	Core intrinsic events

Tags	Attributes	Description
<FONT>...</FONT>		Font
	COLOR=	Color of font
	FACE=	Typeface of font
	SIZE=	Size of font
<FORM>...</FORM>		Form
	ACCEPT-CHARSET=	List of supported character sets
	ACTION=	Server-side form handler
	CLASS= ID= STYLE= TITLE=	Class(es), unique ID, style information, title
	DIR= LANG=	Text direction and language ID
	ENCTYPE=	Encryption type
	METHOD="get | post"	Form data sent to server
	NAME=	Name of form
	TARGET=	Target frame name for rendering
	[events] onsubmit, onreset	Core intrinsic events
<FRAME>...</FRAME>		Frame within frameset
	BORDERCOLOR=	Color of border
	FRAMEBORDER=	Width of border
	HEIGHT=	Height of frame
	MARGINHEIGHT=	Height of margin
	MARGINWIDTH=	Width of margin
	NAME=	Name of frame
	NORESIZE	Prohibits resize
	SCROLLING="yes | no | auto"	Sets scroll
	SRC=	Location of frame source
	WIDTH=	Width of frame
<FRAMESET>...</FRAMESET>		Frameset
	BORDER=	Width of border
	BORDERCOLOR=	Color of border
	COLS=	Number of columns
	FRAMEBORDER=	Width of border
	FRAMESPACING=	Space between frames
	ROWS=	Number of rows
	[events] onload, onunload	Intrinsic events
<HEAD>...</HEAD>		Document head
	DIR= LANG=	Text direction and language ID
	PROFILE=	URL of metadata
<H1>...</H1>		Heading 1
	ALIGN=	Alignment of heading
	CLASS= ID= STYLE= TITLE=	Class(es), unique ID, style information, title
	CLEAR=	Fixes text beside or below image
	COLOR=	Color of text
	DINGBAT=	Adds defined dingbat
	DIR= LANG=	Text direction and language ID

Tags	Attributes	Description
<H2>, <H3>, <H4>, <H5>, <H6>	Same as <H1>	Headings 2 through 6
<HR>		Horizontal rule
	ALIGN=	Alignment of rule
	CLASS= ID= STYLE= TITLE=	Class(es), unique ID, style information, title
	CLEAR=	Fixes text beside or below image
	COLOR=	Color of rule
	NOSHADE=	No shading on rule
	NOWRAP	No wrapping of rule
	SIZE=	Height of rule
	WIDTH=	Width of rule
	[events]	Core intrinsic events
<HTML>...</HTML>		Document container
	DIR= LANG=	Text direction and language ID
	VERSION=	HTML standard version used
<I>...</I>		Italic text
	CLASS= ID= STYLE= TITLE=	Class(es), unique ID, style information, title
	DIR= LANG=	Text direction and language ID
	[events]	Core intrinsic events
<IFRAME>...</IFRAME>		Inline frame
	ALIGN=	Alignment of inline frame
	BORDER=	Size of border
	BORDERCOLOR=	Color of border
	FRAMEBORDER=	Width of border
	FRAMESPACING=	Space between frames
	HEIGHT=	Height of frame
	HSPACE=	Horizontal space
	MARGINHEIGHT=	Height of margin
	MARGINWIDTH=	Width of margin
	NAME=	Name of inline frame
	NORESIZE=	Prohibits resize of frame
	SCROLLING="yes | no | auto"	Sets scroll
	SRC=	Location of inline frame source
	VSPACE=	Vertical space
	WIDTH=	Width of frame
<ILAYER>...</ILAYER>	(same as LAYER tag)	Inline layer positioning (behaves like text element)
<IMG>		Image
	ALIGN=	Alignment of image
	ALT=	Alternate text description
	BORDER=	Size of image border
	CLASS= ID= STYLE= TITLE=	Class(es), unique ID, style information, title
	DIR= LANG=	Text direction and language ID

Tags	Attributes	Description
	DYNSRC=	Dynamic source
	HEIGHT=	Height of image
	HSPACE=	Horizontal space
	ISMAP	Server-side image map
	LOOP=	Number of repetitions
	LOWSRC=	Location of low-resolution image
	NAME=	Name of image
	SRC=	Location of image source
	USEMAP=	Client-side image map
	VSPACE=	Vertical space
	WIDTH=	Width of image
	[events]	Core intrinsic events
<INPUT>...</INPUT>		Form input
	ACCEPT=	Accept input
	ALT=	Alternate text description
	CHECKED	Loads checkboxes already selected
	CLASS= ID= STYLE= TITLE=	Class(es), unique ID, style information, title
	DIR= LANG=	Text direction and language ID
	DISABLED	Disables input
	MAX=	Maximum number of input characters
	MAXLENGTH=	Maximum length of field
	NAME=	Name of form
	SIZE=	Size of field
	SRC=	Location of added images
	TABINDEX=	Explicit tabbing order
	TYPE=" button | checkbox | file | hidden | image | password | radio | reset | submit | text"	Type of input method
	USEMAP=	Client-side image map
	VALUE=	Sets default value
	[events] onfocus, onblur, onselect, onchange Core intrinsic events	
<INS>...</INS>		Inserted text
	CITE=	Change data
	CLASS= ID= STYLE= TITLE=	Class(es), unique ID, style information, title
	DATETIME=	ISO change date
	DIR= LANG=	Text direction and language ID
	[events]	Core intrinsic events
<ISINDEX>		Document is a searchable index—Obsolete, use <FORM> instead
	ACTION=	URL
	CLASS= ID= STYLE= TITLE=	Class(es), unique ID, style information, title
	DIR= LANG=	Text direction and language ID
	PROMPT=	Prompt text

Tags	Attributes	Description
<KBD>...</KBD>		Keyboard
	CLASS= ID= STYLE= TITLE=	Class(es), unique ID, style information, title
	DIR= LANG=	Text direction and language ID
	[events]	Core intrinsic events
<KEYGEN>...</KEYGEN>		Form-generated security key
	NAME=	Required
	CHALLENGE=	Public key challenge string
<LABEL>...</LABEL>		Form field label
	ACCESSKEY=	Keyboard shortcut
	CLASS= ID= STYLE= TITLE=	Class(es), unique ID, style information, title
	DIR= LANG=	Text direction and language ID
	DISABLED	Disables labeling
	FOR=	Field ID
	[events] onfocus, onblur	Core intrinsic events
<LAYER>...</LAYER>		Layer positioning element (behaves like structure)
	Note: Style sheets can also be used to control positioning of layer elements in a manner similar to but not the same as the W3C DOM and CSS-Positioning methods.	
	ABOVE=	Relative stacking order
	BACKGROUND=	Background image
	BELOW=	Relative stacking order
	BGCOLOR=	Background color
	CLIP="n,n,n,n"	Coordinates of viewable area
	HEIGHT=	Height of layer
	LEFT=	Horizontal position of layer in layer
	PAGEX=	Horizontal position of layer in page
	PAGEY=	Vertical position of layer in page
	SRC=	Source of content
	TOP=	Vertical position of layer in layer
	VIEW="hidden | inherit | show"	Define layer visibility
	WIDTH=	Horizontal size of layer
	Z-INDEX=	Absolute stacking order
	onmouseover, onmouseout, onfocus, onblur, onload	Intrinsic events
<LEGEND>		Form fieldset legend
	ACCESSKEY=	Keyboard shortcut
	ALIGN=	Alignment of legend
	CLASS= ID= STYLE= TITLE=	Class(es), unique ID, style information, title
	DIR= LANG=	Text direction and language ID
	[events]	Core intrinsic events

Tags	Attributes	Description
<LI>...</LI>		List item
	ALIGN=	Alignment of items
	CLASS= ID= STYLE= TITLE=	Class(es), unique ID, style information, title
	DIR= LANG=	Text direction and language ID
	TYPE=	Numbering or bullet style
	VALUE="number"	Reset sequence number
	[events]	Core intrinsic events
<LINK>		Link
	CLASS= ID= STYLE= TITLE=	Class(es), unique ID, style information, title
	DIR= LANG=	Text direction and language ID
	HREF=	Hypertext link
	MEDIA=	Supported media list
	NAME=	Name of link
	REL=	Forward link type (application dependent)
	REV=	Reverse link type (application dependent)
	TARGET=	Target frame name for rendering
	TYPE=	Media type
<MAP>...</MAP>		Client-side image map
	CLASS= ID= STYLE= TITLE=	Class(es), unique ID, style information, title
	NAME=	Name of image map
<MENU>...</MENU>		Menu list
	COMPACT	Compact representation
	CLASS= ID= STYLE= TITLE=	Class(es), unique ID, style information, title
	DIR= LANG=	Text direction and language ID
	[events]	Core intrinsic events
<META>		Metadata
	CONTENT=	Content description
	DIR= LANG=	Text direction and language ID
	HTTP-EQUIV=	Server response
	NAME=	Name of document
	TITLE=	Title of document
	URL=	URL of document
<NOBR>...</NOBR>		Inhibits line breaking
<NOEMBED>		Inhibits embedding
<NOFRAMES>...</NOFRAMES>		No frames alternate document body
<NOLAYER>...</NOLAYER>		Inhibits layers
<NOSCRIPT>...</NOSCRIPT>		Noscript data
<OBJECT>...</OBJECT>		Object
	ALIGN=	Alignment of object
	BORDER=	Width of border

Tags	Attributes	Description
	CLASS= ID= STYLE= TITLE=	Class(es), unique ID, style information, title
	CLASSID=	Class identifier
	CODE=	Type of script
	CODEBASE=	Object code base
	CODETYPE=	Media type
	DATA=	Data type
	DECLARE=	References object name
	DIR= LANG=	Text direction and language ID
	DISABLED	Disables object
	HEIGHT=	Height of object
	HSPACE=	Horizontal space
	NAME=	Name of object
	SHAPES=	Name of shaped hyperlink
	STANDBY=	Standby message
	TABINDEX=	Explicit tabbing order
	TYPE=	Media type
	USEMAP=	Image map
	VSPACE=	Vertical space
	WIDTH=	Width of image
	[events]	Core intrinsic events
<OL>...</OL>		Ordered list
	ALIGN=	Alignment of list
	CLASS= ID= STYLE= TITLE=	Class(es), unique ID, style information, title
	COMPACT	Compact representation
	DIR= LANG=	Text direction and language ID
	START=	Starting number
	TYPE=	Numbering style
	[events]	Core intrinsic events
<OPTION>...</OPTION>		Form option
	CLASS= ID= STYLE= TITLE=	Class(es), unique ID, style information, title
	DIR= LANG=	Text direction and language ID
	DISABLED	Disables option
	SELECTED=	Option selected at default
	VALUE=	Value to be returned
	[events]	Core intrinsic events
<P>...</P>		Paragraph
	ALIGN=	Alignment of paragraph
	CLASS= ID= STYLE= TITLE=	Class(es), unique ID, style information, title
	DIR= LANG=	Text direction and language ID
	WIDTH=	Width of paragraph
	[events]	Core intrinsic events

Tags	Attributes	Description
<PARAM>...</PARAM>		Parameter
	NAME=	Name of parameter
	TYPE=	Internet media type
	VALUE=	Sets value
	VALUETYPE=	Interprets value
<PRE>...</PRE>		Preformatted text
<Q>...</Q>		Inline quote
	CLASS= ID= STYLE= TITLE=	Class(es), unique ID, style information, title
	DIR= LANG=	Text direction and language ID
	[events]	Core intrinsic events
<S>...</S>		Strikeout text
	CLASS= ID= STYLE= TITLE=	Class(es), unique ID, style information, title
	DIR= LANG=	Text direction and language ID
	[events]	Core intrinsic events
<SAMP>...<SAMP>		Sample text
	CLASS= ID= STYLE= TITLE=	Class(es), unique ID, style information, title
	DIR= LANG=	Text direction and language ID
	[events]	Core intrinsic events
<SCRIPT>...</SCRIPT>		Script data
	LANGUAGE=	Script language
	SRC=	URL of script source
	TYPE=	Internet content type
	[events]	Core intrinsic events
<SELECT>...</SELECT>		Form selection list
	ALIGN=	Alignment of list
	CLASS= ID= STYLE= TITLE=	Class(es), unique ID, style information, title
	DIR= LANG=	Text direction and language ID
	DISABLED	Disables list
	HEIGHT=	Height of object
	NAME=	Names of object
	SIZE=	Size of object
	TABINDEX=	Explicit tabbing order
	WIDTH=	Width of object
	[events] onfocus, onblur, onselect, onchange	Core intrinsic events
<SMALL>...</SMALL>		Small text
	CLASS= ID= STYLE= TITLE=	Class(es), unique ID, style information, title
	DIR= LANG=	Text direction and language ID
	[events]	Core intrinsic events
<SPAN>...</SPAN>		Generic text container
	ALIGN=	Alignment of container

Tags	Attributes	Description
	CLASS= ID= STYLE= TITLE=	Class(es), unique ID, style information, title
	DIR= LANG=	Text direction and language ID
	[events]	Core intrinsic events
<STRIKE>...</STRIKE>		Strikeout text
	CLASS= ID= STYLE= TITLE=	Class(es), unique ID, style information, title
	DIR= LANG=	Text direction and language ID
	[events]	Core intrinsic events
<STRONG>...</STRONG>		Strong text
	CLASS= ID= STYLE= TITLE=	Class(es), unique ID, style information, title
	DIR= LANG=	Text direction and language ID
	[events]	Core intrinsic events
<STYLE>...</STYLE>		Style sheet definition
	DIR= LANG=	Text direction and language ID
	MEDIA=	Supported media list
	TYPE=	Internet content type
_{...}		Subscript text
	CLASS= ID= STYLE= TITLE=	Class(es), unique ID, style information, title
	DIR= LANG=	Text direction and language ID
	[events]	Core intrinsic events
^{...}		Superscript text
	CLASS= ID= STYLE= TITLE=	Class(es), unique ID, style information, title
	DIR= LANG=	Text direction and language ID
	[events]	Core intrinsic events
<TAB>		Tab value
	ALIGN=	Alignment of tab
	INDENT=	
<TABLE>...</TABLE>		Table
	ALIGN=	Alignment of table
	BACKGROUND=	Location of background image
	BGCOLOR=	Background color
	BORDER=	Size of border
	BORDERCOLOR=	Color of border
	BORDERCOLORDARK=	Dark color for 3-D border
	BORDERCOLORLIGHT=	Light color for 3-D border
	CELLPADDING=	Space between table cell edge and content
	CELLSPACING=	Space between cell borders
	CLASS= ID= STYLE= TITLE=	Class(es), unique ID, style information, title
	COLS=	Number of columns
	DIR= LANG=	Text direction and language ID
	FRAME=	External border around table

Tags	Attributes	Description
	HEIGHT=	Height of table
	NOWRAP	Prohibits text wrapping
	WIDTH=	Width of table
	[events]	Core intrinsic events
<TBODY>...</TBODY>		Table body
	ALIGN=	Alignment of table body
	BGCOLOR=	Background color
	CLASS= ID= STYLE= TITLE=	Class(es), unique ID, style information, title
	DIR= LANG=	Text direction and language ID
	VALIGN=	Vertical alignment
	[events]	Core intrinsic events
<TD>...</TD>		Table cell
	ALIGN=	Alignment of table cell
	AXIS=	Abbreviated cell name
	AXES=	AXIS values
	BACKGROUND=	Location of background image
	BGCOLOR=	Background color
	BORDERCOLOR=	Border color
	BORDERCOLORDARK=	Dark color for 3-D border
	BORDERCOLORLIGHT=	Light color for 3-D border
	CLASS= ID= STYLE= TITLE=	Class(es), unique ID, style information, title
	COLSPAN=	Number of columns spanned
	DIR= LANG=	Text direction and language ID
	HEIGHT=	Height of table cell
	NOWRAP	Prohibits text wrap
	ROWSPAN=	Number of rows spanned
	VALIGN=	Vertical alignment
	WIDTH=	Width of table cell
	[events]	Core intrinsic events
<TEXTAREA>...</TEXTAREA>		Form input text area
	ALIGN=	Alignment of text field
	CLASS= ID= STYLE= TITLE=	Class(es), unique ID, style information, title
	COLS=	Width of text input field
	DATAFLD=	Field of data
	DATASRC=	Location of data source
	DIR= LANG=	Text direction and language ID
	DISABLED	Disables text field
	ERROR=	Error message
	NAME=	Name of text field
	READONLY	Read-only
	ROWS=	Height of text input field

Tags	Attributes	Description
	TABINDEX=	Explicit tabbing order
	WRAP=	Wrap text
	[events] onfocus, onblur, onselect, onchange Core intrinsic events	
<TFOOT>...</TFOOT>		Table footer
	ALIGN=	Alignment of footer
	BGCOLOR=	Background color
	CLASS= ID= STYLE= TITLE=	Class(es), unique ID, style information, title
	DIR= LANG=	Text direction and language ID
	VALIGN=	Vertical alignment
	[events]	Core intrinsic events
<TH>...</TH>		Table cell heading
	ALIGN=	Alignment of heading
	AXIS=	Abbreviated cell name
	AXES=	AXIS values
	BACKGROUND=	Location of background image
	BGCOLOR=	Background color
	BORDERCOLOR=	Border color
	BORDERCOLORDARK=	Dark color for 3-D border
	BORDERCOLORLIGHT=	Light color for 3-D border
	CLASS= ID= STYLE= TITLE=	Class(es), unique ID, style information, title
	COLSPAN=	Number of columns spanned
	DIR= LANG=	Text direction and language ID
	HEIGHT=	Height of table cell
	NOWRAP	Prohibits text wrap
	ROWSPAN=	Number of rows spanned
	VALIGN=	Vertical alignment
	WIDTH=	Width of table cell
	[events]	Core intrinsic events
<THEAD>...</THEAD>		Table header
	ALIGN=	Alignment of header
	BGCOLOR=	Background color
	CLASS= ID= STYLE= TITLE=	Class(es), unique ID, style information, title
	DIR= LANG=	Text direction and language ID
	VALIGN=	Vertical alignment
	[events]	Core intrinsic events
<TITLE>...</TITLE>		Document title
	DIR= LANG=	Text direction and language ID
<TR>...</TR>		Table row
	ALIGN=	Alignment of table row
	BGCOLOR=	Background color

Tags	Attributes	Description
	BORDERCOLOR=	Border color
	BORDERCOLORDARK=	Dark color for 3-D border
	BORDERCOLORLIGHT=	Light color for 3-D border
	CLASS= ID= STYLE= TITLE=	Class(es), unique ID, style information, title
	DIR= LANG=	Text direction and language ID
	HEIGHT=	Height of table row
	NOWRAP	Prohibits text wrap
	VALIGN=	Vertical alignment
	VSPACE=	Vertical space
	[events]	Core intrinsic events
<TT>...</TT>		Monospaced text
	CLASS= ID= STYLE= TITLE=	Class(es), unique ID, style information, title
	DIR= LANG=	Text direction and language ID
	[events]	Core intrinsic events
<U>...</U>		Underline text
	CLASS= ID= STYLE= TITLE=	Class(es), unique ID, style information, title
	DIR= LANG=	Text direction and language ID
	[events]	Core intrinsic events
<UL>...</UL>		Unordered list
	ALIGN=	Alignment of list
	CLASS= ID= STYLE= TITLE=	Class(es), unique ID, style information, title
	COMPACT	Compact representation
	DIR= LANG=	Text direction and language ID
	SRC=	Location of list source
	TYPE="disk|square|circle"	Bullet style
	WRAP=	Wrap text
	[events]	Core intrinsic events
<VAR>...</VAR>		Variable content
	CLASS= ID= STYLE= TITLE=	Class(es), unique ID, style information, title
	DIR= LANG=	Text direction and language ID
	[events]	Core intrinsic events
<WBR>		Conditional break

Cross-Browser Reference

This cross-browser reference includes both tags and attributes and corresponding relevant browser support.

Legend

[nc] = non-conforming (browser doesn't support tag or attribute)

[xx] = obsolete (attribute is considered to be outdated)

* = supported (browser supports tag or attribute)

MSIE = Microsoft Internet Explorer

MS = Microsoft

NSNC = Netscape Navigator / Communicator

NS = Netscape

Lynx = Lynx (text-based browser)

HTML Version = World Wide Web Consortium standard version

Author = author of tag

W3C = World Wide Web Consortium

Cross-Browser Tag and Attribute Support Table

Tag / Attribute	MSIE	NSNC	Lynx	HTML Version	Author
<!—...—>	*	*	*	2	W3C
<!DOCTYPE>	*	*	*	2	W3C
HTML...	*	*	*	2	W3C
<A> ...</A>	*	*	*	2	W3C
accesskey=	4			4	W3C
charset=	4			4	W3C
class=		*3/4	*	3/4	W3C
coords=	4			4	W3C
dir=				4	W3C
href=	*	*	*	2/4	W3C
hreflang=				4	W3C
id=	*3/4	*3/4	*	3/4	W3C
lang=	*3/4	*3/4	*	3/4	W3C
language=	*3/4			[nc]	MS
md=			*	3	W3C
methods=	*2/4	*	*	2	W3C
name=	*	*	*	2/4	W3C

Tag / Attribute	MSIE	NSNC	Lynx	HTML Version	Author
rel=	*	*2/4	*	2/4	W3C
rev=		*2/4	*	2/4	W3C
shape=			*	3/4	W3C
style=	*3/4	4		4	W3C
tabindex=	*3/4	4*		4	W3C
target=	*3/4	*2/4	*	4	W3C
title=	*2/4	*2/4	*	2/4	W3C
urn=	*2/4	*2/4	*	2	W3C
onfocus, onblur	*	*			
{event}=	*3/4	*		4	W3C
<ABBR>				4	W3C
...</ABBR>				4	W3C
class=				4	W3C
dir=				4	W3C
id=				4	W3C
lang=				4	W3C
style=				4	W3C
title=				4	W3C
{event}=				4	W3C
<ACRONYM>			*	3	W3C
...</ACRONYM>					
class=			*	3	W3C
dir=					W3C
id=			*	3	W3C
lang=			*	3	W3C
style=			*	3	W3C
title=			*	3	W3C
{event}=				3	W3C
<ADDRESS>	*	*	*	2/4	W3C
...</ADDRESS>					
align=	*3/4			[nc]	
class=		*3/4	*	3/4	W3C
clear=		*3/4	*	3	W3C
dir=				4	W3C
id=	*	*3/4	*	3/4	W3C
lang=		*3/4	*	3/4	W3C
nowrap		*	*	3	W3C
style=	*3/4	4		4	W3C
title=	*3/4			4	W3C
{event}=	*3/4			4	W3C
<APP>	4			[nc]	SM
...</APP>					
align=	4			[nc]	SM
class=	4			[nc]	SM
height=	4			[nc]	SM
src=	4			[nc]	SM
width=	4			[nc]	SM
<APPLET>	*3/4	*2/4	*	3+/4	W3C
...</APPLET>					
align=	*3/4	*2/4		3+	W3C
alt=	*3/4	*2/4	*	3+	W3C
archive=				4	W3C
code=	*3/4	*2/4	*	3+	W3C
codebase=	*3/4	*2/4	*	3+	W3C

Tag / Attribute	MSIE	NSNC	Lynx	HTML Version	Author
download=	*3/4			[nc]	MS
height=	*3/4	*2/4	*	3+	W3C
hspace=	*3/4	*2/4	*	3+	W3C
name=	*3/4	*2/4	*	3+	W3C
object=		4		4	W3C
title=	*3/4			3	MS
vspace=	*3/4	*2/4	*	3+	W3C
width=	*3/4	*2/4	*	3+	W3C
<AREA>	*	*	*	3+/4	W3C
...</AREA>	[nc]				
accesskey=					
alt=		*2/4	*	3+/4	W3C
coords=	*2/4	*2/4	*	3+/4	W3C
href=	*2/4	*2/4	*	3+/4	W3C
id=	*3/4	*3	*	3	W3C
name=	*3/4		*	3	W3C
nohref=	*2/4	*2/4	*	3+/4	W3C
shape=	*2/4	*2/4	*	3+/4	W3C
style=	*3/4	4		3	W3C
tabindex=	4	4*		4	W3C
target=	*3/4	*2/4		4	W3C
title=	*3/4	*2/4		3	W3C
{event}=	*3/4			3	W3C
<AU>			*	3	W3C
...</AU>					
class=			*	3	W3C
id=			*	3	W3C
lang=			*	3	W3C
<B>	*	*	*	2/4	W3C
...</B>					
class=		*3/4	*	3/4	W3C
dir=				4	W3C
id=	*3/4	*3/4	*	3/4	W3C
lang=		*3/4	*	3/4	W3C
style=	*3/4	4		4	W3C
title=	*3/4	4		4	W3C
{event}=	*3/4			4	W3C
<BANNER>			*	3	W3C
...</BANNER>					
class=			*	3	W3C
id=			*	3	W3C
lang=			*	3	W3C
<BASE>	*	*2/4	*	2/4	W3C
.../BASE>	[nc]				
href=	*	*2/4	*	2/4	W3C
target=	*3/4	*2/4	*	4	W3C
title=	*3/4			[nc]	MS
<BASEFONT>	*	*	*	3+/4	W3C
...</BASEFONT>					
color=	*3/4	*2/4	*	3+/4	W3C
face=	*3/4	*2/4	*	4	W3C
id=	*3/4	*3/4	*	3	W3C
size=	*	*24	*	3+	W3C
title=	*3/4				MS

Tag / Attribute	MSIE	NSNC	Lynx	HTML Version	Author
<BDO>				4	W3C
...</BDO>					
dir=				4	W3C
lang=				4	W3C
<BGSOUND>	*	*2/4		[nc]	MS
loop=	*	*2/4			
src=	*	*2/4			
id=	*				
title=	*				
<BIG>	*	*	*	3+/4	W3C
...</BIG>					
class=		*3/4	*	3/4	W3C
dir=				4	W3C
id=	*3/4	*3/4	*	3/4	W3C
lang=		*3/4	*	3/4	W3C
style=	*3/4	4		4	W3C
title=	*3/4			4	W3C
{event}=	*3/4			4	W3C
<BLINK>		*2/4		NS	[nc]
...</BLINK>					
<BLOCKQUOTE>	*	*	*	2	W3C
...</BLOCKQUOTE>					
cite=				4	W3C
class=				4	W3C
dir=				4	W3C
id=	3/4	*3/4		4	W3C
lang=				4	W3C
style=	*3/4	4		4	W3C
title=	*3/4			4	W3C
{event}=	*3/4			4	W3C
<BODY>	*	*	*	2/4	W3C
...</BODY>					
align=	*3/4			4	W3C
alink=	*	*		3+/4	W3C
background=	*	*		3+/4	W3C
bgcolor=	*	*		3+/4	W3C
bgproperties= fixed	*3/4			[nc]	MS
class=				4	W3C
dir=				4	W3C
id=	*3/4	*3/4		4	W3C
lang=				4	W3C
leftmargin=	*			[nc]	MS
link=	*3/4	*2/4		3+/4	W3C
scroll=	*3/4			[nc]	MS
style=	*3/4	4		4	W3C
text=	*3/4	*2/4		3+/4	W3C
title=	*3/4			4	W3C
topmargin=	*3/4			[nc]	MS
vlink=	*3/4	*2/4		3+/4	W3C
{event}=	*3/4			4	W3C

Tag / Attribute	MSIE	NSNC	Lynx	HTML Version	Author
**\ **	*	*	*	2/4	W3C
class=	*	*3/4		3	W3C
clear=	*	*2/4		3	W3C
none				3+	W3C
dir=				4	W3C
id=	*	*3/4		3	W3C
lang=		*3/4		3	W3C
style=	*3/4	4		4	W3C
title=	*3/4			4	W3C
\<BQ> **...\</BQ>**			*	3	W3C
\<BUTTON> **...\</BUTTON>**	*3/4			4	W3C
accesskey=	*3/4			[nc]	MS
class=	4			4	W3C
dir=				4	W3C
disabled	*3/4			4	W3C
id=	4			4	W3C
lang=				4	W3C
name=				4	W3C
style=	4			4	W3C
tabindex=	4			4	W3C
title=	*3/4			4	W3C
type=	4			4	W3C
value=	4			4	W3C
{event}=	*3/4			4	W3C
\<CAPTION> **...\</CAPTION>**	*	*	*	3	W3C
align=	*	*	*	3+/4	W3C
class=				4	W3C
dir=				4	W3C
id=	*	*3/4	*	3/4	W3C
lang			*	3/4	W3C
style=	*3/4	4		4	W3C
title=	*3/4			4	W3C
valign=	*2/4	*	*	3+	W3C
{event}=	*3/4			4	W3C
\<CENTER> **...\</CENTER>**	*	*	*	3+	W3C
class=				4	W3C
dir=				4	W3C
id=	*3/4	*3/4	*	3	W3C
lang=				4	W3C
style=	*3/4	4		4	W3C
title=	*3/4			4	W3C
{event}=	*3/4			4	W3C
\<CITE> **...\</CITE>**	*	*	*	2/4	W3C
class=		*3/4	*	3/4	W3C
dir=				4	W3C
id=	*3/4	*3/4	*	3/4	W3C
lang=		*3/4	*	3/4	W3C
style=	*3/4	4		4	W3C
title=	*3/4			4	W3C
{event}=	*3/4			4	W3C

Tag / Attribute	MSIE	NSNC	Lynx	HTML Version	Author
<CODE> ...**</CODE>**	*	*	*	2	W3C
class=		*3/4	*	3	W3C
dir=				4	W3C
id=	*3/4	*3/4	*	3	W3C
lang=		*3/4	*	3	W3C
style=	*3/4	4		4	W3C
title=	*3/4			4	W3C
{event}=	*3/4			4	W3C
<COL> ...**</COL>**	4			4	W3C
align=	4			4	W3C
char=				4	W3C
charoff=				4	W3C
class=				4	W3C
dir=				4	W3C
id=	4			4	W3C
span=	4			4	W3C
style=	4			4	W3C
title=	4			4	W3C
valign=	4			4	W3C
width=	4			4	W3C
{event}=	4			4	W3C
<COLGROUP> ...**</COLGROUP>**	*3/4			4	W3C
align=	4			4	W3C
char=				4	W3C
charoff=				4	W3C
class=				4	W3C
id=	4			4	W3C
span=	4			4	W3C
style=	4			4	W3C
title=	4			4	W3C
valign=				4	W3C
width=	4			4	W3C
<COMMENT> ...**</COMMENT>**	*		*	[nc]	
title=	*				
<CREDIT> ...**</CREDIT>**			*	3	W3C
<DD> ...**</DD>**	*	*	*	2/4	W3C
align=	4			3	W3C
class=	4	3		4	W3C
dir=				4	W3C
id=	4	3		3	W3C
lang=		3		3	W3C
style=	4	4		3	W3C
title=	4			3	W3C
{event}=	4				
<DEL> ...**</DEL>**			*	3	W3C
cite=				4	W3C

Tag / Attribute	MSIE	NSNC	Lynx	HTML Version	Author
class=			*	3/4	W3C
datetime=				4	W3C
dir=				4	W3C
id=			*	3/4	W3C
lang=			*	3/4	W3C
style=			*	3/4	W3C
title=			*	3/4	W3C
{event}=				3/4	W3C
<DFN> ...<DFN>	*	*	*	3/4	W3C
class=			*	3/4	W3C
dir=				4	W3C
id=	*3/4		*	3/4	W3C
lang=			*	3/4	W3C
style=	4			4	W3C
title=	4			4	W3C
{event}=	4			4	W3C
<DIR> ...<DIR>	*	*	*	2	W3C
class=				4	W3C
compact	*	*	*	2	W3C
dir=				4	W3C
id=	4	*3/4		4	W3C
lang=				3/4	W3C
style=	4	4		4	W3C
title=	4			4	W3C
{event}=	4			4	W3C
<DIV> ...</DIV>	*	*	*	3/4	W3C
align=	4	*	*	3/4	W3C
justify				3	W3C
class=		*3/4	*	3/4	W3C
clear=		*	*	3	W3C
{measurement}			*	3	W3C
datafld=	4			[nc]	
dataformats=	4			[nc]	
datasrc=	4			[nc]	
dir=				4	W3C
id=	4	*3/4	*	3/4	W3C
lang=		*3/4	*	3/4	W3C
nowrap		*3/4	*	3	W3C
style=	4	4		4	W3C
title=	4			4	W3C
{event}=	4			4	W3C
<DL> ...</DL>	*	*	*	2/4	W3C
align=	4				
class=		3	*	3/4	W3C
clear=		*	*	3	W3C
compact	*	*	*	2/4	W3C
dir=				4	W3C
id=	4	*3/4	*	3/4	W3C
lang=		*3/4		3/4	W3C

Tag / Attribute	MSIE	NSNC	Lynx	HTML Version	Author
style=	4	4		4	W3C
title=	4			4	W3C
{event}=	4			4	W3C
<DT>	*	*	*	2/4	W3C
...</DT>					
align=	4			3	W3C
class=				4	
dir=				4	
id=	4		*	3	W3C
lang=				4	W3C
style=	4			4	W3C
title=	4			4	W3C
{event}=	4			4	W3C
<EM>	*	*	*	2/4	W3C
...</EM>					
class=			*	3/4	W3C
dir=				4	W3C
id=	*3/4			3/4	W3C
lang=				3/4	W3C
style=	4			4	W3C
title=	4			4	W3C
{event}=	4			4	W3C
<EMBED>	*3/4	*		[nc]	NS
...</EMBED>					
accesskey=	4				
align=	4	*			
height=	4				
hidden=	4				
id=	4				
palette=	4				
pluginspage=	4				
src=	4				
style=	4				
title=	4				
width=	4				
{event}=	4				
<FIELDSET>	4			4	W3C
...</FIELDSET>					
class=				4	W3C
dir=				4	W3C
id=				4	W3C
lang=				4	W3C
style=				4	W3C
title=				4	W3C
{event}=				4	W3C
<FIG>			*	3	W3C
...</FIG>					
align=			*	3	W3C
class=			*	3	W3C
clear=			*	3	W3C
height=				3	W3C
id=				3	W3C
imagemap=				3	W3C

Tag / Attribute	MSIE	NSNC	Lynx	HTML Version	Author
lang=				3	W3C
md=				3	W3C
noflow				3	W3C
src=				3	W3C
units=				3	W3C
width=				3	W3C
\<FN\>			*	3	W3C
...\</FN\>					
class=			*	3	W3C
dir=				4	W3C
id=			*	3	W3C
lang=			*	3	W3C
\<FONT\>	*3/4	*	*	3+	W3C
...\</FONT\>					
color=	*	*	*	3+	W3C
face=	*			4	W3C
id=					
size=	*	*	*	3+	W3C
style=					W3C
title=					W3C
{event}=					W3C
\<FORM\>	*	*	*	2/4	W3C
...\</FORM\>					
acceptcharset=				4	W3C
action=	*	*	*	2/4	W3C
class=				4	W3C
dir=				4	W3C
enctype=	*	*	*	2/4	W3C
id=	4			4	W3C
lang=				4	W3C
method=	*	*	*	2/4	W3C
get | post	*	*	*	2/4	W3C
name=	4				
script=				3	W3C
style=	4			4	W3C
target=	4				W3C
title=	4			4	W3C
{event}=	4			4	W3C
\<FRAME\>	*	*	*	4	W3C
...\</FRAME\>					
bordercolor=	*	*3/4			
class=				4	W3C
dir=				4	W3C
frameborder=	*3/4	4		4	W3C
framespacing	*3/4	*			
height=	4				W3C
id=	4			4	W3C
marginheight=	*3/4	*		4	W3C
marginwidth=	*3/4	*		4	W3C
method=				4	W3C
name=	*3/4	*2/4	*	4	W3C
noresize=	*3/4	*		4	W3C
scrolling=	*3/4	*2/4		[nc]	MS

Tag / Attribute	MSIE	NSNC	Lynx	HTML Version	Author
src=	*3/4	*2/4	*	4	W3C
style					W3C
target=	*	*	*	4	W3C
title=	4			4	W3C
width=	4				W3C
{event}=	4			4	W3C
<FRAMESET> ...</FRAMESET>	*3/4	*2/4	*	4	W3C
border=	4				
bordercolor=	4				
cols=	4	*		4	W3C
frameborder=	4				
framespacing=	4				
id=	4				W3C
rows=	4	*		4	W3C
title=	4				W3C
{event}=	4			4	W3C
<HEAD> ...</HEAD>	*	*	*	2/4	W3C
id=	4				W3C
dir=				4	W3C
lang=				4	W3C
profile=				4	W3C
style=	4				W3C
title=	4			4	W3C
<H1> ...</H1>	*	*	*	2/4	W3C
align=	*	*	*	3	W3C
justify				3	W3C
class=				3/4	W3C
clear=	*	*		3	W3C
color=	*			[nc]	
dingbat=			*	3	W3C
dir=				4	W3C
id=			*	3/4	W3C
lang=			*	3/4	W3C
md=			*	3	W3C
nowrap			*	3	W3C
seqnum=				3	W3C
skip=				3	W3C
style=				4	W3C
title=				4	W3C
<H2>, <H3>, <H4>, <H5>, <H6> Same as **<H1>**					
<HR>	*	*	*	2	W3C
align=	*	*	*	3	W3C
class=				4	W3C
clear=				3	W3C
color=	4			[nc]	MS
id=	4			3/4	W3C
md=				3	W3C
noshade=	*	*	*	3+/4	W3C
nowrap				3	W3C

Tag / Attribute	MSIE	NSNC	Lynx	HTML Version	Author
size=	4	*	*	3+	W3C
src=	4			3	W3C
style=	4			4	W3C
title=	4			4	W3C
width=	*	*	*	3+	W3C
{event}=	4			4	W3C
<HTML>	*	*	*	2/4	W3C
...</HTML>					
dir=				4	W3C
lang=				4	W3C
profile=					
TITLE=	4				
version=				4	W3C
<I>	*	*	*	2/4	W3C
...</I>					
class=			*	3/4	W3C
dir=				4	W3C
ID=	*3/4		*	3/4	W3C
lang=			*	3/4	W3C
style=	4			4	W3C
title=	4			4	W3C
{event}=	4			4	W3C
<IFRAME>	*3/4	*		4	W3C
...</IFRAME>					
align=	*3/4			4	W3C
border=	4	*			
bordercolor=	4				
frameborder=	*	4		4	W3C
framespacing=	4				
height=	4				W3C
hspace=	4				W3C
id=	4				W3C
marginheight=	4			4	W3C
marginwidth=	4				W3C
name=	4	*		4	W3C
noresize=	*	4		4	W3C
scrolling=	4			4	W3C
src=	4			4	W3C
style=	4				
title=	4				
vspace=	4				
width=	4			4	W3C
{event}=	4			4	W3C
<ILAYER>		4		[nc]	NS
...</ILAYER>					
<IMG>	*	*	*	2	W3C
align=	*	*	*	2	W3C
alt=	*	*	*	2/4	W3C
border=	*	*		3+/4	W3C
class=				3/4	W3C
controls=	*			[nc]	
dir=				4	W3C
datafld=	4			[nc]	

Tag / Attribute	MSIE	NSNC	Lynx	HTML Version	Author
datasrc=	4			[nc]	
dynsrc=	4			[nc]	
height=	*	*		2/4	W3C
hspace=	*3/4	*		3+/4	W3C
id=	*3/4			3/4	W3C
ismap=	*	*	*	2/4	W3C
lang=				3/4	W3C
loop=	4			[nc]	
lowsrc=	4	*		[nc]	
md=				3	W3C
name=	4				
src=	*	*	*	2/4	W3C
style=	4			4	W3C
title=	4			4	W3C
units=				3	W3C
usemap=	*	*	*	3+/4	W3C
vrml=	4				
vspace=	*	*		3+/4	W3C
width=	*	*		2	W3C
{event}=	4			4	W3C
<INPUT>	*	*	*	2/4	W3C
...</INPUT>					
accesskey=	4			[nc]	MS
accept=				4	W3C
align=	*	*		3/4	W3C
alt=				4	W3C
checked	*	*	*	3/4	W3C
class=				3/4	W3C
datafld=	4			[nc]	
datasrc=	4			[nc]	
dir=				4	W3C
disabled	4			3/4	W3C
error				3	W3C
id=	4			3/4	W3C
lang=				3/4	W3C
language=	4				
max=	*	*		3	W3C
maxlength=	*	*	*	2/4	W3C
md=				3	W3C
min=	*	*		3	W3C
name=	*	*	*	2/4	W3C
readonly=	4			4	W3C
size=	*	*	*	2/4	W3C
src=				2/4	W3C
style=	4			4	W3C
tabindex=	4	4*		4	W3C
title=	4			4	W3C
type=	*	*	*	2/4	W3C
usemap=				4	W3C
value=	*	*	*	2	W3C
{event}=	4			4	
<INS>			*	3/4	W3C
...</INS>					
cite=				4	W3C

Tag / Attribute	MSIE	NSNC	Lynx	HTML Version	Author
class=			*	3/4	W3C
datetime=				4	W3C
dir=					W3C
id=				3	W3C
lang=				3	W3C
style=					W3C
title=					W3C
{event}=					W3C
<ISINDEX>	*	*	*	2/4	W3C
Note: Use <FORM> instead, if possible.					
action=					
class=				4	W3C
dir=				4	W3C
id=				4	W3C
lang=				4	W3C
prompt=	*	*		4	W3C
style=				4	W3C
title=				4	W3C
<KBD>	*	*	*	2/4	W3C
...</KBD>					
class=			*	3/4	W3C
dir=				4	W3C
id=	*3/4		*	3/4	W3C
lang=			*	3/4	W3C
style=	4			4	W3C
title=	4			4	W3C
{event}=	4			4	W3C
<KEYGEN>		*		[nc]	NS
...</KEYGEN>					
<LABEL>	*3/4			4	W3C
...</LABEL>					
accesskey=	4			4	W3C
class=				4	W3C
dir=				4	W3C
disabled				4	W3C
for=	4			4	W3C
id=	4			4	W3C
lang=				4	W3C
style=	4			4	W3C
title=	4			4	W3C
{event}=	4			4	W3C
<LAYER>		4		[nc]	NS
...</LAYER>					
<LEGEND>	4			4	W3C
...</LEGEND>					
accesskey=	4			4	W3C
align=				4	W3C
class=				4	W3C
dir=				4	W3C
id=	4			4	W3C
lang=				4	W3C
style=	4			4	W3C
title=	4			4	W3C
{event}=	4			4	W3C

Tag / Attribute	MSIE	NSNC	Lynx	HTML Version	Author
\<LI\>	*	*	*	2	W3C
...\</LI\>					
align=	4				
class=				4	W3C
dir=				4	W3C
id=	4			4	W3C
lang=				4	W3C
style=	4			4	W3C
title=	4			4	W3C
type=	*	*	*	3+/4	W3C
value=	4			3+/4	W3C
{event}=	4			4	W3C
\<LINK\>	*	*	*	2/4	W3C
...\</LINK\>	[nc]				
class=				4	W3C
dir=				4	W3C
href=	*	*	*	2/4	W3C
hreflang=				4	W3C
id=				4	W3C
lang=				4	W3C
media=				4	W3C
methods=	*	*	*	2	W3C
name=	*			2	W3C
rel=	*	*	*	2/4	W3C
rev=	*	*	*	2/4	W3C
style=				4	W3C
target=	*			4	W3C
title=	*	*	*	2/4	W3C
type=	*			4	W3C
urn=	*	*	*	2	W3C
\<LISTING\>	*	*	*	2	W3C
...\</LISTING\>					
align=	4				
class=		*		3	W3C
id=	*3/4		*	3	W3C
lang=				3	W3C
style=	4				W3C
title=	4				W3C
{event}=	4				W3C
\<MAP\>	*3/4	*	*	3+/4	W3C
...\</MAP\>					
class=				4	W3C
id=	4			4	W3C
name=	*	*	*	3+/4	W3C
style=	4			4	W3C
title=	4			4	W3C
{event}=	4			4	W3C
\<MARQUEE\>	*		*	[nc]	MS*
...\</MARQUEE\>					
align=	*				
behavior=	*				
bgcolor=	*				
datafld=	4				

Tag / Attribute	MSIE	NSNC	Lynx	HTML Version	Author
dataformats=	4				
datasrc=	4				
direction=	*				
height=	*				
hspace=	*				
id=	4				
loop=	*				
scrollamount=	4				
scrolldelay=	4				
style=	4				
title=	4				
vspace=	*				
width=	*				
{event}=	4				
$** ...**$				3	W3C
<MENU> ...**</MENU>**	*	*	*	2/4	W3C
compact	*	*	*	2/4	W3C
dir=				4	W3C
id=	4			4	W3C
lang=				4	W3C
style=	4			4	W3C
title=	4			4	W3C
{event}=	4			4	W3C
<META> ...**</META>**	* [nc]	*	*	2/4	W3C
content=	*	*	*	2/4	W3C
dir=				4	W3C
httpequiv=	*	*	*	2/4	W3C
lang=				4	W3C
name=	*	*	*	2/4	W3C
scheme=				4	W3C
title=	4				W3C
url=	4				
<NEXTID>	*	*	*	2	W3C
n=	*	*	*	2	W3C
<NOBR> ...**</NOBR>**	*	*			NS
id=	4			4	W3C
style=	4			4	W3C
title=	4			4	W3C
<NOEMBED>		*		[nc]	NS
<NOFRAMES> ...**</NOFRAMES>**	*3/4	*2/4	*	4	W3C
id=	4	*		4	MS
style=	4			4	MS
title=	4			4	MS
<NOLAYER> ...**</NOLAYER>**		4		[nc]	NS
<NOSCRIPT> ...**</NOSCRIPT>**	*3/4	*3/4	*		W3C
title=	4			4	W3C

Tag / Attribute	MSIE	NSNC	Lynx	HTML Version	Author
<NOTE>			*	3	W3C
...</NOTE>					
class=			*	3	W3C
clear=			*	3	W3C
id=			*	3	W3C
lang=			*	3	W3C
md=				3	W3C
src=			*	3	W3C
<OBJECT>	*3/4		*	4	W3C
...</OBJECT>					
accesskey=	4			4	MS
align=	*3/4			4	W3C
border=	*3/4			4	W3C
class=	*3/4			4	W3C
classid=	4			4	W3C
code=	4				
codebase=	4			4	W3C
codetype=	4			4	W3C
data=	*3/4			4	W3C
datafld=	4				
datasrc=	4				
declare=				4	W3C
dir=				4	W3C
disabled	4				
height=	*3/4			4	W3C
hspace=				4	W3C
id=	4			4	W3C
lang=				4	W3C
name=	*3/4			4	W3C
shapes=				4	W3C
standby=				4	W3C
style=	4			4	W3C
tabindex=	4			4	W3C
title=	4			4	W3C
type=	*3/4			4	W3C
usemap=				4	W3C
vspace=				4	W3C
width=	*3/4			4	W3C
{event}=	4			4	W3C
<OL>	*	*	*	2/4	W3C
...</OL>					
align=	4				
class=			*	3/4	W3C
clear=			*	3	W3C
compact			*	2	W3C
continue			*	3	W3C
dir=				4	W3C
id=	4		*	3/4	W3C
lang=			*	3/4	W3C
seqnum=	*	*	*	3	W3C
start=	*3/4	*	*	3+/4	W3C
style=	4			4	W3C
title=	4			4	W3C
type=	*	*	*	2/4	W3C
{event}=	4			4	W3C

Tag / Attribute	MSIE	NSNC	Lynx	HTML Version	Author
<OPTION>	*	*	*	2/4	W3C
...</OPTION>					W3C
class=				4	W3C
dir=				4	W3C
disabled				4	W3C
id=	4			4	W3C
lang=				4	W3C
name=	*	*	*	2/4	W3C
selected=	*	*	*	2/4	W3C
style=				4	W3C
title=	4			4	W3C
value=	*	*	*	2/4	W3C
<OVERLAY>			*	3	W3C
<P>	*	*	*	2/4	W3C
...</P>					
align=	*	*	*	3+	W3C
justify				3	W3C
class=				3/4	W3C
clear=		*		3	W3C
dir=				4	W3C
id=	4			3/4	W3C
lang=				3/4	W3C
style=	4			4	W3C
title=	4			4	W3C
width=	4			2	W3C
{event}=	4			4	W3C
<PARAM>	*3/4	*		3+	W3C
...</PARAM>					
data=	4				
datafld=	4				
datasrc=	4				
name=	4	*		3+/4	W3C
object=	4				
ref=	4				
title=	4				
type=				4	W3C
value=	4	*		3+/4	W3C
valuetype=				4	W3C
<PERSON>			*	3	W3C
...<PERSON>					
class=			*	3	W3C
id=			*	3	W3C
lang=			*	3	W3C
<PLAINTEXT>	*	*	*	2	W3C
id=	4				W3C
style=	4				W3C
title=	4				W3C
{event}=	4				W3C
<PRE>	*	*	*	2/4	W3C
...</PRE>					
class=				3/4	W3C
clear=				3	W3C
dir=					W3C

Tag / Attribute	MSIE	NSNC	Lynx	HTML Version	Author
id=	*3/4			3/4	W3C
lang=				3/4	W3C
style=	4			4	W3C
title=	4			4	W3C
width=	4			2/4	W3C
{event}=	4			4	W3C
<Q>	4		*	3/4	W3C
...</Q>					
cite=				4	W3C
class=			*	3/4	W3C
dir=				4	W3C
id=	*3/4		*	3/4	W3C
lang=			*	3/4	W3C
style=	4			4	W3C
title=	4			4	W3C
{event}=	4			4	W3C
<RANGE>				3	W3C
class=				3	W3C
from=				3	W3C
id=				3	W3C
until=				3	W3C
<S>	*	*	*	2	W3C
...</S>					
class=		*3/4	*	3/4	W3C
dir=				4	W3C
id=	*3/4	*3/4	*	3/4	W3C
lang=		*3/4	*	3/4	W3C
style=	4			4	W3C
title=	4			4	W3C
{event}=	4			4	W3C
<SAMP>	*	*	*	2/4	W3C
...<SAMP>					
class=			*	3/4	W3C
dir=				4	W3C
id=	*3/4		*	3/4	W3C
lang=			*	3/4	W3C
style=	4			4	W3C
title=	4			4	W3C
{event}=	4			4	W3C
<SCRIPT>	*	*		3+/4	W3C
...</SCRIPT>					
{event}=	4				
for=	4				
id=	4				
in=	4				
language=	*	*		4	W3C
library=	4				
src=	*	*		4	W3C
title=	4			4	W3C
type=				4	W3C
<SELECT>	*	*	*	2/4	W3C
...</SELECT>					
accesskey=	4			[nc]	MS

Tag / Attribute	MSIE	NSNC	Lynx	HTML Version	Author
align=	4			3	W3C
class=		*3/4		3/4	W3C
datafld=	*			[nc]	
datasrc=				[nc]	
dir=				4	W3C
disabled	4			3/4	W3C
height=				3	W3C
id=	4	*3/4		4	W3C
lang=		*3/4		3/4	W3C
language=	4				
md=				3	W3C
multiple	*	*		2/4	W3C
name=	*	*		2/4	W3C
readonly=	4				
size=	*	*		2/4	W3C
style=	4	4		4	W3C
tabindex=	4	4*		4	W3C
title=	4			4	W3C
units=				3	W3C
width=				3	W3C
{event}=	4			4	W3C
<SERVER>		*		[nc]	NS
<SMALL> ...</SMALL>	*	*	*	3/4	W3C
class=		3	*	3/4	W3C
dir=				4	W3C
id=	*3/4	3	*	3/4	W3C
lang=		3	*	3/4	W3C
style=	4	4		4	W3C
title=	4			4	W3C
{event}=	4			4	W3C
<SPACER>		*3/4		[nc]	NS
<SPAN> ...</SPAN>	*3/4	4		4	W3C
align=				4	W3C
class=				4	W3C
datafld=	4			[nc]	
dataformats=	4			[nc]	
datasrc=	4			[nc]	
dir=				4	W3C
id=	4	3		4	W3C
style=	4	4		4	W3C
title=	4			4	W3C
{event}=	4			4	W3C
<SPOT>				3	W3C
id=				3	W3C
<STRIKE> ...</STRIKE>	*	*	*	3+/4	W3C
class=		*3/4	*	4	W3C
dir=				4	W3C
id=	4	*3/4	*	4	W3C
lang=		*3/4	*	4	W3C
style=	4	4		4	W3C

Tag / Attribute	MSIE	NSNC	Lynx	HTML Version	Author
title=	4			4	W3C
{event}=	4			4	W3C
<STRONG>	*	*	*	2/4	W3C
...</STRONG>					
class=		3	*	3/4	W3C
dir=				4	W3C
id=	*3/4	3	*	3/4	W3C
lang=		3	*	3/4	W3C
style=	4	4		4	W3C
title=	4			4	W3C
{event}=	4			4	W3C
<STYLE>	*3/4	4	*	3+/4	W3C
...</STYLE>					
dir=				4	W3C
lang=				4	W3C
media=				4	W3C
title=	4			4	W3C
type=	4		*	4	W3C
<SUB>	*	*	*	3/4	W3C
...</SUB>					
class=		3	*	3/4	W3C
dir=				4	W3C
id=	3/4	3	*	3/4	W3C
lang=		3	*	3/4	W3C
style=	4	4		4	W3C
title=	4			4	W3C
{event}=	4			4	W3C
<SUP>	*	*	*	3/4	W3C
...</SUP>					
class=		3	*	3/4	W3C
dir=				4	W3C
id=	3/4	3	*	3/4	W3C
lang=		3	*	3/4	W3C
style=	4	4		4	W3C
title=	4			4	W3C
{event}=	4			4	W3C
<TAB>			*	3	W3C
align=			*	3	W3C
dp=			*	3	W3C
id=			*	3	W3C
indent=			*	3	W3C
<TABLE>	*	*	*	3+/4	W3C
...</TABLE>					
align=	[ck}	*	*	3+/4	W3C
class=		3		3/4	W3C
background=	*3/4	4*			
bgcolor=	*3/4	4		4	W3C
border=	*	*	*	3+/4	W3C
bordercolor=	*3/4			[nc]	MS
bordercolordark=	*3/4		[nc]	MS	
bordercolorlight=	*3/4			[nc]	MS
cellpadding=	4	*		3+/4	W3C
cellspacing=	4	*		3+/4	W3C

Tag / Attribute	MSIE	NSNC	Lynx	HTML Version	Author
class=		*3/4		3/4	W3C
clear=				3	W3C
cols=	4			4	W3C
colspec=				3	W3C
datasrc=	4			[nc]	
dir=				4	W3C
dp=				3	W3C
frame=	4			4	W3C
height=	4				
id=	4	*3/4		3/4	W3C
lang=		*3/4		3/4	W3C
noflow				3	W3C
nowrap	*	*		3	W3C
rules=	4			4	W3C
style=	4	4		4	W3C
title=	4			4	W3C
units=				3	W3C
width=	4			3+/4	W3C
{event}=	4			4	W3C
<TBODY> ...</TBODY>	*3/4	4		4	W3C
align=	4			4	W3C
bgcolor=	4				
char=					
charoff=					
class=				4	W3C
dir=				4	W3C
id=	4			4	W3C
lang=				4	W3C
style=	4			4	W3C
title=	4			4	W3C
valign=	4			4	W3C
{event}=	4			4	W3C
<TD> ...</TD>	*	*	*	3+/4	W3C
abbr=				4	W3C
align=	*3/4*	*		3+/4	W3C
decimal				3	W3C
justify				3	W3C
axis=				3/4	W3C
axes=				3	W3C
background=	4				
bgcolor=	4	4		4	W3C
bordercolor=	4				
bordercolordark=	4				MS
bordercolorlight=	4				MS
char=				4	W3C
charoff=				4	W3C
class=				4	W3C
colspan=	*	*		3+/4	W3C
dir=				4	W3C
dp=				3	W3C
height=	4			3+	W3C
id=	4	3		3/4	W3C

Tag / Attribute	MSIE	NSNC	Lynx	HTML Version	Author
lang=		3		3/4	W3C
nowrap	*	*		3+	W3C
rowspan=	4	*		3+	W3C
style=	4	4		4	W3C
title=	4			4	W3C
valign=	*	*		3+/4	W3C
width=	4			3+	W3C
{event}=	4			4	W3C
<TEXTAREA>	*	*	*	2/4	W3C
...</TEXTAREA>					
accesskey=	4			[nc]	MS
align=	4			3	W3C
class=		*3/4		3/4	W3C
cols=	*	*	*	2	W3C
datafld=	*			[nc]	MS
datasrc=	*			[nc]	MS
dir=				4	W3C
disabled	4			3/4	W3C
error=				3	W3C
id=	4	3	*	3/4	W3C
lang=		*3/4	*	3/4	W3C
name=	*	*	*	2/4	W3C
readonly=	4			4	W3C
rows=	*	*	*	2/4	W3C
style=	4	4		4	W3C
tabindex=	4	4*		4	W3C
title=	4			4	W3C
wrap=		*		[nc]	NS
{event}=	4			4	W3C
<TFOOT>	*3/4	4		4	W3C
...</TFOOT>					
align=	4			4	W3C
bgcolor=	4			[nc]	MS
char=				4	W3C
charoff=				4	W3C
dir=				4	W3C
id=	4			4	W3C
lang=				4	W3C
style=	4			4	W3C
title=	4			4	W3C
valign=	4			4	W3C
{event}=	4			4	W3C
<TH>	*	*	*	3+/4	W3C
...</TH>					
abbr=				4	W3C
align=	*	*	*	3+/4	W3C
decimal				3	W3C
justify				3	W3C
axes=				3	W3C
axis=				3/4	W3C
background=	*	*		[nc]	
bgcolor=	*	*		4	W3C
bordercolor=	4			[nc]	MS
bordercolordark=	4			[nc]	MS

Tag / Attribute	MSIE	NSNC	Lynx	HTML Version	Author
bordercolorlight=	4			[nc]	MS
char=				4	W3C
charoff=				4	W3C
class=				4	W3C
colspan=	*	*		3+/4	W3C
dir=				4	W3C
dp=				3	W3C
height=	*	*		3+	W3C
id=	4	3		3	W3C
lang=		3		3	W3C
nowrap	*	*		3+	W3C
rowspan=	*	*		3+	W3C
style=	4	4		4	W3C
title=	4			4	W3C
valign=	*	*		3+	W3C
width=	*	*		3+	W3C
{event}=	4			4	W3C
<THEAD> ...</THEAD>	*3/4	4		4	W3C
align=	4			4	W3C
bgcolor=	4			[nc]	MS
char=				4	W3C
charoff=				4	W3C
class=				4	W3C
dir=				4	W3C
id=	4			4	W3C
lang=				4	W3C
style=	4			4	W3C
title=	4			4	W3C
valign=	4			4	W3C
{event}=	4			4	W3C
<TITLE> ...</TITLE>	*	*	*	2/4	W3C
dir=				4	W3C
lang=				4	W3C
<TR> ...</TR>	*	*	*	3+/4	W3C
align=	4*			3+/4	W3C
justify				3	W3C
bgcolor=	4	4		4	W3C
bordercolor=	4			[nc]	MS
bordercolordark=	4			[nc]	MS
bordercolorlight=	4			[nc]	MS
char=				4	W3C
charoff=				4	W3C
class=		*		3/4	W3C
dir=				4	W3C
dp=				3	W3C
height=	4			3+	W3C
id=	4	*		3/4	W3C
lang=		*		3/4	W3C
nowrap		*		3	W3C
style=	4	4		4	W3C
title=	4			4	W3C

Tag / Attribute	MSIE	NSNC	Lynx	HTML Version	Author
valign=	*	*	*	3/4	W3C
vspace=	*	*		[nc]	NS
{event}=	4			4	W3C
<TT>	*	*	*	2/4	W3C
...</TT>					
class=		*	*	3/4	W3C
dir=				4	W3C
id=	3/4	*	*	3/4	W3C
lang=		*	*	3/4	W3C
style=	4	4		4	W3C
title=	4			4	W3C
{event}=	4			4	W3C
<U>	*	*	*	3/4	W3C
...</U>					
class=		*	*	3/4	W3C
dir=				4	W3C
id=	*	*	*	3/4	W3C
lang=		*	*	3/4	W3C
style=	4	4		4	W3C
title=	4			4	W3C
{event}=	4			4	W3C
<UL>	*	*	*	2/4	W3C
...</UL>					
align=	4		*		
class=		3	*	3/4	W3C
clear=				3	W3C
compact	*	*	*	2/4	W3C
dingbat=			*	3	W3C
dir=				4	W3C
id=	4	3		3/4	W3C
lang=		3		3/4	W3C
md=				3	W3C
plain				3	W3C
src=	4			3	W3C
style=	4	4		4	W3C
title=	4			4	W3C
type=	4	*	*	3+/4	W3C
wrap=				3	W3C
{event}=	4			4	W3C
<VAR>	*	*	*	3+/4	W3C
...</VAR>					
class=		*	*	3/4	W3C
dir=				4	W3C
id=	*	*	*	3/4	W3C
lang=		*	*	3/4	W3C
style=	*	*		4	W3C
title=	4			4	W3C
{event}=	4			4	W3C
<WBR>	*	*		[nc]	NS
id=	4	3			
style=	4	4			
title=	4				

Tag / Attribute	MSIE	NSNC	Lynx	HTML Version	Author
`<XMP>` ...`</XMP>`	*	*	*	2	W3C
id=	4	3		3	W3C
style=	4	4		3	W3C
title=	4			3	W3C
{event}=	4			4	W3C

For the latest official information on HTML 4.0, consult the World Wide Web Consortium at `http://www.w3.org/`.

For current browser capabilities, visit these Web sites:

- **Lynx:** `http://www.crl.com/~subir/lynx.html`
- **Microsoft Internet Explorer:** `http://www.microsoft.com/ie/`
- **Netscape Navigator:** `http://www.netscape.com/`

HTML 4.0 Escaped Entities

Character Entity	Alternate Character Entity	Character
&quot;	&#34;	" (double quote mark)
&amp;	&#38;	& (ampersand)
&gt;	&#62;	> (greater than)
&lt;	&#60;	< (less than)

HTML 4.0 Named Colors

```
Black    = #000000    K = (Black)
Navy     = #000080
Blue     = #0000FF    B = (Blue)
Green    = #008000
Teal     = #008080
Lime     = #00FF00    G = (Green)
Aqua     = #00FFFF    C = (Cyan)
Maroon   = #800000
Purple   = #800080
Olive    = #808000
Gray     = #808080
Silver   = #C0C0C0
Red      = #FF0000
Fuchsia  = #FF00FF    M = (Magenta)
Yellow   = #FFFF00    Y = (Yellow)
White    = #FFFFFF
```

HTML 4.0 Character Entities

Portions copyright International Organization for Standardization 1986

Permission to copy in any form is granted for use with conforming SGML systems and applications as defined in ISO 8879, provided this notice is included in all copies.

Name	Value	Description
Æ	Æ	capital AE diphthong (ligature)
Á	Á	capital A, acute accent
Â	Â	capital A, circumflex accent
À	À	capital A, grave accent
Α	Α	Greek capital letter alpha, Unicode: 0391
Å	Å	capital A, ring
Ã	Ã	capital A, tilde
Ä	Ä	capital A, dieresis or umlaut mark
Β	Β	Greek capital letter beta, Unicode: 0392
Ç	Ç	capital C, cedilla
Χ	Χ	Greek capital letter chi, Unicode: 03A7
‡	‡	double dagger, Unicode: 2021
Δ	Δ	Greek capital letter delta, Unicode: 0394
Ð	Ð	capital Eth, Icelandic
É	É	capital E, acute accent
Ê	Ê	capital E, circumflex accent
È	È	capital E, grave accent
Ε	Ε	Greek capital letter epsilon, Unicode: 0395
Η	Η	Greek capital letter eta, Unicode: 0397
Ë	Ë	capital E, dieresis or umlaut mark
Γ	Γ	Greek capital letter gamma, Unicode: 0393
Í	Í	capital I, acute accent
Î	Î	capital I, circumflex accent
Ì	Ì	capital I, grave accent
Ι	Ι	Greek capital letter iota, Unicode: 0399
Ï	Ï	capital I, dieresis or umlaut mark
Κ	Κ	Greek capital letter kappa, Unicode: 039A
Λ	Λ	Greek capital letter lambda, Unicode: 039B
Μ	Μ	Greek capital letter mu, Unicode: 039C
Ñ	Ñ	capital N, tilde
Ν	Ν	Greek capital letter nu, Unicode: 039D
Œ	Œ	Latin capital ligature oe, Unicode: 0152
Ó	Ó	capital O, acute accent
Ô	Ô	capital O, circumflex accent

Name	Value	Description
&Ograve;	&#210;	capital O, grave accent
&Omega;	&#937;	Greek capital letter omega, Unicode: 03A9
&Omicron;	&#927;	Greek capital letter omicron, Unicode: 039F
&Oslash;	&#216;	capital O, slash
&Otilde;	&#213;	capital O, tilde
&Ouml;	&#214;	capital O, dieresis or umlaut mark
&Phi;	&#934;	Greek capital letter phi, Unicode: 03A6
&Pi;	&#928;	Greek capital letter pi, Unicode: 03A0
&Prime;	&#8243;	double prime, seconds, inches, Unicode: 2033
&Psi;	&#936;	Greek capital letter psi, Unicode: 03A8
&Rho;	&#929;	Greek capital letter rho, Unicode: 03A1
&Scaron;	&#352;	Latin capital letter s with caron, Unicode: 0160
&Sigma;	&#931;	Greek capital letter sigma, Unicode: 03A3
&THORN;	&#222;	capital THORN, Icelandic
&Tau;	&#932;	Greek capital letter tau, Unicode: 03A4
&Theta;	&#920;	Greek capital letter theta, Unicode: 0398
&Uacute;	&#218;	capital U, acute accent
&Ucirc;	&#219;	capital U, circumflex accent
&Ugrave;	&#217;	capital U, grave accent
&Upsilon;	&#933;	Greek capital letter upsilon, Unicode: 03A5
&Uuml;	&#220;	capital U, dieresis or umlaut mark
&Xi;	&#926;	Greek capital letter xi, Unicode: 039E
&Yacute;	&#221;	capital Y, acute accent
&Yuml;	&#376;	Latin capital letter y with diaeresis, Unicode: 0178
&Zeta;	&#918;	Greek capital letter zeta, Unicode: 0396
&aacute;	&#225;	small a, acute accent
&acirc;	&#226;	small a, circumflex accent
&acute;	&#180;	acute accent
&aelig;	&#230;	small ae diphthong (ligature)
&agrave;	&#224;	small a, grave accent
&alefsym;	&#8501;	alef symbol, first transfinite cardinal, Unicode: 2135
&alpha;	&#945;	Greek small letter alpha, Unicode: 03B1
&amp;	&#38;	ampersand, Unicode: 0026
&and;	&#8869;	logical and, wedge, Unicode: 2227
&ang;	&#8736;	angle, Unicode: 2220
&aring;	&#229;	small a, ring
&asymp;	&#8776;	almost equal to, asymptotic to, Unicode: 2248
&atilde;	&#227;	small a, tilde
&auml;	&#228;	small a, dieresis or umlaut mark
&bdquo;	&#8222;	double low9 quotation mark, Unicode: 201E
&beta;	&#946;	Greek small letter beta, Unicode: 03B2
&brvbar;	&#166;	broken (vertical) bar

Name	Value	Description
•	•	bullet, black small circle, Unicode: 2022
∩	∩	intersection, cap, Unicode: 2229
ç	ç	small c, cedilla
¸	¸	cedilla
¢	¢	cent sign
χ	χ	Greek small letter chi, Unicode: 03C7
ˆ	ˆ	modifier letter circumflex accent, Unicode: 02C6
♣	♣	black club suit, shamrock, Unicode: 2663
≅	≅	approximately equal to, Unicode: 2245
©	©	copyright sign
↵	↵	downwards arrow with corner leftwards, carriage return, Unicode: 21B5
∪	∪	union, cup, Unicode: 222A
¤	¤	general currency sign
⇓	⇓	downwards double arrow, Unicode: 21D3
†	†	dagger, Unicode: 2020
↓	↓	downwards arrow, Unicode: 2193
°	°	degree sign
δ	δ	Greek small letter delta, Unicode: 03B4
♦	♦	black diamond suit, Unicode: 2666
÷	÷	divide sign
é	é	small e, acute accent
ê	ê	small e, circumflex accent
è	è	small e, grave accent
∅	∅	empty set, null set, diameter, Unicode: 2205
		em space, Unicode: 2003
		en space, Unicode: 2002
ε	ε	Greek small letter epsilon, Unicode: 03B5
≡	≡	identical to, Unicode: 2261
η	η	Greek small letter eta, Unicode: 03B7
ð	ð	small eth, Icelandic
ë	ë	small e, dieresis or umlaut mark
∃	∃	there exists, Unicode: 2203
ƒ	ƒ	Latin small f with hook, function, florin, Unicode: 0192
∀	∀	for all, Unicode: 2200
½	½	fraction onehalf
¼	¼	fraction onequarter
¾	¾	fraction threequarters
⁄	⁄	fraction slash, Unicode: 2044
γ	γ	Greek small letter gamma, Unicode: 03B3
≥	≥	greaterthan or equal to, Unicode: 2265
>	>	greaterthan sign, Unicode: 003E
⇔	⇔	left right double arrow, Unicode: 21D4

Name	Value	Description
&harr;	&#8596;	left right arrow, Unicode: 2194
&hearts;	&#9829;	black heart suit, valentine, Unicode: 2665
&hellip;	&#8230;	horizontal ellipsis, three dot leader, Unicode: 2026
&iacute;	&#237;	small i, acute accent
&icirc;	&#238;	small i, circumflex accent
&iexcl;	&#161;	inverted exclamation mark
&igrave;	&#236;	small i, grave accent
&image;	&#8465;	blackletter capital I, imaginary part, Unicode: 2111
&infin;	&#8734;	infinity, Unicode: 221E
&int;	&#8747;	integral, Unicode: 222B
&iota;	&#953;	Greek small letter iota, Unicode: 03B9
&iquest;	&#191;	inverted question mark
&isin;	&#8712;	element of, Unicode: 2208
&iuml;	&#239;	small i, dieresis or umlaut mark
&kappa;	&#954;	Greek small letter kappa, Unicode: 03BA
&lArr;	&#8656;	leftwards double arrow, Unicode: 21D0
&lambda;	&#955;	Greek small letter lambda, Unicode: 03BB
&lang;	&#9001;	leftpointing angle bracket, bra, Unicode: 2329
&laquo;	&#171;	angle quotation mark, left
&larr;	&#8592;	leftwards arrow, Unicode: 2190
&lceil;	&#8968;	left ceiling, apl upstile, Unicode: 2308,
&ldquo;	&#8220;	left double quotation mark, Unicode: 201C
&le;	&#8804;	lessthan or equal to, Unicode: 2264
&lfloor;	&#8970;	left floor, apl downstile, Unicode: 230A,
&lowast;	&#8727;	asterisk operator, Unicode: 2217
&loz;	&#9674;	lozenge, Unicode: 25CA
&lrm;	&#8206;	lefttoright mark, Unicode: 200E RFC 2070
&lsaquo;	&#8249;	single leftpointing angle quotation mark, Unicode: 2039
&lsquo;	&#8216;	left single quotation mark, Unicode: 2018
&lt;	&#60;	lessthan sign, Unicode: 003C
&macr;	&#175;	macron
&mdash;	&#8212;	em dash, Unicode: 2014
&micro;	&#181;	micro sign
&middot;	&#183;	middle dot
&minus;	&#8722;	minus sign, Unicode: 2212
&mu;	&#956;	Greek small letter mu, Unicode: 03BC
&nabla;	&#8711;	nabla, backward difference, Unicode: 2207
		nobreak space
&ndash;	&#8211;	en dash, Unicode: 2013
&ne;	&#8800;	not equal to, Unicode: 2260
&ni;	&#8715;	contains as member, Unicode: 220B
&not;	&#172;	not sign

Name	Value	Description
&notin;	&#8713;	not an element of, Unicode: 2209
&nsub;	&#8836;	not a subset of, Unicode: 2284
&ntilde;	&#241;	small n, tilde
&nu;	&#957;	Greek small letter nu, Unicode: 03BD
&oacute;	&#243;	small o, acute accent
&ocirc;	&#244;	small o, circumflex accent
&oelig;	&#339;	Latin small ligature oe, Unicode: 0153
&ograve;	&#242;	small o, grave accent
&oline;	&#8254;	overline, spacing overscore, Unicode: 203E
&omega;	&#969;	Greek small letter omega, Unicode: 03C9
&omicron;	&#959;	Greek small letter omicron, Unicode: 03BF
&oplus;	&#8853;	circled plus, direct sum, Unicode: 2295
&or;	&#8870;	logical or, vee, Unicode: 2228
&ordf;	&#170;	ordinal indicator, feminine
&ordm;	&#186;	ordinal indicator, masculine
&oslash;	&#248;	small o, slash
&otilde;	&#245;	small o, tilde
&otimes;	&#8855;	circled times, vector product, Unicode: 2297
&ouml;	&#246;	small o, dieresis or umlaut mark
&para;	&#182;	pilcrow (paragraph sign)
&part;	&#8706;	partial differential, Unicode: 2202
&permil;	&#8240;	per mille sign, Unicode: 2030
&perp;	&#8869;	up tack, orthogonal to, perpendicular, Unicode: 22A5
&phi;	&#966;	Greek small letter phi, Unicode: 03C6
&pi;	&#960;	Greek small letter pi, Unicode: 03C0
&piv;	&#982;	Greek pi symbol, Unicode: 03D6
&plusmn;	&#177;	plusorminus sign
&pound;	&#163;	pound sterling sign
&prime;	&#8242;	prime, minutes, feet, Unicode: 2032
&prod;	&#8719;	nary product, product sign, Unicode: 220F
&prop;	&#8733;	proportional to, Unicode: 221D
&psi;	&#968;	Greek small letter psi, Unicode: 03C8
&quot;	&#34;	quotation mark, apl quote, Unicode: 0022
&rArr;	&#8658;	rightwards double arrow, Unicode: 21D2
&radic;	&#8730;	square root, radical sign, Unicode: 221A
&rang;	&#9002;	rightpointing angle bracket, ket, Unicode: 232A
&raquo;	&#187;	angle quotation mark, right
&rarr;	&#8594;	rightwards arrow, Unicode: 2192
&rceil;	&#8969;	right ceiling, Unicode: 2309,
&rdquo;	&#8221;	right double quotation mark, Unicode: 201D
&real;	&#8476;	blackletter capital R, real part symbol, Unicode: 211C
&reg;	&#174;	registered sign

Name	Value	Description
&rfloor;	&#8971;	right floor, Unicode: 230B,
&rho;	&#961;	Greek small letter rho, Unicode: 03C1
&rlm;	&#8207;	righttoleft mark, Unicode: 200F RFC 2070
&rsaquo;	&#8250;	single rightpointing angle quotation mark, Unicode: 203A
&rsquo;	&#8217;	right single quotation mark, Unicode: 2019
&sbquo;	&#8218;	single low9 quotation mark, Unicode: 201A
&scaron;	&#353;	Latin small letter s with caron, Unicode: 0161
&sdot;	&#8901;	dot operator, Unicode: 22C5
&sect;	&#167;	section sign
&shy;	&#173;	soft hyphen
&sigma;	&#963;	Greek small letter sigma, Unicode: 03C3
&sigmaf;	&#962;	Greek small letter final sigma, Unicode: 03C2
&sim;	&#8764;	tilde operator, varies with, similar to, Unicode: 223C
&spades;	&#9824;	black spade suit, Unicode: 2660
&sub;	&#8834;	subset of, Unicode: 2282
&sube;	&#8838;	subset of or equal to, Unicode: 2286
&sum;	&#8721;	nary summation, Unicode: 2211
&sup;	&#8835;	superset of, Unicode: 2283
&sup1;	&#185;	superscript one
&sup2;	&#178;	superscript two
&sup3;	&#179;	superscript three
&supe;	&#8839;	superset of or equal to, Unicode: 2287
&szlig;	&#223;	small sharp s, German (sz ligature)
&tau;	&#964;	Greek small letter tau, Unicode: 03C4
&there4;	&#8756;	therefore, Unicode: 2234
&theta;	&#952;	Greek small letter theta, Unicode: 03B8
&thetasym;	&#977;	Greek small letter theta symbol, Unicode: 03D1
		thin space, Unicode: 2009
&thorn;	&#254;	small thorn, Icelandic
&tilde;	&#732;	small tilde, Unicode: 02DC
&times;	&#215;	multiply sign
&trade;	&#8482;	trade mark sign, Unicode: 2122
&uArr;	&#8657;	upwards double arrow, Unicode: 21D1
&uacute;	&#250;	small u, acute accent
&uarr;	&#8593;	upwards arrow, Unicode: 2191
&ucirc;	&#251;	small u, circumflex accent
&ugrave;	&#249;	small u, grave accent
&uml;	&#168;	umlaut (dieresis)
&upsih;	&#978;	Greek upsilon with hook symbol, Unicode: 03D2
&upsilon;	&#965;	Greek small letter upsilon, Unicode: 03C5
&uuml;	&#252;	small u, dieresis or umlaut mark
&weierp;	&#8472;	script capital P, power set, Weierstrass p, Unicode: 2118

Name	Value	Description
ξ	ξ	Greek small letter xi, Unicode: 03BE
ý	ý	small y, acute accent
¥	¥	yen sign
ÿ	ÿ	small y, dieresis or umlaut mark
ζ	ζ	Greek small letter zeta, Unicode: 03B6
‍	‍	zero width joiner, Unicode: 200D
‌	‌	zero width nonjoiner, Unicode: 200C

Numeric Order

Name	Value	Description
"	"	quotation mark, apl quote, Unicode: 0022
&	&	ampersand, Unicode: 0026
<	<	less-than sign, Unicode: 003C
>	>	greater-than sign, Unicode: 003E
		no-break space
¡	¡	inverted exclamation mark
¢	¢	cent sign
£	£	pound sterling sign
¤	¤	general currency sign
¥	¥	yen sign
¦	¦	broken (vertical) bar
§	§	section sign
¨	¨	umlaut (dieresis)
©	©	copyright sign
ª	ª	ordinal indicator, feminine
«	«	angle quotation mark, left
¬	¬	not sign
­	­	soft hyphen
®	®	registered sign
¯	¯	macron
°	°	degree sign
±	±	plus-or-minus sign
²	²	superscript two
³	³	superscript three
´	´	acute accent
µ	µ	micro sign
¶	¶	pilcrow (paragraph sign)
·	·	middle dot
¸	¸	cedilla

Name	Value	Description
¹	¹	superscript one
º	º	ordinal indicator, masculine
»	»	angle quotation mark, right
¼	¼	fraction one-quarter
½	½	fraction one-half
¾	¾	fraction three-quarters
¿	¿	inverted question mark
À	À	capital A, grave accent
Á	Á	capital A, acute accent
Â	Â	capital A, circumflex accent
Ã	Ã	capital A, tilde
Ä	Ä	capital A, dieresis or umlaut mark
Å	Å	capital A, ring
Æ	Æ	capital AE diphthong (ligature)
Ç	Ç	capital C, cedilla
È	È	capital E, grave accent
É	É	capital E, acute accent
Ê	Ê	capital E, circumflex accent
Ë	Ë	capital E, dieresis or umlaut mark
Ì	Ì	capital I, grave accent
Í	Í	capital I, acute accent
Î	Î	capital I, circumflex accent
Ï	Ï	capital I, dieresis or umlaut mark
Ð	Ð	capital Eth, Icelandic
Ñ	Ñ	capital N, tilde
Ò	Ò	capital O, grave accent
Ó	Ó	capital O, acute accent
Ô	Ô	capital O, circumflex accent
Õ	Õ	capital O, tilde
Ö	Ö	capital O, dieresis or umlaut mark
×	×	multiply sign
Ø	Ø	capital O, slash
Ù	Ù	capital U, grave accent
Ú	Ú	capital U, acute accent
Û	Û	capital U, circumflex accent
Ü	Ü	capital U, dieresis or umlaut mark
Ý	Ý	capital Y, acute accent
Þ	Þ	capital THORN, Icelandic
ß	ß	small sharp s, German (sz ligature)
à	à	small a, grave accent
á	á	small a, acute accent
â	â	small a, circumflex accent

Name	Value	Description
ã	ã	small a, tilde
ä	ä	small a, dieresis or umlaut mark
å	å	small a, ring
æ	æ	small ae diphthong (ligature)
ç	ç	small c, cedilla
è	è	small e, grave accent
é	é	small e, acute accent
ê	ê	small e, circumflex accent
ë	ë	small e, dieresis or umlaut mark
ì	ì	small i, grave accent
í	í	small i, acute accent
î	î	small i, circumflex accent
ï	ï	small i, dieresis or umlaut mark
ð	ð	small eth, Icelandic
ñ	ñ	small n, tilde
ò	ò	small o, grave accent
ó	ó	small o, acute accent
ô	ô	small o, circumflex accent
õ	õ	small o, tilde
ö	ö	small o, dieresis or umlaut mark
÷	÷	divide sign
ø	ø	small o, slash
ù	ù	small u, grave accent
ú	ú	small u, acute accent
û	û	small u, circumflex accent
ü	ü	small u, dieresis or umlaut mark
ý	ý	small y, acute accent
þ	þ	small thorn, Icelandic
ÿ	ÿ	small y, dieresis or umlaut mark
Œ	Œ	Latin capital ligature oe, Unicode: 0152
œ	œ	Latin small ligature oe, Unicode: 0153
Š	Š	Latin capital letter s with caron, Unicode: 0160
š	š	Latin small letter s with caron, Unicode: 0161
Ÿ	Ÿ	Latin capital letter y with diaeresis, Unicode: 0178
ƒ	ƒ	Latin small f with hook, function, florin, Unicode: 0192
ˆ	ˆ	modifier letter circumflex accent, Unicode: 02C6
˜	˜	small tilde, Unicode: 02DC
Α	Α	Greek capital letter alpha, Unicode: 0391
Β	Β	Greek capital letter beta, Unicode: 0392
Γ	Γ	Greek capital letter gamma, Unicode: 0393
Δ	Δ	Greek capital letter delta, Unicode: 0394
Ε	Ε	Greek capital letter epsilon, Unicode: 0395

Name	Value	Description
Ζ	Ζ	Greek capital letter zeta, Unicode: 0396
Η	Η	Greek capital letter eta, Unicode: 0397
Θ	Θ	Greek capital letter theta, Unicode: 0398
Ι	Ι	Greek capital letter iota, Unicode: 0399
Κ	Κ	Greek capital letter kappa, Unicode: 039A
Λ	Λ	Greek capital letter lambda, Unicode: 039B
Μ	Μ	Greek capital letter mu, Unicode: 039C
Ν	Ν	Greek capital letter nu, Unicode: 039D
Ξ	Ξ	Greek capital letter xi, Unicode: 039E
Ο	Ο	Greek capital letter omicron, Unicode: 039F
Π	Π	Greek capital letter pi, Unicode: 03A0
Ρ	Ρ	Greek capital letter rho, Unicode: 03A1
Σ	Σ	Greek capital letter sigma, Unicode: 03A3
Τ	Τ	Greek capital letter tau, Unicode: 03A4
Υ	Υ	Greek capital letter upsilon, Unicode: 03A5
Φ	Φ	Greek capital letter phi, Unicode: 03A6
Χ	Χ	Greek capital letter chi, Unicode: 03A7
Ψ	Ψ	Greek capital letter psi, Unicode: 03A8
Ω	Ω	Greek capital letter omega, Unicode: 03A9
α	α	Greek small letter alpha, Unicode: 03B1
β	β	Greek small letter beta, Unicode: 03B2
γ	γ	Greek small letter gamma, Unicode: 03B3
δ	δ	Greek small letter delta, Unicode: 03B4
ε	ε	Greek small letter epsilon, Unicode: 03B5
ζ	ζ	Greek small letter zeta, Unicode: 03B6
η	η	Greek small letter eta, Unicode: 03B7
θ	θ	Greek small letter theta, Unicode: 03B8
ι	ι	Greek small letter iota, Unicode: 03B9
κ	κ	Greek small letter kappa, Unicode: 03BA
λ	λ	Greek small letter lambda, Unicode: 03BB
μ	μ	Greek small letter mu, Unicode: 03BC
ν	ν	Greek small letter nu, Unicode: 03BD
ξ	ξ	Greek small letter xi, Unicode: 03BE
ο	ο	Greek small letter omicron, Unicode: 03BF
π	π	Greek small letter pi, Unicode: 03C0
ρ	ρ	Greek small letter rho, Unicode: 03C1
ς	ς	Greek small letter final sigma, Unicode: 03C2
σ	σ	Greek small letter sigma, Unicode: 03C3
τ	τ	Greek small letter tau, Unicode: 03C4
υ	υ	Greek small letter upsilon, Unicode: 03C5
φ	φ	Greek small letter phi, Unicode: 03C6
χ	χ	Greek small letter chi, Unicode: 03C7

Name	Value	Description
&psi;	&#968;	Greek small letter psi, Unicode: 03C8
&omega;	&#969;	Greek small letter omega, Unicode: 03C9
&thetasym;	&#977;	Greek small letter theta symbol, Unicode: 03D1
&upsih;	&#978;	Greek upsilon with hook symbol, Unicode: 03D2
&piv;	&#982;	Greek pi symbol, Unicode: 03D6
		en space, Unicode: 2002
		em space, Unicode: 2003
		thin space, Unicode: 2009
&zwnj;	&#8204;	zero width non-joiner, Unicode: 200C
&zwj;	&#8205;	zero width joiner, Unicode: 200D
&lrm;	&#8206;	left-to-right mark, Unicode: 200E RFC 2070
&rlm;	&#8207;	right-to-left mark, Unicode: 200F RFC 2070
&ndash;	&#8211;	en dash, Unicode: 2013
&mdash;	&#8212;	em dash, Unicode: 2014
&lsquo;	&#8216;	left single quotation mark, Unicode: 2018
&rsquo;	&#8217;	right single quotation mark, Unicode: 2019
&sbquo;	&#8218;	single low-9 quotation mark, Unicode: 201A
&ldquo;	&#8220;	left double quotation mark, Unicode: 201C
&rdquo;	&#8221;	right double quotation mark, Unicode: 201D
&bdquo;	&#8222;	double low-9 quotation mark, Unicode: 201E
&dagger;	&#8224;	dagger, Unicode: 2020
&Dagger;	&#8225;	double dagger, Unicode: 2021
&bull;	&#8226;	bullet, black small circle, Unicode: 2022
&hellip;	&#8230;	horizontal ellipsis, three dot leader, Unicode: 2026
&permil;	&#8240;	per mille sign, Unicode: 2030
&prime;	&#8242;	prime, minutes, feet, Unicode: 2032
&Prime;	&#8243;	double prime, seconds, inches, Unicode: 2033
&lsaquo;	&#8249;	single left-pointing angle quotation mark, Unicode: 2039
&rsaquo;	&#8250;	single right-pointing angle quotation mark, Unicode: 203A
&oline;	&#8254;	overline, spacing overscore, Unicode: 203E
&frasl;	&#8260;	fraction slash, Unicode: 2044
&image;	&#8465;	blackletter capital I, imaginary part, Unicode: 2111
&weierp;	&#8472;	script capital P, power set, Weierstrass p, Unicode: 2118
&real;	&#8476;	blackletter capital R, real part symbol, Unicode: 211C
&trade;	&#8482;	trade mark sign, Unicode: 2122
&alefsym;	&#8501;	alef symbol, first transfinite cardinal, Unicode: 2135
&larr;	&#8592;	leftwards arrow, Unicode: 2190
&uarr;	&#8593;	upwards arrow, Unicode: 2191
&rarr;	&#8594;	rightwards arrow, Unicode: 2192
&darr;	&#8595;	downwards arrow, Unicode: 2193
&harr;	&#8596;	left right arrow, Unicode: 2194
&crarr;	&#8629;	downwards arrow with corner leftwards, carriage return, Unicode: 21B5

Name	Value	Description
⇐	⇐	leftwards double arrow, Unicode: 21D0
⇑	⇑	upwards double arrow, Unicode: 21D1
⇒	⇒	rightwards double arrow, Unicode: 21D2
⇓	⇓	downwards double arrow, Unicode: 21D3
⇔	⇔	left right double arrow, Unicode: 21D4
∀	∀	for all, Unicode: 2200
∂	∂	partial differential, Unicode: 2202
∃	∃	there exists, Unicode: 2203
∅	∅	empty set, null set, diameter, Unicode: 2205
∇	∇	nabla, backward difference, Unicode: 2207
∈	∈	element of, Unicode: 2208
∉	∉	not an element of, Unicode: 2209
∋	∋	contains as member, Unicode: 220B
∏	∏	n-ary product, product sign, Unicode: 220F
∑	∑	n-ary sumation, Unicode: 2211
−	−	minus sign, Unicode: 2212
∗	∗	asterisk operator, Unicode: 2217
√	√	square root, radical sign, Unicode: 221A
∝	∝	proportional to, Unicode: 221D
∞	∞	infinity, Unicode: 221E
∠	∠	angle, Unicode: 2220
∩	∩	intersection, cap, Unicode: 2229
∪	∪	union, cup, Unicode: 222A
∫	∫	integral, Unicode: 222B
∴	∴	therefore, Unicode: 2234
∼	∼	tilde operator, varies with, similar to, Unicode: 223C
≅	≅	approximately equal to, Unicode: 2245
≈	≈	almost equal to, asymptotic to, Unicode: 2248
≠	≠	not equal to, Unicode: 2260
≡	≡	identical to, Unicode: 2261
≤	≤	less-than or equal to, Unicode: 2264
≥	≥	greater-than or equal to, Unicode: 2265
⊂	⊂	subset of, Unicode: 2282
⊃	⊃	superset of, Unicode: 2283
⊄	⊄	not a subset of, Unicode: 2284
⊆	⊆	subset of or equal to, Unicode: 2286
⊇	⊇	superset of or equal to, Unicode: 2287
⊕	⊕	circled plus, direct sum, Unicode: 2295
⊗	⊗	circled times, vector product, Unicode: 2297
∧	⊥	logical and wedge, Unicode: 2227
⊥	⊥	up tack, orthogonal to, perpendicular, Unicode: 22A5
∨	⊦	logical or vee, Unicode: 2228

Name	Value	Description
⋅	⋅	dot operator, Unicode: 22C5
⌈	⌈	left ceiling, apl upstile, Unicode: 2308,
⌉	⌉	right ceiling, Unicode: 2309,
⌊	⌊	left floor, apl downstile, Unicode: 230A,
⌋	⌋	right floor, Unicode: 230B,
⟨	〈	left-pointing angle bracket, bra, Unicode: 2329
⟩	〉	right-pointing angle bracket, ket, Unicode: 232A
◊	◊	lozenge, Unicode: 25CA
♠	♠	black spade suit, Unicode: 2660
♣	♣	black club suit, shamrock, Unicode: 2663
♥	♥	black heart suit, valentine, Unicode: 2665
♦	♦	black diamond suit, Unicode: 2666

Index

C

G

EVERYTHING YOU NEED TO KNOW ABOUT
good & bad
WEB DESIGN.

Web Pages That Suck
Learn Good Design by Looking at Bad Design
VINCENT FLANDERS, MICHAEL WILLIS

Based on the wildly popular, award-winning site, www.webpagesthatsuck.com, here's the first book to deliver practical advice from two bold and wacky experts who critique and fix real sites.

ISBN: 0-7821-2187-X • 304 pp • 8" x 10" • $39.00

Web By Design
The Complete Guide
MOLLY HOLZSCHLAG

This is the ONLY complete guide to ALL FIVE key aspects of web design: graphics; HTML design and layout techniques; typography; color, shape and space; multimedia and programming.

ISBN: 0-7821-2201-9 • 1,008 pp • 7½" x 9" • $49.99

Effective Web Design
Master the Essentials™
ANN NAVARRO, TABINDA KHAN

"I am constantly being asked to recommend a beginning web design book and haven't been able to, until now. This book delivers on its promise—with it you'll quickly gain the essential knowledge you need for effective web design."
          —Eliza Sherman, President, Cybergrrl, Inc. (www.cybergrrl.com)

ISBN: 0-7821-2278-7 • 400 pp • 7½" x 9" • $34.99

Dynamic HTML
Master the Essentials™
JOSEPH SCHMULLER

Filled with real-world, reusable examples, this clear and concise guide teaches you all you need to take control of what matters most: how your pages look and operate.

ISBN: 0-7821-2277-9 • 608 pp • 7½" x 9" • $29.99

Visit www.sybex.com for details on all titles from Sybex.

SYBEX®

What's on the CD?

The CD is packed with software, which you should check out as you are designing Web pages on Windows 95/NT and Macintosh. This software could make your life a lot easier. The CD includes such items as GIF animators, an image map creator, browsers, and more. To find out how to install the files on the CD, see the readme file.

The CD also contains links to the companion Web site, www.straznitskas.com, and the Sybex Web site, located at www.sybex.com.

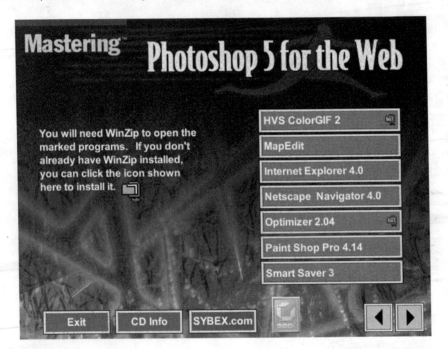

Adobe Acrobat Reader 3.01 allows you to view .pdf files.

Boxtop Software's GIFmation Demo creates and optimizes animated GIFs for cross-platform animation application.

DeBabelizer Pro 4.5 Demo for Windows 95/NT and **DeBabelizer Pro Lite 1.1.3 LE Demo** for the Mac apply filter effects, color corrections, and text overlay to images with scripting.

GIFBuilder 0.5 Demo creates animated GIF files for the Mac.

GIF Movie Gear 2 Demo creates and optimizes animated GIFs.

HTML Power Tools Test Drive Demo aids you in the Web design process.

HVS ColorGIF 2 Demo provides GIF image support.

MapEdit allows you to edit Web image maps.

Microsoft Internet Explorer 4.0 browser allows you to access the Internet.

Netscape Navigator 4.04 is a full-featured Internet browser.

Shop Shop Pro 4.14 Shareware lets you view, edit, and convert images.

Ulead's Cool 3D adds 3D text to your Web pages and more.

Ulead's GIF Animator 2 Trial Version helps you create and optimize animated GIFs.

Ulead's SmartSaver 3 Trial Version optimizes images for the Web.

Ulead's WebRazor Trial Version is for Web imaging and animation.

WebGraphics Optimizer 2.04 optimizes and compresses images for your Web pages.

WinZip 6.3 Shareware Evaluation Version compresses files into archives used for distributing and storing files.

WS_FTP allows you to access ftp sites.